Alice

Also by Hugo Vickers

Gladys, Duchess of Marlborough
Cecil Beaton
Vivien Leigh
Royal Orders
Loving Garbo
The Private World of the Duke and Duchess of Windsor
The Kiss

Alice

Princess Andrew of Greece

HUGO VICKERS

 St. Martin's Griffin ✥ New York

 For information, address St. Martin's Press, 175 Fifth Avenue, New York, N.Y. 10010.

www.stmartins.com

By kind permission of HRH The Duke of Edinburgh: 4, 8, 9, 14, 15, 16, 17, 18, 19, 20, 21, 22, 23, 24, 25, 26, 27, 28, 29, 30, 40; Royal Archives, © Her Majesty Queen Elizabeth II: 1, 2, 3, 11, 12, 13; By kind permission of HRH Princess George of Hanover: 6, 7, 10; Rainer von Hessen: 33; M. Jacques Cohen: 36; Mrs. Maurice Hare: 34; Godfrey Argent: 39; Lady Henderson: 35; Topham Picturepoint: 38; Author's collection: 5, 24, 31, 32, 37

Library of Congress Cataloging-in-Publication Data

Vickers, Hugo.

Alice : Princess Andrew of Greece / Hugo Vickers.

p. cm.

ISBN 0-312-28886-7 (hc)

ISBN 0-312-30239-8 (pbk)

1. Alice, Princess, consort of Andrew, Prince of Greece, 1885–1969. 2. Princesses—Greece—Biography. 3. Princesses—Great Britain—Biography. I. Title.

DF836.A45 V53 2002

949.5'07'092—dc21

[B] 2001048997

First published in Great Britain by Hamish Hamilton Ltd.

10 9 8 7 6 5 4

To William M. Weaver, Jr, godfather and friend

Contents

Acknowledgements

On 9 December 1969, shortly before I left school, I was invited to dinner by the organist of St George's Chapel, Windsor, Dr Sidney Campbell. After dinner, he took me over to St George's Chapel, opening the north door with his key and turning the chapel lights on.

St George's Chapel was arranged for the funeral next day of Princess Andrew of Greece, who had died at Buckingham Palace a few days before. In the quire, before the high altar, stood the bier, placed on the lift which would convey the coffin down into the royal vault below. Surrounding it were the great black and gold candlesticks, lately bequeathed to St George's Chapel by the 7th Earl Stanhope, senior Knight of the Garter. I saw where the Queen and the other royal mourners would sit. The Princess's coffin was then resting, not far away, in the Albert Memorial Chapel.

The following day, in dense fog, the funeral took place. I had never been in St George's Chapel at night, when it was empty. There was then no reason for me to suppose that the memorable scene would take on a greater significance in the years ahead.

In the summer of 1995, nearly quarter of a century later, I was at my desk at home when the telephone rang and Sir Brian McGrath, Prince Philip's treasurer, called me. We had never met, but he told me that Princess Andrew's surviving daughter, Princess George of Hanover, believed the time had come for a biography to be written of her mother. My name had been suggested, and if the idea appealed, perhaps I might like to come and see him and we could discuss it further.

Some days later I went to Buckingham Palace to meet Sir Brian, and he laid out the ground rules. 'Your job is to find a publisher and write the book,' he said. 'My job is to open doors for you.' Five years later, I am happy to report that this arrangement was fulfilled on both sides, Sir Brian not only opening doors for me, but inserting me at lunch tables, arranging interviews and gaining access for me to private archives. My first debt of gratitude is therefore to him.

This book was suggested by HRH Princess George of Hanover, and both she and HRH The Duke of Edinburgh have helped me immeasurably with my work. I enjoyed several meetings with Princess George both in Germany and in London, and she kindly answered a great number of questions, provided me with photographs and even translated an obituary of her mother from Greek into English for me. She and Prince George came over from Windsor to visit me in Hampshire in the summer of 1998 to witness the work in progress.

The Duke of Edinburgh also kindly talked to me about his mother, and was always prepared to answer written questions, of which I submitted a great number. He loaned me his mother's letters to him between 1924 and 1969, and allowed me access to certain other material in his archives, including the photographs in his father's album between 1917 and 1931. He also agreed to read an early draft of the typescript, which prompted further questions and answers.

The support given by Princess Andrew's grandson, Rainer von Hessen, has been immeasurable. He and I maintained a long correspondence throughout the years of research; he translated all the material from the University of Tübingen from German to English; he was ever willing to answer complicated questions about the intricacies of the family; and he guided me on many of the German aspects of the story. He interviewed Mrs Käthe Lindlar, Mrs Almuth Schmidt-Reuter and Mrs Else Stockmann in Cologne, which provided vital information on the Cologne period of his grandmother's life. He came to stay twice in Hampshire to advise me over these middle years and read early drafts of the book. In October 1999 he invited me to Wolfsgarten and guided me around Darmstadt. One of the 'field day' activities of this part of the research was when I climbed a gate in order to find the tombs of Prince Alexander of Hesse and Princess Battenberg, in the grounds of Schloss Heiligenberg, trespassing providing an enjoyable contrast to the more sedentary days spent in archives and libraries.

The late HRH Princess Margaret of Hesse received me twice at Wolfsgarten in January 1996. I am also grateful to members of the royal family who granted me interviews, in particular, HRH The Prince of Wales and HRH The Princess Royal, and His Majesty King Constantine of Greece. Her Majesty Queen Elizabeth The Queen Mother talked of Princess Alice in Scotland and HRH The Princess Margaret, Countess of Snowdon, in Hampshire.

I visited Lady Katherine Brandram, Princess Alice's niece, at her home in Marlow. I talked to Countess Mountbatten of Burma and Lord Brabourne in London in 1998, and Lady Pamela Hicks in London in 1999, as well as other members of the family: HRH Prince Alexander of Yugoslavia, the late HRH Prince Tomislav of Yugoslavia, HRH Princess Margarita of Baden, the late Princess Beatrix of Hohenlohe-Langenburg, Prince Alexander Romanoff, Lady Kennard and Lady Butter. Further help was given me on a non-attributable basis.

I have drawn on the benefit of a long conversation with the late HRH Princess Eugénie of Greece, whom I interviewed on another topic as long ago as February 1980. Princess Irina Bagration kindly gave me access to those papers of her late husband, Prince Theimouraz Bagration, which concerned the burial of Princess Alice in Jerusalem. The Rt. Revd Michael Mann, former Dean of Windsor, related the story of his prolonged negotiations in connection with the transfer to Jerusalem.

I am also very grateful for the help given by Mrs David Griffiths, Prince Philip's archivist, at Buckingham Palace.

By the nature of Princess Alice's life, there were not a large number of survivors who knew her well. In this context, I am grateful to Major Gerald Green, CBE, whose friendship with her dated from 1944 and lasted until her death; also to the late Hon. Sir Steven Runciman and Father Jean Charles-Roux, both of whom knew her in Athens. Mrs Maurice Hare talked to me of Prince Andrew of Greece, whom she knew in the south of France in 1935.

Monsieur Jacques Cohen in Paris was helpful over the period in which Princess Alice hid his mother and other members of his family in Athens during the Second World War. I interviewed him in Paris, and he provided me with important documents and photographs. I also talked to his brother, Monsieur Michel Cohen.

Much of my work was done in archives. I am grateful to Lord Brabourne and Lord Romsey for permitting me to use the Broadlands Archives, which contain the family papers of the late Admiral of the Fleet the Earl Mountbatten of Burma and his family. I spent many days there over a period of more than a year, and received considerable guidance and help from the Broadlands archivist, Mrs Molly Chalk, who delayed her retirement until I came to the end of my labours. There was also useful material in further Mountbatten papers in the Hartley Library at the University of Southampton.

At the Royal Archives, I am particularly grateful for the help and encouragement of Oliver Everett, and Lady de Bellaigue, Miss Frances Dimond, Miss Helen Gray and other members of their staff. I spent a number of days there in 1997. Other important material came from the University of Tübingen, the Hesse family archives at Darmstadt and the Public Record Office.

There was material in the papers of the late Sir Charles and Lady Johnston, which are in my care, and likewise in the papers of the late Sir Cecil Beaton, and of the late Harold Albert, consigned into my care by Mr Robert Tozzi.

My friends Hugh Montgomery-Massingberd and Philip Hoare kindly read some early drafts of the book and were never less than encouraging. My agent, Gillon Aitken, was reassuringly supportive as ever. My ignorance of German was a hindrance to my research, but I was lucky to be able to ask Cäcilie Möbius and Karen McDonald for extensive help with translation.

I am also grateful to the following who helped me with advice, enquiries, access to papers or reminiscences: Mr Kenneth Adams, Mr Godfrey Argent, Dr Marianne Wirenfeldt Asmussen, the Countess of Avon, Philippa Bassett (Archivist Special Collections, the University of Birmingham), Mr Harold Brown, the Earl and Countess of Carnarvon, the late Lord Charteris of Amisfield, Mr and Mrs Simon Courtauld, the Lord Fellowes, the late Revd Canon J. A. Fisher, Mr Alastair Forbes, Sir Edward Ford, Mr Alastair Forsyth, Princess Katya Galitzine, Mr and Mrs Terry Goddard, Mr Robert Golden, Mr Ilya Haritakis, Mr Tim Heald, Lady Henderson, Mr Charles Higham, Mr David Horbury, Mr Richard Howard, Brigadier Miles Hunt-Davis, Miss Claire Hunter-Craig, Father Gerard Irvine, Lt.-Col. Sir John Johnston, Mr Roger Knowles, Mrs Marlene A. Koenig, Viscount Lambton, Mrs Candida Lycett-Green, Mrs Alexandra McCreery, Mrs Linda Mitchell, Mr Tim O'Donovan, Mr James Orr, Dr Mordecai Paldiel (Director, Department of the Righteous, Yad Vashem), Lt.-Commander Michael Parker, RN, Mr Robin Piguet, Mrs Arpad Plesch, Mr John Porter, Mr Robin H. Rodger (Principal Officer Fine and Applied Art, Perth Museum and Art Gallery), Mr Kenneth Rose, Mr Ted Rosvall, Miss Penny Russell-Smith, Dr Eileen Scarff, Mr Ian Shapiro, Sir Sigmund Sternberg, M. Georges-Charles Tomaszewski, Mrs Michael Vickers, the late Captain Andrew Yates and Mr Philip Ziegler.

Because Princess Alice's life was relatively uncharted, the book took a long time to research. This research was punctuated by occasional visits to places connected with her life, in particular Mon Repos in Corfu, Osborne and other places on the Isle of Wight, various locations in the Darmstadt area, the site of the Bellevue clinic at Kreuzlingen, Schloss Salem, Schloss Langenburg, various locations in Netley, the Russian Cathedral in Nice and other places. At the end of my work, I discovered that the garden of Sennicotts (rented by Prince Louis of Battenberg in 1884) was open for the afternoon. Despite my arrival there without an introduction, its owner, Mr John Rank, kindly gave me a spontaneous tour of the house.

I am grateful to Mr Philip Gosling for arranging lectures for me on board *Queen Elizabeth 2*, where, on three separate voyages, most especially in the Pacific in 1999, I wrote many thousands of words in my cabin.

Rebecca Sieff helped me with my research, especially in the Public Record Office, where, over many months, she amassed considerable material on the Greek royal family and twentieth-century Balkan politics. The cream of this appears in the book, with enough left over for a further volume that will alas not be written. I owe her much gratitude for what she found and for the interest she took in the cast of characters.

This book was commissioned by Clare Alexander at Hamish Hamilton but finally published by Juliet Annan, renewing a publishing association dating back to 1981. In her office I am grateful to Keith Taylor, Hannah Robson and Kate Barker. I was lucky to have an especially understanding copy-editor in Anne Askwith.

Charles Drazin, who edited *The Kiss* in 1996, endured the particular burden of reading the typescript in its longest form. This was indeed very much longer than it now appears. He was judicious in his comments and helped sift out much extraneous material. He has the knack of being strict and supportive at the same time, and the book is the better for his insight.

When I began my writing career, I wrote long-hand, but now I depend on machines. I must therefore apologize to my friend and former tenant, David Foster, for the many times I interrupted him with appeals for his help when some aspect of the system failed.

Finally, I am grateful to my wife, Mouse, for her support and for her comments on the developing text. She is a wise editor. As I reached the end of the first draft, so our little boy, Arthur, arrived. As the original draft grew smaller, so he grew bigger. Any author who works at home will know the joy of a little person arriving suddenly at his side to divert him from the contemplation of lives past. This edition contains a few additions and corrections.

Hugo Vickers
April 2001

Introduction

Alice, Princess Andrew of Greece, was a member of the British royal family, but she was also a member of the House of Hesse-Darmstadt and married into the Greek (and Danish) royal family. Her life had a strange symmetry. She was born at Windsor because her great-grandmother, Queen Victoria, ordained that she should be, and after her funeral at Windsor, she lay there for many years for the very different reason that her son, Prince Philip, lived there.

Her life was both conventional and unconventional. She belonged and yet she did not belong. There were times when she lived in the bosom of her family and other times when she had no contact with them whatsoever. There were times when she was there but the world did not know she was there. Seven of her middle years have hitherto been shrouded in complete mystery, and it is arguable that until now, no one in her family, other than Alice's mother, who died in 1950, knew where she was during this period.

In life she had both advantages and disadvantages. She was a beautiful child, but she was isolated by deafness. She fulfilled dynastic obligations but politics intervened to deny her the chance to make a lasting contribution. She married for love, yet eventually she was left on her own. Indeed, so often she set out in what seemed to be a good direction only to be frustrated by outside forces.

The two occasions on which she made the greatest impression on the British public were in November 1947 and June 1953 – at the wedding of Prince Philip and the Coronation of the Queen. On both occasions she had a prominent place, and though they were but six years apart, she effectively changed her guise between them.

At the wedding she can be seen sitting at the head of her family, on the left side of Westminster Abbey, opposite George VI, Queen

Elizabeth (now Queen Elizabeth The Queen Mother) and Queen Mary. She wore velvet, an outfit made for her in Paris from an old royal train – a day dress long to the floor, adorned with the Grand Cross of the Order of the Redeemer, with a hat fashionably trimmed with feathers. Yet she looked matronly and a little severe. She had not been seen at any royal occasions for decades and ill-informed society gossip put it about – unfairly – that she had been released from a sanatorium just for the service.

By 1953 she was unrecognizable as the groom's mother of November 1947, being dressed from head to foot in a long grey dress and a grey cloak, and a nun's veil. Amidst all the jewels, velvet, coronets and fine uniforms present at the occasion, she exuded an unworldly simplicity. As one who witnessed her process alone up the long aisle of the abbey put it: 'She looked as though she were walking into eternity.'[1] Seated with the royal family, she was a part of them, yet somehow distanced from them. Inasmuch as she is remembered at all today, it is as this shadowy figure in grey nun's clothes.

Alice was a very private person. She kept neither diaries nor papers. She destroyed all her letters, save one that she did not have time to tear up and which was still on her bedside table when she died. One of my duties as her biographer was to track her through life. She would be horrified by how much I found out. Yet in her early years, while it is possible to know what she was doing, it is not always possible to know what she was thinking or how she reacted to the events around her. She was part of a large family, almost part of a team, but when in a group, she was usually the quiet one, a little distanced, a little shy, never to the fore.

Alice's story is inevitably overshadowed by the serious religious crisis that caused her to be removed against her will from her family at the age of forty-five and placed in a sanatorium in Switzerland for two and a half years.

It is also overshadowed by wars, revolutions and enforced periods of exile. In the course of her life, virtually every point of stability was overthrown. Though the British royal family remained in the ascendant, her German family ceased to be ruling princes, one uncle was forced to renounce his throne and a German aunt was forced into exile. Two aunts who had married Russian royalty came to savage ends, and soon afterwards Alice's own husband was nearly executed as a political scapegoat.

The middle years of her life, which should have followed a conventional and fulfilling path, did quite the opposite. As her stay in the sanatorium became prolonged, there was a time when it seemed that she might never walk free again. How she achieved recovery is one of the most remarkable aspects of her story. And having done so, how she redirected her life and the good use to which she devoted her time are no less remarkable. In some aspects she succeeded and in others she failed. Ultimately, it is impossible not to admire her courage, her sense of duty and devotion, and the resilience that balanced a certain fragility of mind, spirit and health.

1. The Infant Princess

Empress Frederick of Germany to Queen Victoria: 'I imagine she will be called Alice Victoria Louise Julia. Am I right?'
Queen Victoria to the Duke of Connaught: 'She will be called Alice.'[1]

Two arrivals were expected at Windsor Castle in February 1885. Queen Victoria was due to sail across the Solent and take up residence, and an infant was due to be born at the castle to the Queen's granddaughter, Victoria, Princess Louis of Battenberg.

Queen Victoria had decided that she would attend the birth and such was her domination of her descendants that once this decision was made, what was decided would happen. Young Princess Victoria, daughter of the Queen's deceased daughter Alice, would produce her first baby in her grandmother's home rather than in Hesse-Darmstadt, her paternal home near Frankfurt, where her husband, Prince Louis (sometimes Ludwig) of Battenberg, spent part of each year when not serving elsewhere with the British Royal Navy.

Louis and Victoria were essentially German. But, soon after their marriage in 1884, they had rented Sennicotts, a beautiful Regency-style house near Chichester in Sussex. Louis was either serving in the royal yacht *Victoria and Albert*, which lay off Cowes, or participating in a torpedo course at Portsmouth. They were at Sennicotts when the Queen summoned Victoria to her side.

Queen Victoria is generally perceived as being obsessed with death and the anniversaries of deaths; yet, if anything, she loved the birth of a descendant more and she spent a great deal of time organizing matrimonial alliances amongst her ever-increasing descendants, not always with felicitous results. She played a considerable role in the marriages of Victoria of Hesse and her siblings, and an almost equally influential one in those of the Battenberg brothers of Prince Louis.

Queen Victoria decided that her fourth great-grandchild should be born in the same room, the Tapestry Room, and in the same bed, that Princess Victoria had been in 1863. To this end she had obliged young Victoria to stay with her since before Christmas 1884, first at Osborne, her home on the Isle of Wight, and then at nearby Kent House. On 14 February Princess Victoria was sent ahead to Windsor, where she duly took up residence in the Tapestry Room, in the centre of the George IV Gateway. The expectant mother's room was adorned with gifts specially made by Queen Victoria in anticipation of the birth of the baby.

The staff had been bustling about for some days preparing for the Queen's arrival. A cheery maid, Mrs Brotherstone, was awaiting her and making friends with Mary Adams, who was to be the Princess's nurse.* Every afternoon Princess Victoria was taken for 'solemn drives in a well-sprung phaeton',[2] the Ivory Phaeton, built for Queen Victoria in 1842.†

Since the death of Princess Victoria's mother, Queen Victoria had enjoyed a close, sometimes conspiratorial relationship with her granddaughter, trusting her as her closest link with the Hesse-Darmstadt family. She was receiving regular reports about the princess from the doctors. But, despite her carefully contrived plans, she very nearly missed the birth, being detained at Osborne on the Isle of Wight until 19 February, suffering from 'a cold', in fact a severe neuralgic headache.

The birth of the infant great-granddaughter took place in the late afternoon of 25 February 1885. During the long labour, Queen Victoria's way of inspiring the mother-to-be was to tell her how much she detested the Tapestry Room, because it was here that she had been 'terribly scolded' by her mother, the Duchess of Kent, for making up to William IV, on the disagreeable evening when

* Mary Adams stayed with the family until the summer of 1893. She then became Queen Victoria's dresser.

† The Ivory Phaeton is used by the present Queen at the annual Birthday Parade.

they had dined with him for his seventy-first birthday in August 1836.[3]

Queen Victoria described Alice's arrival in her journal:*

Woke before 7. Hearing that Victoria had had a bad night, I got up & went over to see her. She was very suffering. I had some breakfast, & then went back remaining with dear Victoria on & off, till at length, at 20m to 5 in the afternoon, the child, a little girl, was born. The relief was great for poor Victoria had had such a long hard time, which always makes me anxious. How strange & indeed affecting, it was, to see her lying in the same room, & in the same bed, in which she herself was born. Good Ludwig [Louis] was most helpful & attentive, hardly leaving Victoria for a moment. The Baby is very small, thin & dark. I held it for a few moments in my arms. It is curious that it should be born on dear little Alice's 2nd birthday,† which Helen [the Duchess of Albany] specially came to spend here. As all was going well with dear Victoria, & the evening very fine, I took a short drive with Ly Southampton & Horatia S[topford]. On coming in, went again to Victoria, who had rested & was quite composed & happy. Ludwig is radiant . . .[4]

Arriving in the world in the presence of Queen Victoria was an auspicious if daunting start to life for the infant Alice. Though Alice's childhood was to be peripatetic, the almost goddess-like figure of her great-grandmother loomed over her life and that of her parents, even when they were far away.

Since her father was from a junior branch of the Hesse-Darmstadt family, Alice's parents were never well off. They depended on Queen Victoria for much kindness, for hospitality and occasionally for financial help. Even Louis's future in the Royal Navy seemed to rest in her hands: a nod from the Queen could lead to promotion

*In a busy life, Queen Victoria succeeded in keeping an extensive diary, a valuable source for scholars, even in its surviving form, edited and transcribed by her daughter Princess Beatrice.

†Princess Alice of Albany was born on 25 February 1883. She became Princess Alice, Countess of Athlone, and outlived her namesake by many years, dying in January 1981, aged ninety-seven.

and often did. Being a generation younger, Alice was a little distanced from this, but for her first sixteen years, the Queen-Empress was a benign but powerful influence on her life.

2. The Battenbergs

Alice's mother was a determined young character and she would need all her strength to cope with the many vicissitudes that lay in store for her. She was to be an integral part of Alice's life until her death in 1950, by which time Alice was sixty-five.

Victoria was born on 5 April 1863, the eldest child of Prince Louis of Hesse-Darmstadt, later Grand Duke Louis IV of Hesse and by Rhine, and his wife Princess Alice, Queen Victoria's second daughter. Victoria was one of seven children. She was followed in 1864 by Elisabeth ('Ella'), a pivotal influence on young Alice, and then in 1866 by Irène, the future wife of Prince Henry of Prussia. Ernst Ludwig ('Ernie'), a future Grand Duke of Hesse, was born in 1868, and Friedrich Wilhelm ('Fritz') in 1870. Two more daughters followed: Alix, in 1872, who became Tsarina of Russia, and Marie, in 1874.

In her early years Victoria lived in an annexe of her grandparents' house in Upper Wilhelmstrasse at Bessungen in Germany. In 1866 the family moved to the Neue Palais in Darmstadt, where she and her next sister Ella shared a bedroom.

The Grand Duke of Hesse at this time was Louis III, an immensely tall, stooped, reclusive figure, who was a childless widower. He collected cigar-holders, and travelled about with a small entourage including his hairdresser, whose duty was to ensure that the curls on either side of his bald head were well ironed. Another eccentricity was to ring for a handkerchief when he needed it. He gave a big family dinner every Sunday at the Alte Schloss at 3.00 p.m. In all the many houses where he lived, some twelve of them, he retained an apartment identically decorated in dark green with mahogany furniture. Following his death at Seeheim on 13 June 1877, Victoria's father, Louis III's nephew, became Grand Duke.

The children were strictly brought up, starting lessons at

7.00 a.m., breakfasting with their parents at 9.00 a.m., taking an hour's exercise out of doors, then a light lunch before joining their parents at 2.00 p.m. for a proper meal. There was more exercise in the afternoon, and more schooling, tea at 5.00 p.m., and bed at about 6.30 or 7.00 p.m. Victoria spoke German first, reading it well by the age of six, and English by the age of seven. Religious instruction was given by Pfarrer Sell, a doctor of divinity, who was Professor of Theology in Bonn. The Hesse family belonged to the Lutheran Church, whose ideas were quite close to those of the Anglican church.

The children would often visit the Alice Hospital, which their mother had founded with the advice of Florence Nightingale. Princess Alice had also persuaded the state to take over an 'idiot asylum' and the whole Hesse family helped raise money for it by staging bazaars.

Victoria, a bright girl and an avid reader, took the Oxford exams for younger girls. She enjoyed most of her childhood, but there was sadness. In 1873, when she was ten, her younger brother, Fritz, fell out of a window in Darmstadt while playing hide and seek with Ernie, and died of a brain haemorrhage. He was two and a half. Then in December 1878 Victoria's childhood came to a sudden end. Having nursed the family through diphtheria, her mother lost the youngest daughter, Marie, to the disease in November. Kissing her son Ernie to comfort him, she contracted diphtheria herself, with fatal consequences. 'She had no strength left to resist the disease,' wrote Victoria, 'thoroughly worn out as she was by nursing us all, and died on the 14th of December, the anniversary of the death of her beloved father.'[1]*

Following her mother's death, Victoria looked after her brother and sisters and kept her father company. They spent a lot of time in England with Queen Victoria, and enjoyed stealing lemonade, water and biscuits from a table outside the Queen's room. They ate well in Darmstadt, but less so when staying with Queen Victoria.

* Princess Alice had been a carrier of haemophilia, which gene she passed to her daughters, Irène and Alix. But Victoria and her descendants escaped it.

'We never objected to anything given us at home,' Victoria would later write, 'but the awful bread and butter puddings without a raisin in them or the stodgy tapioca pudding we got in Queen Victoria's houses I still remember with a shudder of disgust.'[2]

Victoria had known Louis of Battenberg, her first cousin once removed, since childhood. He used to pay them family visits when they were in London at the same time. Gradually he developed from being 'our English cousin'[3] into a more romantic figure in Victoria's life. In the spring of 1883, Queen Victoria invited Victoria and her sister Ella to accompany her to Balmoral. Victoria hesitated and Ella told her father: 'If Victoria does not go to Scotland she will become engaged to Louis Battenberg.'[4] Victoria stayed in Darmstadt. Louis had been invited to attend the coronation of Tsar Alexander III, but for the same reason he too preferred to stay in Germany at Schloss Heiligenberg, the family home at Jugenheim near Darmstadt. That June, Victoria and Louis became engaged.

Louis and Victoria were different in character but splendidly compatible. He was popular (though not with certain embittered British politicians in 1914), and he was flamboyant; he adored uniforms and medals and was happy to parade them to his staff before setting off for a formal occasion. Victoria was embarrassed by such exhibitions. She was more down-to-earth, and, despite a tendency to chatter, rather reserved and shy.

Meriel Buchanan, whose father was *en poste* in Darmstadt in the 1890s, admired Victoria for her 'lack of vanity, her firm handshake, her direct, sometimes rather abrupt manner [which] gave an almost masculine impression'. Meriel once heard her say: 'I should have been the man in the family.' Queen Elizabeth The Queen Mother knew her many years later and recalled: 'She was rather like a man – but one isn't allowed to say that these days. She was quite dictatorial. I remember she would say: "Now, I am going to tell you this."'[5]

Louis was to become a distinguished figure in the British navy – an astonishing achievement considering his entirely German origins. He relished its many victories and traditions. Yet at the same time he was eager to look to the future, keeping up with the latest scientific developments and making himself a master of naval strategy and administration. He was a man of action, yet possessed a good sense of fun. A great advantage over many of his fellow officers was his understanding of many different European countries, and a facility with their language and history. He sported the massive tattoo of a dragon across his chest and down his legs, which would delight his future grandchildren. As an older man, he was handsomely bearded, his face exuding gravity tinged with a hint of humour.[6]

Louis was born at Graz on 24 May 1854, the eldest son of Prince Alexander of Hesse and his wife, the former Julie von Hauke, or Haucke. Thus, like Victoria of Hesse, he was a descendant of the Grand Ducal house of Hesse-Darmstadt. But there were rumours about this.

Many said that Prince Alexander and his sister, Marie (later Tsarina of Russia), were sired not by Grand Duke Louis II of Hesse but by the Grand Duchess's chamberlain, Baron Augustus Senarclens von Grancy.[7] Victoria conceded in her unpublished memoirs that he was 'the putative father of my father-in-law, Prince Alexander and the Empress Marie – but *Honi soit qui mal y pense*!'[8]

That most zealous of family historians and genealogists, Earl Mountbatten of Burma, Alice's younger brother, was prepared to recognize the rumour in his privately printed *The Mountbatten Lineage* (1958), though discouraged from so doing by the then head of the family, Prince Louis of Hesse and by Rhine.

Louis's father, Prince Alexander of Hesse, was primarily a soldier. He had begun his service in the Imperial Russian Army and later caused a sensation in Russia, while at court, by eloping with Julie Haucke, one of the maids of honour to the future Tsarina, Marie Alexandrovna.

Julie's origins are even more intriguing than those of her husband.* Prince von Bülow, a source of many outspoken stories about the courts of Europe, gave an account of her ancestry. The

* Many aspersions have been cast on Julie's origins. See Antony Lambton, *The Mountbattens* (Constable, 1989), p. 42 and *passim*.

original Haucke* was one of the many servants of Count Heinrich Bruhle, page and later Prime Minister to Augustus the Strong of Saxony. This Haucke married the daughter of a German baker and confectioner and produced a son, Maurice, born in 1775, whom Count Bruhle placed in the Polish cadet corps. The boy rose to be a general in the Polish army and married Sophie de la Fontaine.

In 1830 the Great Polish Rebellion broke out and Haucke was one of a few officers who remained loyal to Tsar Nicholas I. He was assassinated by the rebels. The Tsar arrived in Warsaw and rewarded the dead Haucke's loyalty by entering his son into the Russian army and appointing his daughter, Julie, a maid of honour to his daughter-in-law.

Julie met Prince Alexander of Hesse in the course of her court duties, and soon afterwards she had to confess that she was pregnant by him. The Prince was banned from court by Tsar Nicholas, but remained loyal, accepted his banishment and married Julie as his morganatic wife. Thus was founded the house of Battenberg.

'Prince Alexander of Hesse was a fine gentleman through and through and kindly as well,' wrote Prince von Bülow, 'Princess Julie a very clever, very ambitious woman.'[9] Lord Mountbatten attributed the brains of the family to Julie Haucke, not to mention the ambition, asserting that his own particular intelligence came from her. Alice was to owe much to her paternal grandmother, who was one of the mainstays of her childhood.

Soon after their wedding Prince Alexander of Hesse joined the Austrian army as a Major-General, which is why Louis was born at Graz. In the 1860s they settled at the Alexander Palais in the Luisen Platz at Darmstadt. They spent the winters there, the season for plays and dances, and the summers at the Heiligenberg.†

Louis's mother, Julie, later styled as Princess Battenberg, was able to help him in his youthful wish to serve in the British navy by consulting Princess Alice. In those days there was only a North

* The name Haucke had the same origin as the medieval word, Hugus, and Hugo. It meant 'thinking or thoughtful spirit' or 'thoughtful man'.

† Julie had a sister called Emilie, whose grandson, Constantine, Baron Stackelberg, known as 'Steno' (1899–1989), will appear later in the story.

German Confederation Navy, consisting of a few Prussian ships, whereas the British Royal Navy offered the possibility of adventures worldwide. It may have seemed a strange idea to admit a German prince to the Royal Navy and certainly the question of a supposed conflict of loyalty would dog his career.*

Louis first served in *Victory*. From early in his career he attracted the 'almost motherly interest'[10] of Queen Victoria, who was forever singling him out for royal duties. This was an advantage in certain ways, but also hindered his career, as did the interest shown in him by the Prince of Wales and the Duke of Edinburgh. His early career was peppered with royal service, notably in the frigate *Ariadne* when the Prince and Princess of Wales (later Edward VII and Queen Alexandra) cruised the Mediterranean in 1869. This experience almost caused him to leave the navy. Only fifteen years old, he was daunted by the hard work in all weathers, the insufficient food, the rough handling meted out in the gun room and his homesickness. Comparing himself to other midshipmen, he felt that his royal service had left him ignorant of the required drill. But the Prince of Wales urged him to stay on, and when he went home on leave and his family treated him as something of a hero in his uniform, he soon felt better about it. In October 1869 he became a midshipman in *Royal Alfred*, sailing on the North American and West Indies station, and he visited the United States. He became something of a protégé of the future Edward VII, endearing himself to him by playing the piano in the ward room.

As was soon evident, Louis was more than able to make his own way in his naval career. He worked hard and impressed those under whom he served. According to his memoirs, he also turned many a pretty head when his ship docked, or when he was stationed on shore. In Bermuda he danced with Emma Astwood, 'the prettiest girl by far'.[11] In New Brunswick there were two pretty Schwabe

*Louis was not the first German prince to serve in the British navy. Admiral Prince Victor of Hohenlohe-Langenburg (1833–91) (later Count Gleichen) was one, and Admiral Prince Ernest of Leiningen (1830–1904) another, the latter largely in the royal yacht. They were both stepnephews of Queen Victoria.

sisters. In Jamaica he fell 'so hopelessly in love'[12] with Julia Hart that he nearly gave up food and drink.

As a sub-Lieutenant, he served in *Serapis*, which in 1875 took the Prince of Wales on a tour of India. Here too his amorous escapades continued. In Kashmir, the Maharajah thoughtfully organized that a young girl of noble birth be placed in the Prince of Wales's bed in his tent. Louis deftly moved her to his own. The memoirs he wrote about his bachelor days include a page marked '*NOT* FOR MY DAUGHTERS'. This concerns a dinner given for the Prince's staff, following which the host led each guest in turn to a compartment, furnished with a divan bed, on which reclined 'a young native girl in transparent white garments'.[13]

For many years the Prince of Wales wanted Louis to join his staff as a kind of ADC, but Louis resisted. Louis was clearly more intelligent than the Prince of Wales and the Duke of Edinburgh, but as royal princes they were invariably favoured over him. He often pandered to their whims, but they respected him and frequently turned to him for advice. Louis felt able to accept the Prince of Wales's offer of a room at Marlborough House and this was his London base until he married.

In the late 1870s his association with the Prince of Wales landed him in a tangled love affair. The Prince introduced him to his mistress, Lillie Langtry, the celebrated actress and beauty, and an affair burgeoned. Meanwhile, Queen Victoria conceived the idea that Louis might be contemplating marriage with her daughter, Princess Beatrice. The Queen was sufficiently concerned about this to instruct the Admiralty to send him abroad and, in future, to employ him only on foreign stations.

Thus Louis went to sea on 24 August 1880. Meanwhile, however, Mrs Langtry was pregnant. Louis longed to marry her, but this did not suit either Lillie's renegade husband, Edward Langtry, or Louis's parents. His father sent an aide-de-camp to arrange an appropriate financial settlement and the affair was hushed up.[14] While Lillie Langtry awaited the birth, Louis departed on a world cruise in the aptly named *Inconstant* in October 1880, during part of which he acted as mentor to Prince Albert Victor and Prince George of

Wales (later George V). Amongst the highlights of the trip was a meeting in Fiji with the old cannibal king, Thakumbow, then in dignified retirement. When pressed by Louis he confessed that 'he could not deny that he had occasional yearnings for babies' legs, which he said were the best dish in the world'.[15]

The child, a daughter, was born at the Hotel Gibraltar in Paris on either 8 March or 31 May 1881. She was baptized Marie Louise, but known as Jeanne-Marie.*[16]

This story remained a secret for many years. In September 1978 Lord Mountbatten publicly acknowledged that Louis was the father of Jeanne-Marie Langtry.† But a recent biography of Lillie Langtry‡ suggests that this was almost certainly not so. The child was probably the progeny of Arthur Jones, one of seven illegitimate sons of Lord Ranelagh.

Soon after Louis's return to Britain in October 1882, he went on half pay, the not infrequent fate of a naval officer, and soon after that he returned to Darmstadt. In March 1883 he joined his brother Sandro in Bulgaria and they set off on an Eastern voyage, which took in the Holy Land, Jerusalem, Jericho, the Dead Sea and Bethlehem, and finally Montenegro.

In the summer of 1883 he was back in Germany and, Lillie Langtry spurned, it was then that he turned his romantic attentions to his Hessian cousin, Victoria. In his memoirs, he described an afternoon in June 1883:

We had many expeditions with the Seeheim party in a variety of pony carts and carriages, with tea baskets, and games to follow. At last one day

*Jeanne-Marie Langtry (1881–1964), married 1902, Sir Ian Malcolm, politician and author.

†Mountbatten made friends with Mary Malcolm, Lillie's granddaughter, and a well-known television announcer, writing to her: 'I think the time has come when it is much better to have the whole thing in the open for there is, after all, a great deal to be said for both sides of the family.' [MtB to Mrs Colin McFadyean (Mary Malcolm), 1 November 1978 – MB, K166a – HL]

‡*Lillie Langtry: Manners, Masks and Morals* by Laura Beatty (Chatto & Windus, 1999).

on a bench in Seeheim grounds, I plucked up courage and asked your dear mother if she would marry me.

All the happiness of my life begins with that memorable day.[17]

At first, Queen Victoria was not pleased: she wanted Victoria to continue looking after her family. But when she heard that Victoria would still be able to keep her father company during Louis's absences at sea, she consented. Even so, she made the young couple wait until the following year before marrying.[18]

In September 1883 Queen Victoria appointed Louis as Lieutenant in her yacht, *Victoria and Albert*. This assured him his promotion to Commander two years later, 'a few months earlier than would otherwise have been the case'.[19] Most of the time, however, he was in another of the Queen's yachts, *Osborne*, as the former yacht was laid up.

As the wedding approached in April 1884, the bride became so excited that she failed to eat for several days. Then she made a sudden late-night feast of a lobster which, not unsurprisingly, made her violently sick. Finally she sprained her ankle trying to leap over a coal scuttle.[20]

For his wedding Louis adorned his naval uniform with suitable decorations, and he and Victoria were married in Darmstadt in the presence of Queen Victoria.

3. Early Days

By 19 March 1885 three-week-old Alice was declared to be now 'quite well',[1] and next day she was taken out in a pony chair. Alice and Princess Victoria stayed at Windsor until 30 March. Members of the royal family came to inspect the baby, including the widowed Empress Eugénie of France, who came from Farnborough. Royal relations who could not come wrote to congratulate the Queen on her new great-grandchild, her daughter the Empress Frederick spicing her pleasure with gloom: 'I cannot think without a pang of this being our darling Alice's *1st* grandchild & she not here to see it & I feel sure this sad thought was uppermost in your mind, when the little one made her appearance!'[2]

Alice was about to go to Darmstadt with her mother and Queen Victoria for her christening, when that perpetual hazard of Victorian life, an unexpected death, intervened. Alice's German great-grandmother, Princess Charles of Hesse,* died suddenly at Bessungen, plunging Darmstadt into mourning. Queen Victoria felt greatly inconvenienced: 'I can hardly believe it! Again such a sad event, throwing a terrible gloom over all at Darmstadt . . . Three successive years, at the same time, all arrangements have to be changed!'†[3] The Queen decided to go to Aix for her holiday and to join the family in Darmstadt later.

On the morning of 30 March, after a service of thanksgiving to mark her recovery from childbirth, Victoria took baby Alice on what would be the first of many travels in her long life. They followed in the wake of Queen Victoria and Princess Beatrice

*Princess Charles of Hesse (1815–85), died on 21 March. She was Elisabeth, daughter of Prince Wilhelm of Prussia, god-daughter of the Duke of Wellington and Field Marshal Blücher, and a deeply religious woman. Through her the famous Holbein *Madonna* came to the Hesse family.

†John Brown died in 1883 and the Duke of Albany in 1884.

and the habitually large household entourage. They entrained to Portsmouth, where they embarked in the royal yacht, *Victoria and Albert*, and sailed to France.

At 11.00 p.m., the royal party arrived in Cherbourg, the baby having travelled well, and joined the royal train. Princess Victoria said goodbye to the Queen, who would be asleep when her granddaughter left early the next day, and to her husband, who was serving in the royal yacht and would join her later. The train then set off for Maisons Lafitte, where, at 6.20 a.m., Prince Henry of Battenberg (then engaged to Princess Beatrice) was waiting to escort his sister-in-law and niece to Darmstadt. Here, Alice was consigned to the care of Mary Anne Orchard ('Orchie'), the family nurse. She was soon the delight of her German family.

Soon afterwards, Victoria received a letter from her grandmother, written on the train to Aix:

> After having seen you almost every day for more than 3 months, & every day for 6 weeks & living in the same House – we shall miss you very much. I hope you & Baby & poor Mary Adams* did not suffer from the very cold night & early move in the cold? . . .
>
> It is very provoking that you shld. have to return alone to Darmstadt without Louis & you will I fear feel the separation much. He is so good & kind & *so* devoted to you. You must be very good & *not* stand abt. yet. But walk a little in the garden.[4]

Before unification, Germany consisted of a number of independent kingdoms duchies and principalities. Hesse-Darmstadt was a Grand Duchy, presided over by Alice's maternal grandfather, Grand Duke Louis IV,† since 1877. When he married Queen Victoria's second daughter, Princess Alice, in 1862, Darmstadt had been elevated from what Sir George Buchanan, the British envoy, described as 'virtually but a small garrison town'[5] to a place with a certain

* Royalty sometimes applied the adjective 'poor' to those not fortunate enough to have royal blood, regardless of their financial circumstances. Queen Mary even described Mrs Cornelius Vanderbilt thus.

† Louis IV, Grand Duke of Hesse and by Rhine, KG (1837–92).

diplomatic prominence, close family ties with the Russian court and a thriving state theatre.

In April 1884 the Grand Duchy had been shaken when the Grand Duke, widowed after Alice's death in 1878, had suddenly married a morganatic wife, unwisely doing so when Queen Victoria was in Darmstadt to attend Louis and Victoria's marriage. Instantly the autocratic Queen commanded that this union be dissolved. The bride was a divorcée, Countess Alexandrine Kolémine, variously described as 'one of the most beautiful and accomplished women of her time',[6] or as 'a Russian divorcée of the worst possible repute'.[7] Nevertheless, the Grand Duke's children hoped that he might find happiness by marrying her. Instead the Countess was pensioned off, continuing to receive money from the Hesse family until her death in 1941, by which time she was an old lady, playing patience in the Hôtel des Trois Couronnes in Vevey, and cheating to win. Meanwhile the Grand Duke was restored to favour with his mother-in-law, who was fond of him, and resigned himself to a life of monogamy.*

The Grand Ducal family occupied some thirty castles or palaces. There was the Neue Palais, a large, white house behind high iron gates in the upper part of the town of Darmstadt, where the Grand Duke lived. Next in importance was the Alte Schloss, a vast, forbidding fifteenth-century building, constructed around several courtyards near the Louisen Platz in the old part of town. It was used for great receptions and state ceremonies, and a number of court officials lived within.

Not far away was the lovely shooting lodge of Wolfsgarten, as beloved by visiting royalty then as it remained into the 1990s. It was built around a grassed courtyard, and guests were bidden to scratch their names on the windows of the state apartments, a tradition which continues.

Hesse-Darmstadt was known for its agriculture, providing an

* The incident was parodied in a novel by Ari Ecilaw, *A King's Second Marriage*, dedicated to 'the great ones of the earth, who think they have the right to violate even the laws, and who forget, in the intoxication of their haughty arrogance, that above them there is One greater than they – God!'

abundance of fruit and cultivated vines. Meriel Buchanan wrote of the countryside round about: 'There were glorious beech woods where violets and lilies-of-the-valley grew in profusion, there were green fields of cowslips and buttercups, there were great pine forests that were full of sandy rides where one could gallop one's horses for miles.'[8] Darmstadt itself was relatively sleepy, with wide streets, avenues of chestnut trees, and little white houses with gardens of lilac, syringa and lime trees.

Besides the Grand Duke, a much loved figure, Alice's family on her mother's side included one surviving son, Ernst Ludwig, known as 'Ernie', then sixteen and about to be confirmed. Of Alice's three Hesse aunts, Ella was the most significant in her life.

Ella was a noted beauty and a widely loved figure. A few weeks after the wedding of Louis and Victoria, she had married Grand Duke Serge of Russia. Queen Victoria disapproved of this union because of her deeply held mistrust of Russians. By marrying Serge, Ella became a rich but doomed woman, and it is fortunate that she did not realize that her marriage to the Grand Duke would eventually lead to the terrible fate of the Russian royal family.

Ella soon became a popular social figure at the Russian court. But hers was a serious character. Worldly riches held no allure for her and she was drawn towards the spiritual life. In society in Moscow and St Petersburg, she was known for her sweet nature. Victoria wrote of her sister's 'unselfishness, her patience, her superiority in fact to our every day motives', and how she sacrificed her own pleasure and comfort to serve others. 'How often has she gone to a party or ball, amiable & kind to all whilst suffering from a raging headache, merely that others should not be disappointed.'[9]

Ella took a keen interest in her niece Alice from the start, writing to Queen Victoria from St Petersburg:

You can well imagine how happy I am to be an aunt & long for the moment when I can see the dear Baby. I would very much like to be one of the godmothers if even she has not amongst her names mine, don't you think it could be managed? I would be oh so glad.[10]

Queen Victoria fixed it, though she hoped that Grand Duke Serge of Russia would not come to the christening, on account of Russia's warfaring activities. However, he was there.

Neither of her other aunts took as strong a part in Alice's life, though she often stayed with Aunt Irène, then eighteen, after her marriage in 1888 to Prince Henry of Prussia, a younger son of the Empress Frederick (Queen Victoria's eldest daughter) and thus a brother of the Kaiser. Alix, a nervous child of twelve, was the future Tsarina, who then thought of Alice as 'a delightful toy'.[11]

Also in Darmstadt were Alice's paternal grandfather, Prince Alexander of Hesse, and his wife, Princess Battenberg.* Their home, Heiligenberg, was a villa set around a courtyard, high in the hills, and approached by a winding drive through hazel trees. From the terrace there was a fine view over the Klosterburg with just a glimpse of the distant Rhine. It was a romantic place which Alice thought of as home even after she married.

The Heiligenberg was originally a farmhouse, bought by Grand Duchess Wilhelmine and bequeathed to Prince Alexander and his sister, the Empress Marie Alexandrovna of Russia. The Grand Duchess had converted it into a fine country house. Meriel Buchanan recalled: 'There was a lovely terrace there shaded with lime trees, a long hazel walk that was a fairyland of green, shimmering shadow, the ruins of an old nunnery, and a little wooden cottage in the garden where we played at cooking and housekeeping.'[12]

Also in Darmstadt was Louis's youngest brother. Prince Franz Josef of Battenberg ('Franzjos'),† and his sister, Marie, Countess of Erbach-Schönberg,‡ with her husband, Gustave. Alice's father

* Princess Battenberg (1825–95), the former Julie Haucke.

† Queen Victoria was also involved in the marriage of Franzjos to Anna of Montenegro in 1897, and, in the 1880s, with a proposed marriage between Louis's other brother, Sandro of Bulgaria, and Princess Victoria of Prussia. This marriage did not take place, but became a five-year fiasco, ruining the life of that Princess Victoria, while Sandro married a soubrette from the Darmstadt theatre.

‡ Princess Marie of Battenberg (1852–1923), author of *Reminiscences* (1925), married 1871, Gustave, Count of Erbach-Schönberg (1840–1908).

completed the group when he arrived from his naval duties.

Most of these figures were assembled on the platform of Darmstadt station when Queen Victoria's train drew in at 8.00 a.m. on 23 April 1885.

Young Ernie was confirmed in the morning of 25 April, and Alice was christened the same afternoon. Staying at the Neue Palais, Queen Victoria wrote at length:

A day of great emotion. Dear beloved Alice's birthday & her darling boy to be confirmed & 1st grandchild christened. But she was not there to see it! . . .

Went downstairs with Louis at 1.30. Ernie had put on his uniform & looked so tall & broad. He is now the same height as his father. The whole family numbering 17, lunched in the big Dining room, below, a very handsome luncheon. I sat between Ernie & Serge.* After talking a little in the Drawing room, went upstairs to rest a little. At 4, we came down again for the Christening of Victoria & Ludwig's dear little Baby, which took place in the same room, in which we lunched. At the upper end of the room, an altar had been placed, on which stood the beautiful old rock crystal crucifix which, as well as the silver brocade altar cloth (made out of her wedding dress) had belonged to Pss. Charles. Dr Bender, who had christened Victoria herself, at Windsor, performed the service, which was very short. Louis, Pce Alexander, Pss Battenberg, Ella, Marie Erbach & myself were sponsors, & stood together, while Victoria (with a little cap on, looking very pretty), Ludwig, Beatrice, William of Hesse,† Liko & Franzjos, stood opposite. The suites, Ministers, & some of the servants, were also present. The very nice nurse held the Baby & handed her to me. She received the names of Victoria Alice Elizabeth Julie Marie, but she is to be called Alice.[13]

On 1 May, once Queen Victoria had completed her round of

* Victoria's promise to her grandmother, 'we can easily manage that you need not see him much', had not worked. [VMH to QV, 8 April 1885 – RA U 166/7]

† Prince William (1845–1900), the Grand Duke's younger brother. A passionate Wagnerian, who otherwise did little in life.

visits to family coffins at the Rosenhöhe, the park where the Hesse family are buried, her train left Darmstadt by moonlight. Louis, Victoria, Alice and Princess Beatrice were aboard. They all crossed the Channel in the royal yacht, Queen Victoria disembarking at Sheerness. Alice sailed on with her parents to Portsmouth, where the family settled back at Sennicotts, near Chichester. There they enjoyed life in the tranquil countryside of West Sussex, a welcome contrast to court life whether at Windsor or Darmstadt.

At Sennicotts Louis was happy 'in the proud position of a father of a family'. He found that he and Victoria had become thoroughly English, conversing in that language rather than German. He appreciated the interest Victoria took in all naval matters, and did not mind that they had to live 'in a small way'. He wrote to a friend:

> It is certainly a mighty fine 'loaf' in the *Victoria and Albert*, and I should not care ever to go back to her. It is, of course, very pleasant, when one is married and has an opposite number who is a regular ship-keeper, but it unfits one for any other work.[14]

Though Louis was happy, Queen Victoria felt the need to admonish her granddaughter: 'Let me again ask you to remember that your *1st duty* is to your dear and most devoted *Husband* to whom you can *never* be *kind enough* & to whom I think a *little* more *tenderness* is due *sometimes*.'[15] Princess Victoria was quick to reply: 'I shall not forget what you said about my duty to Louis, & indeed it will be easy to fulfil it, for I love him with all my heart & if I have seemed to think of Papa more than him, it is only because I am so afraid of my happy married life making me neglect poor Papa, who has always been the best & kindest of fathers to me.'[16]

Queen Victoria lived until Alice was nearly sixteen. Alice saw her at Windsor, Osborne, Balmoral, Buckingham Palace, in Darmstadt and in the south of France. There were times when she spent weeks on end in Queen Victoria's company. Equally, more than a year could go by without her setting eyes on her. But never was her presence unfelt.

Alice's emergence from childhood into adolescence coincided with the last years of the Queen's life. As she grew older, Alice took stock of this complex figure, whose every whim was treated as a command. In later life, when Alice referred to 'The Queen', she thought first of Queen Victoria.

Alice was one of the many descendants who pointed out that Queen Victoria was a much sweeter person than her traditionally austere image suggested, just as Meriel Buchanan was startled by the melodious youthfulness of her voice. Alice would recall that her great-grandmother was fond of a ribald story, just as her own mother was, speaking with glee of the stationer in Copenhagen who wrapped his customer's purchases in paper bearing his name: W.C. Stinks.[17]

It is a tribute to Queen Victoria that so many of her descendants believed that she loved them the best. Alice's mother maintained that she had a special affinity with the Queen, having been brought up by her as a daughter, following her own mother's death. She found Queen Victoria less and less austere as the years went by.

In the privacy of her sitting room the Queen would take off her widow's cap and wear a simple bow arrangement at the back of her head. Princess Victoria remembered 'a faint perfume of orange blossom',[18] which the Queen had found in Grasse. She had a good sense of humour, though hated to laugh at the misfortunes of others. Recalling her childhood, Alice once told her granddaughter the Princess Royal that she was sitting behind her great-grandmother at Osborne when an ambassador came for an audience. The man was so nervous that he tripped and fell flat on his face. Alice watched her great-grandmother, whose face did not flinch, though there was 'a slight trembling of the veil'.[19]

When she was older, Alice would 'drive out' with the Queen. Sometimes a female member of the family sat with her, while a male relation might walk along outside. At Balmoral the Queen would be seated in a pony carriage, followed by a group of Highland servants and a troupe of dogs running in and out of the flowerbeds.

The Queen had her own brand of charm which endeared her to those who served her. The Dean of Windsor, Randall Davidson, concluded that there was 'a combination of absolute truthfulness and simplicity with the instinctive recognition and quiet assertion of her position as Queen'. He believed that her lack of 'stately or splendid appearance' may have been another factor:

> People were taken by surprise by the sheer force of her personality. It may seem strange, but it is true that as a woman she was both shy and humble. Abundant examples will occur to those who know her. But as Queen she was neither shy nor humble, and asserted her position unhesitatingly.[20]

Princess Victoria put it slightly differently: 'Grandmama was essentially what was called a womanly nature, and her likes and dislikes were influenced by personal contacts. This was the secret of Lord Beaconsfield's charm for her, he never overlooked the woman in the Sovereign.'[21]

At the time of Alice's birth in 1885, the Queen was still in good health, but rheumatism, failing eyesight and dental problems caused a gradual decline.[22] The Queen grew increasingly lame, having injured both legs in falls, and relied on her Indian servants to support her from room to room. In her last years she moved about the house in a wheelchair. She feared that she might go blind like her grandfather, George III. Having suffered badly from gout, she drank only whisky and water at meals.

Because Queen Victoria liked to know every detail in the progress of her descendants, Alice's development was recorded in her diary and letters to her and can therefore be traced from vaccination to first tooth to tentative steps. By June 1885 she was 'growing nicely & is very merry, laughing & crowing all day'.[23] On the Queen's instructions, she was put into short clothes at three months, Princess Victoria using some of the embroidery from her dead mother's trousseau for frocks for her.

At five months, in July, Alice was at Kent House for the wedding of Princess Beatrice, for which Queen Victoria only gave permission when it was agreed that Prince Henry (or 'Liko') would come and live with the family. At the wedding breakfast, the Queen had a chance to inspect 'the dear pretty little Baby, who sits up now'.[24]

Alice spent the winter of 1885 in Darmstadt and at the Heiligenberg, where her father was on half-pay again, having relinquished his command of the royal yacht. In November, Victoria sent a new picture of her to Queen Victoria.

I think you will find her much altered & she has almost an older look on the photo than in reality. I fear she is very backward with her teeth, which show no signs of coming through yet. Otherwise she is well advanced, sits up nicely if supported in the back, laughs & produces many funny sounds, is very little shy with strangers & plays with everything you give her . . . Her attempts at crawling are feeble still, but she rolls about like a porpoise.[25]

For Alice's first birthday in 1886, her great-grandmother sent her a hood that she made herself and a brooch, which Alice 'laughed over delightedly & touched daintily with one finger'.[26] Princess Victoria sent a further report: 'Baby brightens the house up wonderfully & is universally admired. She is getting quite strong & if holding on to a chair can stand alone.'[27]

Alice's parents lived adequately on an allowance from Louis's father, but were concerned when Queen Victoria demanded their presence in England in the summer of 1886: 'Baby is just at the age when she cannot be left alone one minute, without risk of accidents, especially as she is restless & lively as quick-silver, & we should be obliged to take the nursery maid too, as Jones [the nurse] could not do the packing etc. & look after the child at the same time.'[28] The Queen paid their travel expenses and thus Alice passed that summer at Osborne, Windsor Castle, Cumberland Lodge (the Windsor Great Park home of the Queen's third daughter, Helena, Princess Christian) and Balmoral (Alice's only sojourn there under the aegis of Queen Victoria).

She was just beginning to walk, and at Cumberland Lodge in May she had a rare encounter with a baby of her own age. Victoria recalled:

Aunt Helena's faithful lady-in-waiting, Emily Loch had a little niece of Alice's age to tea one afternoon and we thought it would be nice for the babies to play together. The idea was not a success, for after crawling towards each other, they proceeded to poke their fingers at each other's eyes and grab hold of each other's hair. I fancy each thought the other a live doll![29]

A while later, in Malta, Alice went on to bite her Edinburgh cousin, Baby Bee.* Victoria was a little wary of Alice's playmate: 'Bee was somewhat critical at that early age already, declaring that Alice ate butter and bread, not bread and butter.'[30] A fondness for over-eating was a habit that Alice carried through life.

Perhaps the most alarming such incident involved Queen Victoria herself, as her mother described:

She [the Queen] was not always so lenient towards the behaviour of small children. I remember when Alice was a little girl of about four, she, like many grandchildren and great-grandchildren before her, refused to kiss Grandmama's hand, and when Grandmama, in a severe voice, said 'naughty child' and slapped her hand, Alice slapped back, saying 'Naughty Grandmama'. I had hurriedly to remove the offender.[31]

No one had yet noticed that Alice was deaf. The first hint came in a letter to Queen Victoria in January 1887, though the cause was still undeveloped in her mother's mind. Victoria wrote:

Baby looks so nice in the pretty frocks you gave her. She is very slow in learning to talk, but on the other hand very clever with her fingers. She unties a bow without ever pulling it into a knot & now & then succeeds in buttoning her own dressing gown. This sort of amusement she is particularly fond of & spends any amount of time patiently at it, which is very funny.[32]

* Princess Beatrice (1884–1966), married 1909, Infante Alfonso of Bourbon-Orleans (1886–1975), a distinguished pilot.

It was not until Alice was four years old that her mother began to articulate her concern. In a progress report to Queen Victoria, she wrote:

The child has grown very much since last you saw her, is very lively & quick with her fingers, but decidedly backward of speech, using all sorts of self-invented words & pronouncing others very indistinctly, so that strangers find it difficult to understand her. We make great efforts to improve this & I think the society of her little Erbach* cousin is helping her on.[33]

Alice's grandmother, Princess Battenberg, was the person who identified the problem as deafness, taking Alice to an ear specialist in Darmstadt. Alice had been born with the defect, though some in the family assert that her hearing was damaged on one of her early sea voyages. The deafness was due to the thickness of the Eustachian tubes and would always be a problem.

Her mother spent long hours with her, teaching her to lip-read, and she learned to follow conversations. By May 1889, Alice was speaking 'quite nicely at last',[34] and her hearing was deemed better a year later. But in 1893, when she was eight, Victoria took her to an aurist in London, her lack of progress remaining a 'great worry'[35] to her parents. They discovered that no operation was possible. By the age of fourteen there was a marked improvement, but it was not until as late as 1922 that Alice announced that she had heard a cuckoo for the first time.

The deafness isolated Alice from the usual friendships of childhood but she learned to fall back on her own resources. Besides this, she was neither a problem child nor in any way unintelligent.

Her mother had to decide how to treat her within the family circle. Alice's younger brothers and sister were told that they must talk normally amongst themselves, making no concessions to Alice.

*Princess Elisabeth (Edda) of Erbach-Schonberg (1883–1966), daughter of Alice's aunt, Princess Marie of Battenberg. In 1910 she married Wilhelm, Prince of Stolberg-Wernigerode (d. 1931). They had one son.

She would either join in or not. This family edict was something that her brother Dickie (Lord Mountbatten) found hard to understand and which continued to disturb him in later life.

As she grew older, Alice could hear certain voices according to pitch. In the 1950s she surprised her family in Baden by hearing the guards march outside. It was the echo of the stamping boots that she detected.[36] And her lip-reading became so good that people put their hands over their mouths when imparting secrets across the room, aware that she could lip-read not only in English and German but in several languages. 'You had to be very careful what you said,' recalled Alice's niece, Princess Eugénie.*[37]

Alice's disability worried Victoria more than Alice herself: 'I know . . . from experience that to see one's children not quite strong, or with some little ailment, like Alice's hearing, is a cause of worry & pain to the parents.'[38]

Alice's father was rising fast in the Royal Navy. His occasional attendance was required in England, but more often in Malta with the Mediterranean Fleet. But for all his success, Louis's progress to the top of his profession was far from smooth. When, in August 1887, he was appointed Commander of *Dreadnought* under Captain Sir Harry Stephenson, in the Mediterranean, there was an outcry in the House of Commons. He was accused of having been given preferment over thirty other officers and it was maintained that this was because he was a prince. Willie Redmond, the Irish Nationalist MP, asked 'whether a German has ever before been placed in command of a British man-of-war, over the heads of British officers equally qualified'. The First Lord praised Louis's career and pointed out that Captain Stephenson had specifically asked for him.[39]

Louis and Victoria spent most of their summers in Hesse-Darmstadt, where both had family responsibilities. Sometimes Alice travelled with her parents and sometimes, as when her mother had

*Many years later Alice relished watching silent films, where she was able to lip-read what the characters were really saying. She amused her family by relating how in a passionate love scene in Von Stroheim's film, *Greed* (1923), in reality the hero was telling the heroine that he was being evicted for not paying his rent.

typhoid in the summer of 1887, she was left with her grandparents. Because of the travelling and because her parents could not employ a large staff, she spent more time with them than she would have done had she been raised in a large Victorian household with distant nurseries and green baize doors.

In 1887 there occurred the great royal milestone, the Golden Jubilee of Queen Victoria, which kept Louis and Victoria in England for a whole month from mid-June until mid-July. While her parents stayed at Buckingham Palace, Alice and her cousin, Feo Meiningen,* were placed with the mistress of the robes, the Duchess of Buccleuch, in her mansion at Whitehall. From there the children watched the Jubilee procession to Westminster Abbey, dazzled by the carriages and horses and the royal guests in their fine uniforms. For her brief attendance of this event, Alice was given the Queen's Golden Jubilee medal, a trophy which delighted her.

The island of Malta played an important role in the family's life. Alice was first taken there in October 1887, returning to Europe in April 1888, and stayed there with her mother and father through the winters of 1888, 1890 and 1891. There were four more consecutive winters there between 1894 and 1897. Thus from an early age Alice became accustomed to life in a hot climate, which prepared her well for the heat of Greek summers to come.

Malta was the most vital strategic point in the Mediterranean for maintaining sea power. It was a place of festivals, notably the carnival in Valetta, with processions, a battle of confetti and three days of dancing in the streets.

When the family first arrived there in the autumn of 1887, they found Alfred (the Duke of Edinburgh) living in some splendour at San Antonio, as Commander-in-Chief of the Mediterranean Fleet. San Antonio became a focal point for their lives: 'with its lovely garden [it] looks very much like an oasis in this yellow stone desert,

* Princess Feodora of Saxe-Meiningen (1879–1945), a granddaughter of Empress Frederick of Germany, married in 1898 Prince Heinrich XXX Reuss. She achieved posthumous fame as a sufferer of porphyria [see John C.G. Röhl *et al*, *The Purple Secret* (Bantam, 1998)].

but there are plenty of small hills & dells to relieve the apparent monotony.'[40] The Battenberg family settled at 1 Molino Avento, a small corner house, on the battlements of Valetta, renting the flat next door for the nursery and knocking a hole through. Alice enjoyed outdoor pursuits, which were punctuated by lessons with her mother and later a governess. She rode with Uncle Alfred's children, whose ponies had been brought from England.

Life in Malta revolved around the Mediterranean Fleet. Alice became familiar with bearded naval officers in their whites, on visits on board the great vessels, celebrating 'Bescheerung' (the distribution of presents at Christmas) with the ratings, going from ship to ship, nibbling plum puddings. At times their routine was disrupted by a terrifying royal aunt coming to stay or the arrival of a whiskery figure such as the old Duke of Cambridge, who nodded off during concerts. Alice was too young to take note of one shy, bearded young lieutenant, who spent time with her family and was to be seen gazing lovingly at the eldest Edinburgh girl, Marie (later Queen of Romania). Nor did either she or young Prince George of Wales himself divine that one day he would be her king and, years hence, play a significant role in the fate of her family.

4. Growing Up

Alice was not old enough to form an impression of her paternal grandfather, Prince Alexander of Hesse. This genial figure, living under the shadow of his youthful transgressions, fell ill with cancer of the kidney in the summer of 1888, suffering valiantly. In order not to alarm him, the family left for Malta on 21 November that year, Louis and Victoria taking leave of him as if all was well.

Within a few days Louis and Victoria were summoned back. On 15 December Prince Alexander died at the Heiligenberg, aged sixty-five. 'Poor Louis is terribly unhappy,' wrote Victoria. 'He always got on so well with his father.'[1] Queen Victoria, who lived with an expanding portfolio of grief, sympathized with Louis for the loss of his 'paternal roof' and urged Victoria: 'Try & keep lovingly together, helping one another & do all you can for your poor dear Mother-in-law for whom the loss is dreadful.'[2] Louis went on half-pay in order to do that. The family spent the severe winter of 1888–9 with Victoria's father.

Louis inherited the Heiligenberg, where he and Victoria had spent their honeymoon in 1884, and so, at last, Alice had a home of her own. For most of 1889 they were based there or in Darmstadt, and it was at the Heiligenberg that Alice's sister Louise was born on 13 July 1889.

Queen Victoria had been pressing Victoria to have another child for some time. She had complained of the lack of playmates for Alice on her birthday in February 1888: 'her birthday, her 3rd already & she has *no* little Brother or Sister!!'[3] Louise was born prematurely as the result of Victoria going on a rough drive to Felsberg.

Alice's mother judged Louise 'not as pretty as Alice was, having a big nose, & is said by most people to be very like me'.[4] Nor did she revise her opinion in her memoirs: 'Unlike Alice, who was a fine sturdy baby, Louise was rather a miserable little object, and the nickname "shrimp" which Louis then gave her remained attached to her during her childhood.'[5] Alice witnessed the christening at the Heiligenberg on 9 August, greatly interested by 'the man who washed little sister's head'.[6]

When Louis and Victoria went to Malta that October and he assumed command of the small cruiser, *Scout*, Alice and Louise stayed behind with Princess Battenberg. They were separated from their parents for five long months. It seems extraordinary that a mother could leave a baby as yet unweaned, a mere four months old, so early in her life, but as Victoria assured the Queen: 'we could not manage otherwise.'[7] She added: 'We thought the baby too young for such a long journey.'[8]

Princess Battenberg took a particular interest in Alice. In turn Alice learned much from Princess Battenberg, who spoke German, Russian, Polish and French, and read Dante in Italian and Shakespeare in English, and of whom it was said that Bismarck was afraid. It was a special friendship as can develop between a granddaughter and grandmother, and it much pleased Queen Victoria, who held Princess Battenberg in high esteem.

It is invariably asserted that Alice's Aunt Ella was the religious influence on her life. But Princess Battenberg, a deeply intelligent woman, was equally devout. She had suffered two shocks in the months before taking Alice into her care. The first was the death of her husband in December 1888, and the second was the marriage of her son, Sandro of Bulgaria, to the soubrette, Johanna Loisinger. This union had shocked her despite – or perhaps because of – her own morganatic status. She never saw Sandro again, and though Queen Victoria later met the soubrette, finding her 'pleasing',[9] she did not. She retired for a time to a deaconesshouse, 'broken in mind and spirit',[10] in the words of her daughter Marie, who eventually persuaded her to come out. Looking after Alice constituted her return to normality and for Alice there was the added bonus that she tended to spoil her.

On 8 April 1890 Alice was reunited with her mother, back from

Malta. For days Alice scarcely left her side. 'I find her grown & her figure less round & babyish,'[11] reported Victoria. Soon afterwards in September there was a further separation when Victoria accompanied her father, Ernie and Alix on a visit to Ella at Ilinskoe, in Russia, and in October, when she returned, the children's nurse, Mary Jones, originally found by Queen Victoria, left to be replaced by Ellen Hughes just before the family set off for another Malta winter. Hughes was a success.

Alice's education at her mother's knee continued in Malta. Now she was able to read German fluently, and began English and writing, taking an hour's lesson each day.

Alice was again left in Darmstadt in the summer of 1891, when her mother went to England. She passed her time with another new nurse, Sophie Hahn, and went on expeditions with her grandmother to Schönberg (the ancient castle on the hill where Louis's sister, Marie Erbach, lived), Seeheim and elsewhere. Her mother came home for but two days before departing for Venice, arriving back in time for Louise's second birthday in July.

Alice was developing into a truly beautiful child. The Empress Frederick, who saw her at Schloss Homburg in August, sent an enthusiastic report: '*What* a *beautiful* child little Alice is! She has the most perfect little face, & those beautiful brown eyes & dark eyebrows!'[12] To her daughter, Crown Princess Sophie,* in Athens, she added: 'One can hardly take one's eyes off little Alice's face, it is so interesting and picturesque. If she remains so, she will be one of the prettiest girls in Europe.'[13] The future Edward VII endorsed this, declaring at about this time that 'no throne in Europe was too good for her'.[14]

In February 1892, after another stint in Malta, the family moved into a new apartment at the Alte Palais, loaned to them by Victoria's father. Presently Louis went to London, but Alice and Louise stayed in Darmstadt with their mother. Alice began regular riding lessons on a pony called Marstall, 'a most gentle, docile little animal',[15] sent

* Crown Princess Sophie (1870–1932), later Queen Sophie of Greece. Married 1889, Constantine I, who succeeded in 1913.

over by Queen Victoria. And when she went to visit her cousins, Alice was conveyed through the snow on a sleigh.

In the autumn of 1891, Louis IV had suffered shooting pains in the heart while attending Imperial manoeuvres at Kassel, and again when ascending a mountain during a shoot with his cousin, the Prince of Leiningen. On 4 March 1892, he suffered a paralysing stroke during lunch at the Neue Palais. His family gathered at his bedside. A long vigil began until the Grand Duke died, aged fifty-four, at 12.45 a.m. on 13 March.

Darmstadt descended into deep mourning. The Grand Duke lay in state, hands folded, head slightly raised, adorned in the uniform of his Hessian regiment. Tall, lighted tapers gave the only light, clergymen in black robes and guards with fixed bayonets stood by the coffin, and one thousand soldiers filed past. Queen Victoria published her grief in the Court Circular: 'Another heavy blow has fallen on the Queen in the loss of Her Majesty's beloved son-in-law . . . in whom the Queen feels she loses a real son.'[16]

On the day of the funeral on 17 March, shops closed and black drapes hung from private houses. The coffin, resting on a huge bier, covered with flowers, was conveyed to the Rosenhöhe by six horses, draped in black cloth and caparisoned with black plumes. The soldiers wore the old-fashioned uniforms of the day, with helmets and white plumes. The choir sang and the veterans wept. The much loved ruler of Hesse-Darmstadt was laid to rest in the mausoleum built for his wife Alice.

A few days later, an even younger member of the family died, for this was an age when one in three children failed to reach adulthood. Alice's subnormal cousin, Maxi, the fourteen-year-old son of Marie Erbach, died twelve days after the Grand Duke. His had been a hopeless life, his mother describing him euphemistically as 'Maxi, an angel in human guise, who was sent to us, with shadowed mind, from the great beyond by God.'[17]

The new Grand Duke was Louis's only surviving son, Ernst Ludwig, then twenty-three, and in the view of Empress Frederick 'much too young and inexperienced for his position'.[18] In April Queen Victoria visited Darmstadt and invested Ernie with his father's insignia of the Order of the Garter, enjoining him: 'Wear it as honourably as your father did.'[19]

Ernie was still unmarried and, though at the time he seemed more preoccupied with a nasty abscess and a swollen tooth than marriage, Queen Victoria undertook the leading role in negotiations to find him a bride. Victoria Melita was one of the Edinburgh cousins whom Alice knew from Malta days. Queen Victoria had contemplated a union between Ernie and 'Ducky', as she was known, when she saw them making friends at Balmoral in 1891. She now proceeded to make this match a reality.

Ducky and Ernie were eventually married in Coburg on 19 April 1894, but soon discovered that they were an ill-matched pair. Historians have constantly averred that Ernie was homosexual, which his penchant for the arts and delight in fancy dress might support. Ducky was variously described as a 'rather passionate . . . often misunderstood' child,[20] 'somewhat farouche',[21] and capable of using 'strength and withering contempt when disappointed'.[22] She liked to climb out of the window at Wolfsgarten and ride her horse in the small hours of the night. The mismatch finally convinced Queen Victoria that she would never again dabble in marital unions.

The Battenbergs remained in Darmstadt until the summer of 1892. Alice was still too young to be greatly affected by the court mourning. Her main preoccupation was having milk teeth removed in Frankfurt. 'She was so good and quiet,'[23] recorded her nanny, Sophie Hahn.

The most memorable incident for the children was the dramatic fire that took place at the Heiligenberg at the end of July. Princess Beatrice and her husband, Prince Henry of Battenberg, were staying with them on one of their rare escapes from Queen Victoria. With them was their young son, Drino,* who played with Alice

* Prince Alexander of Battenberg (1886–1960), later Marquess of Carisbrooke.

and Louise. What should have been a welcome respite for Princess Beatrice turned grim when she was 'dreadfully stung'[24] by gnats. With her maid she pursued the gnats with a lighted candle. The result was catastrophic. The candle caught a mosquito curtain, fire blazed and in minutes the Princess's rooms and the roof of the pavilion near the clock tower were consumed by flames. Sophie Hahn was woken by the cry of fire: 'How my knees were trembling. The Princess [Victoria] came quickly and ordered the children to get dressed and take any valuables from our room and put them in a basket which we did.'[25]

Alice, Louise and Drino looked on from a safe vantage point, 'wide-eyed and interested',[26] and found much to engage them. Princess Beatrice darted about in a nightgown covered only by Princess Battenberg's cloak. 'It was awful hearing Princess Beatrice shouting after her pearls and jewels, but no one could save them,'[27] wrote Sophie Hahn. Onlookers caused the traditional havoc, one of the maids was convinced that she would get bronchitis despite the warmth of the night and the fire, and finally, Victoria inadvertently terrified young Drino by telling him that the firemen had come – 'his idea of firemen being some sort of imps that came out of the fire!'[28]

The damage would have been worse, but there was no wind, and by 5.00 a.m. the Jugenheim fire brigade had extinguished the blaze. The next day Princess Beatrice assessed her losses: emeralds split in two, pearls crumbled to chalk and many clothes lost. Her misery was completed by having to talk to the fire insurance assessors wearing a hat, her false fringe having been burnt.

More seriously, Victoria, who was pregnant again, worried that she might give birth prematurely. But it was not until a Sunday in November, when Princess Battenberg was on her way to church, that her old servant stopped her to announce: '*Es ist ein Prinz im Alten Palais angekommen.*' The old Princess was shocked that her daughter-in-law was being troubled by visitors so soon before giving birth. Only when Ernie and Alix rushed up to her excitedly did she realize that the 'prince' was the new baby. Prince George of Battenberg – or Georgie, as he was called in the family – arrived safely on 6 November 1892 at the Alte Palais in Darmstadt. With pride, Queen Victoria noted the birth of her thirteenth great-grandchild.

Alice, now aged seven, undertook more serious lessons with a tutor, Miss Robson, who had been out in India as governess to Princess Margaret of Connaught.

Early in 1893, Alice acquired a playmate in Meriel Buchanan, when her father, Sir George, arrived to assume his duties as Chargé d'Affaires. Meriel recalled many visits to the Heiligenberg and to the small wooden cottage in the grounds, 'where Princess Alice and I played at being housewives, sweeping the floor with miniature brooms and, under the guidance of a nurse, trying to make scones for tea'.[29]

Meriel became an admirer of her young companion:

> [Princess Alice] was my ideal, a paragon of perfection, whose golden hair and big, dark-brown eyes filled me with admiration and envy. I wanted to copy her in all things, to wear a comb or a slide instead of a ribbon round my hair, to be as tall and slender as she was, to hold myself with that grace and dignity, that seemed to come to her so naturally. Even her slight deafness, which gave her sometimes a rather faraway look, as if she was living in a world of her own, was an added attraction in my eyes.[30]

Soon after Georgie's birth, Louis took up his latest post as Naval Adviser to the Inspector-General of Fortifications, with an office at the Horseguards in Whitehall, renting a house in Pimlico. Victoria joined him in March 1893, but the children stayed in Darmstadt until May.

There now began a phase which kept the family mainly, though not exclusively, in England until the summer of 1894. Thus once again Queen Victoria loomed large in their lives, and they made the rounds of her many residences. But before this, they enjoyed a three-month phase as a 'normal' family, living by the sea in a rented house on the Under Cliffe at Sandgate, near Folkestone.

Presently, the demands of royal life encroached. Alice was bidden to be a bridesmaid to Princess May of Teck when she married the Duke of York. 'Poor little Alice Albany', who was on holiday in Arolsen, had been invited to be a bridesmaid at this wedding but was then sent a telegram telling her not to bother.* Queen Victoria informed the groom that 'little Alice Battenberg, dear *Aunt* Alice's grd. child, *wd* take her place' as one of the ten bridesmaids. 'She is lovely & already 8 years old.'[31]

The wedding took place at the Chapel Royal, St James's Palace, on 6 July 1893. The bridesmaids played their part well, Queen Victoria noting that Alice looked 'very sweet in white satin, with a little pink and red rose on the shoulder and some small bows of the same on the shoes'.†[32] On the return journey there was tremendous cheering for the royal family, and particularly for Princess May, who would one day be England's queen. The occasion did not instil a lifelong love of ceremony into Alice. Little Alice of Albany, on the other hand, relished such occasions until well into the 1970s.

After the wedding, Queen Victoria entertained Princess Victoria and 'her 3 sweet children'[33] at Windsor for ten days, during which Alice had dancing lessons, at least one of which was performed under the watchful eye of her great-grandmother. It was at this time that, back in London, Alice went to an ear specialist. While staying at Buckingham Palace, both Alice and Louise had their tonsils removed by Queen Victoria's doctor, Sir James Reid. They were soon back at Sandgate, where the sea air effaced their slight paleness after the operation.

Later that July, after a brief return home to Germany, Victoria and the children settled into 37 Eccleston Square, the Pimlico home rented by Louis for the next year. Victoria told her grandmother:

* Princess Alice (later Countess of Athlone) recalled that her cousin Alice of Battenberg was 'a much prettier girl anyway, but I never got over the disappointment' [*For My Grandchildren* (Cassell, 1966), p. 80].

† The four little ones were Alice, Princess Margaret and Princess Patricia of Connaught, and Princess Ena of Battenberg.

We are very comfortably established here & the house though small is a very nice & clean one & the rooms are of a fair size. The garden in the Square is quite private & a very nice place for the children to play in & Battersea Park, which is a very quiet & prettily laid out one, is only a quarter of an hour's walk from our house.[34]

The Prince of Wales, with no consideration of the relative lack of income of the Battenbergs, decried the cheap neighbourhood, describing the square as a place where 'only pianists lived'.[35] Queen Victoria preferred the children to play in the gardens of Buckingham Palace and gave the family a key. Even so, London was so dirty that playing in the soot-covered bushes of the palace gardens made the children filthy.

For Christmas 1893, the family went to Osborne. Alice was now old enough to enjoy Queen Victoria's Isle of Wight home, which was something of a haven for children. The Prince Consort had designed it as a retreat for the monarch and her family away from the more formal life of the capital, though cabinet ministers frequently crossed the Solent on government business.

The nursery floor was directly above the Queen's apartments, with a schoolroom (used regularly by Princess Beatrice's children) and a dormitory full of beds, where the numerous little ones slept. On the first floor there was another schoolroom for those over the age of six. All these rooms were well stocked with toys.

In the grounds, there was the Swiss Cottage, built by the Prince Consort as a play place for his nine children. It had a pantry, kitchen and dining room, and there they learned about domestic matters. Underneath was a museum containing all kinds of artefacts brought back by different members of the royal family from every corner of the world. There was also a small fort with miniature cannons, and near by an elaborate bathing machine, used by the Queen for discreet dips in the sea on the warmer days of the summer.

Christmas 1893 was a time of some sadness for the Queen. She mourned Louis's brother, Sandro of Bulgaria, who had died in

November, and was depressed by her increasing lameness and bad eyesight. But in the Osborne nursery Alice and the other children played happily, attending the Christmas service at 11.00 a.m. and the lighting of the tree at 6.00 p.m.

On 2 January 1894 the Queen went to watch Alice and her cousins, Drino and Ena, being drilled by a sergeant from Parkhurst; there were tea parties and much scampering about. Now that she was approaching her ninth birthday, Alice accompanied her mother and Queen Victoria on an afternoon drive through Newport and West Cowes, the first of many such drives in the remaining seven years of the Queen's long life. Presently, Queen Victoria wrote: 'I love these darling children so, almost as much as their own parents.'[36]

After Osborne, Alice was taken to Sandringham for her first weekend with the Prince and Princess of Wales. There she found a more sumptuous way of life than at any of Queen Victoria's residences. There was a tea party at the Big House, the Duke of York showed them round the stables, kennels and pheasantry, and before they left, some 400 partridges were shot.

Just before Easter 1894, the Battenbergs moved from London to Elm Grove, Walton-on-Thames, a spacious house, with 'scanty and old-fashioned'[37] furniture, comfortable and with a small garden. The Thames was a short walk away through the town. One of their treats was to take a boat and go up river.

In April, Alice's Aunt Alix came to stay. She was now engaged to the Tsarevich of Russia. This was another of those controversial Russian alliances that so displeased Queen Victoria. Alix had loved the Tsarevich since 1888. At first she had been reluctant to change her religion to Orthodoxy. But she overcame this misgiving after her brother Ernie married, realizing that he no longer needed her as a companion, and accepted the Tsarevich. Queen Victoria was thunderstruck when Ella told her.

In Walton Alice enjoyed some of the excitements of the occasion, especially when the Tsarevich arrived from Russia in mid-June. The young couple were clearly deeply in love, and their informal stay was a rare period of freedom, as Nicky brought only his old valet with him. Alice watched them roaming about as they pleased, undeterred by English rain, happy to be together. She and Louise went with the couple for drives around Walton, the Tsarevich writing: 'The little girls jumped around terribly in the carriage.'[38]

Another guest at Walton was Alice's uncle, Franzjos. The Battenbergs took him on the river, where he proved such a hopeless oarsman that Alice was put ashore with a rope to pull them upstream.* But she ran so fast that she was forever pulling the bows into the bank.

In due course, the family and the inhabitants of Walton watched in amazement as a royal carriage and outrider arrived to whisk the Battenbergs, Alix and Nicky to Windsor Castle.

Following Louis and Victoria's return to Darmstadt at the beginning of August 1894, the remains of Prince Alexander of Hesse were buried in a new mausoleum at the Heiligenberg. Alice watched with her family as the coffin was borne up the hill, and saw her grandmother, Princess Battenberg, weep as the coffin came in sight.

Soon after this, Alix made a precipitate journey to Livadia to join the Tsarevich, whose father, Tsar Alexander III, had fallen suddenly and gravely ill. She arrived in time to receive his blessing. Events then moved quickly. The Tsar died on 2 November and was buried in St Petersburg. Alix married the new Tsar, Nicholas II, in the Chapel of the Winter Palace on 26 November.

In the meantime, the Battenbergs had gone again to Malta, where Louis commanded *Cambrian*. But they returned the following summer, staying at the Heiligenberg, where, in September, Princess Battenberg died. Though not unused to death, Alice had to face the first real loss of an ally in the world of grown-ups.

She saw Princess Battenberg lying dead in her open coffin in the terrace room. The family placed flowers round the coffin, but her

* Prince Franz Josef was also 'particularly poor as a shot. The cooks came to recognize only too clearly the birds which had eventually been brought down by his gun,' recorded the royal chef, Gabriel Tschumi [Gabriel Tschumi, *Royal Chef* (William Kimber, 1954), p. 63].

brother, little Georgie, placed a pear at her side, insisting that she would prefer this to flowers.[39] Princess Victoria wrote to her own grandmother to tell her how sad Alice was. 'Poor little Alice too,' replied the Queen, 'it is touching to hear of her sorrow. I hope this feeling of affection & gratitude will always be encouraged as her dear Grandmama was so fond of & kind to her.'[40]

Thereafter life continued with further visits to Malta, returns to Darmstadt, stays at the Heiligenberg and Wolfsgarten, visits from the aunts in Russia and a new treat – the occasional excursion to Aunt Irène at her new home, Hemmelmark in Schleswig-Holstein, where they bathed in the sea, fished in the lake or went out in Prince Henry's new sailing yacht, *Esperance*, bought at Cowes in an era when German princes were welcome there.

Queen Victoria continued to be sent progress reports about Alice. She heard from Princess Victoria that after a fractious phase, Alice was now more settled and reasonable, and her hearing seemed to have improved. As Empress Frederick observed: 'Alice is so handsome and one really cannot call her deaf, she is only not very quick of hearing, that is all. She is 11 but as big as a girl of 14.'[41]

5. Alice with Queen Victoria

One of the naval duties that irked Alice's father more than anything was to be summoned from active service in the Mediterranean to attend upon Queen Victoria's annual spring holiday on the French Riviera. In 1895 he complained to Princess Beatrice about having to go. She informed him that it was the Admiralty's idea and not the Queen's, but that the Queen would see that he was not kept away too long.

The following year he was allowed to bring Victoria and Alice with him. They made their home with the lately widowed Princess Beatrice* and her four children – the 'little fatherless ones',[1] as Queen Victoria called them – at Villa Liserbe, near the Queen's hotel at Cimiez, high above Nice.

Every afternoon the Queen drove out in her carriage, often accompanied by her granddaughter Victoria. This was a magnificent spectacle, the legendary Queen-Empress seated in her carriage with two outriders in front and two behind. The local children ran up, presenting flowers snatched from anywhere, and were rewarded with a franc piece, given by the Queen. Occasionally a newfangled motor car would pass them, smothering the Queen and her companion in dust.

The next year, Victoria and Alice again joined the Queen in a newly built hotel, the Excelsior Hotel Regina, an edifice like a wedding cake. As usual, Princess Beatrice was with her and Princess Christian's daughter, (Helena) Victoria, made up the party. Alice was presented to her great-grandmother in the hall and pronounced

* In December 1895, Prince Henry of Battenberg, bored by prolonged attendance at Queen Victoria's court, saw in the Ashanti Expedition a chance to escape and prove himself. But he succumbed to malaria before seeing a shot fired and died at sea on 20 January 1896. His body was preserved in rum and brought home for burial at St Mildred's Church, Whippingham.

to be 'grown very tall'.[2] Though still not old enough to dine with the Queen, she accompanied her on afternoon drives in the carriage. One afternoon the royal party went to La Turbie with Alice's only surviving Battenberg uncle, Franzjos, and Princess Anna of Montenegro. While most of them went to a booth containing a 'camera obscura', Franzjos and Anna broke away from the main party. Soon afterwards, at breakfast, Louis announced their engagement and presently Anna's wily father, Prince Nikola, arrived to charm Queen Victoria.

Ten years had passed since Alice acquired her Golden Jubilee medal. In the celebrations of Queen Victoria's Diamond Jubilee, she took a larger part. The Battenbergs were amongst the many members of Queen Victoria's extended family who made their way to London, lodging with Queen Victoria's daughter, Princess Louise, at Kensington Palace.

The Jubilee was celebrated at St Paul's Cathedral on 21 June. Queen Victoria, who had been so reclusive in the middle years of her reign, came out into the midst of her people, surrounded by troops from every part of her Empire. The tiny figure was cheered in her carriage by vast, enthusiastic crowds as a beloved and respected Queen and Empress, the ruler of two thirds of the world's population.

For Alice, the day began when she joined the entire royal family in the Bow Room of Buckingham Palace to await the arrival of Queen Victoria in her wheelchair. Then came the procession to the steps of the cathedral. Louis was mounted; Victoria was in one carriage, and Alice was in another with Princess Beatrice's children, supervised, as a decade earlier, by the Duchess of Buccleuch.

When Alice stayed with Queen Victoria, she played with Princess Beatrice's children. The two families were on good terms, but over the years everyone from Prince Louis downwards took a disparaging view of young Drino and his sister Ena. During the Jubilee celebrations, Ena bowed from right to left in the carriage, a fact noticed in the press. This queenly behaviour impressed neither

Alice nor Louise and would take on a larger significance when, in 1906, Ena became the wife of the King of Spain.

The service of thanksgiving was held at the foot of the steps to St Paul's Cathedral, out of deference to the lameness of Queen Victoria. A few days later, Alice, Louise and Georgie attended the Queen's garden party at Buckingham Palace, and then, on 26 June, they saw the great naval review at Spithead, lunching on board *Majestic*. After these magnificent events, they would need little convincing that their great-grandmother ruled the world.

It was during the Jubilee summer that a lifelong ally entered the Battenberg household in the form of Nona Kerr. Princess Victoria had never had a lady-in-waiting before. Now she found a lady of breeding who could double as such and as governess. Nona was born in 1875, the youngest of the six sisters of Mark Kerr, Louis's closest naval friend. She was a granddaughter of the 6th Marquess of Lothian; her father, an admiral who had died not long before, had served Queen Victoria as groom-in-waiting. Princess Victoria employed her for a wage of £210 a year.

Nona's early days with the Battenberg family were suitably terrifying. Her first duty was to attend a dinner for 270 in a tent in the gardens of Buckingham Palace, the night before the Jubilee. Speaking no German, she found herself seated between two enormous German officers. Afterwards she was presented to Queen Victoria. Within three weeks, she found herself living in Germany in a household where she heard a babble of French and German spoken, but all too little English.

Princess Victoria was not there long enough to help her settle in, but soon Nona became the mainstay of the Battenberg family. She remained Victoria's lady-in-waiting for nineteen years and was her 'closest friend'[3] all her life.* All the family confided in her.

This friendship was strong enough to weather the mildly illicit devotion that the mousy Nona inspired from Louis. In 1905 he wrote to her from Canada: 'I miss you quite as much as my children

* Her papers are now in the Broadlands Archives.

and *her*,'[4] and when she married in 1915, he compared his feelings to losing a daughter in marriage, 'torn asunder in one's feelings of joy at her happiness and grief at one's own loss'.[5]

Throughout 1898 and until October 1899 Alice was based in Germany with her family, but they contrived to visit Queen Victoria at Osborne in both January 1898 and January 1899. Alice frequently joined her mother to drive out with Queen Victoria from Osborne House.

In Darmstadt in the autumn of 1898, Alice was joined by Louise in lessons with Fräulein Textor, a large lady with a beaming smile and booming voice, related to Goethe, who ran a finishing school for English girls. The girls performed in amateur theatricals, after which there were parties, with simnel cake, buns, honey and jam, and cups of chocolate and whipped cream. To widen Alice's education, Victoria began to take her to the opera, further testament to a gradual improvement in her hearing. Alice was now of an age to dine with her mother, Uncle Ernie and Ducky at the Neue Palais.

For recreation, Alice played tennis at the Neue Palais, swam in the new pool at the Heiligenberg until the weather turned cold, and rode a new pony called Cheril, brought from England. Meriel Buchanan observed her again: 'She was always at her ease, and never tongue-tied, self-conscious and awkward.'[6]

In June 1899 Louis was appointed Assistant Director of Naval Intelligence in London, causing another upheaval for the family, which settled at 40 Grosvenor Gardens in October in 'a very comfortable house',[7] not far from Louis's office. Louis had to spend a great deal of his time dealing with troops and officers departing for the Boer War. The whole family used to watch as the regiments marched to Victoria station, with bands playing 'God Save the Queen'.

The highlight of the year was joining the entire royal family at Windsor for Christmas. Queen Victoria, spending a rare Christmas at the castle, distributed gifts from the Christmas trees to the wives and children of soldiers at a tea party. She was pushed up and down the St George's Hall in her wheelchair and left the party for a while to take tea in her private apartments. Alice joined in the festivities with a host of cousins.

The atmosphere was lighter still for New Year's Eve at Sandringham, where there was energetic discussion as to whether 1900 was the last year of the old century or the first of the new. The general view, supported by the Prince of Wales, was that it heralded the new. For Alice it marked the dawn of a new age, as the days of childhood slipped away and she looked towards a grown-up life of long skirts, court parties and the fulfilment of what was accepted as her ultimate destiny, a suitable marriage.

It was hard to suppose that Queen Victoria would not reign for ever. Nevertheless there was a general sense of the Queen's gradual decline. The short period that the Battenbergs spent at Frogmore in the summer of 1900 was therefore a memorable one, especially in retrospect.

Frogmore House nestled in the Queen's private garden in sight of Windsor Castle, near the Long Walk and two Mausoleums. For the children excitement centred round the menagerie of animals, which included two large ostriches, two kangaroos, the late Emperor of Germany's charger and a magnificent South African zebra. Their attention was often diverted by the 'thrilling' sight of a brougham with shuttered blinds, said to contain the Munshi's* wife driving in the park.[8]

The Battenbergs were well established at Frogmore by the time Queen Victoria returned to Windsor from her last major public expedition, to Ireland. They saw more of her that summer than normally. On her morning drives the Queen breakfasted in the grounds of Frogmore and then visited her animals. She remained in her pony carriage, attending to her papers, before returning to the castle for lunch. She came back to Frogmore for tea, and a

* The Munshi was Queen Victoria's overbearing Indian servant, a controversial figure at court.

further ride in the cool of the evening. Sometimes Alice and Louise would accompany her to church, and sometimes they attended evensong at St George's Chapel with their mother.

The summer was enlivened by the arrival of Victoria's fourth child. On 25 June Queen Victoria was happy to record: 'I heard on waking that dear Victoria had got a little boy, born at 6 this morning, and it was a great pleasure.'[9] Later in the day, and again the next day, the Queen saw the latest addition to the family, who weighed in at over eight pounds. He was the last great-grandson born in her reign.

The boy, named Louis after his father and innumerable Hesse ancestors, was to be the most potent force of all the Battenbergs, to rise in time to be Viceroy of India and First Sea Lord, and to end his days as Admiral of the Fleet Earl Mountbatten of Burma. In later life he used to say that he and Louise took after their mother, who 'babbled endlessly', while Alice and Georgie emulated their father, being 'extremely quiet, deep thinking and not very talkative'.[10]

Princess Victoria wanted the new boy to be called Louis in the family, but the other children protested that it was his father's name and he should have his own. Victoria then suggested Nick after the Tsar, one of his godparents, but this was rejected. Instead they agreed he should be called Dick. This became Dickie when he went to school.

Dickie's birth was the spur that finally placed Alice at Queen Victoria's table for dinner. The following day Princess Victoria was still resting, and Alice was taken up the hill by her father to join the Queen, Prince and Princess Christian, young Arthur of Connaught and Alice's cousin, Ena. When dinner was over at nine, the group made their way to the Waterloo Chamber. The old Queen observed with delight the flowers in front of the stage and they heard a performance of the first act of *Carmen*, followed by *Cavalleria Rusticana*. 'Calvé* was more charming then ever,' recorded the

*Madame Emma Calvé (1858–1942), French soprano, who made her Covent Garden début in that role in 1892.

Queen, 'her voice even more beautiful and powerful than before.'[11]

Dickie was christened by the Dean of Windsor at Frogmore on 17 July. The choir of St George's Chapel sang. Queen Victoria held the infant and handed him to the Dean. In later life, Dickie would relate that he knocked Queen Victoria's spectacles off the end of her nose. Nevertheless she noted: 'He is a beautiful huge child and behaves very well.'[12]

A family holiday at the Yorkshire sea resort of Filey followed, and after a final stint at Frogmore, the Battenbergs settled at 4 Hans Crescent in Knightsbridge.

Time was running out for Queen Victoria and the Victorian era. In July 1900 the death of her son, Affie, formerly Duke of Edinburgh but by then Duke of Coburg, was a cause of distress to her. The health of her daughter, Vicky, the Empress Frederick, was also in sharp decline and cancer had been diagnosed. She worried too about the outcome of the South African war and the fate of the young men who had to serve in such dangerous conditions. She lost her own grandson there in October – Prince Christian Victor. For many years the mainstays of her court had been falling away, men like her stalwart private secretary, Sir Henry Ponsonby, who died in 1895.

The Queen went up to Balmoral as usual on 1 September and came back to Windsor on 7 November. On 18 December she left the castle and crossed the Solent to Osborne for Christmas. On the last day of the year, she appointed Alice's father a trustee of her private money. On 3 January 1901 Lord Roberts, Commander-in-Chief of the army in South Africa, returned home triumphant, but by 11 January the Queen's health had declined to a point that caused anxiety.

Louis and Victoria were summoned to Osborne to join a prolonged family vigil. The Kaiser arrived uninvited, tipped off by the Queen's doctor, Sir James Reid. Alice's mother resented the Kaiser's presence, aware that he was no favourite of her grandmother.

Queen Victoria finally died, literally in the Kaiser's arms, on 22 January, aged eighty-one. An era was over.

Though the Queen's death was not unexpected, it was nonetheless a profound shock. Cosmo Gordon Lang, Vicar of Portsea and the Queen's honorary chaplain, was present at Portsmouth when the funeral cortège crossed the Solent bringing the Queen-Empress to the land of her resting place. He wrote:

> There was the strangest silence I have ever known. It could literally be *felt*. It was so deep and tense that when two children talked at a distance of some 300 yards it seemed an intolerable intrusion. The German Emperor afterwards said that nothing of the kind had ever impressed him so deeply as that wedge of black silent humanity through which the Royal yacht passed into the harbour.[13]

Battleships were lined from Cowes to Portsmouth and through the centre came six torpedo boats escorting *Alberta*. The silence was broken distantly by the sound of the guns of the warships saluting the Queen and the strains of Chopin's funeral march from each ship as she passed by. As *Alberta* sailed into Portsmouth harbour, 'the sun set in a rich glow of tranquil glory'.[14]

6. Falling in Love

From Alice's childhood and adolescence, no letters written by her survive. She could be observed only through the eyes of others. But, from the reign of Edward VII onwards, there are letters with her thoughts and opinions. It is as though Queen Victoria had to die to allow Alice to come alive in her own right.

On 2 February 1901, Alice went to Windsor for Queen Victoria's funeral. She described it to her friend, Jo Riedesel,* in Darmstadt:

> We had to wait three hours in St George's Chapel until the train arrived. The coffin was covered with a white and red silk cloth, on which there was a large crown, sceptre and two orbs. All the friends followed behind. In the chapel everything was white as the Queen insisted there was to be no black. The coffin did not arrive until 3 p.m., a lot later than was expected, and so we had to eat lunch at 4.30 and thus arrived home exhausted by 9 p.m. However, it was worse for Papa, as he had to go two hours by train from London, not riding as he had thought, and another hour from Windsor to the Chapel.†[1]

Queen Victoria was laid to rest beside the Prince Consort in the Mausoleum at Frogmore.

The new reign heralded not only a new sovereign but a subtle reshuffling of relationships within the royal family. Everyone moved up a step. Alice, who had counted Windsor and Osborne as homes where she would be welcome, now came only by the

*Jo Riedesel, daughter of Moritz Riedesel, Master of the Horse in Darmstadt. Alice wrote to her in German.

†When the horses at Windsor station kicked over their traces after waiting for three hours, Louis offered the naval guard of honour to pull the gun carriage. A new tradition was established.

invitation of her great-uncle. The whiff of cigar smoke permeated the rooms of Buckingham Palace.

Edward VII swept away the austerity of his mother's court and with it the aura of sanctuary that it had held for many of her descendants. The Battenbergs noticed the change when they were invited to stay at Windsor that March. 'It was a strange sort of visit, so different from old times,' recorded Victoria. 'Uncle Bertie was very busy planning rearrangements of the rooms and we and the suite dined in the big dining room and afterwards played cards in the drawing room.'[2]

Queen Alexandra's influence was now unchecked. Drino Carisbrooke noted a greater influence over King Edward than was generally supposed: 'She was so jealous of the English Royal Family that she never asked any of her sisters-in-law to Sandringham, whereas she would fill the place with her Danish relations.'[3] One of these Danish relations was her nephew, young Prince Andrew of Greece.

The death of Queen Victoria effected a change of fortune for the Battenbergs. As a beneficiary of her grandmother's will, Victoria's annual income rose by £2,000 a year. She increased Nona's salary to £15 monthly.

The Queen's death also provoked a dramatic change in the life of Alice's Uncle Ernie in Darmstadt. He and Ducky, who had long been unhappy together, felt able to separate. By the autumn of 1901, Ernie had retreated to Capri, and Ducky was asking for a divorce. When the break came, sympathy rested with Ernie, while Ducky was castigated in the courts of Europe as a reckless and irresponsible wife. Years later, Victoria concluded: 'I can only say that I thought then, and still think, that it was best for both that they should part from each other.'*[4]

By the end of 1901 Alice had seen change all around her, an early lesson that nothing remains in place for long. There reigned a king in Britain awaiting his coronation, and Darmstadt was the

*In 1905 Ducky married Grand Duke Cyril of Russia, whom she had met in 1896.

home of a lone Grand Duke with only his little daughter, Elisabeth, for company six months of the year.

Alice began the new reign in London with her parents in Knightsbridge at 4 Hans Crescent, studying with governesses and attending McPherson's Institute in Sloane Street for drill and gymnastics. Pastor Frisius, the chaplain of the German Chapel Royal at Marlborough House, prepared her for confirmation in the Protestant faith. Back at the Heiligenberg in April, Alice was further examined by Pfarrer Matthes of Jugenheim and duly confirmed in a simple service in the village church there on 9 April.

In the summer of 1901, during the early part of which the family went down with measles, Darmstadt came alive with Ernie's great Art Nouveau exhibition. Alice disapproved of this and the way he redecorated Wolfsgarten with leather wallpaper, though she respected his right to innovation. More exciting was her first visit to Russia, with her family and Nona.

Alice knew her two aunts in Russia well but had only previously seen them at Wolfsgarten, or other family homes. Their first stay was at Ilinskoe, the home of Serge and Ella outside Moscow, where they went fishing and bathing. The visit was a chance for Alice to get to know the children of Serge's brother Grand Duke Paul, Dimitri and Marie,* who were spending summers there. After a brief stay with the Tsar and Alix in Peterhof, they travelled by yacht to St Petersburg to attend a memorial service on 13 August for the Empress Frederick, who had died while they were away. Thus in the first of only two visits she would make to Russia, Alice had her first glimpse of Russian Imperial life. She travelled in the Imperial train with her uncle and aunt and her parents. They lived on board for several days and viewed the military manoeuvres at Narva. The Tsar was still all powerful and there was not a hint of the horrors to come.

★

*Dimitri (1891–1942) and Marie (1890–1958) were adopted by Ella after their father, Grand Duke Paul, Serge's brother, was banished from Russia for marrying morganatically in 1902.

In September 1901 Louis went to Plymouth to commission *Implacable*, in preparation for joining the Mediterranean Fleet, and in October the family settled once again in Malta. Their home was 52 Strada Mezzodi, which Louis furnished. This year there was a buggy for Alice, Louise and Nona to ride about in, while their governess, Fräulein Grau, was lodged in Valetta so that the girls could continue their studies.

As she approached her seventeenth birthday, Alice was still under the wing of her parents. Though her sister Louise thought that Alice would become a queen one day, Alice herself showed no such ambition. She was content to watch the great seas at St Elmo breaking in the storms that beset Malta at the beginning of 1902.

Edward VII was due to be crowned on 26 June and to this great ceremony Victoria and Alice were summoned. They set off to England on 22 June, with Nona in attendance, and were joined at Flushing by Henry and Irène of Prussia.

Victoria and Alice stayed at Buckingham Palace. They were shocked when the King arrived there in time for luncheon on 23 June, looking desperately ill. The next day, in grave danger for his life and yet reluctant to disappoint his people, he was operated on for peritonitis and the coronation ceremony was cancelled. Meanwhile, Victoria and Alice stayed on at the palace.

Also at the palace were a number of visiting royal guests, notably Crown Prince Constantine of Greece (the Duke of Sparta) and his wife Sophie, daughter of the Empress Frederick. Travelling with them were two of the Duke's brothers, George and Andrew. The latter, known in his family as Andrea, was then a newly joined subaltern in the Greek Army, just twenty years old.

It has been suggested that Alice first met Prince Andrew while he was on military service in Germany. This is not impossible, but since he only joined the Greek army in May that year and since he was not stationed in Germany until June 1903, it is unlikely. Whatever the case, it was at Buckingham Palace in June 1902 that they fell in love. In old age, Alice described her first sighting of Andrea to her grandson the Prince of Wales. 'He was exactly like a Greek God,'[5] she said.

Great gatherings of royalty for events such as coronations and weddings have traditionally afforded parents the opportunity to conspire about marital alliances. This time the enforced proximity combined with tension for the King's health and long hours with nothing to do provided Andrea and Alice with plenty of opportunity for romance to develop. But there was no parental conspiracy. This was a genuine love match between a handsome army officer and a beautiful girl. Alice's mother later confirmed this: 'It was then that Alice & Andrea became privately engaged, somewhat against my wish, as I considered them too young.'[6]

The coronation was postponed indefinitely and Alice returned to Darmstadt on 5 July. Her friends at once noticed a change in her. They had 'little doubt of her radiant happiness'.[7] She caused her mother many worries, and Victoria was relieved that Louis was able to come to the Heiligenberg from naval duties in Corfu for a five-day family summit on how to direct Alice's future, proving that even the destiny of a minor, morganatic princess was subjected to dynastic pressure.

Alice never wavered in her love for Andrea and was heart-set on marrying him. Victoria reported the latest developments to Nona in England, confirming that Alice was 'much in love', and concluding, 'Anyhow I think there is little doubt of Andrea by & by becoming my son-in-law.'[8] Victoria consulted her sisters and the Tsarina wrote reassuringly: 'May she be as happy as we are, more one cannot wish.'[9] Yet no announcement was made.

Alice waited anxiously for news of the postponed coronation. She was relieved to hear that it would take place in Westminster Abbey on 9 August. Fewer guests were invited from overseas and the sermon was dropped, but Alice and her mother were included, and so too was Andrea. Better still it was decided that Alice and her mother would travel to the abbey in the same carriage as Andrea and his brother George.

An impressive part of the ceremony in the abbey was the procession of Princes and Princesses of the Blood Royal. The King's three daughters were followed by his three sisters and their families. Then came the royal duchesses and their daughters, and finally there walked two aged royal figures, the 83-year-old Duke of Cambridge, leaning heavily on his stick, and his sister, the Grand Duchess of Mecklenburg-Strelitz, then seventy-nine, both of whom had been present at Queen Victoria's coronation in 1838.

As Alice and her mother followed at the end of the procession, attended by Nona, they played their small part in this great occasion, which marked the transition from the dowdiness of the Victorian age into the full magnificence of the Edwardian era. Mother and daughter made their way to the royal box, Victoria sitting in the second row, while Alice sat in the third next to her cousin, Alice of Albany.

The King was crowned with the Imperial state crown, rather than St Edward's crown, and any worries that the family may have endured for Uncle Bertie were diverted by concern for the greater frailty of the Archbishop of Canterbury, who faltered on several occasions and nearly fell over when attempting to kiss the King's cheek. Amongst the accounts of the ceremony, Andrea was singled out for his 'manly bearing'.[10]

In their few days in London, Alice and Andrea spent as much time as possible together. By the time Alice returned to Germany on 13 August, she was unofficially engaged, though a seemingly endless separation of ten months stretched before her, due to Andrea's military service in Greece.

There were times when she suffered deeply. A friend told Meriel Buchanan that she had gone into a room at Fräulein Textor's school and found Alice crying bitterly, her fair hair dishevelled and her muslin dress crumpled:

> She had not had a letter from Andrew for over a week, in spite of the fact that she had written to him every day. He must be ill, he might have had a serious accident, or perhaps he had changed his mind. Even when she was told that it was probably only due to some delay in the post, she refused to be comforted, but the next morning she arrived at school with her face transfigured, all tears forgotten, for the mail had brought five letters which had been held up in the post from Greece.[11]

The man upon whom Alice had set her heart was the fourth son of George I of Greece. Yet on his father's side he was not Greek at all; nor were any of the Greek royal family.

The Greeks had achieved independence from Turkish domination by 1827 and were declared an independent kingdom by the London Protocol of 1830. Prince Otto of Bavaria was their first king, elected to serve by the Allies (France, Great Britain and Russia) in 1832. But he left the country following an insurrection in 1862. The Greeks then looked around for a new king and settled on Prince William of Denmark. He arrived in Greece as George I in 1863, aged but seventeen.

Andrea's father and grandfather were Danish, but his grandfather, Christian IX of Denmark, from whom so many royal dynasties descend, was only Danish through the female line, twice over,* his father being Wilhelm, Duke of Schleswig-Holstein-Sonderburg-Glücksburg, whose line was deemed to be a minor branch of the Danish royal house. The so-called Schleswig-Holstein question had dominated European politics for many years in the nineteenth century, a complicated issue of the possession of the lands in the south of Denmark and the north of Germany, of rights of succession and the Salic Law. At a glance, Andrea's paternal origins were two parts Danish, one part Dutch and five parts German. If he was primarily German on his father's side, he was Russian on his mother's. His mother was the former Grand Duchess Olga of Russia, a granddaughter of Tsar Nicholas I. And yet, dividing the blood into eight separate parts, six parts were German and one Nassau-Weilburg (arguably Dutch).† One of Andrea's aunts was Queen Alexandra, which explains his presence at the coronation; another was Empress Marie of Russia, mother of Tsar Nicholas II.

Andrea was born in Athens on 2 February 1882. Of all his brothers and sisters, he was the most identified with Greece, learning the

* King Christian's mother was Louise of Hesse-Kassel (1789–1867), and her mother was Louise (1750–1831), daughter of Frederik V of Denmark. It was through this line that Christian IX inherited the Danish throne.

† Prince Philip is arguably quarter Danish and quarter Russian. He has no Greek blood at all.

language and speaking it more fluently than English. He spoke only Greek to his parents. He had been raised in the uncomfortable Royal Palace in Athens, which, in those days, had but one bath which few felt inclined to use as the taps scarcely ran. The corridors were draughty and the state rooms cold. In 1896 Andrea suffered from typhoid, caught from the palace drains. Andrea and his brothers were impressive-looking men, tall, with high-domed foreheads. Short-sighted, Andrea wore spectacles in early life, though later he adopted a monocle, which added an aura of distinction. He was quick-witted and intelligent.

His education had been directed only towards the military. He was drilled at the Military Academy by German instructors and consigned to the care of a fierce taskmaster called Panayotis Danglis, who put him through a strict training in artillery work, military history, technology and geography and fortifications. Even on holidays in Corfu, Danglis was on hand to drill him while his brothers enjoyed picnics.

Not surprisingly, Andrea emerged as a professional soldier with one thought in mind – to serve in the Greek army. 'He took his duties very seriously as he loved his profession,' wrote Alice, 'and he wished to earn his promotion like any other officer.'[12]

Alice spent her last Christmas with her family at Kiel, with her Aunt Irène. She threw herself into the spirit of it. They drove out in Prince Henry's new steam car, making frequent stops at farmhouses to refill the boiler. The family went out on Uncle Henry's boat, attending church, distributing presents on board, and drinking tea in the officers' mess. Kaiserin Auguste Viktoria gave Alice a fur coat and muff for Christmas, but Alice was more enthusiastic when gifts arrived from Greece, as she wrote later to her friend, Jo Riedesel: 'The King sent me a bracelet, the Queen some Greek silk for a dress and a paper-knife, from Andrea I got a brooch and a duck's head for an umbrella handle. I always so love what he gives me but don't know what I should do. He always knows what I like.'[13]

In January 1903 Louis was appointed Director of Naval Intelligence at the Admiralty in London. In January 1903, the Battenbergs settled at 70 Cadogan Square, London. Alice resumed her studies with a variety of teachers, taking piano lessons, history of music, art and English literature. She also studied French and Greek. To her German friend, she wrote: 'It is not yet clear when my fiancé will be arriving, but I think it will be the beginning or middle of March.'[14]

King Edward was delighted to have Louis and his family in England, describing Louis as 'invaluable in the important post he now holds. He is quite one of the best officers we have in our Navy.'[15] He invited the Battenbergs and Alice to a small family dinner followed by a dance for four hundred to celebrate his fortieth wedding anniversary on 10 March. Seated at various tables were Lord Rosebery, Arthur Balfour, Austen Chamberlain and Winston Churchill. Waltzes, polkas and quadrilles were played and the evening ended with the enticing gallop, *Lebenslust*. Yet as the London season had still not begun, there were few other distractions for Alice. These were months of endless waiting, and to her consternation Andrea's arrival was put off until May due to 'unpleasant political situations in Athens, which are to do with the Army'.[16] She was frequently 'very depressed'.[17]

In April the Battenbergs moved to Sopwell, the dower house of the Earl and Countess of Verulam on the Gorhambury estate, near St Albans, which they rented for three months. They acquired their first motor car, a four-seater Wolseley wagonette, with a 12 hp engine, in which Louis often drove Alice and Louise.

At last, on 8 May, Andrea arrived, without even an ADC, to stay with the family. Two days later his engagement to Alice was officially announced. She was eighteen and he was twenty-one. The King, who was in Scotland, gave his approval and there was a dinner given by the Prince and Princess of Wales at Marlborough House. On 15 May the young couple had a foretaste of what was expected of them. Victoria took them to a solemn Te Deum in honour of their engagement at the Greek Church in Moscow Road, Bayswater. Alice would sit through a great number of Te Deums in Athens in the years to come.

The engaged pair were received by two archimandrites and if the service itself was short, the deputations that followed were not. The honorary secretary of the Byron Society addressed Andrea:

> That your choice should have fallen upon the Princess Alice, the accomplished daughter of Prince Louis of Battenberg, a distinguished officer in His Majesty's Navy, and the granddaughter of our own beloved Princess Alice, Grand Duchess of Hesse, whose memory will ever be revered by the British people, is a source of intense gratification . . .[18]

The fiancé thanked them in a firm voice.

News of the engagement soon spread to other royal houses. In May the old Grand Duchess of Mecklenburg-Strelitz berated her niece, the Princess of Wales: 'You do not mention the very youthful betrothal, so odd, no money besides! George [the Prince of Wales] writes full of praise of her as bright and pretty, a pity she is not young enough to wait for *my* Fred,* who can't marry yet, of course.'[19] In a later letter the Grand Duchess cast her mind back to the coronation: 'So the Greek-Battenberg engagement was settled last year. I remember her, such a pretty girl, only rather deaf.'[20]

Andrea left for Darmstadt on 19 June, where, with the King of Greece's permission, he was attached to the Hessian Rote Dragoner, the Red Dragoons. Alice longed to go to the Heiligenberg, but her parents kept her in England. They took her to the state ball for President Loubet of France and 1,100 guests at Buckingham Palace, where the Australian soprano, Nellie Melba, sang. 'Alice danced a great deal,' reported Victoria, '& her father too. It was never too hot & was a very pretty sight. We remained until the end, which was after 3 a.m.'[21]

At the end of July, Alice was at last able to return to Germany. The wedding was fixed for 7 October so that the Tsar of Russia

* Adolf Friedrich VI (1882–1918), grandson of the Grand Duchess. This would not have been a good fate for Alice. He succeeded his father as Grand Duke in 1914, abdicated in 1918, and shot himself in the chest, as a result of profound melancholia, brought on by a thwarted love affair 'which had obscured his judgement' [*The Times*, 7 March 1918].

could shoot with the Emperor of Austria in September. Nona arrived to help with the plans and Andrea came over when military duties permitted for seven brief visits in August and a week in September. Alice could not wait to be married, as she explained to Jo Riedesel:

We are so happy to be back here. It is so nice here & I was so homesick in England, though I have many lovely girlfriends there. However I am really happiest in Hessen. My groom is in Darmstadt as you know & is busy with his work. He took a couple of days holiday, however, to visit me and as he had ridden through the night and as tomorrow is Saturday, he will arrive in the afternoon and stay here over Sunday.[22]

Alice was nervous that she might be lonely after the wedding as Andrea would be working each morning. She counted on Jo as a rare friend to visit her: 'I won't come across as funny to you as a married woman, and I am still such a young girl. Imagine, in 2 months and it seems so unbelievable. I will get used to it.'[23]

7. The Wedding

One of the largest influxes of royalty for many years descended on Darmstadt for the wedding. The carriages came out, the royal residences were prepared and an air of excitement permeated the normally sleepy city.

The Grand Duchess of Mecklenburg-Strelitz, having decried Queen Alexandra's presence at the wedding – 'Why? There is surely no reason for it, a Battenberg, daughter of an illegitimate father, he a fourth son of a newly baked King!' – went on to complain about the expense to Ernie as host and the problems of protocol, and ended despairingly: 'I hear the young couple have been given a Palace to live in by themselves, all this only for 6 months!'[1]

Uncle Ernie handed over the Alte Schloss to the entire Greek royal family, including Queen Olga's sister, Vera, Duchess of Württemberg. At the Neue Palais, where Ernie lived, there stayed the Tsar and Tsarina and their children, Ella and Serge with Marie and Dimitri (their adopted children), Queen Alexandra and her daughter, Princess Victoria. The Alte Schloss also housed the Henrys of Prussia, Princess Beatrice and her daughter Ena, the Duke of Teck and Prince Albert of Schleswig-Holstein.

For days there were spectacular parties. '[Darmstadt] being a charming and old-fashioned town, the royal visitors could enjoy themselves without being cramped by the strict ceremony that is in force on like occasions in the great capitals of Europe,' recalled Nona's brother, Mark Kerr, invited as Louis's oldest naval friend. 'They all appeared to be on holiday, and the atmosphere was full of fun and merriment.'[2] Ernie gave a dinner for all the royal relations and their suites at the Alte Schloss, and then, on the eve of the wedding, Louis and Victoria gave a reception and buffet for 260 people in the ballroom of the Alte Palais. Victoria was horrified to realize that the fish was less than fresh. 'Alice looked charming and radiant,' recalled her Aunt Marie, 'and not less handsome and radiant was her father, my dear brother Louis, who wore the uniform of the Hessian artillery.'[3]

King Edward's representative, the Duke of Teck, spent a lot of time writing to his wife, wondering whether or not he would be fed properly before or after the opera, and having to put on full-dress uniform not only to greet Queen Alexandra, but also again later for the King and Queen of Greece. 'We are fairly kept on the run here,'[4] wrote the Duke.

On the morning of 6 October the civil marriage took place, with only near relations attending. Next day there were then two religious ceremonies. King Edward had wanted a fourth ceremony at the British Legation, because the bride was a British subject, but at this the young couple demurred. First Alice and Andrea were married by Protestant rite in the chapel in the Alte Schloss, and then they went to the new Russian chapel on the Mathildenhöhe, a newly laid-out garden area in Darmstadt. For the occasion the Battenbergs produced the old state carriage of Prince Alexander of Hesse to convey the bride to the church. The groom wore his Red Dragoons uniform, and the riband and star of the Grand Cross of the Royal Victorian Order, given him by Edward VII. Alice wore a beautiful lace dress with a veil of myrtle and orange blossoms.

The procession into the chapel began with thirty members of the royal families of Europe, advancing in pairs. The more minor members went first, the order gradually rising in importance to Ernie escorting his sister Alix, and the Tsar escorting Queen Alexandra, who was gloriously dressed in a tight-fitting gown of mauve sequins, and adorned with amethysts. Then came the groom, with his parents, the King and Queen of Greece, on either side, and finally Alice walking between Louis and Victoria.

The bridal procession was greeted with a wedding song composed by William de Haan with words from the book of Ruth, sung by the choir of the Court Theatre. The royal guests then formed a semi-circle around the bridal pair for the ceremony itself. In the organ loft sat a clutch of children, the ill-fated younger offspring of the Tsar and Tsarina. At this service Alice misheard the questions, and said 'no' instead of 'yes' when asked if she assented freely to marriage, and 'yes' instead of 'no' when asked about having promised her hand elsewhere.

The Russian service was more exotic and more intimate, with the rites said by a high priest and an archimandrite. Alice's aunt Marie Erbach recalled: 'We were received by Russians and Greeks, blazing with gold, and led into the rich, beautiful chapel, where we were greeted by three priests in golden vestments. The bridal couple, who, of course, came last, stood on a carpet of rose-coloured silk – a symbol of the path of life.' Four princes held the heavy wedding crowns of Catherine the Great over the heads of the young couple, 'who held candles in their hands. The circling of the altar three times, during which the crowns were held over their heads, was a little difficult. After the concluding Te Deum, Andrew led his wife to the parents on both sides.'[5]

After the ceremonies, there was a large family dinner, with no suites in attendance. The departure was the opportunity for merry high jinks amongst the royal guests, Prince Henry of Prussia setting the tone with a mighty cry of 'Hoch!' Prince George of Greece seized Andrea's hat and planted it on the head of his Aunt Vera, knocking her spectacles off her nose. Duchess Vera thought Mark Kerr was responsible and hit him on the head with the hat. Queen Alexandra told Nona that her brother was the culprit and she rushed forward to sort the matter out, convinced he had drunk too much.

Shoes were tied to the back of the carriage. When they set off, rice and slippers were thrown at them. Ernie and the Tsar were to the fore, rushing after them into the crowd, hotly pursued by excited policemen and plain-clothes Russian detectives, clutching umbrellas. Mark Kerr told the tale:

The Emperor went straight for the backs of the people, who were anxiously awaiting the passing of the Royal carriage. Putting his head down, he rammed them and gradually pushed his way through the six files of human beings, shedding the children from his coat-tails on the way, and reached the street at the moment when the carriage was going by with Princess Alice bowing her acknowledgments to the cheering crowd. At this moment she received the full bag of rice, which the Emperor had carried, in her face, followed by the satin shoe. Casting dignity aside she caught the shoe, and leaning over the back of the carriage hit the Emperor on the head with it, at the same time telling him exactly what she thought of him, which so over-came him that he stood still in the middle of the road shrieking with laughter.[6]

After this the bride and groom transferred into their new Wolseley car, a gift from the Tsar in a soberer moment before he began to enjoy the wedding, and departed for the Heiligenberg. While Ernie continued to entertain his royal guests for another week, Alice and Andrea began their brief honeymoon in the familiar surroundings of her family home. They returned to Darmstadt in time for Ernie's big evening party at the Alte Schloss for the departing guests.

After their honeymoon Alice and Andrea settled in Louis and Victoria's apartment in the Alte Palais, and Andrea resumed service with the Red Dragoons.

Alice's wedding would be recalled as one of Darmstadt's finest celebrations, made the more poignant since it was the last occasion on which all the branches of the Hesse family were together. Terrible fates awaited many of the guests, and one little witness survived the wedding by just five weeks.

Ernie's only comfort since Ducky left him had been his daughter, Elisabeth, now aged eight. But she died of ambulatory typhoid, while staying with her father at Skierniewice, the Tsar's shooting box in Poland, on 16 November. Alice and Andrea went to Darmstadt station to meet Victoria, who came to help with the funeral arrangements. Ducky, the child's mother, joined her ex-husband at Frankfurt and they arrived in Darmstadt together. Six horses, draped in white, bore the funeral bier through the streets of Darmstadt, the coffin completely obscured by a mass of flowers. It was a marked contrast to the festive arrivals of a few weeks earlier.

Ernie was completely alone until he found a second, quieter wife, Princess Eleonore of Lich, whom he married in February 1905. Known as 'Onor', she was maternal and cosy, and the family thought her charming and kind. 'She understood him perfectly,' recalled Victoria, 'thanks to her unselfish but very intelligent nature and they were deeply devoted to each other.'[7] Queen Mary was sterner in judgement, meeting Onor at Windsor in 1907: 'She is ugly but quite nice & well dressed. He [Ernie] tells me he is quite happy in everything and at last has a "companion" who takes interest in what he likes.'[8] Onor bore Ernie two fine sons, one of whom would become Alice's son-in-law.

But that December of 1903, Ernie needed comforting. Victoria stayed in Darmstadt until after his birthday, as did Ella and Serge. Alice and Andrea spent Christmas with him.

Early in the new year of 1904, Alice and Andrea prepared to depart for Greece. They were all packed and ready to go, when they were suddenly told that the Greek royal yacht, *Amphitrite*, had to go to Odessa first to pick up Queen Olga.

8. The Greek Royal Family

Alice surrendered the life of Europe and England for a hot-house existence in Greece. At once she transferred her loyalties to the country which she would call her home for the next sixty-three years. She had never been there before and was ill prepared for the primitive conditions and the lack of intellectual stimulus. But Alice was trained to do her duty and thrilled to be at Andrea's side.

On 6 January 1904, a day later than scheduled, Alice and Andrea arrived at the Piraeus in *Amphitrite*, having been detained by boisterous weather at the entrance of the Corinth Canal. They were accompanied on board by Grand Duke and Grand Duchess George of Russia.*

A spirited welcome, combining elements of ceremony and religion, awaited the young couple as they stepped ashore. The King and Queen of Greece accompanied them in a state procession to the cathedral, where they were received by the Metropolitan and other members of the Holy Synod. In the presence of Greek ministers, the diplomatic body and court officials, they heard a Te Deum chanted. The Athenians cheered the young couple to the cathedral and later to the palace. The Mayor gave an address welcoming 'a handsome and graceful Princess sprung from Princely Families beloved by the Greek Nation'.[1]

Besides the official welcome, all the guilds and schools in Athens took part, and in the evening there was a display of fireworks, illuminating the city. Thoughtfully, the King of Greece telegraphed Alice's parents in London to announce that she was safely with them.

* Grand Duchess George of Russia (1876–1940), born Princess Marie of Greece. The Grand Duke was murdered by the Bolsheviks in 1919. She then married Vice-Admiral Pericles Joannides.

Alice found herself a member of the Greek royal family, which consisted of George I and Queen Olga, Crown Prince Constantine and his wife Crown Princess Sophie; Prince George ('Big George'), Prince Nicholas and his wife, Grand Duchess Helen of Russia; and Prince Christopher (known as 'Christo'). All of these lived in Athens, though 'Big George' was based in Crete. The King and Queen's surviving daughter Marie, Grand Duchess George of Russia, also had a house in Athens and spent a large part of the year there, to escape court life in Russia.

In the next generation were Constantine's children, George, Alexander and Paul (all of whom were destined to be kings of Greece), Helen (later Queen of Romania) and baby Irene (later Duchess of Aosta), who was christened that April. Such was the disparity of ages that Christo was less than two years older than his nephew, George. Prince and Princess Nicholas had one small daughter, Olga (later Princess Paul of Yugoslavia), and the Princess was pregnant with her second daughter, Elisabeth, born in May that year.

George I created a strong family life about him, holding regular Sunday lunches together. The family were a team and he was especially kind to Alice, making a point of taking her round personally to meet guests at receptions, aware of her deafness and how daunting it must be to arrive knowing no one in a strange land.

The Greek royal family were never wholly accepted by the Greeks. The King used to remind his sons: 'Never forget that you are foreigners among the Greeks, and never let them remember it.'[2] In choosing Prince William of Denmark in 1863, the Greeks were aware that their candidate had close links with the British, his sister Alexandra being about to marry the Prince of Wales. They hoped this would ensure a greater measure of British protection.

George I, as William became, was a democratic sovereign with greater power than most other European monarchs. He had a prominent role in the constitution, which often placed him uncomfortably in the maelstrom of Greek politics. He was an informal man, who kept ceremonial to a minimum and who liked to walk unaccompanied in the streets.

King George was a kind man, as calm as his father, Christian IX, and as intelligent as his mother, Queen Louise. According to Prince von Bülow: 'Like his father, he was a perfect "gentleman". This impressed the Greeks, of whom it cannot always be said.'[3] As a young man, his ministers had sometimes found it hard to treat him with the reserve and dignity due his station, so boyish was he and 'full of animal spirits'.[4]

The British gave Greece the Ionian Islands (which included Corfu) when George I became king. Greece gained a sense of order, yet George I's reign was dominated by the control exerted by the guaranteeing powers, Great Britain, France and Russia, who were continually vying for the upper hand. The ownership and rule of Crete was another problem: whether it should be under Greek rule or controlled by the Allies.

The King was straightforward and truthful by nature. As such he was popular, though never secure. In 1898 he had survived an assassination attempt in Athens and forty years on the throne did nothing to make him withdraw his offer to depart if no longer wanted.

In 1867 George I had married a Russian Grand Duchess, thus strengthening his links with Russia. Queen Olga came to Athens as a sixteen-year-old bride with a trousseau that included her childhood dolls. While the Greeks had periodic dislikes for their royal family, they were consistent in their love for Queen Olga. She was intensely Russian and lived surrounded by icons. Amongst numerable charitable works, she founded the Evangelismos Hospital in Athens, two military hospitals and the Russian Hospital at the Piraeus, and she built a boy's reformatory school and a prison specifically for women.

Queen Olga, her daughter Marie and daughter-in-law Sophie were energetic nurses in the 1897 Turko-Grecian war, establishing a precedent which Alice later adopted. In her later years, as a widow, Queen Olga wore black with the traditional Mary Stuart cap. Her granddaughter, Princess Eugénie, once wrote to her as a little girl saying: 'I'm looking forward to seeing you and hope you will come paddling with us,'[5] which conjures an unlikely image.

The King and Queen were happily married, but the King permitted himself what Prince von Bülow called 'an occasional relaxation', on his annual holiday without the Queen at Aix-les-Bains. When the Crown Prince, Constantine, followed his father's example, Sophie, his wife, asked her father-in-law how she should handle the situation. King George told her: 'You must consult your dear mother-in-law; she will be able to give you the best advice on this point.'[6]

Crown Prince Constantine, sometimes known as the Duke of Sparta or the Diadoch or 'Tino', was first and foremost a soldier. He was not bright, but, as Queen Victoria wrote to the Empress Frederick, 'a good heart and good character . . . go far beyond cleverness'.[7] He had the advantage of being the first member of this new Greek royal family to have been born in Greece, in August 1868. He commanded the Greek army in the Turko-Grecian war of 1897, in which they were defeated, but later he was given the chance to redeem himself.

In 1889 Constantine married the Kaiser's sister, Sophie. The wedding was celebrated in both Protestant and Orthodox services. A year later problems developed between the Kaiser and his sister, the Kaiser refusing Sophie permission to enter Germany because she had adopted the Orthodox faith. Sophie did not mind as she disliked her brother. Yet, sometimes, even within the Greek royal family, there was antagonism towards her for being German, and she was unfairly blamed as a pro-German influence on her husband during the First World War.

It was inevitable that Sophie found the life of Athens rather provincial after Berlin. Some years later she told Marie Bonaparte (who married her brother-in-law Prince George) that Athens society was not very lively and consisted primarily of the wives of tobacco merchants. Sophie was energetic, astute and practical. Inspired more by her mother, Empress Frederick, than by the example of her mother-in-law, she was actively engaged in charity and welfare work, especially hospitals and afforestation. But she was often depressed at the laziness of the Greeks in making the necessary effort.

All Andrea's other brothers, soldiers like himself, were larger-than-life figures. They acted from the best of intentions. They were hostile to most of the Greek politicians, a treacherous and duplicitous band throughout modern Greek history, and later they caused the British Foreign Office numerous headaches with their unwillingness to adapt to modern constitutional ways. 'Patriots to a man,' wrote Christo's son, Prince Michael, 'great-hearted and erudite, they were always more at ease amid simple surroundings: they shared with all Greeks a taste for frankness and warm humanity, qualities they reflected in their own large natures.'[8]

Big George was born in Corfu in June 1869 and after serving in the Greek navy in the Turko-Grecian war of 1897, was appointed High Commissioner of Crete, then under Allied control, an unenviable task for a twenty-seven-year-old. He was treated as a figurehead by the Great Powers and came into opposition with a wily Cretan lawyer, Eleutherios Venizelos, who would come to play a leading role in the affairs of Greece – invariably at odds with the Greek royal family. Big George remained in his post in Crete until 1906, returning to Athens, worn out. Thereafter he spent as little time in Greece as possible.

The next brother, Nicholas, was born in January 1872. Besides being a professional soldier, he was a good painter and playwright. He is remembered for the two volumes he wrote about his time in Greece, and as the father of Princess Marina, Duchess of Kent. The year before Alice's arrival in Athens, he had married Grand Duchess Helen of Russia. Known as Ellen, she was an austere, beautiful and commanding woman, the daughter of Grand Duke Vladimir and his formidable wife, Grand Duchess Maria Pavlovna.

Of all the members of the family, Ellen was to play the longest part in Alice's life. Even the most forgiving of biographers concede that there was no great affection or rapport between the sisters-in-law. Princess Nicholas was both an Imperial and Royal Highness. Her priorities were 'God first, then the Russian Grand Dukes, then the rest'.[9] For her, as for so many princesses in Europe, the word 'morganatic' was a pejorative one. She was therefore disinclined to show much respect to a Battenberg, born a mere Serene Highness and only elevated to Royal Highness on marriage.

Alice took a philosophical approach to Ellen. Over the years she observed that in the eyes of her Russian sister-in-law, her status improved a little when her sister Louise became Crown Princess of Sweden, and rather more so when her son married Princess Elizabeth.*

The youngest brother, Christopher, born in August 1888 and thus only fourteen at this time, was a benign and harmless soul. Christo became a dabbler in the occult, fascinated by the world of ghosts and automatic writing. His main achievement was to marry a very rich woman, Mrs Nancy Leeds. He too wrote some memoirs.

There had been three girls in the family. Alexandra, born in 1870, had married Grand Duke Paul of Russia but had died in 1891, leaving two children, Marie and Dimitri, by then the wards of Alice's Aunt Ella. The second sister, Marie ('Minnie'), born in 1876, was Grand Duchess George of Russia, and the youngest daughter, Olga, lived only a few months in 1880.

In Athens George I lived in the large and unmanageable Royal Palace, an impressive building in the middle of the city, with marble porticoes and handsome pediments, built by King Otto. The rooms were large and cold; nor was it known for its comfort. Here the royal family held occasional state balls, to which guests were bidden at 8.30 p.m. There was a moment of ceremony, when, on the dot of 9.00 p.m., the folding doors opened and the royal family processed in. Andrea and Alice and Christo also lived in the Royal Palace, the Crown Prince having his own palace near by, and Nicholas setting up home at the Nicholas Palace, also in Athens.

All the family preferred Tatoï, their country home fifteen miles outside Athens, where they lived simply in a series of villas, forming a complex. Tatoï was set in an estate of 40,000 acres, with a sloping

* Ellen was similarly disinclined to show much respect to her Prussian sister-in-law, Sophie, and was offensively unfriendly, as we shall see, to Princess Marie Bonaparte, when she married Big George in 1907.

woodland of pine trees, a Danish-style home farm, deer paddocks and vineyards. Prince Nicholas called it 'a refuge, a haunt of freedom, where the mountains and trees were as dear to our hearts as we felt we were dear to theirs'.[10]

Alice celebrated her nineteenth birthday that February, and liked to recall that when she woke, still in the dark, Andrea pretended that his gift to her was a motor-bicycle and that this unsuitable object was actually in their bedroom.[11] 'So fond of jokes he was,' recalled his niece, Queen Helen of Romania.[12]

Alice was happy to see her Uncle Ernie in Athens during March and April, and the following month Prince Francis of Teck reported that at Tatoï he had found the newly-weds 'as happy as possible'. Of Alice he commented that she looked 'radiant & extremely handsome'.[13]

Presently Alice joined her sister-in-law, Ellen, in Greek lessons. In the fullness of time, both princesses spoke it fluently. As soon as Alice gained confidence, she threw herself into social welfare work, this being the role for British princesses established for them by the Prince Consort. In particular she worked at the Greek School of Embroidery, which had been started by Lady Egerton, the wife of an earlier British Ambassador. This was a school where girls from poor families could learn a skill which would help them support their families. Alice spent hours there, learning how to embroider, and how to mingle the colours and all the different stitches. The school flourished for many years.

The early days of marriage were relatively carefree. Andrea loved to ride and Alice used to accompany him to the Actaeon Palace Hotel at Phaleron Bay, about four miles from Athens. In attendance was Andrea's ADC, Captain Menelaos Metaxas,* a highly respected friend of the family, who served as Andrea's right-hand man for many years. Andrea and his friends were experienced riders, while Alice was not, though she raced with them so hard

* Captain Menelaos Metaxas (1876–1938), a cousin of the later dictator. He had a passion for motor cars, and later became successful importing German cars into Greece.

that on one occasion Andrea asked Metaxas: 'Help my wife down, will you? If she's not careful, she'll break her neck.' Andrea spoke in Greek which Alice still did not understand, but Metaxas made him repeat it in English, saying: 'You must tell her nothing but the truth.'[14]

The Greek royal family invariably decamped from Greece every summer, often for months on end. This tradition was adopted by Alice and Andrea, who, as the ways of Greek politics made their lives more complicated, came to long for this annual respite from the fray. In that summer of 1904 they stayed with her parents at their rented home in Hertfordshire, and then accompanied Victoria to Wolfsgarten, where Alice fell ill with a bad fever. They returned to Athens in mid-October.

Alice was in Athens when she heard the news of the murder of Ella's husband. Serge of Russia, on 17 February 1905. The murder caused Ella to withdraw from all forms of social life in Moscow and instead to become active in charitable work.

For some time Serge had been a deeply unpopular Governor of Moscow. He therefore forbade Ella to accompany him on his excursions into the city. She was at home in the Kremlin when a bomb was thrown at his carriage and exploded, and at once rushed out and cradled Serge's dead body, his blood soaking her dress. Her first thought on seeing the body was: 'Hurry, hurry, Serge hates blood and mess.'[15]

Then, in an act of saintliness, which nevertheless became the subject of bizarre gossip in Russia, she visited Serge's assassin, Kaliaev, in prison, asking him to pray with her for God's forgiveness for his crime. Her motive was to help his soul, so that he would not die unconfessed. Victoria went to Russia to comfort her sister, and was soon able to report to Nona: 'With her unselfish character, high sense of duty, healthy nerves & energetic mind, I have no doubt of her being able to shape her future life wisely & well by herself, & her great sorrow she has borne bravely from the first.'[16]

Ella was soon distributing 4,500 free dinners to the poorest people in Moscow. In the October Revolution, later in 1905, Ella was blockaded in the Kremlin. Each day she slipped out to visit the wounded in hospital. In 1906 she nursed invalids rendered incurable by the Russo-Japanese war of 1905, and was criticized for spoiling them. All this Alice knew, and when confronted with similar crises in Greece some years later, would follow her aunt's example virtually to the letter.

Athens life was at its most glamorous in the years 1905 and 1906. It was a city bidding for international recognition, attracting distinguished visitors from far and wide. There were memorably exciting events, but it is a sad truth that Alice missed most of them, because these were the years of pregnancy and babies.

In April 1905 she had missed the opening of the International Archaeological Conference, though she attended the inauguration of a new library at the British School of Archaeology. She missed the Kaiser's unwelcome visit the same month, and most of Queen Alexandra's more popular one, and the Panhellenic Games in May. In April 1906 she missed the opening of the Olympic Games, one of the highlights of modern Greece's history, with echoes of its classical past. While she witnessed the arrival of the Prince and Princess of Wales the same month, on their way back to England from India, she missed the banquet at which Edward VII spoke.

Alice gave birth to her first daughter, swiftly named Margarita, at the Royal Palace at 1.00 a.m. on 18 April 1905. Her mother arrived in Athens a fortnight before to be with her and Queen Olga stayed with Alice throughout what turned out to be a long labour. The Queen obliged Andrea to attend part of it too, telling Victoria: 'It is only right that men should see the suffering they cause their wives and which they completely escape.'[17] Presently, Louis sailed into Athens aboard his flagship, *Drake*, and was able to attend his granddaughter Margarita's christening on 11 May.

Alice was soon up and about again, and so, on 16 May, her mother left for Germany. Louis also sailed away, conscious that the family was now often apart. Missing Louise's confirmation at Jugenheim, he wrote to her: 'It will always be a comfort to me to know that Mama has a helpful companion in you especially since Alice found her happiness & thus left us so early.'[18]

Hardly had Alice recovered from the birth when there was a stark example of the turbulence of the country in which she now lived. On 13 June, the Prime Minister of Greece, Theodore Delyannis,* alighted from his carriage to enter the Chamber, when a man approached him from the crowd as if in greeting and plunged a knife into him. He was dead within the hour. The assassin was the keeper of a gambling house who resented the Prime Minister's rigorous measures against such places. Four days later, the King, Nicholas and Andrea walked behind the coffin to the cathedral, with huge crowds along the route.

Alice longed to show Margarita to her family, but when five-year-old Dickie met his niece at the Heiligenberg in August, he commented: 'This house was much pleasanter before a crying baby came into it.'[19] Louise gave a more favourable impression in a letter to her father: 'The baby is so very nice. It smiles, laughs all day long and hardly ever cries.'[20] Alice left Margarita, not to mention Andrea's cockatoo which travelled with them, and the couple made a two-week expedition to Copenhagen in mid-August to visit Andrea's 87-year-old grandfather, Christian IX. He was then suffering badly from lumbago and would die the following January.

Soon after their return to Greece in September, Andrea was transferred from the 2nd to the 1st Cavalry Regiment. He took up his position as a squadron-commander in the garrison town of Larissa, in Thessaly, near Mount Olympus, from the autumn of 1905 until the spring of 1906. His task was to train recruits, most of whom were, as Alice put it, 'raw peasants from the mountains, who had never left their goats and had never even seen a horse in their lives'.[21]

Alice moved to Larissa with him, and spent her time with Margarita. Although the child was not yet one, she was able to walk a little if held by the hand and enjoyed playing with Billy, the

* Theodore Delyannis (1826–1905), Prime Minister of Greece 1885–6, 1890–92, 1895–7 and 1904–5.

largest of Andrea's several dogs, all of which he treated as children. This was an even simpler life for Alice than that in Athens. Andrea had a motor car and they went on excursions. She enjoyed playing with a friendly monkey that belonged to the cook. Meanwhile she had become pregnant again.

In the summer of 1906 Alice and Andrea were back in Athens. Theodora was born at Tatoï at 11.45 p.m. on 30 May, while Andrea was away in Madrid attending the wedding of Alice's cousin Ena to Alfonso XIII of Spain, after which the bridal couple narrowly escaped death from an assassin's bomb. Andrea did not therefore see his second daughter until she was a fortnight old. Theodora soon acquired the family nickname of 'Dolla', as Margarita mistook Theodora for 'dear Dolla'.

Because of her confinement Alice remained quietly at Tatoï with Andrea and the children that summer. In September she wrote to Jo Riedesel in Darmstadt, congratulating her on becoming engaged and adding: 'My two little ones are such good & funny & strong, healthy children – Thank God.'[22] When not occupied with her babies Alice extended her charity work by helping a society which trained girls as private nurses, an organization perpetually in need of additional funds.[23]

The early months of 1907 gave Alice a foretaste of how the Greek press would in the years to come undermine the Greek royal family. There were numerous attacks inspired by a rumour that the King's sons were to receive annuities. The princes were accused of not doing enough for Greece. *Acropolis* stated: 'The Princes deserve no compensation because they show no interest in matters of general concern. To be remunerated for doing nothing is the privilege of Russian Grand Dukes.'[24] *Chronos* wrote:

Nobody ever hears of the Princes. They never take the lead in times of disaster. The Bulgarians set Salonika in a blaze in 1902, and the Princes were loafing about the boulevards of Paris. Anhialo has been burnt, and no Royal Prince goes to visit the refugees, to whom the Greeks are giving their shirts. Yet the Greek Princes are far richer than any other European Princes.[25]

Sir Francis Elliot, the British Ambassador to Greece from 1903 to 1917, whose role was to put Greek affairs into perspective for the benefit of the Foreign Office in London, was a supportive and perceptive ally to the Greek royal family and to the King. On this occasion he thought that the princes did what they could 'within the limited sphere which is open to them',[26] and concluded that the attacks were symptomatic of a country 'where liberty is confounded with licence, and disrespect for authority mistaken for independence'.[27]

9. Political Intrigue

The Greek press and the machinations of the politicians made the years between 1907 and 1912 difficult ones for the Greek royal family. Alice was not much in Greece for the first two years, since she and Andrea were travelling to England, Germany, Malta and Russia.

Alice had a more interesting time away from Athens than in it. In the summer of 1907 she had the strange experience of being entertained in England as the wife of a Greek prince – almost as a foreigner in the place where she had been born.

Alice and Andrea arrived at Windsor Castle for the royal meeting at Ascot on 18 June and on the next day they were conveyed up the course in a Windsor landau with the Princess of Wales. There was a large house party at the castle, including what the Princess of Wales described as 'a numerous array of royalties',[1] from Ernie and Onor to the King of Siam.

It may have been on this visit that Alice acquired another story she liked to tell into old age. A tiny piece of spinach landed on the boiled shirt of Edward VII. To the surprise of the guests, he then deliberately put more spinach on it, exclaiming: 'As I've got to change it, I might as well make it worthwhile.'[2]

Presently the whole party moved to Buckingham Palace, attending a ball at the Russian Embassy and the King's Birthday Parade, in which Andrea rode to Horseguards Parade in the procession directly behind the King, little realizing that this would one day be the annual duty of his yet unborn son. Alice went down the Mall in Queen Alexandra's carriage, with Aunt Onor and Queen Alexandra's unmarried daughter Princess Victoria. In the evening the Queen took the same three to *Un Ballo in Maschera* at Covent Garden. They went to the Duchess of Westminster's ball for five hundred at Grosvenor House on 1 July, and two days later returned to Germany.

At the Heiligenberg, Alice was reunited with her mother, who wrote to Alice's brother Georgie that Alice had 'grown in height & breadth so that Louise looks a good deal smaller than her'.[3] By now Louise and Dickie were firm friends with Margarita and Theodora.

Alice sat for the Hungarian artist, Philip de László, who had lately moved to London and painted Edward VII. The fashionable artist was commissioned by the family to paint a half-length portrait of Alice in a white dress. During his stay at the Heiligenberg, he sang Hungarian songs accompanied by Conny Pauer.* He began sketching Alice on 15 July and finished the portrait on 20 July. Alice made Louise sit in her place when he was doing her knees, though in the portrait these are covered by the dress.

The result is a fine one, though Alice did not particularly like it or admire the artist's work. She would not have disagreed with the verdict that de László's status as a portrait painter was 'not with the more eminent masters, for he had neither deep psychological penetration nor a highly nervous and individual line'.[4] In later life she told a friend that de László's method was to paint the outline of a beautiful woman, and then to fill in the distinctive features of the sitter.†[5]

In August 1907 Alice returned to Greece and settled into a large newly built house at Tatoï. In the autumn her father paid her a rare visit on his way to Malta, while Andrea set off on army manoeuvres with his brothers, the Crown Prince and Christo.

Another sister-in-law joined the Greek royal family that autumn when 'Big George' married Princess Marie Bonaparte. She was a most unusual girl, destined to enjoy an equally unusual marriage. She was extremely rich, owing to her descent from François Blanc, who owned the casino in Monte Carlo. A passionate woman, she

* Conny Pauer, sister of the musician Max Pauer (1866–1945) and daughter of the Viennese pianist Ernest Pauer (1826–1905), who all lived at Jugenheim.

† Prince Philip has the portraits of both his parents and of Prince Louis in his study at Buckingham Palace. De László went on to paint Louise, Victoria, most of the Battenberg family and many members of the Greek royal family. He even sketched Nona in 1909. Lord Mountbatten amassed an impressive collection of family portraits at Broadlands, including several de Lászlós.

hoped for too much from Big George. Not a ladies' man, he was devoted only to his uncle, Prince Valdemar of Denmark. Presently Marie was experimenting with complicated gynaecological operations, Freudian analysis and a passionate love affair with Aristide Briand.*

The French princess arrived in Athens in December and recorded her impressions of her new family in her diary. She described Andrea as 'like a thoroughbred horse' and Alice as 'a beautiful blond Englishwoman with ample flesh, smiles a lot and doesn't say much since she's deaf'.[6] Ellen she thought 'superb', but added that she was scared by 'her beauty and her pride'.[7]

Marie Bonaparte's arrival led to more dissension between the press and the princes. At the station the Crown Prince saw a crowd gathered and asked: 'Who are those?' 'Reporters, Your Royal Highness.' 'Tell them to go to the Devil!' he cried. Unfortunately he was overheard and the press did not report the bride's arrival in any Greek paper. An ingenious official then assured the journalists that what the Crown Prince had in fact said was 'What the devil do they want here?', after which matters proceeded more amicably.[8]

Almost immediately there was trouble within the royal family, as Sir Francis Elliot reported to the Foreign Office in London, in a letter which included some details 'not suitable for official despatch':

> Rumour has it that some of the King's daughters-in-law of longer standing are not particularly pleased at [the princess's] intrusion into their midst, and my daughter tells me of an incident she noticed last night, which seems to forebode some want of harmony. The Royal Family were retiring, and Princess Nicholas was approaching the door, when Princess George came hurriedly up from behind and passed through first without a smile or word to her sister-in-law, who drew back her skirts as if not to be touched by her.[9]

Alice, ever generous, would never have been less than welcoming to a newcomer, but it is no surprise to find Ellen behaving in

* See Celia Bertin, *Marie Bonaparte* (Harcourt Brace Jovanovich, New York, 1982).

this haughty style. In England the letter was shown to King Edward. On it the King wrote: 'As the King's new daughter-in-law is immensely rich she will have no difficulty in maintaining her position with her sisters-in-law.'[10] He was right. Marie did exactly as she pleased.

Alice was again away from Greece for a large part of 1908. In March she took her daughters to Malta to visit her parents. Her father was now a vice-admiral, living aboard his flagship, *Prince of Wales*, when not confined to a wheelchair with grievous attacks of gout.

This private visit landed Alice in a diplomatic incident, which rumbled on for several weeks. The King of Greece consigned a Greek decoration to her care, and asked her to present this to a certain British naval officer, Captain Robert Hornby. Alice duly decorated him. She was not aware that this would cause headaches in the Foreign Office when the King heard about it from the Prince of Wales. Thereafter Hornby was uncertain whether or not to wear it when meeting the King of Greece. Alice sailed back to Greece at the end of March.

In April, with most of the Greek royal family, she attended the wedding of Grand Duchess Marie to Prince William of Sweden in St Petersburg. The bride was Andrea's niece, the daughter of Princess Alexandra of Greece, who had died in 1891. Marie was also a niece of Grand Duke Serge, whom Ella had adopted following the disgrace and dismissal from Russia of Marie's father, Grand Duke Paul.*

Alice had met Marie on her previous visit to Russia in 1901 and Marie had attended Alice's wedding. She was sorry to find that Marie believed she was being forced into a loveless marriage by Ella. Marie was the only person who did not hold Ella in high

* Grand Duke Paul sired an illegitimate son, Vladimir, by his mistress, Olga von Pistohlkors, the divorced wife of one of Grand Duke Vladimir's ADCs. In 1902 he married her in contravention of the Tsar's wishes and was banished from Russia, the Dowager Empress judging that he had neglected his fundamental obligations, his children, country, service and honour.

esteem and of these negotiations she left a brutal account in her memoirs.*

The wedding was celebrated at the Palace of Tsarskoe Selo on 3 May, the bride bedecked in crown jewels and adorned in the crimson velvet robes of a Russian grand duchess, so heavy that she needed help to rise to her feet.

Alice witnessed the indifferent bride undergo first the Russian Orthodox and then the Protestant marriages, preceded and followed by a banquet and a gala reception, an exhausting process by which the welfare of a lost and unhappy girl was consigned to a prince she hardly knew.† But Alice lost no affection for Ella over this. Neither was she prepared to warm to Grand Duke Paul's morganatic second wife, who came with him from France; nor did it sour her belief in the merits of arranged marriages.

Alice and Andrea stayed on in Russia until August, affording Alice her one real chance to understand the lives of the Tsar and her Aunt Alix and the work of her Aunt Ella. She observed the perpetual dilemma of royalty at its sharpest: the conventional role in conflict with the desire to contribute to the welfare of the people of the country.

Alice and Andrea stayed at the Nicholas Palace in Moscow in early June. Alice's mother and their children joined them there, while the entourage were housed at the Tsar's palace in such cramped conditions that Victoria's maid, Edith Pye,‡ known in the family as the Pye-Crust, had to sleep in the bathroom.

While Andrea played a 'frivolous' hand of bridge with Nona and others, Alice observed her Aunt Ella. The Grand Duchess had undergone an operation for a non-malignant internal growth earlier

* *Things I Remember* by Grand Duchess Marie of Russia (Cassell, 1931), pp.91–100.

† The marriage was not a happy one, lasting only until 1914. The Grand Duchess remarried in 1917, escaped the Revolution and lived variously in London and America, earning her living as a journalist. She was the author of *A Grand Duchess Remembers* and other books. She died in Germany in 1958.

‡ Edith Pye (d. 1962). She stayed with Victoria all her life and occasionally came out of retirement in the 1950s to look after Alice when she was in London.

that year. This had left her less slim and sometimes she looked tired, but her thoughts were preoccupied with the convent of nursing sisters she was establishing. She had bought a property in Moscow with two houses on it. One would be a hospital and in the other she would live as active head of her community. And she was about to build a church.

Ella explained that the nurses would be trained in the hospital, but their role would be to go out to tend to the wounded and suffering and to oversee the parish institutions in the Moscow district, such as infant schools. Ella's idea had been inspired by her mother's 'Alice Nurses' in Darmstadt, who were district nurses working in the community. The nurses would take vows, but these would not be severe. They would serve for between two and five years, and the vows could then be renewed for a further five years.

Alice listened to Ella carefully, but was aware that almost the entire family and court were against her aunt's plan. Only Victoria was of the view that her sister was 'perfectly right to fill her life with useful work'.[11] The others were afraid that Ella intended to shut herself up, but this was not her intention.

On 10 June the foundation bricks were laid for Ella's church on a cold, but fine morning. Alice attended the ceremony and the long service. From a chapel near the Kremlin came 'the fearfully holy image of the Virgin', brought there for the occasion 'in a quaint old carriage with six horses'.[12] The architect employed by Ella for part of this work was Alexei V. Shchussev, who was later called upon to design Lenin's tomb, evidence of a life of contrasts.

Alice took Ella's work to heart. She longed to undertake something similar in Greece, but it was to be many years before she could do so. She relished Ella's exploration of the spiritual, and the practical aspect of helping the less fortunate. The visit seeded thoughts and ideas in her.

Later that year, Alice would hear that Ella had given Ernie a picture by Sir Edward Burne-Jones of St George and the Dragon, and valuable gifts to other members of the family. She was divesting herself of her worldly goods. Rumours soon spread to Darmstadt that she was retreating from life and taking the veil, but Victoria pointed out that all this was merely an extension of the nursing work that she had begun in the Russo-Japanese war. However, two years later Ella would take the irrevocable step of renouncing her other life. She told her nursing sisters: 'I am about to leave the brilliant world in which it fell to me to occupy a brilliant position, but together with you all I am about to enter a much greater world – that of the poor and the afflicted.'[13]

During their remaining days in Moscow, Alice was impressed by a visit to the fortified Monastery of St Serge, some miles outside the city. This opened her eyes to new forms of religion. To get there, they took a long, slow train journey, then travelled in two coupés along a bumpy road, past little wooden shops selling cotton to pilgrims, and arrived at the oldest church in the complex. Nona kept a record of the visit:

> There were the Archimandrite & all the priests of the community & they led us into the church which was small & full of people & immediately a service began. The church is very beautiful & very richly decorated with images & gold. As soon as the short service was over, the Archimandrite showed Pr.A. [Andrea] the sarcophagus where the body of St Serge is buried & each of the party who were Orthodox Church knelt down crossing themselves & touching the ground with their foreheads before the Saint & in getting up kissed the relique.[14]

From Moscow, the whole party moved to St Petersburg, where Alice deposited her daughters at the Winter Palace, and left with Andrea for Sweden and Denmark. Towards the end of July she joined her mother and Ella at Hapsal, in Estonia, where the Grand Duchess was taking the waters. Alice rejoined Andrea in St Petersburg and they returned to Greece at the end of August via Constantinople, where they were welcomed with enthusiastic demonstrations by the Greek communities. To the annoyance of the Greek press, however, the Sultan 'did not find occasion' to receive them.[15]

★

Alice stayed quietly at Tatoï for the rest of 1908. In the new year of 1909 the Greek royal family entered a period of intense political antagonism.

The King had been unpopular for returning to Greece in December 1908 after an absence of four months with no tangible resolution of the ever-prolonged Cretan question. There were rumblings that not only the King but also the Crown Prince should be ousted and that the Crown Prince's eighteen-year-old son, Prince George, should be placed on the throne.

Young Prince George joined the Infantry as a second lieutenant on 27 May 1909. It was not a propitious time for a prince to enter the army. Soon afterwards some dissatisfied officers formed a Military League. Their grievance was that the princes retained the same officers as ADCs year after year, denying other officers the chance to serve in this way. This became an issue in the Greek elections. The victorious party had campaigned for the removal of all the princes from high command. But when the new Prime Minister, Dimitrios Rhallys, took office at the beginning of August, one of the promises he failed to keep was to oust the princes. On 28 August the officers launched a *coup d'état.*

Athens fell into disarray. Edward VII offered the services of the Mediterranean Fleet to help restore order and the King of Greece asked that two British battleships remain in Phaleron Bay. This was partly to reassure Alice and Ellen, the only royal ladies left in Athens because of the customary summer exodus. According to the King of Greece, they 'had been made very nervous by what had occurred'.[16]

In later life, Alice maintained that 'revolutions & wars have never disturbed me',[17] and whatever fears she may have had at the time, she revealed her keen political antennae in assessing the situation. She believed that the Military League was determined to get rid of the Crown Prince and Prince Nicholas, but seemed inclined to keep Andrea, a situation which was unacceptable to him.[18] Writing of this in 1929, she observed: 'The ostensible aim of this league was to upset the Government, under the pretext that it was weak and not governing the country in a satisfactory manner.' The position of all the princes in the army soon became untenable, as Alice went on to recall:

[Andrea] soon discovered that one of the aims of the league was to prevent the sons of the King from doing any responsible work or holding any high commands in the army. Wishing to lighten the task of his father, King George I, who was trying to come to an understanding with the insurgents and accept Mr Venizelos, whom they had secretly sent for from Crete, as Prime Minister, he voluntarily sent in his resignation. His brothers, Nicholas and Christopher, also resigned from the army and his brother George from the navy at the same time.[19]

The brothers resigned their various posts on 1 September.* The press claimed that they had 'yielded to the will of the people', but the British Ambassador asserted that they resigned, 'feeling it impossible any longer to associate on the old terms with their brother officers'.[20]

The Crown Prince resigned as Commander-in-Chief, following criticism that he had administered reproof 'in intemperate language'[21] and ignored his military units, except during the autumn manoeuvres. Soon afterwards, he left Greece, apparently for Germany, with crowds crying out: 'We will not let you go.' In fact, Constantine headed for the sybaritic delights of Paris. 'Even his friends cannot find excuses for his unwisdom in seeking in Paris distractions unsuited either to his age or to his position, during a time of such anxiety,'[22] commented the British Ambassador Sir Francis Elliot. The Crown Prince did not return until April 1910.

The King himself remained calm, though he confided to Elliot that he contemplated abdication. He was 'deeply pained at the prospect of such an ending to the labours of 46 years, and he would have liked to complete the 50 years of his reign, but he felt so humiliated that it was hateful to him to meet anybody'.[23] In

* Nicholas resigned as Colonel and Inspector of Artillery and joined the Russian army; Christo set off to Germany to study for three years, and the younger Prince George joined the 1st Regiment of Footguards in Berlin; Big George was already *en disponibilité* but he resigned as Rear-Admiral.

mid-September 1909 Andrea cancelled a visit to Berlin, afraid lest the entire royal family be thrown out of Greece.[24] Nor was Alice able to go there for Christmas.

On 27 September there was a mass meeting of the guilds of Athens and the Piraeus in the Champs de Mars. A crowd of 50,000 gathered to applaud a resolution supporting the actions of the Military League. The resolution was presented to the King and he was cheered by the crowd. There seemed a genuine wish in Athens that new ideals should be sought in government. Even so, rumours circulated in Athens as to who might replace the King. As Sir Francis Elliot put it: 'Fantastic stories are of daily invention.'[25]

By Christmas Day the King had resolved to stay on as a constitutional monarch. By March 1910 the Military League was disbanded and its exhausted officers renounced politics in favour of more congenial military duties. Order returned to the Greek capital. At the end of March the King rode in state to the Chamber and convoked the new National Assembly, instigating reforms to render the constitution more effective both in home and foreign affairs.

The most significant result of this débâcle was the rise to power of Eleutherios Venizelos. He had been able to effect an agreement between the King and the Military League, leading to the formation of the National Assembly. When it met, he became Prime Minister. The figure of Venizelos would hover over Greek politics for some decades. But the rebellions left Andrea without a job. As Alice put it: 'His work was stopped, just when it was beginning to bear fruit.'[26]

Alice was still at Tatoï with Andrea, the King and Queen and Christo on the night of 6 January 1910 when the telephone rang and they were told that the entire centre block of the Royal Palace in Athens was ablaze. The curious design of the building made it exceptionally vulnerable to fire. There were three parallel blocks, running from east to west, connected by façades at both sides. The fire started in the roof of the Orthodox Chapel, spreading with terrifying rapidity the length of the upper floor of the centre block, which was completely destroyed.

Fortunately the two British warships that had been stationed in

Phaleron Bay in the aftermath of the *coup d'état* were still there. An hour later some four hundred men arrived to assist the single hand-engine. Earth and sand were piled up by the men and drenched to contain the fire.

The royal family rushed to the palace from Tatoï. Alice, Andrea and Christo were 'busily and usefully employed',[27] according to the Ambassador. With the rescue party came twenty armed Marines in case the fire had been caused by an insurrection and they might be needed to protect the King. Andrea was quick to see the bad effect this might create and asked them to leave. And sure enough, there was some adverse comment in the Greek press that the presence of these men undermined the nation's sovereignty.

Meanwhile the archives were brought to safety, along with pictures and furniture. The King's apartments were safely cleared, whereas the Queen lost personal possessions by breakage and theft. The roof fell in at midnight, and the royal family finally returned to Tatoï at 3.30 a.m.

Sir Francis Elliot reported to London the extraordinary rumours that were circulating about the fire:

> I was not surprised to hear, before I had been half an hour on the spot, that it was being said that the King had had the Palace set alight in order to attract sympathy. Today the legend is circulating in various forms that it was known beforehand that the Palace would be burnt down on Christmas Eve – the actual date according to the Orthodox Calendar. The real cause of the fire has not yet been discovered.[28]

Since the beginning of the political unrest in the previous year, the royal family had kept out of Athens, largely because the princes hated to attend public events in civilian clothes, where previously they had worn uniforms. In November 1909 though, Andrea, Alice, Nicholas and Ellen had begun to accept invitations to evening parties at the British and Belgian Legations for the first time since the coup.

April 1910 found the family installed in Corfu, where the King received frequent reassurances that the general public still wanted him as their king. But Alice and Andrea were not happy. Andrea was suspicious of Venizelos, and wondered what use he himself was in Greece. Alice told her family how restless they were, and how they could hardly 'bear being there any longer'.[29]

Alice and Andrea were due to visit Alice's parents in England. They were to accompany Queen Alexandra, who came to Corfu on 20 April, on a leisurely voyage, stopping for a few days in Venice. The news that King Edward was ill, and later seriously ill, changed Queen Alexandra's plans, and Alice and Andrea found themselves hastening to England with her more quickly than anticipated. They all arrived in London on the late afternoon of 5 May, Alice and Andrea and their daughters going to stay with Alice's parents at their rented house in Chesham.

Within a day of their return, the King's condition suddenly deteriorated and he died at Buckingham Palace. Alice and Andrea were joined at the King's funeral by George I, the Crown Prince and Christo. In the procession through the streets of London to the lying-in-state at Westminster, Louis, as personal ADC, walked alone, immediately before the King's charger and his rough-haired terrier, Caesar. Andrea also walked, while Alice travelled in a carriage. With Victoria and Nona they went to the funeral at St George's Chapel, Windsor, on 20 May, joined by Alice's brother Georgie, who obtained leave from HMS *Superb* at Portsmouth. Nine foreign sovereigns gathered in England for the occasion.

George V and Queen Mary ascended the throne, and much of the ebullient gaiety of the Edwardian era was replaced by a more serious monarchy, with a king whose professed interests were shooting and stamp-collecting. The glamorous women of dubious virtue that were such an adornment of the Edwardian court found that their day was done. England was presided over by a monarch who adhered to his marriage vows, and though probably a better man than his father and certainly a more dutiful sovereign, he somehow lacked the late King's presence and panache. Louis, a perceptive judge, came to think of him as a cipher.

As had happened nine years before with the death of Queen

Victoria, all the relationships in the British royal family were again subtly reshuffled. Alice was now but one of the many cousins of the new King. This was distancing, especially at a time when the position of the Greek royal family was so tenuous.

Alice and Andrea stayed on in England after the funeral. Victoria found that Alice's two girls had reached a most entertaining age: 'Dolla was full of quaint ideas such as that she had seen fairies flitting about in the grounds. She used to have the funniest fits of absent-mindedness too, for which she was much derided by her very sprightly sister.'[30]

On 24 June Victoria took Alice, Andrea, Louise and Nona to Windsor for the confirmation of the new Prince of Wales (later the Duke of Windsor). As the ladies were still dressed in deep mourning and Andrea in evening tails with the riband of the GCVO, they made a curious impression. Andrea, who never missed the chance for a joke, said the general public would assume that 'this must be a party of widows, accompanied by a conjurer'.[31]

It was by no means certain that Alice and Andrea would return to Greece. They were not needed there, it seemed, and during their travels they even contemplated staying away. Thus the next weeks were a mixture of amusement, tempered by indecision and increasing listlessness on the part of Andrea.

From London they went to Paris, where they enjoyed a reception that contrasted markedly with the city in mourning, not to mention the hostility of the politicians and press in Greece. They were invited everywhere, more or less adopted by the American Princess Isembourg* and had a good time until Alice fell ill with influenza.

The Heiligenberg, to which they repaired in July, missing Louise's twenty-first birthday by a day, was the usual haven, though Alice still felt ill and Andrea now had a vile cold. Louis arrived from the Home Fleet, Georgie secured a week's leave from the Royal Navy and Dickie was on holiday from naval college. There were

* Princess Isembourg-Birstein (1872–1939). Bertha Lewis, born in New Orleans. Married 1895, Prince Charles Isembourg.

visits to Wolfsgarten and most mornings Alice and Louise rode together before breakfast.

Hanging over both Alice and Andrea was the uncertainty of the future. Andrea felt duty-bound to return to Greece and duly went back early in August. His example was followed by his brothers Nicholas and Christo, who, according to Louise, only ever followed his lead.[32]

Andrea's plan was that he would return to Germany in September to collect Alice and his daughters and escort them to Greece. There then began a phase of muddled telegrams, messages and changes of plan. Andrea cabled Alice that she must return to Athens alone. She sent for a maid for the journey. Alice then cabled back, but Andrea did not receive the telegram. He then cabled saying he was in 'a great state of mind' and wanting to know if she had got his message. She cabled back that she did not understand his cable and had had no message. The cables crossed. At the end of it all, Louise concluded that 'it may mean she is to join him somewhere soon'.[33]

There was probably no more to all this than a case of bad communications. Nevertheless it highlighted the problems of returning to Greece and the uncertainty of what Alice would find when she got there.

Before her departure, Alice saw the Tsar and his family with Uncle Ernie at Friedberg, a castle with a fortified gateway, near Nauheim, where the Tsarina was undergoing a cure that August. Then Andrea returned for Alice on 15 September, at about which time she became pregnant for the first time in four years and they left for Greece together ten days later.

Venizelos now held sway in Athens. He was worried that the royal family were becoming too isolated, partly because of the problem over uniforms. He persuaded the King and Queen, Andrea and Alice to spend more time in Athens. A big effort was made by most of the royal family to play a fuller part in the social life of the city, Nicholas, a talented amateur artist, taking on the presidency of the National Picture Gallery of the School of Fine Art.

In April 1911 only the King and the Crown Princess attended the annual Independence Day celebrations, the princes 'still impeded by the difficulty about uniform'.[34] But, at the end of June, after a stormy debate and an all-night sitting in the Chamber, Venizelos pushed through a bill by which the Crown Prince was appointed Inspector-General of the army.

Alice was safely delivered of a third daughter at Tatoï on 22 June 1911, the very afternoon of the coronation of George V in England. The child was given the name Cecilia, but always known in the family as Cécile. Alice recovered her health rapidly and was out of bed, though still in her room, within ten days of her confinement. In those days that was unusual.

In honour of the coincidence of Cécile's birth, Andrea asked George V to be one of her godparents, the others being Uncle Ernie, Prince Nicholas and Queen Olga's fat sister, Vera, Duchess of Württemberg.* On Sunday 2 July Cécile was baptised at Tatoï by the Metropolitan of Athens. Alice's mother saw the baby at Wolfsgarten that August and declared her 'a pretty, healthy & most cheerful little soul, smiling & cooing when awake, in fact as Mr Patterson once said "good enough to be a poor man's child"'.[35]

In September Alice and Andrea accompanied Victoria to the Heiligenberg, and on 1 November they took their growing family to Venice, returning to Athens on 28 November. In an otherwise uneventful autumn, the Crown Prince, Nicholas and Andrea attended a ball for officers of the Greek navy, the first such occasion they had graced since 1909.

In February 1912, Louise came to stay with Alice. Athens was cold when she arrived, but she was fascinated to stay at the palace, the burnt middle part of which was still not wholly rebuilt, so that to get from one side to the other meant a walk outside. Louise spent as much time as possible with Margarita and Theodora, who were now old enough to lunch downstairs. She went with them to the carnival procession where they threw confetti, papers and ribbons into the crowd. And on another occasion she took them

* A few days later, Queen Olga's mother died in Russia aged eighty-one. Vera died in April 1912, aged fifty-eight.

to Phaleron, where they had tea on the beach and climbed the rocks looking for crabs.

At other times, Margarita and Theodora undertook English and Greek lessons with their governess, and gymnastics in the long corridor of the palace with a Swedish woman. Of Cécile, Louise wrote to her brother Dickie: 'The baby is quite delightful, she crawls all over the place & is always cheerful.'[36]

She did not refer to a plot that Alice was hatching, to marry her to Andrea's youngest brother, Christo – not an overly appealing prospect, according to contemporary witnesses: 'a big fat boy',[37] wrote the Tsarina, and a sufferer from 'plumpness and slight myopia',[38] according to the writer Compton Mackenzie. The lack of money of both parties meant that the cause had few promoters and was soon forgotten.*

Louise stayed with Alice and Andrea until 6 May. During her visit, Alice worked at the Greek School of Embroidery every morning.

In March 1912 there was a general election in Athens and the King felt that at such a time he should be away from the capital. He dragooned Alice, Andrea, Louise, Christo and Minnie (Grand Duchess George) to accompany him on a four-day cruise in his yacht until the votes had been counted. He was delighted when Venizelos was re-elected Prime Minister. The Greek press were calm, too. They pronounced that a change in attitude at the heart of government had been achieved. Old hostilities towards the King and the Crown Prince were treated as if they had never occurred, though the Crown Princess was still criticized for her inflexible determination not to mix with the Greeks.

For Alice the summer was uneventful, but in October the First Balkan War began, ending Andrea's period of enforced idleness and giving Alice the chance to perform valuable service to the Greeks.

* Mention was made of it in the Swedish edition of Margit Fjellman's biography of Queen Louise, but King Gustaf asked that this be excised from the English edition. It was.

10. The First Balkan War

The Balkan Wars came about because of the long-held dream of the Greeks to expand their territories. Venizelos was to the fore in the quest to advance towards Constantinople. Now the Greeks joined the other members of the Balkan League – Bulgaria, Montenegro and Serbia – and declared war on Turkey.

Greece had endured troubled times since its defeat by the Turks in 1897. During the ensuing years the question of the ownership and rule of Crete had loomed over the political arena. By 1912 the Greeks were determined to liberate their occupied territories, to attack the Slavs in the Balkans and the Turks in Thrace, Macedonia and the Aegean. They also sought to unite Crete with the Greek mainland.

By the end of September 1912, complications with Turkey were growing, securities were falling sharply on the Bourse and war seemed inevitable.

On 2 October Andrea arrived in Athens from Corfu and offered his services to the Minister of War, even as a simple volunteer if so required. Venizelos promised to reinstate all the princes into the army, and thus Nicholas and Christo also returned to Athens. The Crown Prince was promoted to Commander-in-Chief. On 17 October Turkey declared war on Serbia and the next day Greece declared war on Turkey.

The princes were officially reinstated into the army on 21 October, Andrea becoming a Lieutenant-Colonel with the 3rd Regiment of Cavalry. Such was their enthusiasm that they all set off to Larissa the day before, without waiting for the appointments to be gazetted.

The royal ladies immediately set to work nursing and organizing hospitals. The School of Greek Embroidery had prospered with Alice's help, and by 1912 a great number of women were employed there. Alice immediately directed them to make garments for the troops and the refugees. Within a month of the outbreak of war, the ladies had made 80,000 garments, and on her travels through the Greek countryside, Alice spotted soldiers wearing bashliks (hoods) made at the school.

Alice accompanied Andrea and his brothers to Larissa on 20 October, but soon pushed on to Elassona on her own mission to collect warm clothing for the reservists and to establish a first-aid hospital at the front. She was joined by two nurses from the Alice Hospital created by her grandmother in Darmstadt.

Alice's experiences were gruesome, and in long letters to her mother she gave a vivid account of her ordeals. The story began at Larissa on 22 October:

I went to the Military Hospital and saw the arrival of some 15 to 20 wounded soldiers from a skirmish at Elassona who had taken 14 hours coming here over utterly impossible roads, over a fearful mountain pass – Melouna – at the frontier, where huge boulders and rocks stuck out of the road, and on hearing of their agony and the impossibility of bringing severely wounded at all to Larissa, and news which reached us of the army's tremendously rapid advance, I instantly decided to move my hospital to Elassona. So I hurriedly got hold of a motor to go and find a house in Elassona, as I was told there would not be a big battle for two days at least and I would have time to move all the things there and my first-class operation room. So I left with Madame Agyropoulo, the wife of the Prefect of Larissa, in whose house I had been living; also my surgeon and his assistant and 'Schwester Margarethe', the surgical Alice Hospital nurse, and we set off at 11 o'clock and reached Elassona at 4.30 p.m. over impossible roads; we nearly fell over precipices and stuck twice in sandy river beds for an hour. In all the villages we passed we were nearly kissed by the inhabitants, who yelled and wept with joy: 'Free at last!' 'God says it is enough after 500 years!' and so on, and they showed me scars of the terrible ill-treatment of the Turks. When I arrived at Elassona and saw the Greek flag flying over my principal house it was the most impressive moment of my life.[1]

In Elassona Alice was horrified to hear that a fierce battle was raging. The wounded would be too far from Larissa and she still had not established her hospital at Elassona. So she commandeered a school and pillaged Turkish houses for mattresses, eiderdown coverings and long pillows, big enough for two men to sleep on. They were thus prepared for 120 men, and Alice summoned her nurses overnight from Larissa. Alice continued:

In the meantime I sent my surgeon to the battlefield with a motor of the General Staff, which I took upon myself to sign an order for. For here I must explain a moment, that although the Army had very good surgeons and men nurses with lots of bandages to make the first bandages on the battlefield; they had no means of transport to the nearest town, nor *one single plan* for improvising a hospital, with food and bandages, in such a town; and the Red Cross of Athens and other countries were so slow, they had not a single hospital nearer the scene of War than Athens, for the Larissa Hospital I myself forced the Military Authorities to fit out an operation room in 24 hours. So you understand nobody was officially there to organize the transport, no one to house and feed the lightly wounded who were able to walk about, and no one who had cognac, milk, soup, coffee and tea and chocolate for the severely wounded. This, to show you clearly the awful state of affairs I found. All this is the fault of the French General, Eydoux, and the chief doctor, Arnaud, whom we had plagued for two weeks before the war to get things ready quickly, because the Queen and we all *knew* the French had nothing at all for the Red Cross things, and though we begged and argued, and even told him he was telling lies, he swore that everything was ready.

Alice heard guns firing all day long until battle ceased at 6.30 p.m. The first wounded arrived by motor with Alice's surgeon, Meerminga, two hours later:

Of course there were no nurses except Schwester Margarethe, and as we had hundreds coming all together at a time, Madame Agyropoulo and I put on aprons and caps and started to help the doctors in that school I mentioned, where we had put the mattresses and bandages ready. And we took the bandages off the wounded, and put fresh ones on after the doctor had examined the wounds – ghastly ones from shells, then fractured bones and ordinary Mauser wounds etc. We helped the doctors in fearful operations, hurriedly done in the corridor amongst the dying and wounded waiting for their turn, for we could not spare a single room. We had no light, only one or two miserable lamps, and they all wanted something to eat or drink, for they were wet through from the *pelting* rain pouring for hours on them. I found a small spirit lamp in a corner of one room and took spirits of wine from a lamp in another and a small Turkish coffee pot with water, and I possessed one tin of condensed milk which had to do for 250 men. They came steadily from 8.30 till 3.30 at night. The operation was going on at one moment, and a man dying on the other side of me on a stretcher, and I trying to cook with such a miserable small quantity of water in a tiny pot, and the dying man wanting to hold one of my hands for comfort, and I had to stir with the other hand, and the blood from the operation table dripping on me. And this sort of work went on for three days and three nights with a couple of hours between the arrivals at night for sleep.[2]

Alice remained in the same clothes for days, sleeping in the freezing house of a peasant with nothing to eat. During three days she consumed but one crust of dry bread and one small cup of Turkish coffee. More wounded arrived, some dying *en route* because of the rain and cold. Alice commandeered four more houses and put the less badly wounded there, covering them with blankets and folding their overcoats into pillows. They were lightly fed and those requiring operations came to Alice's operating room, the only one near the battlefield. Presently a man appeared who helped with the cooking, boiling water in a large kettle over a fire. The work of cooking, bandaging and operating continued, and as more injured were carried in, and all the beds filled, so the next batch were placed on mattresses on the floor and made comfortable. Alice continued:

We gave each man in both hospitals a glass of brandy after the pain of bandaging, and a glass of hot milk in bed to make them sleep, and actually, the rest after the bad roads made most of them sleep. But, God! What things we saw! Shattered arms, and legs and heads, such awful sights – and then to have to bandage those dreadful things for three days and three nights. The corridor full of blood, and cast-off bandages knee high. Then two charming Greek ladies came, one from Rome and one from Paris, who had been Red Cross nurses for three years, and we gave over the work to them, but only after *all* the wounded had arrived and been bandaged by us.[3]

The Crown Prince asked Alice and her doctors to set up another hospital in Servia, and to arrange housing, feeding and transport.

The war was a turning point for Alice. It plunged her into an activity that remained close to her heart all her life. Writing to her mother within days of the events she had described, Alice commented that she was 'too exhausted to follow the Army to any more battles, although 800 cases have given me experience enough to make me now a first-class Nurse; I, who had never set my foot in hospitals, because I could not stand the sight of wounds and pain.'[4]

Hardly had she arrived in Servia on 25 October than Alice learned that the Turks had scattered in disarray as far as Monastir and Salonika, often without food, arms and ammunition, and sometimes without clothes. There would therefore be no great battle. Alice was aware that there were still some Turks lurking in Servia, and they had been 'massacring Christians here in a most awful way, the streets are full of priests, women and children, and rivers of blood'. In revenge the Christians were burning the deserted Turkish houses.

On 26 October, King George arrived in Servia to review the troops and to thank them for their bravery. He made a ceremonial entry into Elassona, Servia and Kozani, the three conquered towns. Alice joined the King and the princes on their ceremonial entry through a triumphal arch at Kozani with schoolchildren lining the route. There was a Te Deum in a beautiful church, with the Bishop adorned in full finery. For a few days Alice was able to sleep in a proper bedroom with sheets of lace and embroidery.

On 25 October Alice had been reunited with Andrea, then working on the Crown Prince's staff and lately promoted to Colonel. He told her how the Crown Prince had won a great military victory against all odds at Elassona the day before. Andrea had been present throughout, riding the Irish hunter given to Alice by the Tsar. This fine beast had behaved well even under shell fire.

The Greek infantry had traversed virtually impassable mountain ranges around Mount Olympus with scant cover from their artillery, and had got through by doing so at great speed. However, all the captains and sergeant-majors had been killed, and four hundred men were either killed or wounded. Andrea calculated that he had heard or seen a thousand shells bursting in the night. Eventually the Turks were routed and their retreat cut off, and panic ensued. Four hundred Turks were taken prisoner and many were killed. The Crown Prince rode to victory. As Alice described it: 'When Tino rode down into the Pass this morning, the bodies of the Turks were piled up all down the road, ten deep, high as a wall. Awful! Awful!'[5]

On 2 November Alice wrote a second letter to her mother from Verria, in Macedonia, somewhat west of Salonika. In it she described the events of the past few days. At Kozani Alice found a new military hospital and new barracks, constructed a few days earlier by French engineers:

Lovelier still, all the necessary materials had already arrived, beds, blankets, dressing gowns, mugs, basins, bandages, lamps, etc: mostly still in packing cases in a big depot room, but all rummaged by the Turks before leaving and in a frightful mess. And the floors of the empty wings (there are four buildings forming a square) were literally knee-deep in filth. So Mme. Agyropoulo and I got some charwomen to sweep and wash all the floors and some soldiers to put up over 200 bedsteads and then for two whole days we made up those beds with mattresses, blankets, sheets and pillows. We made some ourselves and filled them up with cotton until every bed was ready. We hung up the lamps and washed the mugs and put one by each bed, also spittoons, and we put shirts and under-drawers in a cupboard for each room etc. Tino and the boys went when the King came, and so we had meals with the King who was much nearer the hospital than our house, which was right in the town, half an hour off.[6]

News then arrived of victory by the Greeks at Kailar on 26 October. Alice and her team returned to the hospital, put on their aprons and caps and slept for half an hour until the steady stream of 175 wounded began to arrive for bandaging. This work continued through the night until 6.00 a.m. Some 160 sick cases also arrived and had to be housed in a wing to themselves. After snatching sleep for an hour and a half, they returned to the hospital for more bandaging and feeding. The next day Alice endured her worst nursing experience:

Our last afternoon at Kozani was spent in assisting at the amputation of a leg. I had to give chloroform at a certain moment and prevent the patient from biting his tongue and also to hand cotton wool, basins, etc. Once I got over my feeling of disgust, it was very interesting, of course. It was not done in a special operation room but in one of the wards, screened off from the other patients, and after all was over, the leg was forgotten on the floor and I suddenly saw it there afterwards and pointed it out to Mme. Agyropoulo, saying that somebody ought to take it away. She promptly picked it up herself, wrapped it up in some stuff, put it under her arm and marched out of the hospital to find a place to bury it in. But she never noticed that she left the bloody end uncovered, and as she is as deaf as I, although I shouted after her, she went on unconcerned, and everybody she passed nearly retched with disgust – and, of course, I ended by laughing, when the comic part of the thing struck me.[7]

More wounded came in the evening, but by midnight they were in care, so Alice managed to get a whole night's sleep. Then eight doctors and three nurses arrived from the Athens Red Cross and the two Red Cross ladies from Elassona, so by 1 November Alice was able to move on to Verria in the direction of Salonika to await more wounded men, who could later be moved to Salonika itself and then by sea to the Piraeus. Here she spent four nights with the

King at a tiny station in cramped conditions, made worse by unceasing rain.

The army was marching towards Monastir and Salonika, through another narrow mountain pass. The Crown Prince advanced his men one by one along the top of the mountains, while sending a division round to cut off a Turkish retreat. From Verria Alice could see the fighting through field glasses, and, though she herself could not hear the guns, others could. Once again Alice prepared for an influx of wounded soldiers. She ended her letter with some urgency:

It has begun to snow on the pass I came through yesterday, by motor, and the cold here is terrible. I get neuralgia but Aspirin cuts it off in half an hour. I feel very well otherwise, but I am thinner than Louise and flat as a board; I think you would not know me any more, and yet I eat splendid hearty meals with a beautiful appetite.

I just hear that the battle is won and the Turks are running away and the wounded are beginning to come and I am off to receive them at the hospital.[8]

Alice's two letters were copied by Victoria and widely distributed amongst the British royal family. Alice's brother, Georgie, commented: 'I have never read anything so interesting. It filled me with an intense admiration and sympathy for Alice; she has surpassed herself in bravery & tirelessness of effort.'[9]

Further testimony of Alice's courage came from Schwester Anna, one of the Alice Hospital nurses, who sent a report to her hospital in Darmstadt: 'We are becoming real soldiers. Princess Andreas is setting the finest example.' The nurse recorded Alice telephoning from Elassona at 7.00 p.m. 'Depart immediately and bring essential things as destitution is great.' After a hair-raising journey across swamps, made irksome by punctures, they joined her at 11.30 a.m. the next day.[10]

Salonika fell on 9 November, the Crown Prince taking the surrender of 25,000 men. Alice entered the newly taken city as part of the

King's entourage during his grand entry two days later. Prince Nicholas was appointed Governor, while the Crown Prince, presently promoted to general *honoris causa*, advanced to Monastir.

At the beginning of the war, Alice had been short of helpers. Nona had immediately volunteered to come from England, and was not dissuaded by a predictable telegram from Alice reading: 'Don't come.'[11] A Miss Boase, trained at Charing Cross Hospital, came with her. Victoria sold some jewellery and gave Nona £100 for deserving causes encountered on her travels.

Alice had settled with Andrea and the King in a villa in Salonika formerly owned by the old Sultan. She came out to greet Nona, who arrived from Athens with Queen Olga and a group of doctors and nurses on 13 November. Nona wrote back to Victoria: 'It would make you proud to hear the way everyone speaks of Pss Alice. Sophie Baltazzi, Doctor Sava, the officers, *everyone*. She has done wonders and at each place she has been through has left a well organized hospital.'[12]

In these days Alice was sustained by a certain manic energy, as Nona observed:

> Princess Alice is *very* thin but says she is perfectly well & I think she is *now*, but when the excitement is over she will be run down & feel very flat. At present she simply can't stop doing things. Pr. A [Andrea] wants to send her back to Athens to the babies soon, but I don't think he will succeed just yet. She is taking a tonic & I think is going to have some cocoa when she goes to bed to fatten her up a bit. She does not seem to have suffered much from the horrors she went through but of course the reaction may still come.[13]

Nona was relieved that Andrea was with them, 'because I am sure he is *very* necessary as he has got such a good head on his shoulders'.[14]

Within a couple of days Alice and Nona were busy reorganizing the hospitals in Salonika, which were very badly run. At the Jewish Hospital the patients were starving to death. Sanitary conditions were poor, and typhoid and dysentery were rife. Alice arranged a priest for each hospital as so many people were dying and needed to be buried quickly. Thirty Greek patients were then judged fit and discharged from hospital to make way for others. Immediately they set off on a three-mile walk to complain to the King. Andrea intercepted them and sent them packing.

On 23 November Nona accompanied Alice on her return to Athens for a much needed rest. In Athens, Venizelos came to see her and made her 'a beautiful speech . . . thanking her from himself as Prime Minister, Greek & Cretan, & from the whole ministry for all she had done. He added tactfully that of course they thanked all the other princesses, but not in the same way.'[15] Venizelos told Alice there would be fighting near Jannina. She made him promise carts and horses, and set off to Previsa on 6 December to set up a hospital, which could follow closely behind the army if necessary.

And so the efforts continued, Alice and Nona arriving in Previsa in pouring rain, and inspecting improvised hospitals at Philippiada, by which time Alice was hiding behind a substantial veil because of nettle-rash.

Back in Athens, there was a row between Alice and the Crown Princess over the deployment of some of the Crown Princess's nurses from Cairo. Unreasonably, the Crown Princess was furious when Alice sent them to Salonika, where they were desperately needed, without first obtaining the Crown Princess's permission.

Alice herself went to Salonika, inspecting a camp for refugees and satisfying herself that the homeless were being properly fed. Alice and Nona stayed in Salonika, celebrating Christmas and the King's birthday on the same day. Then they returned to Athens, where a Christmas brooch sent by the Tsarina awaited Alice. But, noted Nona: 'We have not got any cards or telegram or sign of life from the Grand Duchess. It is funny that she has not sent Pss. Alice a word at all since the war broke out.'[16]

A week later they returned to Salonika, where the Turks were delaying signing the peace indefinitely. Alice's children also came and were delighted to see their father – especially Cécile, who ran to Andrea despite bad seasickness on the voyage. By this time both Alice and Andrea were thoroughly run down. Alice needed shots of arsenic as a tonic, while Nona judged Andrea as bored with nothing to do and 'awfully depressed & in such a state (inwardly) of nerves'.[17]

The final mission was to Epirus on 23 January. Alice intended to sort out the hospitals there, but because of the earlier row with the Crown Princess, the Crown Prince suddenly entrusted all the military hospitals in Epirus to Big George's wife, Marie, who was only there because she was prevented from leaving by a cold. The entire staff of the hospital in Philippiada heard the Crown Prince say: 'Why the devil is Alice coming here to mix up everything as she did in Saloniki?'[18] In spite of this, the local doctors and nurses asked Alice to visit their hospitals and the work of checking, feeding patients and inspecting refugee kitchens continued apace.

At the end of February, Alice and Nona moved on to Eminaga. On 4 March there was more fighting and the next day about a hundred slightly wounded needed care. But the war news was good: three forts were taken, and on 6 March the Greeks made progress. Nona recorded:

> At 6.30 a.m. rifle fire began all round us & we dressed in 3 seconds! We then discovered that Jannina had fallen! Why we were not shot I do not know, everyone was letting off their rifles in all directions. We stayed all that day at Eminaga feeding people, & on Friday we came here [Jannina]. It was a wonderful entry. We have seen awfully interesting things & very terrible ones also . . . We passed many bodies of Turks lying in every position. In the afternoon we went to see the prisoners & that was horrible, as many were dying from exhaustion & want of food & water. In the barracks they found 150 corpses that no one had bothered to bury.[19]

Alice and Nona witnessed the entry into Jannina, before returning to Athens. The war was finally over. A second Balkan War would follow, but Alice would be prepared with the personal experience she already had of what she called 'all the horror'.[20] She was exhausted by her experiences, but she had matured. From now on she would take wars, revolutions and other uprisings in her stride.

As a result of this war, and the Second Balkan War which followed, Venizelos negotiated substantial territorial gains and the annexation of Crete by Greece in the Treaty of London in 1913. Alice's nursing activities were in due course recognized. In November 1913, George V decorated her with the Royal Red Cross. The citation read: 'in recognition of her services in nursing the sick and wounded among the Greek soldiers during the recent war'.[21]

On 16 March Alice said goodbye to Nona, who returned to England, her job done. Two days later, the reign of George I of Greece came to an abrupt and shocking end.

11. The Murder of King George

King of the Hellenes since he was seventeen, George I had weathered many storms and, despite being forced to contemplate abdication once or twice before, he had hoped to remain king until his Golden Jubilee at the end of October 1913, when he intended to abdicate. An assassin's hand thwarted his plan.

The King liked to take an afternoon stroll in Salonika, just as he enjoyed walking informally on his long holidays in Aix-les-Bains. Accompanied only by an equerry and two gendarmes, he was walking through the streets on the afternoon of 18 March 1913. When he reached the White Tower he turned back and passed a café from which a scruffy individual emerged and shot him in the back at close range. He died almost instantly.

The assassin was promptly arrested. The politicians feared that he might prove to be either a Bulgarian, or possibly a Turk, but he turned out to be a deranged Greek. In Athens, Venizelos, emerging from a ministerial council in a state of some emotion, said to Sir Francis Elliot: 'It is a terrible thing to say, but it is a cause of great thankfulness that he is a Greek.'[1] On 6 May the man in question, Alexander Schinas, was taken from prison to the Prefecture to be examined. He was detained on the second floor, where he sauntered towards the window and suddenly leapt on to the window ledge and hurled himself to his death thirty feet below.

Andrea, Alice and young George were at the palace when news of the King's death arrived. They broke it to Queen Olga, and the next morning they all left together for Salonika. The Crown Prince, now Constantine I (or XII),* returned to Athens and took the oath.

* King Constantine was sometimes hailed as Constantine XII in deference to a much earlier dynasty, but, wisely, discouraged this as meaningless.

Politicians who had criticized George I now heaped eulogies upon him. The press did likewise. Sir Francis Elliot wrote:

Tragic as was the manner of the King's death, he was at least happy in the moment of it. He had seen the edifice he had laboured to construct for fifty years crowned by the victories of his army under the leadership of his Son and Successor. He had the assurance that his dynasty was at last firmly seated upon the throne which he had often during his long reign been tempted to abandon in despair. He had seen his aspirations realized beyond his most ambitious dreams. He will live on in the memories of his people as a martyr to the national cause.[2]

Athens experienced its first royal funeral on 2 April. Alice wore the Grand Cross of the Order of the Redeemer, which the dead King had given her. Alice had always been fond of him, and likewise he had been good to her. Huge crowds gathered as his body was moved first from Salonika to Athens, and thence to the pine-tree-covered hillside of Tatoï, where he was committed to the ground, all his sons throwing bunches of violets and earth into the grave.

On 13 April the King's political will was published and well received. There was a message to the new King urging him to love his country 'wholeheartedly', to respect the interests of the people, to give his children a good Greek education and, moreover: 'Be calm and never forget that you are reigning over a southern people who are easily roused and may in a moment do and say many things which they will probably forget a few hours after. For this reason never fall into a passion and never forget that it is preferable that the King should suffer rather than his people.'[3]

The King's private will was not published, though its contents were soon widely known. He left no more than £80,000, most of which went to his impecunious younger sons, Andrea and Christo. The will granted Alice and Andrea an annuity of £4,000 and gave them Mon Repos, the King's home on Corfu, with all the silver, linen and glass in it. From now on this was their home.

★

The new King came to the throne at a curious moment in his fortunes. He had lived down the defeat in the earlier war with the Turks in 1897, and in the First Balkan War was hailed as Greece's victorious general. 'It is astonishing how *strong* the Crown Prince is now,' Nona had written. 'Everyone has the greatest respect for him & he is wonderful here, so just & yet firm, & manages this difficult situation extremely well.'[4]

But no sooner had he won back general respect than he put it all at risk by embarking on an affair in the last days of the Balkan War with 'a most *un*attractive female* working in Pss Ellen's hospital'. His father was kept in the dark, but the entire army knew. It became a considerable scandal. 'Of course,' noted Nona, 'the Crown Princess has only herself to thank for all this as she had made his life unbearable for some years.'[5]

The situation took a strange twist when it was discovered that the Crown Princess was going to have a baby in April. Alice felt she should therefore be forgiven much of her spleen, while her astonished mother commented from England: 'It certainly must excuse a good deal of her bad temper & touchiness, for many people are most trying & irritable at such times & if she had an inkling of her husband's 'goings on', that will not have made her feel more amiable or happy.'[6]

Meanwhile Constantine continued his dalliance, inflicting the presence of his mistress on Alice and others of the family. Nona reported that he was 'failing horribly, & it is such a despicable, low story'.[7] However, when he ascended the throne, affairs of state precluded the new King from seeing much of his mistress.

King Constantine had two advantages over his father. First, he was wholly Greek and secondly he practised the Orthodox religion. In this respect it also helped that he was married to a wife called Sophie, as there was a myth in Greece that when a Constantine

* It seems most probable that the mistress was Paola von Ostheim, since she knew him from 1912 until his death. Sometimes described as Paola, Princess of Saxe-Weimar, she published *A King's Private Letters* (1925), which aimed to do justice to a much maligned monarch. The last letter reached her after his death. In these letters he often apologized for not having seen her.

shared the throne with a Sofia, it would be a time of plentiful prosperity.

This was Sir Francis Elliot's verdict on the new King:

> Inferior in intelligence to his father, and wanting in his dexterous pliability, he is a man of stronger character, and may be well fitted to deal with the new problems which will arise in the new situation. It is to be hoped that there will be no conflict of opinion between him and Monsieur Venizelos, a man of equally strong character, until the development of the new Greece has been fairly started.[8]

As usual, Sir Francis had outlined the problems with some prescience.

The new Queen Sophie had a yet more complicated position. Notwithstanding the good omen of her name, the Greeks would never trust her since she was the Kaiser's sister: they refused to accept that her relations with the Kaiser were often strained and ignored her professions of total loyalty to Greece. Her attitude only added to her difficulties. She was frequently not on speaking terms with Venizelos. Her conduct in the Balkan War had considerably annoyed Alice and Queen Olga. In December 1912, in Salonika, Andrea told Nona 'that the row with the Crown Princess had got much worse – that she had been beastly to Alice & then had gone for him . . . I think she is really a bit mad'.[9] From London, Victoria attempted to put this into perspective: 'Sophie indulges in the true German "Empfindlichkeit", a defect which really is at times worse than a vice. *Entre nous* it may have come out so strongly because she is probably somewhat jealous of Alice's great popularity. Any how it is despicable & monstrous.'[10]

On 4 May Queen Sophie gave birth to her baby, Katherine,* who was christened at the Crown Prince's palace on 14 June, with George V and the entire Greek army and navy as godparents. The new princess, who was nearly twenty-three years younger than

* Princess Katherine of Greece married 1947, Major Richard Brandram (1911–94). Now known as Lady Katherine Brandram. She lives in England.

her eldest brother, Crown Prince George, completed the family of six.

In the early days of the new reign, Alice set up a hospital in Athens and paid a brief visit to Salonika in July to organize her hospital there. In August all the royal family left Greece for a variety of destinations, Andrea, Alice and their three children heading for Germany and then England.

Andrea was worried that if another war broke out between Greece and Turkey he might have to hurry back to Greece. He was anxious to visit his tailor and do vital shopping before that. In London, the family stayed at Mall House, Spring Gardens, where Louis lived as First Sea Lord, having lately succeeded Sir Francis Bridgeman. Victoria had the pleasure of presenting Alice's little girls to her uncle, the Duke of Connaught, hailing him as their great-great-uncle. Horrified, the Duke exclaimed: 'My dear, you are making an ancestor of me!'*[11]

Andrea paid a formal visit to his cousin, George V, and returned to him his father's Garter insignia and other British orders. On 15 October he and Alice attended the wedding of King George's niece, Alexandra, Duchess of Fife in her own right, to Prince Arthur of Connaught at the Chapel Royal. To this wedding of another princess devoted to nursing, Alice wore white satin trimmed with embroidery.

While in London, Alice made a public appearance at the Greek Legation and toured Charing Cross Hospital and the London Hospital. During these weeks de László painted a portrait of Andrea to go with Alice's and its progress was frequently inspected.† They also found time to take the children by bus to St Paul's Cathedral and to visit the zoo. They returned to Greece on 17 November.

*

* The Duke of Connaught lived long enough to be made godfather to Prince Ludwig of Hesse, the infant son of Cécile, who was born in October 1931. He was his great-great-great-nephew. Tragically, the child died before the Duke.

† Soon afterwards, de László went to Athens to paint King Constantine, and later painted Queen Olga and Princess Nicholas.

Since 1912 Andrea's main occupation had been his regimental duties as Colonel commanding the 3rd Cavalry. As Alice wrote: 'For four years he was strenuously occupied in raising his regiment to the highest degree of efficiency.'[12] In January 1914 he was appointed to command the Cavalry School, with a French officer underneath him.

Alice's fourth baby was expected in early June, and her mother came from the Isle of Wight to be with her daughter at Mon Repos. The baby was late, causing Andrea to prolong his leave from the army more than once. Alice's gynaecologist, Dr Louros, was in residence but was hardly seen except at meals, as he was busy writing a book and went out to attend other patients on the island. 'Alice is much put out at this delay in the arrival of the baby,' Victoria wrote to Nona. 'They think now that the very latest date at which it can come is June 29th. It is the first time she has been mistaken in the date & has emulated Sophie, who sometimes kept people waiting a month.'[13]

There was good news on 26 June. 'Well, the baby is there at last,' wrote Victoria. 'She (alas!) made her appearance at 6 a.m. Of course it is a disappointment her being another girl; she is a fine, healthy, large child.'[14] The baby was given the name Sophia, though more usually known as Sophie. In the family they called her Tiny, because she was the 'tiny baby' of the family.*

Hardly had Sophie been born than external events caused great concern. Victoria noted: 'The political situation is critical & may end in war, but I hope not. The worst of it is that it looks as if the Turks meant to drag on matters until their Dreadnoughts have come & then would like a war, which would be a naval one & the Greeks believe that these ships will make their enemies almost invincible.'[15] In fact it was the assassination of Archduke Franz Ferdinand of Austria at Sarajevo on 28 June that precipitated the First World War.

* 'Please congratulate Alice from me,' wrote Dickie, 'but it was silly not to have a boy for once in a way.' [Richard Hough, *Louis and Victoria* (Hutchinson, 1974), p. 221.]

12. The First World War

King Constantine believed that neutrality would best serve Greece in the First World War. The Allies wanted him to join them, but he refused, partly from fear that the Kaiser might emerge as ultimate victor. He feared that the Allies would not send enough support, and he feared annihilation by Germany. It was a decision that would cost him dearly.

Though born a minor German princess, Alice had begun life as primarily English with the added cachet of being a descendant of Queen Victoria. However, she was fiercely loyal to Greece. But she was to suffer a problem that would intensify as the politics of Europe became more fraught, a problem that confronted most royal families – close relations finding themselves on opposing sides in wartime.

Alice's parents lived in England. They were firmly allied to the British cause; her father was the British First Sea Lord. Her mother's cousin was George V and Alice had numerous relations in England, many of them playmates since childhood days at Windsor and Osborne. But she also had two aunts in Russia – Alix, married to the Tsar, and Ella, now busily occupied with her nursing sisterhood.

Another aunt, Irène, was married to the brother of the Kaiser, and living at Kiel. Prince Henry of Prussia was serving as an admiral in the German navy. He had been a popular figure at Cowes for some years and considered himself on good terms with George V. In December 1912 and again in July 1914, he called on George V and asked him for an indication of what Britain would do in the event of Germany and Austria going to war with Russia. On both occasions, he returned to the Kaiser with an incorrect version of George V's views. This, combined with the Kaiser's wish to read only that which suited him, led the German Emperor to believe that Britain had given an assurance of neutrality, and Prince Henry that he had done his best to avoid the war.

Alice's uncle was Grand Duke of Hesse. Early in the war, news reached her that Uncle Ernie had left Aunt Onor in charge of government and joined the German army. Matters were little better in Greece itself, where her sisters-in-law were variously Prussian, Russian and French. Queen Sophie was a sister of the Kaiser.

Although Alice's loyalty to Greece meant that during the war, whatever she might have thought privately, she was a strictly neutral figure, for her the ties of blood surmounted political considerations. She was able to serve as an important, harmless means of communication between different members of the family. In particular she was able to keep in touch with her aunt Onor in Darmstadt, which Louis and Victoria were not.

Aunt Onor asked Alice for help in obtaining parcels to alleviate the plight of their prisoners. Alice informed her aunt of her calmer existence:

> Here in Corfu where we are living such an idyllic and quiet life, my thoughts are still with our relations, as I have seen two wars and so can sympathize with you and imagine all the horror. Next week we are going back to Athens as Andrea has to return to duty. The children are all very well and have spent four months enjoying the sea, are as black as Negroes, and swim as fast as fishes. Sometimes they speak of Don and Lu and were amused that they wanted a little sister of their own. The little one is called Sophia and is growing up well, thank God.[1]

In September Louise wrote to Alice, outlining where various British relatives were serving, and asking about the German relations, informing her that their aunt, Marie Erbach, had turned the Heiligenberg into a Red Cross home, and beseeching her: 'Don't please forget to give us any scrap of news you may get through Sophie. We have heard nothing from anybody.'[2] Shortly before this, the Tsarina had written to Alice from Tsarskoe Selo, reporting that she and her daughters, Olga and Tatiana, had been to the hospital 'to bind up wounds', that Ella had been with her for two days and that all the men of the family had left to serve.[3]

Alice's brother, Georgie, was serving in the British navy, and experienced his first sea battle at Heligoland in August 1914, both he and his ship emerging uninjured. 'His captain reports that he worked his gun-turret very well & coolly – 200 Germans wounded & prisoners have been landed in Scotland, amongst them Admiral Tirpitz's son,'[4] Alice wrote to Aunt Onor.

The war was to undermine almost every aspect of life that had given Alice security. A particularly big blow was the collapse of her father's naval career. Louis resigned as First Sea Lord in October 1914. He had been responsible for mobilizing the fleet prior to 4 August and ensuring that the Royal Navy was prepared for instant action. But since the outbreak of war he had been portrayed in the press as a German in charge of British naval forces with a home in Germany and German servants.

Louis had been an outstanding First Sea Lord, wholly loyal to the British navy for forty-six years. But, in his own words, he realized that the British government looked on him as 'a Jonah', and so 'decided to jump overboard the same day'.[5] He asked only that he be made a Privy Councillor as a sign that he still commanded the trust of the King and his ministers. This was done.

The traditional reason for Louis's downfall is always given as the German connection. This had all but prevented his appointment in April 1912, when a new Sea Lord was needed, Lloyd George telling the Prime Minister, H. H. Asquith, that he was horrified at the idea of a German holding 'the supreme place'.[6] However, by 1914, Asquith was finding it hard to work with him and feared that he was not doing a good job. Although Louis considered Winston Churchill a supporter, the First Lord of the Admiralty was pressing for his replacement by the controversial Admiral of the Fleet Lord Fisher. Churchill believed that Fisher, then seventy-four, would inspire much-needed confidence and that he would be more supportive than Louis. Victoria was furious about Louis's resignation, describing the government as men 'few greatly respect or trust', and adding: 'The King is a nobody.'[7]

Young Dickie was then a naval cadet, tear-sodden at his father's plight. He vowed he would rise to the top of the navy to avenge his father's honour.

The day before the resignation, Princess Beatrice's son, Maurice of Battenberg, died of wounds in the retreat from Mons. In November Victoria swapped her German maid, Eugenie, with her sister Irène's English maid called Knight.

Alice did what she could from afar, selling a Brussels lace dress and sending the money to Nona, who was nursing in Rouen. But there was little that she could do as grim news reached her of the plight of her relations in Europe.

Until the war her academically inclined uncle, Franzjos, and his Montenegrin wife Anna spent some time at Prinz Emils Garten. But at the outbreak, they were outside Germany and Ernie advised them not to return. Later Ernie gave Franzjos permission to come back, but he decided not to. When Italy joined the war, he and Anna found themselves permanent exiles. They settled in Switzerland, where he pursued academic studies. They had never been prosperous, and now their fortunes went into sharp decline. By August 1916, Franzjos was described as 'awfully badly off'.[8]

Uncle Ernie hated the war. He was interested in all the arts as well as technical innovations, a man inclined towards tranquil contemplation, but he accepted his obligation to go into the field. 'He is always with his troops,' wrote Victoria, '& full of admiration for their bravery & for the spirit of unity & self-sacrifice the whole country [Germany] is showing; & he feels as if they are undefeatable. For his sake I am glad he has these impressions to counteract the horrors of the battlefield.'[9]

Deeply depressed, Ernie had written to his sister, the Tsarina: 'You can't think what I go through when I am out there, sometimes walking quite alone in the fields & no one to speak to & my heart goes out to my dear ones & I break my head how one could bring peace to the world & I find no answer.'[10]

On 13 May 1915 Ernie suffered the humiliation of having his banner as an Extra Knight of the Garter removed from St George's

Chapel, along with that of the Kaiser, Henry of Prussia (Irène's husband), the Duke of Coburg* and others.

Most of all though, Alice worried about her mother. In the middle of the war, Victoria described to Nona how she felt having two sons serving in the British navy:

I can't be grateful enough that I was given the nature of a fatalist. All my life I have felt that all of us have our appointed time on earth & that nothing will alter it. Perhaps the way my mother & little sister were swept away by that vile diphtheria has helped me to strengthen the feeling. Now we are so many falling in war & are apt to forget, how many have been taken before by the attack of disease – though you know it, for your mother too was taken by an epidemic.

I feel too if it is Georgie's time to go, he will go & my Dickie too, but not otherwise, & so I hope I shall not worry more than is inevitable when Dickie goes to sea.[11]

On 24 January 1915 Nona married Captain Richard Crichton, a friend from childhood, who had previously asked her to marry him in peacetime. Wounded in the South African war, he wore an iron down one leg, causing Louis to describe him as Nona's 'lame Dick'.[12] Nona had nursed him before. Now she would look after him permanently.

Alice described Nona as 'truly happy'.[13] Victoria wrote to Nona: 'You know, don't you, that I consider you one of us, as much mine as the girls & so of course you will remain that, just like Alice,

*In 1959 Prince Louis of Hesse wrote to Dickie: 'This was brought on by Charley Coburg's idiotic act of sending back his British Orders and decorations after the declaration of war (so Papa told me). All the same Papa always considered himself as a Knight of the Garter as he had received it from Queen Victoria who had said to him 'Wear it as honourably as your father did' – and Papa thought he had done so. I remember he had a talk about this with George V after the war and the King thought the whole thing rather ridiculous.' [Prince Louis of Hesse to MtB, Wolfsgarten, 19 March 1959 – MB/I70 – HL.]

though she is married.'[14] In June 1915 it became clear that Nona would never have a child, due to a fibroid growth on the 'inner organs', but the marriage was nevertheless a happy one. And Dick joined Nona in the close inner circle of Battenbergs for life, as cherished as Nona.

Alice's sister, Louise, now twenty-five, had followed her sister's adventures as a nurse in the Balkan Wars. In March 1915 she set off to nurse in Nevers, France, in a team organized by Lady Paget.* Frailer in health than Alice, Louise was soon coping with inoculations, amputations and the removal of shrapnel from the wounded. She was undeterred by the smell of fetid wounds.

In the course of the year, first Louis and later Victoria, with her maid, the Pye-Crust, came to see her. Victoria was impressed that her younger daughter was 'thoroughly at home in her hospital'.[15] She met Louise's colleagues and one in particular appealed to her, a male nurse. She described him as

> the quaintest of men – a Parisian painter of the ultra-modern school, Scotch by birth, affected in manner, with a head like the picture of Shakespeare, witty & shy, & withal a thoroughly good fellow, who will do readily the most prosaic & dirty work in spite of beautiful long, manicured nails on his white hands.[16]

Because of his looks, this man was nicknamed Shakespeare. Unaware of a growing affection between Louise and Shakespeare, Victoria was unusually inspired in her description of him.

The painter's real name was Alexander Stuart-Hill. He was the son of a fish merchant, born in Perth in 1888, and he had studied at the Edinburgh School of Art, where he had won a scholarship. He then went abroad to work in Europe. He loved France best and so stayed to work in the hospital in Nevers during the war. Later he exhibited every year at the Royal Academy and cut a swathe as

*Lady Paget (d. 1918). Viti, daughter of Rt. Hon. Sir William Macgregor. Married 1906, Admiral Sir Alfred Paget (1852–1918).

'a figure unique for distinctive appearance, for witty conversation and personal charm, and for essential kindliness of nature'.[17]

Louise saw a great deal of Shakespeare during her war work and in due course their friendship caused a crisis.

Alice remained in Greece until the summer of 1917, occupied in bringing up her four girls. The political situation in the country became increasingly difficult as King Constantine remained resolutely neutral. When in April 1915 he blocked Venizelos's plan to offer Greek help in the forcing of the Dardanelles and in support of Serbia, that powerful politician resigned, causing a general election. After winning that election, he returned to power and promised aid to Serbia.

For some time Venizelos had wanted to invite an Anglo-French force of 150,000 men to land at Salonika to aid Serbia. The King forbade this, but in October, without his permission, such a force did indeed land there. The King believed that this was a violation of Greek territory and he immediately dismissed Venizelos from office. Venizelos retreated to Crete.

If the King thought he had seen the last of his erstwhile Prime Minister, he was mistaken. By October 1916 Venizelos had set up a provisional government in Crete which was recognized by France and Britain. He bided his time, awaiting the King's downfall and his own return to power.

For the previous four years Andrea had been busy bringing his regiment to a high peak of efficiency. In September 1915 he was sent with his men to Salonika, still considered to be a garrison town since its conquest in 1912. He was living in a rented house for six months, engrossed in military duties and on one occasion nearly being killed by a bomb while drilling his men.

The same month Alice joined Andrea in Salonika, leaving the children behind in Corfu. 'All the trains & ships are in the hands of the military,' she wrote, 'so that at the moment it is impossible.'[18]

The presence of Allied troops made Alice feel that she should explain Greece's wartime stance to the British. On two occasions she summoned the Earl of Granard (then Assistant Military Secretary to the Commander-in-Chief, British Salonika Force) to visit her. At their second meeting, which took place at the Greek headquarters, she discussed the proposed visit of King Constantine to see his army.

Alice took the opportunity to tell Granard her views on the state of the King of Greece's thinking, all of which he relayed to George V:

> Princess Andrew went on to say that she is absolutely convinced that the King [of Greece] is in no sense pro-German, but that he is working for the best interests of his country . . .
>
> HRH was inclined to complain of the actions of our Minister at Athens in dealing on this matter, with M. Venizelos not with the King. I felt, however, obliged to point out that such procedure was usual in a Constitutional Country. HRH seemed also to consider that Sir Francis [Elliot] was very much in favour of M. Venizelos, as opposed to the King.
>
> The Greek Royal Family seem inclined to look upon their late Prime Minister as a very dangerous man and they do not seem to realize that he is the biggest man in Greece today.[19]

Alice also outlined her views regarding the treaty with Serbia entered into by Venizelos. She said that 'when the Greeks asked Serbia to help them about 2 years ago in some quarrels which were likely to arise between the Greeks and Bulgaria dealing with Turkey, they refused to do so. Hence the Princess concluded that Greece had no more loyalty towards her neighbour.'[20]

Alice was so involved in what might happen at Salonika that she stayed on there well into the new year of 1916, leaving her children to spend Christmas in Athens without her. There were camps all around Salonika, which was further surrounded by barbed wire and trenches. 'It is most interesting,' wrote Alice to her brother Dickie. 'We are waiting patiently for the attack, but what a noise the guns will make. We won't be able to hear ourselves think even.'[21] But by May, although Andrea worried about the defences, still no attack had come and Alice was hearing rumours that the

German government might be 'throwing out renewed feelers about peace'.[22]

Early in July a mysterious fire broke out at Tatoï, destroying the main residence and much of the surrounding forest. Eighteen people lost their lives, including the King's ADC. King Constantine and Queen Sophie were there and the Queen ran from the house for a mile and a half with her little daughter, Katherine, in her arms. The fire raged for forty-eight hours and it was unclear why it started. It was judged likely to have been 'a calculated act of incendiarism'.[23]

Andrea became more closely concerned with Greece's international position when King Constantine sent him to Paris and London in July 1916 to reassure the Allies that Greece would remain neutral and that there was no secret pact with either Germany or Bulgaria. This diplomatic move was another example of the King acting independently of his government.

On 22 July Andrea had a walk in the garden with George V, which achieved nothing, a good talk to the Foreign Secretary, Sir Edward Grey, but a less good one with the former Viceroy, Lord Hardinge of Penshurst, the Permanent Under-Secretary of State at the Foreign Office, who accused the Greek government of forcing the demobilized soldiers to vote against Venizelos. He was soon deflated by placards announcing 'Tino's new treachery'.[24]

Next he went to Paris, where he was greeted with suspicion, but was suddenly recalled indefinitely to London, where he told his father-in-law that he was 'very sick of his job'.[25] He was a guest at Windsor Castle at the end of August, where he was urged by the Marquis de Soveral,* a fellow guest, to advise King Constantine to join the Allies.

The political intent of Andrea's visit was soon over and the rest of it was spent meeting Dick Crichton, sleeping with his feet

* The Marquis de Soveral (1853–1922), Portuguese Minister in London, intimate friend of Edward VII and a much sought after guest in the Edwardian era. Known as 'The Blue Monkey'.

protruding through the iron end of a bed in Georgie's room while staying with Louis and Victoria at Kent House, on the Isle of Wight, sneaking whisky into his sister's room at Windsor, and losing his ADC, Major Metaxas, to the labyrinth of castle corridors so that the poor man was obliged to spend the night on some stairs until apprehended as a burglar in the morning.

He returned to Greece at the end of August. His sister-in-law Louise summed up the situation succinctly: 'I simply can't understand at all what is happening there,' she wrote from France. 'That wretched country is simply going to be ruined. Goodness only knows what is going to happen to the family. It is truly dreadful. Tino apparently must have waited too long & now won't & can't give in.'[26]

Back in Greece, Andrea rejoined his regiment. Alice and the children were now more often than not in Athens. This was a turbulent period in Greece's history. Two crises were developing: King Constantine's continued refusal to join the war on the side of the Allies, and the conflict between him and Venizelos. Alice was present during this tense and difficult period which soon led to the royal family's exile.

Venizelos moved from Crete to Salonika and established his provisional government. There were thus two governments in Greece, the King's neutral government in Athens, and Venizelos's government in Salonika, which was at war with the central powers and supported by the Allies.

In September 1916 Alice followed news of the huge protest meeting in Athens in which Venizelist volunteers marched through the streets, pleading that Venizelos save them now as he had saved them six years before. Sir Francis Elliot continued to press the King into joining the Allied cause and the King continued to dither.

There were meetings between the King and the French in Athens in October, aimed to smooth relations between Greece and the Allies and to prevent war breaking out between them. There were stories of French reservists bursting into the garden of the French Legation during this meeting, shouting 'Long Live the King' and

'Down with France and England', firing revolver shots into the air and departing. There were rumours that Tatoï was being extensively defended with trenches, troops, anti-aircraft precautions and convoys of small-arm and artillery ammunition, the reason being 'the fear of civil war accompanied by an attempt to seize the King'.[27]

With increasing concern, Alice noted the arrival of Allied armed forces in November, creating a police control presence in Athens under Allied supervision. This was in order to prevent collisions between royalist and provisional government troops.

Alice became more urgently involved in the crisis when Allied warships bombarded Athens on 1 December, in an attempt to gain control of the city, most of the shells falling near the palace. It began amid 'considerable excitement in town and some desultory firing including machine-gun and one round of field gun'.[28] Alice was working quietly at the embroidery school when she saw wounded people in the streets and heard that the palace was in danger. She rushed home 'through a rain of bullets',[29] and swiftly steered her children into the palace cellar, where she found Queen Sophie and others already in hiding.

The situation worsened, though Alice herself remained stoically in Athens, her spirit unbroken, and never at any point did she consider leaving. The crisis had led to malnutrition and exhaustion amongst the Greek people. Alice joined Queen Sophie in soup kitchens trying to provide food for starving children. And she waited for the inevitable conclusion, vigilant at all times for the safety of her little ones.

In the new year of 1917, the power structure of Europe was altered by the Russian Revolution, a time of great anxiety for Alice, since she feared for her aunts and cousins. As far as Greece was concerned, it meant that King Constantine lost a potential ally.

It was not long before King Constantine realized that he must accept defeat. He had tried to save his country from war. He believed himself no traitor. But the Greeks were in despair and public opinion was against him.

In April a plan was formed to spirit the King and the entire royal family out of Greece. Monsieur Ricaud, the Principal French Intelligence Officer, revealed that 'if a single shot was fired in the town [Athens], [the] Palace would be destroyed by bombardment'.[30] By 2 May a story reached Sir Francis Elliot that the King was thinking of going to Switzerland.

The King's new government, headed by A. Zaimis, was formed two days later and shortly afterwards there was a meeting of the Military Club, at which Andrea conveyed the King's wish that discipline should be maintained and superior orders obeyed.

When, in June, Greek marines fired on some French sailors who had arrived in the Piraeus, the Allies closed in on the King and sought his abdication. The French occupied Thessaly, and Monsieur Jonnart, the Allied High Commissioner in Salonika, arrived in Athens. Jonnart presented the ultimatum to Zaimis that the King abdicate in favour of one of his sons. A scheme was mooted by Zaimis whereby the King might appoint one of his sons as Viceroy until the end of the war. The Crown Prince (George) was deemed unacceptable as he had been trained in the military in Berlin.

It was therefore decided that the second son, Alexander, would become King. On 11 June Alexander duly took his oath at the palace, with none of his family in attendance. He was but twenty-four years old.

Since a few days before the abdication all the Greek royal family, including Alice and Andrea and their family, had taken refuge in the palace. At the moment when the Greek people realized that their King was about to leave, they thought only good of him. Indeed a large group of reservists surrounded the palace in an attempt to prevent him from going. Some ring leaders were arrested but then a dense crowd gathered, and in the end it proved impossible to get either the King or any members of his family out on the night of 12 June.

The next day, at 5.00 p.m., King Constantine eluded the crowds and made his way to Tatoï. After several changes of plan, he and his party left Oropos at 1.30 p.m. on 14 June, in two Greek ships escorted by two French destroyers. The King was accompanied by Queen Sophie and his children, the Crown Prince, Prince Paul and Princesses Helen, Irene and Katherine, with a household that brought the number to forty-five. They made their way to Switzerland.

The dignified manner of the King's departure minimized the fuss attendant on it. Compton Mackenzie wrote that the King left behind him 'a long glamorous vista of lost causes'.[31] And in one of the last despatches before he too left Greece, Sir Francis Elliot noted:

On Tuesday, May 29th 1433, Constantine Paleologus, Emperor of Constantinople, lost his throne and his life to the Turks. On Tuesday, May 29th (C.S.) 1917, King Constantine, King of the Hellenes, was driven from his throne by the Franks, and terminated in humiliation a reign begun only four years ago amid all the circumstance of triumph and omens of prosperity.[32]

13. The First Exile

At first it seemed possible that Alice and Andrea might stay in Greece during the reign of King Alexander. However, Andrea and his brothers soon found themselves dubbed 'wicked uncles', a characterization which they never succeeded in escaping. Hardly had the new reign begun than the princes were given polite intimation from the government that they should 'temporarily absent themselves from Athens pending a solution of crisis'.[1]

Big George was already out of Greece, and Nicholas and Christo left for Switzerland. In the first days of the new reign, Alice's father was optimistic that Andrea would stay, writing: 'Venizelos will be Prime Minister and the new King will be a George Rex.* It seems that Andrea is the only Prince to remain. He will be a great help to Alex. & Venizelos respects him. They ought to have made *him* King.'[2] But perhaps because he could have supported the inexperienced young King, Andrea was also asked to leave. With Alice and their young family, he left for Switzerland a fortnight after the other princes.

Naturally, Alice saw Andrea's role as in Greece and deeply resented the exile, which, as when he had relinquished his command in the army, subjected him to a period of enforced idleness. The new King had been assured by the government that his uncles were just taking a trip abroad and could come back after a month or so, but, in practice, the government was resistant to such a course. The new British Ambassador, Earl Granville,† pointed out that 'it was very undesirable for their own sakes that the Princes should return yet as there was still so much unrest in the country',

* A family nickname for George V, implying that Alexander would be a cipher.

† 3rd Earl Granville (1872–1939). Minister in Salonika 1916–17, Ambassador in Athens 1917–21.

since 'ill-conditioned partisans of the present Government would certainly fabricate stories against them which would make mischief'.[3]

Alice and Andrea began their exile in St Moritz. Andrea had saved some money, which was a bonus. With the help of his ADC, Metaxas, he had sold his cars well before leaving Athens, and the Swiss hotel was not unduly expensive. Metaxas accompanied them into exile.

Alice sought permission to visit her parents in the Isle of Wight. She was nervous as to whether it would be granted since the British Foreign Secretary had refused Christo permission to enter Britain on the grounds that all the Greek princes had supported the neutrality of their brother, while professing a wish to support the Allies. However, in her case, the Foreign Office advanced no objection and George V wrote personally to her parents giving his blessing.

Alice travelled from St Moritz to Paris with Big George, joined her father at the Hotel Lotti in Paris, and on 5 September they crossed to Southampton and thence to the Isle of Wight. Her parents now lived in Kent House, a grey stone building which Princess Louise, Duchess of Argyll, had given them, situated between the gates of Osborne and the town of Cowes.

For over thirteen years, Alice had been preoccupied with the political problems of Greece. Temporarily relieved of these, she was soon faced with others. She had not seen her parents since before the war. Her father was occupied compiling a book on medals and as treasurer of the Isle of Wight branch of the Red Cross, while her mother worked hard each day in the garden and undertook charitable works. They were both well, but her mother seemed considerably diminished: 'I was very shocked how thin & tiny she has become. Her figure is hardly recognizable but her face is still the same, her hair a bit greyer, but apart from that she is in excellent health. Her emaciation, she tells me, only began when she had to worry so much about her sisters in Russia.'[4]

In turn, Victoria examined Alice. 'Switzerland has done her nerves & health a lot of good already,'[5] she reported, adding later that Alice looked 'well but a little anaemic'.[6]

Alice had arrived at a moment of major readjustment in the life of her parents. A few weeks earlier, on 14 July, Louis had renounced the title of Prince Louis of Battenberg to be created Marquess of Milford Haven. Victoria could have kept her style of Grand Ducal Highness and Princess of Hesse, but decided to drop her titles too and take Louis's new name. From now on she was Marchioness of Milford Haven. Their children lost their princely titles, Louise becoming Lady Louise Mountbatten, Georgie Earl of Medina, and Dickie Lord Louis Mountbatten. Alice, being already married into another royal house, was not affected.* No Battenbergs thus remained, other than Franzjos and Anna, the latter bearing the name into the 1970s.

The Milford Havens, as they must now be called, minded the change. In June Victoria had written to Nona:

> It is possible that Prince & Princess Louis of Battenberg may never again visit you in England or meet you again there, but that these friends will be replaced by some new-fangled British Peer & his wife, whose very family name (like Schmidt – Smith) will be transmogrified & anglicized into Mountbatten. It is a queer topsy-turvy world this world at war & I own that when such great & serious changes are taking place this change affecting our name etc. leaves me more indifferent than I might have expected.[7]

The reason for the name change was that George V had become sensitive about the German names and titles used by many of his relations. He consulted Asquith and Lord Rosebery, who supported

* Alice was never a Mountbatten. Princess Beatrice relinquished her style as Princess Henry of Battenberg, her son Drino became Marquess of Carisbrooke, which he deeply resented, and his brother Lord Leopold Mountbatten. Princess Christian became Princess Helena when Prince Christian died and her daughters Princess Helena Victoria and Princess Marie Louise, without the Schleswig-Holstein suffix. Queen Mary's brothers became Marquess of Cambridge and Earl of Athlone. There were other minor adjustments. Mindful of the resentment of Drino, Louise wrote: 'I shriek with laughter when I think of Drino.' [L to NK 13 June 1917 – BA.]

the changes. The King also changed the name of the British royal house from the House of Wettin to the House of Windsor. He summoned Louis from the Isle of Wight and after being closeted with him for some time, explained to him that because he was 'being attacked as being half-German & surrounding himself with German names, &c, he must ask us Holsteins, Tecks & Battenbergs to give up using in England our German titles & to assume English surnames'.[8] Louis was pleased to have a peerage but aware that he was at the King's mercy: 'We are only allowed to use our German titles as the Sovereign has recognized it, but he can refuse this recognition any moment. If so we are plain Mister which would be impossible. Peerage seems the only possible compensation.'[9]

During her ten-day stay with her parents, Alice was told of the problem concerning Louise. Her younger sister had fallen in love with her artist friend, Alexander Stuart-Hill, whom the family had called Shakespeare. Alice had the opportunity to meet Shakespeare for herself when she and Louise went to London for two days. She summed up Louise and her predicament in a letter to Aunt Onor in Darmstadt:

She has become much more beautiful, her character so refined and nobly developed, so independent & competent and sensible in her work. I haven't asked Mama for her permission, but I will tell you that as the war broke out she fell in love with a very nice man & he with her, but he was killed within the first few months before they could become engaged. My parents were very upset as they had liked him very much.* But now Louise has become engaged to a Scottish artist who lives in Paris. He is quite well known in artistic circles & they predict a famous future for him. But he looks so odd and is such an eccentric that only now, after two years has Louise had the courage to tell her parents, just before I

* There is no hint as to the identity of this man in the various Mountbatten papers. Louise's biographer claims that King Manoel of Portugal asked Edward VII for her hand in 1909, but Louise refused [Margit Fjellman, *Louise Mountbatten, Queen of Sweden* (Allen & Unwin, 1968), p. 79]. Again there is no mention of this in the papers. Christo was another mooted suitor.

arrived. I found them all very upset because they fear that an artistic temperament like his might be rather difficult in marriage & they are so afraid that Louise may not be happy. They asked him to wait until the war is over and so the engagement has not been publicly announced. Only Nona, Georgie & Dick [Dickie]* know about it. I went to London with her & met him and went around with the two of them, but everyone turns in the street and laughs at him when they see him. We call him Shakespeare because he has a little beard just like him, but his name is Stuart Hill. Louise was shaking with fear before the first meeting with Nona & the brothers so I had to be there. He is very easy to talk to and interesting and she is madly in love with him, but he is so incredibly affected.[10]

Victoria discussed the Shakespeare problem with Alice before she and Louise went to London and found her 'most sensible & nice about it & she & Louise have had a long talk, which I think will be a help to Louise'.[11] Louis had probably suspected that Louise loved Shakespeare as early as May, since he wrote to her, offering to take her for a winter sea voyage, revisiting his haunts as a midshipman, round the West Indies, America and Canada. It was the kind of invitation that looked generous, but was almost certainly received with a sinking heart. Shakespeare came to stay at Kent House from 27 to 31 July.

Just before Shakespeare's visit, Louise poured out her heart to Nona, apologizing for having kept it secret for so long. She told her that she loved Shakespeare and that they would marry after the war, when they could 'scrape up enough money'. Louise continued:

He is just the one & only person I could ever marry & really be happy with. He is the person I have always looked for & thought I should never find. He understands love & marriage in the same way as I do & like me has never really cared for or wished to marry anyone up till now.

I wish you knew him. I know you will really like him when you get

* Alice also noted Dickie's thick straight eyebrows running right across his brow.

to know him well. He is the most charming & fine character & he is not a tiny bit what one expects artists to be, though he loves his art & it means nearly everything to him.

I have known him now for two years & we have got to know & understand each other really well. Marriage has always frightened me because so often it is not a success & people give up their independence for nothing. But I think it is bound to be a success when one's love is built on a real & great friendship like yours & Dick's. To marry anybody one has only just fallen in love with is a great risk because it may not be anything really deep & lasting.[12]

Louise told Nona that while Shakespeare's father lived, he was not independent and they thought marriage was impossible, but the father had died just when last she returned to Nevers. She realized that her parents were likely to be somewhat disappointed in her choice 'because Shakespeare is not exactly a "*parti*"', but found them 'too charming & nice & kind & understanding' and their reaction totally 'unselfish' and 'wonderful'. She believed that they trusted her in her judgement, but in this she was self-deceiving. Louise concluded:

Though Shakespeare has very little money of his own, about £400 a year, he is, I think, bound to get on in the world. His artist friends & other people consider that he has a very great talent & that he is bound to make a name for himself. His father never gave him a penny & the money he has lived on & had for travelling he made by his paintings. Just before the war he saved £1,000 which he alas invested in Germany. He was going to have an exhibition at one of the small good galleries in London in the autumn of 1914 & was painting for it in Italy when the war broke out.[13]

Alice took a middle line on this matter, sympathetic to Louise, while sharing her parents' concern. The engagement survived through 1918, and Shakespeare spent a further holiday with the Milford Havens at Kent House between 13 and 24 June 1918, when the weather conspired to be its most disagreeable.

Presently, the family became preoccupied by events in Russia, which pushed the question of Louise's matrimonial plans into the background. Finally, Louis was forced to tell Louise that she could not marry Shakespeare because he was homosexual. In those unsophisticated times, Louise had grown up unaware of what homosexuality was or indeed that such a possibility existed. In December 1918 Alice wrote to Aunt Onor: 'I had a letter from Louise who broke her engagement. She understood that it would not work but is *very* unhappy nevertheless.'[14] Later she clarified this: 'The parents found out that her fiancé was not a decent man.'[15]*

During Shakespeare's engagement to Louise, she gave him a gold and chagreen cigarette case and a gold matchbox. When Shakespeare died in February 1948, he did not forget his erstwhile fiancée: 'To Her Royal Highness Louise, Crown Princess of Sweden, one of my landscapes of London, to be selected by my executors',[16] proving that, even if they were not in touch, at least he retained a fond memory of her. Louise was left to the fate of perpetual spinsterhood – or so it seemed at the time.

After their stay in London, Alice and Louise went to Edinburgh for five days to stay with Georgie, and Alice met his wife Nada for the first time. Alice laughed to see her younger brother sitting at

* The families' predictions were fully justified. Alexander Stuart-Hill became a painter of distinction. The Perth Art Gallery in Scotland has several of his pictures. He became part of the set of 'Colonel' George Kolkhorst, the eccentric Oxford don, affectionately mocked by John Betjeman and Osbert Lancaster. He created a studio from an old stable at 41 Glebe Place, London, where he entertained widely. Sir Steven Runciman recalled 'a vague picture of a very *petit maître* figure' [Hon. Sir Steven Runciman to author, 10 July 1997]. Father Gerard Irvine recalled his fondness for needlework. In later life, Shakespeare was inclined to spend an hour and a half each day applying his make-up. And he set up home with a Russian pianist called Ivan Phillipowsky (1895–1951), who gave frequent recitals in London and of whom it was said: 'His treatment of the piano belied his powerful physique for he was more interested in handling Mozart's delicate figuration with clarity and care than in achieving the massive effects of the romantic school' [*The Times*, 12 February 1951].

the head of the table. Nada she thought 'too nice. So jolly & funny, *very* intelligent and tactful. She adores her parents-in-law, and vice versa.'[17]

Georgie had married Countess Nadejda (Nada) Torby, in 1916. She was daughter of Grand Duke Michael and his wife, Countess Torby, then living in Kenwood House,* their rented home in Hampstead. Her father, who was heir to properties in the Caucasus, gave her £2,000 a year, with extra for travel, motor cars and jewels. Besides this, a large sum had been laid aside for each of his children at birth – 'a great relief to know',[18] wrote Victoria at the time. Nada was a great-granddaughter of Tsar Nicholas I of Russia, through her father, second son of the Tsar's fourth son. She had an elder sister, Anastasia, known as Zia, who was shortly to marry Sir Harold Wernher, Bt, then considered the richest bachelor in England, having inherited a mining fortune in South Africa, along with the magnificent Bedfordshire seat, Luton Hoo, where they would live in some splendour.

From Scotland, Alice went to Sandringham to visit Queen Alexandra: 'Aunt Alix is . . . grief-stricken about her sister in the Crimea [The Dowager Empress Marie] and although she was still wonderfully beautiful . . . she is completely broken & moans that she feels she is going mad, there is such pressure in her head. And the poor dear is not exaggerating: we all think that, should anything happen to her sister, she couldn't bear it.'[19]

Then Alice went to stay with Nona, who was living in Cambridge, and gave her some money for her charitable work. In October she returned to Switzerland. Having travelled for eight weeks, she was 'mad with fatigue'.[20] The return journey was fraught with the problems traditionally associated with wartime travel.

Alice's visit to England landed her in diplomatic trouble. The British Consul-General in Zurich heard a story from 'an important Venizelist'[21] that Alice had seen King George during her visit to

*Kenwood belonged to the 6th Earl of Ilchester. It was later rented by Mrs Nancy Leeds, who married Prince Christopher.

England and that he had promised to support the restoration of King Constantine to Greece. Alice had not seen the King while in England, though possibly Queen Alexandra had said something, both encouraging and muddled, concerning the plight of her nephew, King Constantine. The supposed remarks were passed back to England through the traditional (official espionage) route of the Foreign Office.

Lord Stamfordham, the King's private secretary, was quick to confirm that neither had the King seen Alice nor was there any truth in the story that King George supported restoration. On 3 December, Lord Hardinge wrote back saying that royalist intrigues in Switzerland 'seem to be assuming alarming proportions'.[22] He instructed Lord Acton, the Consul-General, to deny the allegations.

But the story rumbled on. According to Lord Granville in Athens, Nikolaos Politis, the Greek Minister of Foreign Affairs, had received a delegation reporting that King Constantine's restoration was 'only a question of time', that all the powers except France 'were anxious for it' and that 'Princess Andrew of Greece, on Her Royal Highness's return from England, had announced that "the English Court" had assured her that this was their desire there'.[23] But Granville also reported that Politis was aware that this story had become exaggerated.

Meanwhile Alice and Andrea had to endure their continuing exile, with no idea how long it would last. They worried about King Constantine, who was also in Switzerland. He was either sunk in apathy or inveighling against Venizelos, his general condition not helped by his doctor's diagnosis that he was suffering from raging consumption. Like all exiles, he dreamed only of returning to his country.

During these months, Alice and her family had worried about the fate of the two aunts in Russia. The situation had been getting steadily worse there for some time. In December 1916, they had heard of the murder of the sinister monk Rasputin (who had acquired a hold over the Tsarina, who thought he would cure her haemophiliac son), by two members of the Russian royal family, Prince Felix Yusupov and Grand Duke Dimitri (brother of Marie, and childhood ward of Ella). Of the murder Victoria wrote: 'I do hope that this time the news of Rasputin's death is true, though poor Alix will probably fall ill at it. What harm he has done her. I fear that among the masses in Russia she is hated, chiefly due to that vile creature & a set of people who have always tried to injure her.'[24]

The Tsar abdicated on 28 March 1917, which caused more worries. 'My poor Ella must be feeling so solitary, so anxious for them,' wrote Victoria, 'but she is so good & so deeply & truly religious that she will find strength & comfort, where we who are less good than she could not find it in the same degree.'[25] In April 1917 Ella acknowledged the new government and asked to be allowed to continue as the head of her sisterhood.

In November 1917, Alix sent a message to Victoria that she had received the good wishes sent on her birthday, the only message to reach her. Occasionally a figure would arrive in England asking to see Victoria, bringing news of Ella. After the fall of the Tsar, Ella lived in increasing danger, but refused all offers of rescue, most notably one from the Kaiser, who had been a youthful admirer. In about April 1918 she was arrested.

The Tsar and Tsarina and all their young family were executed at Ekaterinburg on 16/17 July 1918, and news of the Tsar's death reached Victoria on 24 July. Alice heard about it in Lucerne and wrote at once to Uncle Ernie in Darmstadt:

> I don't know what to say. After all this plotting & planning to have this terrible news sprung upon us. We refused to believe it for a long time & have waited with the hope that a denial would appear in some paper or other & now we are beginning to fear there is no more hope left. I think so much of you & understand so well, what it meant to you. I have seen you together too much & too often not to know. Words fail me to say more. I have not had the courage to write to Mama yet.
>
> My poor mother-in-law* would not let me telegraph to you for news.

* Queen Olga was now living with the Greek royal family in exile in Switzerland.

She dreaded what the answer might be. We got the news before dinner of the day in which we had finally draughted a letter to you. She had delayed so long after I had received your dear letter, because she had received a long letter from Georgi Michaelovitch,* which he had managed to smuggle out to Aunt Elisabeth in spite of his guards, saying he had heard rumours that the Tschecko-Slovaks were advancing & probably going to try & liberate U. Nicky & that this was a little dangerous. This made my mother-in-law hesitate in telling me what to write to you, because she refused to take the responsibility of any suggestion which might endanger his life.

Finally that day she came to my room, telling me to write to you to explain matters & to warn you of the danger & to ask you to use your own judgement before undertaking anything. She hopes you will forgive her in having been so long in telling me to thank you for your kind offer of help. In the meantime I enclose two photos of their house at Ekaterinburg, of which she begs you to give one to Auntie Irène. She has also received a letter from her nephew Kostia† from Alapayeosk, which is near Ekaterinburg, where A. Ella also is. They are all well & allowed to walk a little way out of the village, where he says the air is good & they prefer it to Ekaterinburg, where they were before & where the air is bad. He enclosed a drawing of the school where they live & which I copied for you.

And now the newspapers say all the men were removed from there by an unknown band. Some telegrams say they were murdered & others that they were taken to the Tschecko-Slovak camp & now my mother-in-law is in an awful state of mind these days. She can only get her news from Russia from Serbia & does not like to ask the German Legation at Berne, because it's so small a town & everybody gossips with all the other Legations in it, so if you hear anything about her nephews, do be nice & let her know.[26]

For years afterwards the relatives in England, Germany and Switzerland were given contradictory versions of what may or may

* Grand Duke George (1863–1919), Queen Olga's son-in-law, husband of Princess Marie. He was murdered in St Petersburg in January 1919.

† Prince Constantine (1891–1918), 3rd son of Grand Duke Constantine, brother of Queen Olga. He was murdered with Ella at Alapaievsk.

not have happened, their hopes raised, only to be dashed again.

Alice did not know that Ella was in fact already dead. After her removal from the convent in Moscow in about April 1918, Ella was imprisoned at Alapaievsk with Sister Barbara, the most loyal of her sisters at the convent, and five other members of the Russian Imperial family. These were Grand Duke Serge,* Prince John† and his younger brothers, Constantine and Igor, and Prince Vladimir Paley.‡ On the evening of 17/18 July they were all taken from the school house to the edge of the mine shaft and thrown in. They did not die instantly. They were heard singing psalms, and Ella used part of her dress to bandage the arm of Prince John, which was broken in the fall. The soldiers threw a grenade into the mine shaft and finally they all died.

This news was not confirmed until 10 November, by a sad coincidence the day before the armistice was signed and the so-called Great War came to an end, yet as late as December, Ella was described as 'living and staying in the Urals'.[27]

Alice minded the death of her Aunt Ella more than she would say, but she submerged her grief in concern for her mother's feelings. Victoria was 'dazed' when the fear that had haunted her was finally confirmed as reality. In a letter to Nona she paid tribute to Ella:

> If ever anyone has met death without fear she will have & her deep & pure faith will have upheld & supported & comforted her in all she has gone through so that the misery poor Alicky will have suffered will not have touched Ella's soul & maybe, had she lived, years of solitary suffering

* Grand Duke Serge (1869–1918), son of Grand Duke Michael, and an uncle of Nada, Georgie's wife.

† Prince John (1886–1918), Prince Constantine (1891–1918) and Prince Igor (1894–1918), sons of Grand Duke Constantine ('K. R.'). Prince John was married to Elena, daughter of Peter I of Serbia. She survived and died in Nice in 1962. The other two were unmarried.

‡ Prince Vladimir Paley (1897–1918), son of Grand Duke Paul by the morganatic marriage, which had caused so much difficulty in 1902. Grand Duke Paul was murdered in St Petersburg in January 1919.

would have been her lot, for I have recently heard that all her work in Moscow has been destroyed, the sisterhood scattered, the home given over to lay purposes.[28]

The bodies of Ella and her companions were found in September, when the White Russians, under the command of General I. S. Smolin, occupied Alapaievsk. At a dinner, an engineer became intoxicated and revealed that the bodies were buried nearby, 'in the deepest shaft', one that had been abandoned long ago. The shaft was identified and the clearing operation began. They had to remove rubbish, stones and earth piled to the top, work which took several days. Then they had to pump out a great deal of water. Eventually the bodies were brought to the surface – the six royal victims, the physician, the valet and Sister Barbara. Smolin recorded:

The sight of the dead bodies was dreadful . . . All except Grand Duchess Elizabeth Feodorovna and the nun [Sister Barbara] were in travelling clothes. Grand Duchess Elizabeth Feodorovna wore a grey dress with a white neckerchief: a cross of cypress wood hung on her breast. The nun was dressed in the same manner, and on her breast were a gold cross and a watch. When the other bodies were examined some valuable gold and silver objects were found on them. It was obvious that the executioners were in such haste to fulfil their brutal and ghastly task that they had not had sufficient time to rob the victims.[29]

The royal victims were given a solemn burial mass in the local church, which was attended by an enormous throng of town dwellers and people from the nearby countryside. Eventually the bodies were removed to Peking and most of them were reburied in the Russian Orthodox Mission cemetery there. Ella's earthly travels, however, were not over.

One day, back in London a few years later, Princess Beatrice spotted a picture of the cemetery in her copy of the *Illustrated London News*. In January 1921 Victoria arranged for the coffins of Ella and Sister Barbara to be brought to Jerusalem and buried on the Mount of Olives at the Russian Orthodox Convent of Saint Mary Magdalene. Victoria, Louis and Louise were there for the service.

Ella was recognized as a saint by the Russian Orthodox Church Abroad in 1984 and by the Moscow Patriarchite in 1992. In July 1998, she was one of ten twentieth-century Christian martyrs whose effigies above the Great West Door of Westminster Abbey were dedicated in the presence of The Queen and Prince Philip.

As the war with Germany drew to a close, Uncle Ernie and Aunt Onor fared better than Ella or Alix. 'You know how much I think of you two who are so *innocent*,' Alice wrote to Aunt Onor in Darmstadt. 'God help you and hopefully the times won't become too bad in Hesse.'[30]

Ernie was in Darmstadt in November 1918 when a Council of State was formed, followed in December by the People's Council for the Republic of Hesse to represent all classes. Cars were at the ready and he could have sped off to hiding, but he preferred to remain and face the mob that approached the Neue Palais. He waited for them in the throne room with Onor at his side. Eventually they burst down the door and streamed in crying, 'Down with the Grand Duke!' and 'Kill the Grand Duke!' As they approached him, a kind of shame came over them and they fell silent. Ernie then addressed them in a loud voice:

> I can see no Hessian uniforms amongst you, but you will form a deputation and tell me what you want. In the meantime, as no one has ever been to the palace without being entertained, my wife will make you tea.[31]

A committee was formed which protected Ernie and Onor, though they were held prisoner at home in Darmstadt throughout that winter. In January 1919 he registered as a voter for electoral purposes. In June it was reported that he was well, and that his old team, including his chamberlain, Graf von Hardenberg and Onor's lady-in-waiting, Georgina von Rotsmann, were with him. In 1919 Hesse declared itself a republic.

Ernie was deposed and lost some of his properties, but he never formally abdicated. He set aside politics and his military life, and began to re-establish himself in the affection of the people of Darmstadt as a patron of art, philosophy and science, architecture and opera, all of which were a great deal more congenial to him.

The last of the German family to depart was Aunt Irène with Henry of Prussia, who proved less dignified in defeat. He and his two sons had served in the German Imperial Navy, which had suffered the ignominious defeats of mutiny, scuttling and surrender. In November 1918, he and Irène fled from Kiel in a motor car, flying red flags. There were two sailors on the footboard and one of them was shot dead as they crossed the Dutch border.

By December they were based in Amsterdam, from where Henry issued the first of several statements, declaring loyalty to the Kaiser and promising to do everything to save him from harm. In February 1919 he argued in public for the restoration of the monarchy in Germany, the removal of the 'parasitical soldiers and workers' councils'[32] and the re-introduction of well-disciplined military power. In July he begged George V 'to desist from any demand for the extradition of HM the Emperor William',[33] claiming that the Kaiser had done all in his power to avoid war.

In August Henry went further, claiming that documents proved that Britain had spent years preparing for war, in order to 'eliminate Germany as a troublesome competition from the world market'. He continued: 'Germany and her brave people have been severely hit, but are not yet dead. The German spirit which at present still lives, and will one day awake to full consciousness of the disgrace and shame which have been inflicted by its victors. It will one day demand a reckoning from its torturers, even if after many years.'[34] Even in Germany the Prince was dismissed as a 'danger for the German people',[35] and nobody regretted when he retired from the public fray and settled quietly with Irène at Hemmelmark, their country property in Germany. He died there in 1929.

Thus, by the end of the war, Alice was still living in exile, with her uncle deposed, two aunts murdered and another likewise in exile. Little remained of the fabric of her youth.

14. Veering towards Religion

The years of exile left Alice in a kind of limbo. After the foregoing tragedies, it is not surprising to find her seeking solace in religion. In 1917 Alice found a book called *Les Grands Initiés* by Édouard Schuré, which appealed to her particular approach to religion, being more philosophical than strictly doctrinal. She relished exploring all the different religions, what they had to offer and how they came to be.

Les Grands Initiés was first published in France in 1913 and within nine years had gone into twenty-four editions. It was translated into German, Italian, Spanish and Russian, and eventually into English. It mirrored a widespread interest in comparative religions.

Schuré himself was born in Strasbourg, and became a friend of Richard Wagner and wrote about his work. The mystical side of Wagner's music intrigued him and led him to study the occult and transcendental philosophy. This in turn drew him into the circle of a Greek lady called Margherita Albana Mignaty, who was the centre of a literary circle in Florence. Influenced by her, he produced this book.

Schuré took as his text the conflict between science and religion in the intellectual mind. He argued that originally Christianity affirmed the Christian faith in the midst of Europe, which was then semi-barbarian, and thus acted as the mightiest of moral forces. From the sixteenth century, experimental science established a claim to 'the legitimate rights of reason' and as an intellectual force. The conflict resulted because, as he put it:

> Science, dazzled by her discoveries in the physical world, and forgetting the very existence of the psychic and the intellectual worlds, has become agnostic in her methods and materialistic both in her principles and in her goal; since Philosophy, bewildered and powerless between the two,

has, in a measure, abdicated her rights and fallen away into a vague kind of scepticism, a profound rupture has been brought about in the soul of society as well as in the individual.[1]

Schuré then outlined the history of the various religions and doctrines, from the Aryan cycle, Rama, through Krishna, Hermes, Moses, Orpheus, and through Pythagoras, Plato and finally to Jesus. Christ, he concluded, ruled supreme and opened his heart to all the preceding religions. He hoped to solve some mysteries: 'Religion responds to the needs of the heart, hence its eternal magic,' he wrote. 'Science, to those of the spirit, hence its eternal might. These two powers, however, have long been unable to come to a mutual understanding. Religion without proof and Science without hope are now face to face, each challenging the other, without being able to gain the victory.'[2]

While Alice found much in *Les Grands Initiés* that was constructive and informative, she was also subject to the less helpful influence of her brother-in-law, Christo, who was living with them in exile. He was a friendly soul, cherubic in appearance, myopic, but not a man of intellect. When he died in 1940, Lincoln MacVeagh,* the acerbic American Ambassador to Greece, assessed him brutally:

He was twice married, to Mrs Leeds, widow of a tin-plate King, and to Princess Françoise of France, daughter of a hundred real ones, achieving notoriety from the first and a son from the second. His military career as aide to his brother Constantine during the Balkan Wars appears to have been as unproductive of service to his country as of distinction to himself. In Greece he was neither loved nor hated, but rather regarded with indifference . . . His studies seemed to have extended no further than an amateurish and occasional investigation of spooks.[3]

It seems strange that someone as intelligent as Alice should be so influenced by Christo. Partly, it was because she wished to experiment and partly, no doubt, because there was so little else of

* Lincoln MacVeagh (1890–1972), Ambassador to Greece 1933–47.

interest to do. Alice joined Christo at the table, where they performed automatic writing together. This involved a glass moving round the table, steered by the divine, though held there by one finger of each participant, until a message was spelt out, letter by letter.

In 1929 Louise recalled 'the writings [Alice] used to do with Christo one summer at Tatoï [1912], & then the time when Big George got messages from some spirit whom Alice firmly believed in'.[4] Alice was also keen on Christian Science.

A later medical report reveals that Alice was introduced to spiritualism during this first exile in Switzerland by an American lady who arranged sessions with Christo, and who subsequently became insane. Alice did not participate in these sessions directly, but read extensively about the process and practised automatic writing when she had an important decision to make. She became superstitious and was often to be seen dealing cards and seemingly getting messages from this.[5] Thus Alice began a gradual descent into more serious religious torments.

In their exile, Alice and Andrea moved between Lucerne and Rigi-First, taking boat rides with the family on Lac Lucerne, sometimes going to the Dolder in Zurich, where the children took donkey rides. By 1919 their main base was the Grand Hotel in Lucerne. The hotel became the base in exile for most of the Greek royal family, including King Constantine and Queen Sophie.

Dickie sometimes visited Alice and her family, sharing their skiing and skating expeditions. The children were growing up, all of them well educated, divided as ever into two families – the elder two girls and then the younger two. Margarita wrote to Dickie that she preferred summer in Switzerland to the winter, but missed the sea 'after two years of beastly little lakes'.[6] This aimless existence was at least soothing, after the tragedies which they had endured.

Andrea could do little that was constructive and his every move, however innocent, like those of his brothers, was monitored by the diplomats in Greece, Switzerland and Italy. A line of communication between King Constantine in Switzerland and King Alex-

1. 'The four generations. April 1886'. A matriarch and her descendants: (*left to right*) Queen Victoria, Princess Beatrice, Princess Louis of Battenberg and her infant daughter, Alice.

2. Alice as a youngster, *c.* 1887.

3. Julie von Hauke, Princess Battenberg, Alice's paternal grandmother, *c.* 1875.

4. Prince and Princess Louis of Battenberg with their daughters, Alice (*right*) and Louise, and their son, Georgie.

5. Ella: Grand Duchess Elisabeth of Russia, Alice's aunt, godmother and inspiration, 1887.

6. Alice, a radiant beauty, Darmstadt, December 1902.

7. Alice as a bride, October 1903.

8. The bridal couple emerge from the Russian chapel in Darmstadt, October 1903.

9. Alice, Princess of Greece, in her tiara, *c.* 1905.

10. Margarita and Theodora in Corfu.

11. Alice with Theodora in the boat to England, photographed by Queen Alexandra's daughter, Princess Victoria, May 1910.

12. Alice as a nurse in the Balkan Wars, with Andrea, 1913.

13. (*left*) The Russian sister-in-law, Princess Nicholas of Greece.

14. (*above*) Mother and daughters in exile, 1917: Theodora, Sophie, Alice, Cécile and Margarita.

15. (*below left*) Alice with her brother-in-law, 'Big George', in exile.

16. (*below right*) Alice with her brother-in-law, 'Christo', in Switzerland. He taught her magic writing.

17. (*above left*) Exile in Switzerland. Andrea on the lake.

18. (*above right*) Alice on the lake with her daughters, Theodora and Margarita.

19. (*left*) A visit home. Alice with her parents on the Isle of Wight, 1917: (*left to right*) Louise, Dickie, Victoria, Louis and Alice.

20. (*below*) Greece in débâcle. King Constantine returns, 1920.

21. Andrea during the Asia Minor campaign, 1921.

22. Andrea faces trial in Athens, December 1922.

ander in Greece was discovered via Big George in Paris, the Papal diplomatic bag in Rome, various couriers and 'the slow but sure channel'[7] of Alexandria. In 1919 Andrea petitioned the Foreign Office that he be allowed to return to Corfu, an idea seemingly supported by Venizelos, though it came to nothing.

In June 1919, Louis and Louise came to Lucerne to see Alice. Louise, who stayed for more than a month, judged Alice 'not looking very well, but not thin like two years ago'.[8] The visit of Alice's father paved the way towards a reconciliation between the English and German families following the war. Inevitably there was residual bitterness, though this was partly negated by the shared tragedy of the murders of Alix and Ella. Alice was anxious to help where she could, though nervous about the outcome. But she was encouraged by a successful reunion between Louis and his brother Franzjos and Anna, living in voluntary exile from Darmstadt in Lausanne, though then at Thun, south of Berne. This prompted Alice into effecting a more important reconciliation between her parents and Uncle Ernie.

Uncle Ernie and Aunt Onor were on their way to their mountain-top castle, Tarasp, in the Engadine, near the Austrian-Italian border, where they duly arrived in mid-July. Alice changed her holiday plans to lodge at nearby Vulpera in order that they could all meet for the first time since before the war. Ernie hoped that Alice's mother might join them too, but Alice warned Onor:

I suppose it would be better if I told you now that Mama's nerves are terribly strained and, although physically she is all right and has a good appetite and works in the garden several hours a day, she could not even make up her mind to join us here [Lucerne]. It is sheer agony for her to discuss the sad Russian thing. She had to go over it with A[unt] Minny and S[ophie] Buxhoeveden* & didn't have the strength to do so with me & my mother-in-law again. Papa & I are afraid that she will not have the courage to talk about it to Uncle Ernie & so it would not come as a

* Baroness Sophie (Isa) Buxhoeveden (1884–1956), principal lady-in-waiting to the Tsarina until her murder. Later a staunch ally to Victoria.

surprise to us if Mama now wrote that she would rather come next summer when her *very* strained nerves have recovered from her awful distress about her sisters.[9]

Louis found he had to go back to London, but Alice and her family arrived in Vulpera on 17 July, and Victoria plucked up courage and came later in order to see Ernie and then to take Louise home. But Victoria did not want to be Ernie's guest, which caused some offence at first. In the end, she settled with Alice and her family at the Pension Villa Maria in Vulpera, which was close to the castle.

For days Alice and Louise had been in two minds about whether they wanted their mother to come. They feared the strain this would impose. Uncle Ernie still did not know how Ella had died, as Onor had kept the details from him. No one wanted this story to slip out.

Gradually a pattern was established. Alice and her family stayed together during the day, the four girls becoming immensely bronzed. They made friends with Don and Lu, Ernie's sons, whom everyone liked. At teatime they all went up to the castle and walked together and stayed until dinner. Louise explained to Nona:

> Like that one has the pleasure of being with them for not too long to avoid talking about the painful subjects of the war. Though the Revolution [in Germany] has made it so much easier meeting because one has all that to talk about & their experiences which are most interesting. I feel one looks upon them as *individuals* one is fond of, not as being one with their natives, & individuals who have suffered so much through it all, which makes it easier. The bitterness & hate this monstrous war has brought for us all makes one want all the more to keep the love one has for those one is fond of above it all & they have done nothing of their doing.[10]

Andrea enjoyed some long walks, a welcome change from Lucerne, and Louise herself enjoyed a physical rest, if not what she called 'a mental rest'.[11] Victoria liked the pensione and the wild flowers and found the air refreshing. 'Now the ice is broken, I like meeting Ernie & Onor, who are quite unchanged in character,' she wrote to Nona. 'Ernie's news about Russia is as sparse & unreliable as all that one has received. Being here is doing him much good as he has gone through very hard times during the revolution & he does not expect things to quiet down this winter yet.'[12]

At the end of the break, Alice returned to the Grand Hotel in Lucerne with her girls. King Constantine and Queen Sophie were in residence, the King railing against the way Greece had been treated at the Peace Conference. Back in England, Victoria sold some shares and was able to give £800 to each of her four children. All but Alice could use it as capital, but Victoria wished she could see Alice's face when her share arrived to help with her expenses in exile.

Alice suffered from influenza at the beginning of 1920, as did Andrea and the younger two children. She hoped to join her parents in Rome, following their visit to Corfu with Louise, but she was refused permission to go to Italy. Instead, Alice left Margarita and Theodora with Queen Olga, while she and Andrea took the younger two with them to Lugano, and Louis, Victoria and Louise joined them there. Only then did Alice regain her strength, at which point Cécile fell ill with a mild case of scarlet fever.

During 1920, unexpected happenings in Greece altered the political situation relating to King Constantine and the Greek royal family in exile. Just as they had left Greece precipitously, so did they suddenly find themselves poised to return. By various means, the Greek royal family had followed the plight of young King Alexander since he had assumed the throne three years before.

Since July 1917 Venizelos had been Prime Minister once more. When Lord Granville arrived in Athens to take up his duties as British Ambassador in October that year, he found King Alexander isolated but doing his best, prepared to listen but full of grievances, and minding the exile of his uncles. The King was presently undermined when a series of damaging telegrams between the Kaiser and King Constantine were published. These purported to confirm what King Constantine had always denied – that there was a link between him and the Kaiser, albeit only when Greece was in dire straits in the spring of 1917. The effect was to denigrate King Constantine for having 'deceived the representatives of the people, his Ministers, his Generals and the Representatives of the Entente'.[13]

King Alexander persisted in believing that the Germans might win the war and it was learned that he received letters from his father written in invisible ink.

A worse crisis loomed when he announced his wish to marry. The King's chosen bride was a beautiful Greek girl called Aspasia Manos, a childhood playmate and the daughter of Colonel Petros Manos, grand equerry to King Constantine, who had accompanied the King into exile in Switzerland. Venizelos forbade the marriage. Aspasia was twenty-two, and already the subject of some diplomatic concern. In London Arthur Balfour had heard that she was 'likely to exercise influence whereas her relatives will probably alter their attitude when once identified with the present regime'.[14] Only the Duke of Connaught offered encouragement when he came to Athens to present the King with the Grand Cross of the Order of the Bath and was much taken with Miss Manos.

Soon the situation became muddier when a story emerged from Switzerland that Aspasia's father had been 'forced to commit suicide owing to a scandal connected with Princess Helen'.[15] In May 1918 Lord Granville met the King and Aspasia in the Royal Garden to discuss how the marriage might proceed, but when the King became 'very unruly', he told him 'plainly that His Majesty's Government support him as a constitutional sovereign and if he behaves unconstitutionally we shall wash our hands of him'.[16]

By September 1918 King Alexander was no further forward and was feeling thoroughly disgruntled. It was not until a year later, on 4 November 1919, that he married Aspasia Manos in secret at the palace. For a while she moved in with the King, but when gossip pursued them, she retreated to Naples with her mother.

The wedding remained a secret until May 1920, when King Alexander finally succeeded in his long-held wish to get to Paris on what Venizelos described as a well-earned 'pleasure trip'.[17] It was then revealed that he was joining his bride of six months. In

June Aspasia became pregnant and a month later, Alexander returned to Greece alone, after which he performed his kingly duties in a perfunctory manner, complaining that he had become a cipher in the hands of Venizelos.

In the same month martial law was abolished in Greece and the opposition openly demanded the return of the ex-King. This prompted the British government to give assurances that it was against restoration and that it deplored the ex-King's wartime behaviour, and that it would not recognize him as King.

By September the Greek government was convinced that ex-King Constantine was instigating plots against it and was even behind a recent attempt on the life of Venizelos. He was moving about freely, had his own couriers and published a weekly newspaper. There was discussion as to how to curb the King's activities and isolate him from the more active agitators.[18]

Towards the end of September, Andrea became embroiled in the intrigues, when he and Christo moved to Rome. Foreign Office reports described the princes as 'believed to be trying to create atmosphere in favour of ex-King'.[19] They were warned not to take any steps 'which might entail action by the Italian authorities'.[20] Another report stated that Andrea and Christo were 'trying to create a strongly pro-Constantine atmosphere in Rome'.[21]

Since 1914 Christo had wanted to marry a rich widow called Nancy Leeds,* but had been prevented by the laws of the Greek royal house. In February 1920, he had been given permission, and they were married in Vevey. This made Christo more powerful, since Nancy's money enabled the princes to spend considerable sums on press coverage. They were said to be meeting important political figures, and to be in communication with Gounaris.† The

* Nancy Leeds (1873–1923), widow of William Bateman Leeds, a tin magnate in Ohio. Christo was fifteen years her junior.

† Dmitrios Gounaris (1867–1922), Prime Minister of Greece from 1915–17 and 1921–2, described by Prince Nicholas as 'a striking personality; a straightforward gentleman and a Statesman of no mean capacity, a distinguished orator, a man of exceptional culture' [HRH Prince Nicholas of Greece, *My Fifty Years* (Hutchinson, 1926), p. 306].

Italian government promised the British government that King Constantine would not be permitted to come to Rome from Lucerne.

In October, while these supposed intrigues were going on, tragedy struck unexpectedly in Greece. King Alexander was walking his dog at Tatoï, when it was attacked by a pet monkey. He tried to separate dog and monkey, when another monkey joined the fray and bit him in the stomach and the thigh. Five days later the wound turned septic and fever set in. The King was diagnosed as suffering from cellulitis, an infection by which the poison spreads through the limbs and into the bloodstream, causing fever. His temperature soared to 103°F and fell, only to rise again to 105°F. The operation of curettage was performed on 10 October, but his condition did not improve. And so it continued for three long weeks, while his young and pregnant bride returned to nurse him.

It was not long before the Greek government and press began to wonder what would happen 'should any change occur in the occupancy of the Hellenic throne'.[22] On 21 October, Queen Olga was permitted to visit her grandson, being the only member of the family whom the Greek politicians would tolerate in Greece at that time. In due course a cerebral crisis was followed by delirium and on 25 October 1920 the King died. Queen Olga and Aspasia, who met for the first time at the King's bedside, followed the cortège to Tatoï.

Venizelos had panicked when he realized that the King was likely to die. He knew that the Allies would not accept King Constantine and sought his formal abdication. Nor was Prince George wanted, because of his military training in Germany. Venizelos therefore settled on Prince Paul as the next candidate for the throne. But Prince Paul declared that he would accept only if the Greek people freely announced that it did not want either his father or elder brother 'in a free expression of its will'.[23]

Events now moved fast. Christo was reported as pouring his new wife's money into anti-Venizelist funds. Venizelos was roundly beaten in the postponed elections, which took place in November, and Rhallys became Prime Minister. Queen Olga, still in Greece following her grandson's death, became Regent.

In Lucerne, ex-King Constantine was asked what he would do if the Allies objected to him becoming King again. He stated: 'It has nothing to do with me. Ask the Greek people.'[24] He stressed publicly his wish to be a good ally to Britain. At length, despite the Allies refusing to recognize King Constantine as King of Greece, the Greek government decided to have him back.

On 22 November, Andrea and Christo arrived in Corfu by Lloyds steamer, received an 'enthusiastic reception'[25] and went on to Athens, arriving the next day. Alice recalled: 'They were accorded an enthusiastic reception, and were dragged from their car and borne on the shoulders of the populace, frenzied with joy, the whole way from Phaleron Bay to Athens and [Andrea] was forced to make a speech from the balcony of the palace to the vast crowds gathered below.'[26] Andrea was reinstated into the Greek army. She and the children followed a few days later on *Lloyd Triestino* with Christo's wife, and likewise travelled from Corfu to Athens.

Diplomatic problems remained. Lord Granville politely refused an invitation to be received by Queen Olga because she was described as 'Regent in the name of her son King Constantine', and he was anxious not to commit himself or his government 'in one sense or the other'.[27] The French refused to recognize King Constantine and on 2 December the Foreign Secretary, Lord Curzon, clarified the British position by declaring that the restoration would 'create a new and unfavourable situation in the relations between Greece and the Allies.'[28] After many diplomatic wrangles and changes of mind, Lord Granville was instructed to remain in Athens, but to have no dealings with King Constantine.

When King Constantine arrived back in Greece on 19 December, Athens was, in the words of the *Times* correspondent, 'bursting with Royalist enthusiasm'.[29] The King's picture adorned most windows, olive branches decorated balconies, and the Athenians could be heard singing local songs. A cartoon depicted a tomb opening, King Constantine rising from it while Venizelos and other ministers fainted at the sight.

King Constantine arrived in Athens wearing the uniform of a

full general, with a smiling Queen Sophie at his side. In a speech he declared that he would nurture good relations with the Allied powers and referred to future ties with Romania, which were to be cemented by the marriage of his son the Crown Prince to Princess Elisabeth, and his daughter Helen to Crown Prince Carol of Romania.

Events had been dramatic in the latter months of 1920. Within a mere three months of Alexander's death, the unthinkable had happened: King Constantine had been restored to Greece to wide public approbation.

15. The Birth of Prince Philip

Alice settled back at Mon Repos, as delighted as her daughters to be basking once more in the warmth of Corfu. In all senses, it was a time of new beginnings.

In February 1921 Alice told her parents that she was expecting an addition to the family towards the end of June, the first for seven years. This news reached them on their return to England from burying Aunt Ella in Jerusalem. 'I hope it will be the longed-for boy,' wrote Victoria to Nona. 'She says she is feeling very fit. She is just a year younger than I was when Dickie was born & there will be about the same difference in age between the baby & Tiny as between Dickie & Georgie.'[1]

Andrea became a Major-General in the Greek army, but he was not given a command. He found himself appointed to the Cavalry Brigade, where his influence would be minimal. The reason for this was no secret to him: 'The prejudice against those officers dismissed from the army in 1917, of whom I was one, was deliberately greater in my own case,'[2] he wrote. Not until June 1921 was he appointed to command the XIIth Division and 2nd Army in Thrace.

King Constantine strove in vain for better relations with the Allies, while Venizelos, now in self-imposed exile, kept suggesting that he should abdicate. This cry was soon adopted by all Venizelists, who further sought the exile of Crown Prince George and all the royal family.

Soon, two royal alliances were forged, both of them ultimately unsatisfactory. The Crown Prince married Princess Elisabeth of Romania in Bucharest on 27 February and his sister, Princess Helen, married Prince Carol of Romania in Athens on 10 March, Alice and Andrea being present at the latter occasion. Both these occasions were dominated by Queen Marie of Romania, who told Lord

Granville that the King and Queen of Greece were 'rather stupid' and did not get on with their son, George.[3]

Another crisis loomed in the domestic life of the Greek royal family, as they awaited the outcome of the pregnancy of Aspasia Manos, King Alexander's widow. Her marriage to the King had been recognized as legal by the Court of First Instance, despite some irregularities in its religious celebration. Aspasia was not popular in the Greek royal family, but Alice felt sorry for her.

The family worried that the child might be a boy, thus potentially raising problems of succession, so there was relief when, on 25 March, Aspasia gave birth to a daughter. She was named Alexandra* and was the only Princess of Greece to have been born with Greek blood.

Years later, Alexandra wrote that Alice, likewise pregnant, had stayed in Athens for Christmas in 1920 in order to comfort the young widow. She added that 'not all the royal relatives troubled to do so'.[4] Aspasia was always grateful to Alice for this.

As Alice's pregnancy continued, the Greeks and Andrea became more deeply involved in the ill-fated Asia Minor campaign. This campaign was meant to fulfil the great Byzantine dream, the conquest of Turkey by Greece. Venizelos had instigated it in June 1920, before his fall from power. King Constantine, nothing if not an experienced warrior, advised against pursuing this endeavour but was ignored. When the second advance began in March 1921, Andrea wanted to be a part of it. He only achieved his wish as the hour of Alice's delivery approached.

Alice was resting at Mon Repos on 6 April, when a shocking report appeared in the newspapers announcing that Andrea had died from

* Princess Alexandra of Greece and Denmark (1921–1993), married 1944, King Peter of Yugoslavia (1923–1970). Author of two books, *For A King's Love* (Odhams Press, 1956), and *Prince Philip: A Family Portrait* (Hodder & Stoughton, 1959). The former was ghosted by Joan Reeder, a *Daily Mirror* journalist, and the latter by Harold Albert, alias Helen Cathcart.

wounds in the Asia Minor campaign. This report did not worry Alice, since she knew he was safe, but it was upsetting for the rest of the family, reading it at home. 'I never really believed the news about Andrea,' wrote Victoria to her elder son Georgie, 'for he was not to have left Athens except in company of his brother, but it will have given you a great shock.'[5]

Alice gave birth to the long-awaited son, Philip, on the dining-room table at Mon Repos, Corfu, on 10 June. 'He is a splendid, healthy child, thank God,' she wrote. 'I am very well too. It was an uncomplicated delivery & I am now enjoying the fresh air on the terrace.'[6]

Victoria wrote to Nona:

> I knew you would rejoice with us at Alice having a boy. Poor Andrea had the bad luck of leaving the day before the event & so has not seen his son. This is the 9th year he & Alice were passing in an atmosphere of war, a sore trial & I do hope that this — campaign may be a victorious one for the Greeks & Andrea get through it safely.[7]

Alice passed her time in the seclusion of Mon Repos, surrounded by the scent of orange and wisteria. Two days after Philip was born, she was dictating replies to telegrams of congratulation and then wrote three or four letters a day for the next three weeks. As she recovered from the birth, she worried about Andrea, who was now at the front awaiting the moment of attack.

There was reason for concern. Andrea's division consisted of men from the new provinces, Thrace, Eastern Macedonia and Asia Minor. They were raw recruits and hardly knew how to shoot. Some of the officers were unable to read or write. 'A's letters are slightly desperate,' wrote Alice, 'but he is hoping philosophically that his men will stand their ground, but as far as the real Army is concerned, he is positive that they will eventually win.'[8]

But as the campaign progressed, it became clear to Andrea that the whole exercise was a fiasco. It could only end in the deaths of numerous Greeks. He remained on active service until the end of September, away from his family and friends, still without a glimpse of his son, becoming increasingly gloomy as the campaign became more bogged down.

On 10 September Alice was at home in Corfu, where no doubt a fine day dawned. She could not have known that elsewhere in the world, two more vital points of stability were being taken from her. On that day Andrea made a stand against his commander-in-chief, opening himself up to accusations of disobedience. The next day Alice's father died.

Alice left for London as soon as she could after hearing the news of her father's death, but she knew that she would not get there in time for the funeral. With her came the infant Philip, as she was still nursing him.

Alice had loved her father. She wrote:

> The world has become such a sad place lately. We are so grateful that the good Lord has taken him now. One can never know what other calamities may befall us & he could hardly have been happier than he was this summer. Mama, too, says that this was probably the right moment for him. But Oh God what an effort it will mean for our poor bereaved family to get used to a life without him. I am so terribly sorry for poor Dickie, as he is so young & had such a wonderful and faithful friendship with his father. He would sit at his feet for hours on end and ask him about things. The first blow in his happy youth . . . I simply dare not write about Louise.[9]

Louis was only sixty-seven. He had begun to slow down a little, but had enjoyed a busy summer and remained full of plans for the future. He had been intensely moved, when on 4 August, at the instigation of the First Lord of the Admiralty, Lord Lee of Fareham, the King had appointed him Admiral of the Fleet, the highest rank available to a naval officer. Once the decision had been made, the Admiralty went in search of him to give him the news. As it happened, Louis received Lee's hand-delivered letter in London and turned up in his office twenty minutes later. With tears in his eyes he sank down on to the sofa and told Lee: 'I think you know what this means to me. It is the greatest moment of my life.'[10]

Alice heard how her father had died in his rooms in Half Moon Street, shortly after a holiday in Scotland with her mother. Louis had a chill which turned into influenza. He stayed in his rooms and the housekeeper brought him soup and toast, which he tried to eat. She left him for a while and, on returning to the room, found him dead in his chair. Louis was clasping a silver cross attached to a golden chain that he wore round his neck. He had succumbed to a sudden heart attack.

Louis was hailed in the press as 'the very pattern of the best class of British officer'.[11] The King wrote to Victoria, recalling that they had been shipmates together, '& I remember how much I admired him then both as a sailor & as a man, when he was a Lieutenant'.[12]

Alice was still on her way over when Louis's coffin was borne in procession to Westminster Abbey and, after the funeral, taken across the Solent to the Isle of Wight, where he was buried in an outdoor grave in the churchyard of Whippingham Church, inside which his brother Henry lay. It was a place filled with memories of Queen Victoria and Osborne days, of royal marriages and church services, a tranquil and beautiful spot not far from the sea that Louis knew and loved so well.

Alice inherited one tenth of his estate, which comprised some £6,535 in England, half a million roubles in Russia, and 734,613 marks in Darmstadt (the Heiligenberg having been sold the previous year). His jewellery, pictures, prints, books and works of art were divided equally between his four children.

Alice only reached Paris on 22 September, making her way to Hampshire, to stay with her mother at Fishponds, Nona's home in Netley, near Southampton. Victoria thus saw Philip before Andrea did. Presently they all went to London, where Alice and baby Philip stayed at Spencer House, loaned to them by Christo's wife, along with a cook and servants. The only relief from the sad business of probates came when, on a Sunday early in October, Dickie invited his mother, Alice and Louise on board *Renown*, in which he was shortly to sail to India with the Prince of Wales.

There Dickie's family met and formed a favourable impression of Edwina Ashley, with whom Dickie was much stricken. She too was in mourning, her grandfather, Sir Ernest Cassel, having lately died, leaving her the largest part of his fortune in trust. Soon afterwards, Alice and Philip returned to Greece.

Some months later, the King offered Victoria an apartment at Kensington Palace, and she and Louise moved into it in December 1922. This was Victoria's home for the duration of her widowhood. 'It is hard to move into a new place, where my dear husband never lived with me. This is, however, the fate of most widows & I have much to be thankful for. I think of all that others have had to lose and suffer.'[13] She thought of Ella, who had had no children to help her when Serge was murdered in 1905.

Alice returned to Greece to find Andrea on leave from the army, deeply depressed by the progress of the war, but cheered by his first sight of Philip. He had led a successful advance to Eski Shehr and been promoted to Lieutenant-General, but there was political intrigue among his fellow officers, which he was unable to check. Finally General Papoulas ordered him to advance, but he knew this would lead to slaughter. He refused.

His chief of staff was sacked and he asked to be allowed to resign. But the Commander-in-Chief refused to allow him to go, without giving him an explanation for this. Finally, however, he obtained permission to go on leave. Alice, fiercely loyal as ever, wrote later that he did this 'not wishing to bear the responsibility of the serious consequences which would inevitably ensue'.[14]

To this end, the Greek army advanced across the Aegean Sea to Smyrna and into Asia Minor. It pressed ahead and seemed to be making progress in 1921, but the further it went in, the longer the lines of communication became. It achieved early victories, but these proved short-lived. In September the army was forced to retreat and then to hold its ground, not just for a short time but for almost a year. By 1922, when the men were weak and feeble, the Turks advanced, reinforced by aid from France. In effect they drove the Greeks back into the sea with huge loss of life; the victories of the past decade were wiped out. Winston Churchill described the fiasco as 'true Greek tragedy, with Chance as the ever-ready hand-maid of Fate'.[15]

From now on, Andrea was considered a controversial figure in Greece. At the end of October, he was criticized in the Greek press (with the Crown Prince and his brother Nicholas) for giving an anti-Venizelos interview in the *Giornale d'Italia*. More trouble would follow.

Andrea remained convinced of the hopelessness of the Asia Minor campaign. In January 1922, he wrote to the future dictator, Ionnis Metaxas, pointing out that the Greeks would be forced to retreat and that the army was in disarray. 'Something must be done quickly to remove us from the nightmare of Asia Minor,' he wrote. 'I don't know what, but we must stop bluffing and face the situation as it really is. Because finally which is better? – to fall into the sea or to escape before we are ducked? I am afraid I shall be labelled a defeatist for saying this.'[16]

In December Andrea was transferred to the 5th Army Corps of Epirus and the Ionian Islands, stationed at Jannina. From there, he observed the disaster unfold, while he bemoaned his own lot: 'My God, when shall I get away from this hell here?'[17] The Greek army in Asia Minor was overcome by the Turks, exactly as he feared would happen. Andrea did not therefore witness the ultimate tragedy first-hand.

Fifteen months later, he would be accused of having 'abandoned a position without orders when in contact with the enemy',[18] but he took comfort from a letter from King Constantine: 'I regret that you considered it necessary to give me your assurance that the accusation against you of abandoning your position before the enemy is not true. You might have known my opinion of you by now, that I consider you . . . an honourable, conscientious, and able soldier.'[19]

Alice could but watch these developments from her haven at Mon Repos, amongst the fruit trees and Judas trees, the grass studded with wild flowers and irises and the burgeoning wisteria. She did accompany Andrea to Athens, where he was treated for pyorrhoea of the gums, and she went with him to Jannina for a fortnight to organize a house for him. Alice was still in Jannina on 19 March 1922 when her mother and Louise came to stay with her in Corfu, bringing with them pre-war trunks filled with silver from the Heiligenberg and numerous gifts for Philip's nursery.

The recent sorrows of the family were somewhat mitigated by news from the royal tour in Delhi that Dickie had become engaged to Edwina Ashley, a considerable improvement, thought Victoria, on his previous attachment, Audrey James.* Edwina was a considerable heiress and Dickie described himself to Nona as 'the luckiest fellow alive'.[20] Victoria confirmed this, adding a further benefit: 'One can be very happy, without much money, but of course it is a relief to know her well off & that Dickie may be able to help Louise when I am gone if necessary.'[21]

Dickie was determined to marry Edwina that very summer and asked Alice to come to England for the wedding. As Victoria put it, 'Alice who is so like him in loving to settle up plans beforehand intends to do so.'[22] Alice's daughters were thrilled about the marriage and yet more so when they were invited to be bridesmaids. Margarita saw Edwina's picture in the *Sphere*, and pronounced her 'lovely'.[23] Cécile declared: 'We have never had such a pretty aunt in the family.'[24]

Alice's daughters were growing up fast. Margarita was nearly seventeen and Theodora nearly sixteen. Their hair was fashionably turned up and their grandmother described them as 'quite natural & unaffected girls, really children, that do Alice credit, but though nice looking, they have merely the good looks of youth'.[25] Victoria also described the younger two: 'Cécile will certainly be the prettiest of the lot, Tiny is great fun & the precious Philipp [*sic*] the image of Andrea.'[26] Victoria took solace in watching Philip standing up by himself, sitting with bare legs on the hard road, and crawling along it without minding the stones. 'He is in fact just as advanced

* Audrey James (1902–68), daughter of Mrs Willie James, of West Dean Park. She made three marriages, to Captain Dudley Coats, Marshall Field of Chicago, and to the Hon. Peter Pleydell-Bouverie. A beautiful, sophisticated and flighty girl, who had caused some concern in the Milford Haven household. Later she had a torrid fling with the Prince of Wales.

& sturdy for his age as all the others were.'[27] Louise loved the new baby: 'Philip has of course grown enormously, crawls about fast & is always standing up, laughs all day long. I have never seen such a cheerful baby. He has kept his blue eyes & his hair is white like Dolla's as a baby.'[28]

On 4 April Alice and Andrea returned to Corfu for Easter and Victoria's birthday. Louise described Alice as 'looking well & so is Andrea & in quite good spirits'.[29] It was a calm period, with the children excavating bits of pottery, bronze nails, coins and human bones from an ancient Greek cemetery. The best they achieved was half a pot intact. Some of their finds Alice sent to the Director of the American School in Athens, though this worried Andrea since he pictured hordes of archaeologists descending on Mon Repos to dig up the garden.

Early in May Alice went with Andrea to Jannina, where she gave some tea parties for the local authorities, returning to Corfu on 16 May. King Constantine, whose health had declined steadily since the previous autumn, fell ill again, and the new Crown Princess of Greece almost died of typhoid fever. Alice discovered that she and Andrea would lose a quarter of their income because of the new forced Greek loan, but remained generally optimistic and resourceful.

Andrea was not able to accompany Alice and the children when they settled at Spencer House in London in June for Dickie's wedding. The occasion was one of high glamour, setting the pace for that brand of high life which would epitomize the Mountbattens from now on, a mixture of royal and service life with high living – and at times 'Curzon Street Communist' life, so favoured by Edwina. Dickie had wanted to be married in Westminster Abbey, but conceded that the abbey was 'only for the really big fish'.[30] The Chapel Royal was too small for his purposes, so they settled on St Margaret's, Westminster.

The wedding took place on 18 July 1922 in the presence of the King and Queen and Queen Alexandra, and a great many members of the royal family and society. Alice's daughters were amongst the bridesmaids, dressed in delphinium blue to match Edwina's eyes.

Their flapper outfits were hard to control, while the silk stockings kept wrinkling at the ankles. Philip, too young for the ceremony, remained at Spencer House.

Afterwards Alice visited Scotland, where she enjoyed glorious weather and touring. The only cloud on the horizon was the news from Greece, which was, in the words of Louise, 'hateful'.[31] On 19 September Alice took the family back to Greece, where they faced the most considerable drama of Alice's and Andrea's life. Victoria was already worried: 'I can't imagine what the results of the Greek débâcle in Asia Minor will be & can only hope the King & the family may not have to suffer for it.'[32]

16. The Greeks in Defeat

When Alice returned to Greece, she found the country in disarray. The Greeks and Armenians were being massacred by the Turks. Venizelos, the man who had started the war, was still lurking in retirement, following his 1921 election defeat. From afar he observed the chaos and blamed it on the return of King Constantine. The King himself was a sick man, his spirits bruised by defeat.

During this phase, Britain was represented in Athens by two able diplomats, Francis Lindley,* the new Ambassador, a fiercely patriotic man of consummate common sense, and his Counsellor, Charles Bentinck,† a vigorous character, whose joy in life was to set off on horseback to winkle out an obscure ecclesiastical ceremony or a liturgy being sung in some remote church.

In London, matters were overseen by Sir Eyre Crowe,‡ Permanent Under-Secretary of State for Foreign Affairs, a skilful negotiator at a number of international conferences, described by the writer, Harold Nicolson, then at the Foreign Office, as a 'man of extreme violence and extreme gentleness . . . so human . . . so superhuman . . . a man of truth and vigour'.[1] When the King wished to discuss foreign affairs, he summoned Crowe to the palace. These men monitored the last months of King Constantine's reign and the dangers that befell Andrea.

* Hon. Francis Lindley (1872–1950), later Rt. Hon. Sir Francis Lindley. He was posted in Petrograd in 1915, stayed in charge of the British Mission when Sir George Buchanan was withdrawn in 1918 and was Consul-General in Russia 1919–20. Later he was Ambassador to Portugal and Japan.

† C. H. Bentinck (1879–1955), later Revd Sir Charles Bentinck. Diplomat in Berlin, St Petersburg and the Hague. Served in Athens 1917–23. Counsellor from 1920. Ordained 1941.

‡ Sir Eyre Crowe (1864–1925), diplomat and one of the most distinguished public servants of his day. When he died, Stanley Baldwin said, 'We have lost the ablest servant of the Crown.'

It was a frantic year. By June 1922 Lindley was convinced that the militant wing of the Venizelist party were now anti-Constantine, indeed definitely Republican, but doubted that the country was yet ready for 'the adventure of revolution'.[2] Curiously, the King had remained popular despite a year and a half of war and other internal difficulties. But when the discontented soldiers returned from Asia Minor in August, his popularity went into sharp decline. So did his health.

Andrea's standing in Athens was now at low ebb, since he was generally 'criticized for remaining on leave and absent from his command in Epirus while such tragic events'[3] were happening in his country.

Early in September, there was a meeting at the palace in Athens at which the King, Andrea and Prince Nicholas received Monsieur Vlachos, the editor of *Kathemerini*. Andrea advocated the King abdicating in favour of the Crown Prince. He suggested that the King should go for a cure in some foreign country and then abdicate on grounds of ill health. Nicholas was against abdication, while the King himself refrained from discussing it.

On 10 September King Constantine issued a proclamation to the Greek people, explaining that the army had met with misfortune, having fought victoriously for freedom for a decade. He promised to do whatever was necessary in the interests of the nation within the bounds of the constitution and appealed for patriotism.

Meanwhile a Revolutionary Committee had been formed, led by Colonel Plastiras* and Colonel Gonatas,† representing the younger officers who demanded revenge for the shame of their defeat. When the Revolutionary Committee dropped leaflets over Athens demanding that the King go, Lindley telegraphed for British men-of-war to be sent to Athens 'to save bloodshed and if necessary to take off Royal Family'.[4] Finally, on 27 September, King Constantine agreed to abdicate. The Crown Prince was summoned

* Nikolaos Plastiras (1883–1953), soldier turned politician, who led the 1922 revolt. He served under Andrea in the Asia Minor campaign.

† Stylianos Gonatas, revolutionary leader and later Prime Minister.

from Bucharest, accepted the crown and took the oath of allegiance.

The new King, George II, would be little more than a puppet. The Foreign Secretary, Lord Curzon, then presiding at the Lausanne Conference, refused to recognize him any more than he had his father, while Harold Nicolson thought that 'his wife and very dominating mother-in-law* will see to it that he behaves sensibly'.[5]

It was arranged that King Constantine and Queen Sophie would leave on board a Greek merchant vessel, accompanied by Andrea and Nicholas. Lindley hoped that all the princes would go, because 'I consider any delay as most dangerous to their lives.'[6] But when the royal party left Greece on the evening of 30 September, Andrea was not of the party.†

Alice and Andrea remained in Corfu, where they had been assured by the new government that they would be out of danger. They found themselves under siege. On the instructions of the Revolutionary Committee, their letters were opened and read and their every move watched. Alice's mother received a letter from her in October, delivered by hand, and wrote in turn to Dickie:

> Andrea & she are almost isolated at Mon Repos & have to be most careful in all they say & do. Some thousands of refugees are to be moved to Corfu & I hope she will be allowed to occupy herself with them. Louise is sending out useful clothing material to her with the money Edwina & you & some other generous friends gave her.[7]

Victoria then reported to Nona:

> Alice says the violent Venizelists are in power & all the extreme measures & people of his regime active again. Elections are to be hurried on. Co-ertion, intimidation etc will of course be used fully & as soon as this so-called 'Revolutionary' party gets in officially, Venizelos, who now

* Queen Marie of Romania.

† Only the King and Queen, Princess Katherine and Prince Nicholas sailed in *Patris*, a troop ship with shocking sanitary arrangements. They arrived in Palermo, where after a few days of excitement they faded into obscurity.

keeps in the background to humbug the Powers, will have himself recalled & probably proclaim the Republic. After a while I feel sure a reaction will set in again, but meanwhile I am rather anxious as to what may be done to Andrea.[8]

Victoria was right to worry. On 26 October Colonel Loufas of the Revolutionary Committee came to interview Andrea about the Asia Minor débâcle. After a preliminary examination Loufas took Andrea to Athens in the Greek destroyer *Aspis*. Alice described what happened in another letter to her mother, delivered by Christo, passed on to George V by Victoria and finally to Lord Curzon:

Andrea was taken away from Corfu in a destroyer 2 weeks ago. They said it would be for 2 days but he has not returned. We are now shocked to find that he is probably going to be accused and not a witness, as he was told by the Revolutionary officer, who took him away in the destroyer. In a pencil note now received from him, brought by a Greek lady and which she with much difficulty smuggled out of Athens, he says he is kept strictly alone and does not know whether he is going to be accused or only examined. He is lodged in the house of a former Aide-de-Camp [General Palli] of Prince Nicholas, but the police insisted upon his living separately in two rooms with a guard at the door and no one is allowed to visit him except in the presence of a police officer. Mr Lindley has been very kind and has protested to the Foreign Minister about the treatment of Andrea and so has the Italian Minister; and the American Minister was so indignant that he has said he had a good mind to telegraph to America and stop the subsidy to the refugees. The Royalists are anxious about his detention and think the Revolutionaries may want him as a hostage to prevent a counter revolution.[9]

Loufas maintained that Andrea was taken because he had been unable to give satisfactory explanations to certain points in connection with the Greek offensive on the River Sakharia in 1921. It was further stated that, disregarding General Papoulas's order to advance, Andrea had acted on his own initiative 'with disastrous results not only to the corps under his command but to the entire Army'.[10] The British consul in Corfu reported that the arrest was for 'several grave charges both military and political.'[11] These charges were disobedience to orders and abandoning his position in the face of the enemy.

The Revolutionary Committee also arrested various ministers and army officers connected with the Asia Minor campaign.* Frank Lindley was swift to protest about the composition of the proposed court martial and made it clear that any executions that followed would be regarded as 'acts of revenge which would split the country'.[12] The prisoners were interrogated by General Pangalos, described by Lindley as 'a fanatic Venizelist who is charged with the duty of Public Prosecutor'.[13]

At the beginning of November, Alice hoped that Andrea would be freed and would be able to take the two older children to Paris, while she held the fort at Mon Repos with the three younger ones. In London, Alice's brother, Georgie, went to see George V, who had been briefed by Curzon. The King told him that he foresaw no problem in Andrea coming to London. But as the month went on, the situation worsened.

Harold Nicolson was then at the Lausanne Conference helping Lord Curzon with the business of reorganizing the boundaries of various Balkan countries. Writing on 14 November, he compared conditions in Greece to those at the time of the 1909 revolt, and concluded: 'We are thus faced with the menace of complete chaos in Greece.'[14] Throughout November there were fears of execution, threats of the removal of the Minister in Athens, and reassurances

* The arrested men were Dimitrios Gounaris (1867–1922), the former Liberal Prime Minister, Nikalaos Stratos (1872–1922), the Minister of the Interior, Nikalaos Theotokis (1878–1922), the War Minister, Georgios Baltazzi (1866–1922), the Foreign Minister, Michael Goudas (d. 1922), a Minister, Petros Protopapadakis (1860–1922), another former Prime Minister, Nikalaos Kalogeropoulos (1852–1927), a former Prime Minister said to be in his dotage, General Georgios Hatzianestis (1863–1922), the Commander of the Asia Minor and Thrace armies, Xenophon Stratigos (1869–1927), Minister of Communications, and Colonel Constantinopoulos, late Chief of the Military District of Athens.

from Lindley that executions were unlikely to take place. George V wondered if the British should recognize George II, but Curzon squashed the idea.

In mid-November, Christo came from Paris and called on Alice at Mon Repos. He found her living under police surveillance and she was 'very uneasy and sensed the coming storm just as I did'.[15] Christo then went to Athens, where he was forbidden to see Andrea, though they communicated via a message concealed inside a packet of cigarettes. Andrea was resigned to his fate and recorded that General Pangalos had said to him: 'How many children have you?. . . Poor things, what a pity they will soon be orphans!'[16]

Christo himself was safe because he was carrying a large cheque for the Red Cross in Greece, given to him by his rich wife. He was able to see the new King at Tatoï, finding him a virtual prisoner and afraid of the Greeks. Before making a precipitous departure, Christo retrieved his securities and Princess Nicholas's prize possessions, her substantial collection of jewels and her Persian cat. He stopped at Corfu, but was forbidden to land. Alice came down from Mon Repos to hear his far from reassuring stories. She gave Christo the letter to her mother about Andrea's detention.

On 22 November, the King discussed the matter with Sir Eyre Crowe, who cabled to Lindley that the King was 'most anxious concerning Prince Andrew'. He asked to be kept informed at all times and added: 'It seems difficult to believe that Greek government will show such criminal folly as to permit extreme measures. But can you make any suggestions as to way open to us, and to you personally, to influence Greek authorities to get the Prince released and allow him to leave the country.'*[17]

Andrea was due to be brought before the court martial at the end of November, a week after the trial of the ministers, who were described, worryingly, as the 'more guilty parties'. Frank Lindley still thought that exile was the most likely punishment and believed that the object of the trial was to show that revolution is no respecter of persons. Andrea would only be in danger if there was 'an upheaval'.[18]

* A copy of this telegram was passed on to Victoria.

Meanwhile the Foreign Office had received a note from a Mr H. G. Mayes, addressed to them from the Junior Naval and Military Club in London, which gave a succinct account of the trials that had been taking place since 13 November. He warned the Foreign Office that 'the packed court has . . . been given the dangerously elastic instruction to apply "the cannons of substantial justice"'.[19] His warnings should have been heeded, but, typically, the Foreign Office chose to ignore him on the grounds that the Prime Minister knew nothing about Mayes, other than that he was an organizer of the Olympic Games.

On 25 November the new government in Greece resigned and General Gonatas formed a government. The new Minister of War was General Pangalos, who was 'the most violent of all soldiers',[20] reminded Frank Lindley. Two days later the Ambassador was pleading for the lives of the imprisoned ministers. He failed.

On 28 November, the arrested ministers and army officers were taken in lorries to the plains at Goudi, below Mount Hymettus. Nikalaos Stratos, the former Minister of the Interior, helped out Dimitrios Gounaris, the former Prime Minister. 'Where are we going?' he asked. 'To the next world,' replied Gounaris, turning up his collar against the cold. Hatzianestis was the next to arrive. He was to be degraded from the post of general, but as they approached him, he tore off his own epaulettes. Holes had been dug for each man to fall into, and each was placed in front of the allotted hole. Stratos again helped Gounaris, positioning him before taking his own place. Five soldiers stood before each condemned man. All six refused the offer to have his eyes bandaged. Baltazzi wiped his monocle and put it on. The general stood to attention, and thus they met their deaths.[21]

News of the executions led to considerable discussion across Europe. In Paris it was reported that there was some regret 'that the chief culprits, namely Constantine and Princes Nicholas and Andrew, have escaped a similar fate'.[22]

Of the three, it was Andrea who remained in danger. On the day the ministers were shot, diplomatic relations between Britain and Greece were immediately severed. On the same day Alice arrived in Athens from Corfu to see what she could do. Frank Lindley sought assurances that the British would look after George II if necessary. A British man-of-war was finally sent to Athens.

Lindley was even more concerned about Andrea:

> There is no doubt that Prince Andrew's position has become much more dangerous since execution of Ministers and I hear his trial is to begin on November 30th. Mr G. Talbot,* who arrived this morning after execution is concentrating on saving Prince Andrew and I think he will have a better chance of succeeding than Legation now that rupture of diplomatic relations has taken place. We both agree that a show of force such as presence of man-of-war would do more harm than good. On my suggestion he is considering possibility of bribery.[23]

Following this, Lindley sailed away, leaving Charles Bentinck in Athens as Chargé d'Affaires.

Commander Gerald Talbot came to Athens from Lausanne. He was an intriguing figure in this drama. He was in Lausanne because Venizelos was the Greek delegate at the conference. Harold Nicolson had thought that someone should keep an eye on him and 'ascertain his views'.[24] Talbot was set to work.

Talbot had become a close friend of Venizelos in the winter of 1916–17 when he was there to oversee newspaper propaganda for the Foreign Office. In effect he was a Secret Service officer. Compton Mackenzie recalled seeing him seated at the Penhellenion, late at night, in earnest discussion with newspaper editors and was impressed by his 'great domed forehead'. He wrote:

> His was the kind of personality that completely defies translation to the printed page. I have alluded to the dome of his forehead. It was really enormous. Khubla Khan did not decree a statelier pleasure-dome in

* Commander Gerald Talbot, RNVR (1881–1945), Naval Attaché in Greece, later knighted.

Xanadu. This forehead was rendered more impressive by the majestic stolidity of the demeanour it crowned.[25]

In 1917 Talbot was appointed Naval Attaché in Athens, where he remained until October 1920. Venizelos attended his wedding to a rich French widow, Hélène Labouchere, in 1920. Thereafter Talbot and his new wife divided their time between Felix Hall in Essex and a flat in Paris.

In Lausanne Curzon had heard about the death sentences about to be imposed on the ministers. On 28 November he had told Venizelos that if he failed to use his influence to prevent the executions, he would be responsible for 'an abominable crime'.[26] Venizelos told him that he had already sent Talbot to Athens 'to urge counsels of moderation'.[27] By the time Talbot arrived in Athens, on 28 November, the ministers were dead, but it was not too late to devote his energy to rescuing Andrea.

The Prince was still under house arrest, living under close supervision in two rooms and convinced that he would be shot. In a later report, the *Daily Express* wrote of his plight: 'He is a brave man but his friends assert that not only did he anticipate death, but there was always the disagreeable feeling that for three weeks death might come suddenly, perhaps in his quarters.'[28]

On 29 November a 'most urgent' telegram from Bentinck to Sir Eyre Crowe showed more promising news. Talbot had obtained a promise from General Pangalos, the Minister of War, and Colonel Plastiras, another of the rebels, that Andrea would not be executed but would be allowed to leave the country in the care of Talbot. The plan was as follows:

Prince will be tried on Saturday and sentenced probably to penal servitude or possibly to death. Plastiras will then grant pardon and hand him over to Mr Talbot for immediate removal with Princess by British warship to Brindisi or to any other port en route to England. British warship must be at Phaleron by midday on Sunday, December 3rd and captain should report immediately to legation for orders, but in view of necessity for utmost secrecy, captain should be given no indication of reason for voyage.

This promise has been obtained with greatest difficulty and Talbot is convinced it is essential that above arrangement be strictly adhered to so as to save Prince's life. As success of plan depends upon absolute secrecy of existence of this arrangement, even Prince and Princess cannot be given hint of coming. Talbot is convinced that he can rely on word given him and I see no other possibility of saving Prince's life.[29]

By 1 December Talbot had extracted a promise that no more political prisoners would be shot, and thus the life of the senile Monsieur Kalegoropoulos was spared. Bentinck reported that Pangalos was keen to keep George II on the throne, and that General Papoulas (who had given evidence against Andrea) had been arrested.

HMS *Calypso* was then sent to Phaleron Bay and the battleship HMS *Malaya* was in the vicinity in case George II and Queen Elisabeth needed to be rescued. George V was kept informed of this. He telegraphed to King Constantine in Palermo that he would do all he could. That King's distraught daughter Helen wrote: 'But what can he do? The revolutionaries declare any foreign intervention will be fatal.'[30] George V also received a nervous telegram from his maternal aunt, Queen Olga, then in Paris and fearing the worst for her boy: 'Knowing your warm interest implore you to save him Aunt Olga.'[31]

On 3 December Andrea went for trial at the House of Parliament. In the courtroom Colonel Kalogeras accused him of refusing to advance against the enemy on 3 August 1921, despite the orders of the Commander-in-Chief, General Papoulas. Andrea replied that the orders were that the Third Army Corps were to defend, while the First and Second Army Corps attacked. He added that the Third Corps would notify the other two corps when the Turkish attack began. Colonel Sariyannis, the former Sub-Chief of Staff in Ionia, stated that had Papoulas's order been carried out successfully, the Sakharia battle would have been won.

Andrea was unanimously pronounced guilty of disobedience and abandoning his post in the face of the enemy. It was allowed that he lacked experience in commanding a large unit, and he was therefore 'degraded and condemned to perpetual banishment'[32] from Greece. While it is true that Andrea took the initiative not to pursue a futile course in battle, his trial was designed to make him a political scapegoat and to cover up the incompetence of the Greek generals and politicians.

Talbot obtained an interview with the Prime Minister and Colonel Plastiras. Charles Bentinck was present. They renewed pledges about the other ex-ministers, and promised that all civilians would be safe. They gave reassuring promises about the King 'whom they had placed on the throne and intended to keep there'.[33] Bentinck further reported: 'I consider the situation has undergone distinct change for better and I cannot speak too highly of the services rendered by Mr Talbot. He has saved Prince Andrew's life and arrested revolution in its insane course.'[34]

Alice and Andrea left Greece via Phaleron with Gerald Talbot, who would escort them on their journey to safety. The *Calypso* called at Corfu, where Alice hurriedly packed up a few belongings and gathered her family together. In an atmosphere of some tenseness, the four daughters and baby Philip left the house and boarded the vessel. The youngest member of the family was put to bed in an improvised cot made from an orange box. Without further delay they sailed away in the direction of Brindisi.

The accepted view of the rescue is that it was George V who rescued Andrea with the help of Talbot. In fact, the impetus came from Venizelos. Years later Andrea's daughter, Margarita, wrote: 'Mama always insisted it was a Secret Service man sent by Uncle George [George V] . . . Fancy he's being such a friend of Venizelos. Papa would have had a fit!!'[35]

17. 'Alice's Royalist Plots'

Alice and Andrea were fiercely aware that another period of exile stretched before them. They did not know for how long it would last or whether they would ever see Greece again. On the other hand, the political situation could have brought them back again as suddenly as they had left. In America a few months later, when Andrea was asked by the press if he intended to return to Greece, he replied without hesitation that he 'would not risk the chance of being executed'.[1]

As they sailed towards Brindisi, the family relaxed a little from the atmosphere of intense fear of recent weeks. But hardly had they escaped than new problems arose. The family party of seven with a further six servants arrived in Rome without passports to learn that, despite assurances, no provision had been made for them. They were penniless. It fell to the British Ambassador, Sir Ronald Graham, to advance funds and arrange travel to Paris. The French Embassy facilitated their entry into France, where they planned to spend only the night of Friday 8 December, proceeding to London the next day by the midday train. There was, in fact, a guarantee given by Talbot to the Greek government that he would take Andrea directly to London.

They counted without George V and Bonar Law, the British Prime Minister. George V had been concerned himself with Andrea's plight, but he was still nervous about foreign princes coming to Britain. A message from Downing Street did not help. The Prime Minister expressed the hope that the King would not encourage members of the Greek royal family to seek domicile in England, 'if it can possibly be avoided'.[2]

Alice and Andrea were again the victims of political manoeuvrings outside their control. In London, a question was asked in the House of Commons by Commander Kenworthy, a Labour

MP, as to why a British warship (as opposed to a Greek one) had been sent to rescue Prince and Princess Andrew.

The question was answered, but it alarmed the Foreign Office. Miles Lampson, Counsellor there, commented: 'In the circumstances, is it desirable that Prince Andrew should come here? I really don't see how we can stop him now – unless the Government prefer that, having saved him, he should go elsewhere – say to join the ex-King Constantine, who I believe, is still at Palermo.'[3]

Even before this, George V had sent a message to Victoria to say that it would be better if Andrea and Alice did not come to Britain at this time. Then Lord Stamfordham informed the King that the Prime Minister agreed that it was 'undesirable' for Andrea to come to England while Parliament was sitting, and that the Prime Minister had agreed, 'subject to Foreign Office concurrence, to send a message to Lord Hardinge to say that both the King and the Prime Minister think it would be prudent for the Prince not to arrive for the present'.[4]

Victoria 'rejoiced' that her daughter and family had been rescued, but was livid to hear that they were not welcome on British soil. She telegraphed Alice and Andrea on 4 December: 'I suggest, by desire, you break journey arriving here a fortnight hence.'[5] The 'by desire' was inserted to indicate that it was the King's wish not hers. When she spoke to Lord Stamfordham, she did not disguise her anger:

> Though I feel my tone was wrong and after the trouble you have taken to keep me informed of my son-in-law's fate, very ungrateful, yet I must adhere to the substance of what I said and decline to urge my daughter and her unfortunate family, who are penniless until they can make some arrangement with her bankers here, to try and lodge themselves in Paris after Prince Christopher has left. They have after all a certain pride and cannot ask Prince Christopher's wife to go on spending money on them.[6]

Victoria was convinced that rich Greeks in London were trying to alarm the government, and pointed out that when Kenworthy spoke he was not even supported by the 'other solitary Communist', and therefore 'I cannot feel in sympathy with the desire to keep Prince Andrew etc. away and consider it not my duty in assisting to do so.'[7]

On 8 December a telegram was sent to Lord Hardinge in Paris telling him that the Prime Minister agreed with the King 'in thinking it most undesirable' that Andrea should come to Britain and begging him to do all in his power 'to dissuade him from doing so'.[8] On the same day Lord Stamfordham informed Victoria that she might be underrating 'the disagreeable attitude of the Labour party and extreme politicians to our relations with the Greek Royal Family'. He continued:

The only time during the War that there were the least signs of antagonism to the King was when the Greek Princes came here and the present Government *would* no doubt be glad if the arrival of the Prince and Princess *could* have been delayed if only until after Parliament prorogues, I hope on the 14th.

The King's view is that through his personal action Prince Andrew's life has been saved – We have a telegram from Athens saying King George had sent his Marshal to our Minister to express to *our* King George his sincere thanks for all that had been done for himself and his family – and that if, in order to allay political susceptibilities, HRH's arrival here were delayed for a time, the consequent inconvenience should not be unduly estimated by them: especially as a somewhat deferred arrival would avoid any possible comment which might be painful to the Prince and Princess themselves.[9]

The machinations continued. Andrea, Alice and entourage arrived in Paris on 8 December and found themselves stuck there. Gerald Talbot was still with them and became concerned. He contacted Lord Hardinge at the British Embassy to ask for assistance with the party leaving for England the next day. Hardinge sent for him and questioned him. Talbot told him that they had received Lady Milford Haven's telegram but intended to disregard it, because he had 'promised the Revolutionary Party in Greece to take Prince Andrew to England, and therefore he had to fulfil his pledge, and as he stated, unless his pledge was fulfilled, other Greek personages might suffer capital punishment in Greece'.[10]

Hardinge rejected this and made it clear that his embassy would not give any visas without the approval of the Foreign Office.[11] Alarmed at being thwarted in the fulfilment of his pledge, Talbot went first to Lausanne to see Lord Curzon. The Foreign Secretary told him that he did not share his apprehensions and that all would be well if Prince Andrew came to England as rapidly as circumstances permitted. Talbot then went to London and saw Sir Eyre Crowe on 11 December. All these meetings were reassuring.

After a delay of six days, Alice and Andrea finally heard that the King had given permission for them to come to London on or after Sunday 17 December, Parliament having been prorogued two days before. It was arranged that the family's entry to Dover be facilitated at both passport and customs control in order to avoid publicity.

On the same day, Talbot was received at Buckingham Palace, where the King appointed him a KCVO and knighted him, an honour well deserved. Talbot was then sent by the King to see Victoria and Louise at Victoria's new apartments at Kensington Palace, where he told his tale. 'He must have enormous force of character & personality & it is entirely owing to him that Andrea got off with his life,'[12] reported Louise to Nona. Talbot told them that the problem had been that the head people were answerable to a mass oflower-grade officers, who were determined that Andrea be the scapegoat for King Constantine, who had eluded them.

Alice and Andrea arrived in London on Sunday 17 December, as secretly as possible, and moved into rooms at the Stafford Hotel. The King's private diary of 19 December records the following: 'Andrea came to see me, he has just arrived from Athens where he was tried and very nearly shot, his life was saved by Commdr. Gerald Talbot, RNVR.'[13] Unlike Talbot's visit to the King, Andrea's was not published in the Court Circular.

Despite the problem of getting into England, both Alice and Andrea credited their survival to the kindness of the King and were never less than grateful for what they perceived as his timely intervention. But the business had taken its toll on Alice. A while later, Louise went to inspect some de László sketches of her made in London at the time of Dickie's wedding. The contrast between the relaxed Alice in the sketches and the worn look on her sister's face at the end of 1922, less than six months later, gave Louise a shock. 'I am so glad they were done while Alice was still looking her very best last summer,' Louise wrote to Nona. 'At least now there will be something really like Alice to have for always.'[14]

It was never the intention of Alice and Andrea to settle permanently in Britain. Having won the battle to come to London they set off again. They left Margarita and Theodora with Victoria, and took the younger children to Paris, consigning them to the care of Andrea's sister-in-law, Princess George of Greece. She loaned them a small house on her land at St Cloud, 5 rue du Mont-Valérien, which was to be their permanent home for the next seven years, the entire time that the family lived in France together. Presently the two older children joined them there.

In January 1923 Alice and Andrea sailed from Cherbourg to the United States for a much-needed two-month holiday, as guests of Prince and Princess Christopher. On their sea voyage to New York aboard *Olympic*, Andrea received a cable with the news that King Constantine had died suddenly in Palermo from heart failure. The King had been living quietly at the Hotel Villa Igiea in Palermo since his exile from Greece the previous October and was just about to leave for Naples to settle in Florence. Though only fifty-four, he had suddenly become old, walking slowly about Palermo, with bent shoulders, leaning on his stick. 'Poor Father. He died of a broken heart,'[15] said his daughter Helen.

The American press were waiting for Andrea when he and Alice, and Prince and Princess Christopher, docked at Pier 59, North River, New York on 17 January 1923. Andrea paid tribute to King Constantine, suggesting that he had never recovered from his serious illnesses of 1915 and 1917. He went on to say that he believed the Greeks were now tired of fighting. He spoke at length of the Greek débâcle and his trial and rescue.

Unfortunately his remarks were picked up in the press and used against him. Later, after his return to Europe in the summer, the American Chargé d'Affaires in Athens accused him of making propaganda. Andrea protested, writing both to Bentinck in Athens and to Gerald Talbot. To his mother-in-law he wrote: 'My only crime in America was that to the question whether I had been imprisoned and narrowly escaped being shot, I answered in the affirmative. I don't think this is propaganda considering the whole world knew about it.'[16] Andrea suspected that certain Greeks might be stirring up trouble for an excuse to seize Mon Repos.

In New York, Alice and Andrea stayed at the Ambassador Hotel, accompanied by just one maid and a valet, a small entourage for those days. They took an automobile ride, ascended the Woolworth building for a rather cold view of the city and bought replicas of it for their children. Andrea told the press that he admired Broadway and the high buildings and thought the women's outfits were 'very neat indeed'. He was asked why he did not have a gentleman-in-waiting and replied with a laugh: 'I am a democrat.'[17]

Andrea and Christo walked over Brooklyn Bridge one Sunday afternoon and returned in a Fifth Avenue bus. Though recognized by a Greek, who saluted them on the bridge, they did not acknowledge him, preferring to remain incognito.

The Greek royal family were in mourning for six months. Memorial services were held for King Constantine, and Christo, Andrea and Alice even took the train to Montreal on a bitterly cold morning in February to attend one organized by the Greek community there. A crowded service took place, followed by a lavish luncheon at the Ritz Hotel, which they could not enjoy because of the profusion of speeches and presentations.

Back in the USA, they travelled to Washington and Palm Beach, staying at the Poinsiana Hotel in a group which included Lady Sarah Wilson, the former heroine of the Relief of Mafeking. The hotel was so large that the pages cycled along the corridors. The holiday was refreshing for Andrea and Alice, but not for Christo, since he was living with the secret that his wife Nancy had been dying of cancer for two years.* Nancy's illness meant that Alice and Andrea returned alone to Europe, sailing in *Aquitania* on 20 March, with Lady Sarah Wilson again a travelling companion.

Andrea and Alice returned to their new home at St Cloud. From now until the end of the 1920s, they would divide their time between this home on the outskirts of Paris and London, with occasional excursions elsewhere.

At St Cloud they lived in cramped conditions, with too many family and staff in too few rooms. They were not well off, but they were well looked after. Andrea's sister-in-law, Marie, was generous to them. Her son, Prince Peter, remembered: 'She put them up in a house of hers, next to our own, and paid all their expenses for years. It was definitely not "a struggle to make ends meet" because my mother never allowed it to be so.'[18] Yet Alice's daughter, Sophie, recalled: 'There were staff of different nationalities. One of the maids came in and said that a footman had attacked her with a knife. There were always problems paying the bills.'[19]

Alice continued to work on her Greek embroidery and helped in a charity shop called Hellas in the Faubourg St Honoré, selling Greek wares, tapestry, medallions and other items in aid of Greek refugees. Occasionally Prince Nicholas sent one of his paintings, and the establishment was widely recommended by those members of the family with a civic sense. This enterprise, recalled Prince Peter a little disparagingly, 'was only a side-show to mark from exile our continued connection with Greece'.[20]

In 1927, when stationed in Malta, Dickie issued his mother, Georgie and Alice with a copy of a restricted code so that they could communicate in secret on private matters. One such he cited as: 'Alice's Royalist plots & requests for funds.'[21]

It would be wrong to suggest that Alice was forever plotting in the political arena, but her interest in Greece found occasional outlets, not always constructively. In the way of exiles, she and

* Princess Christopher died in London on 29 August 1923.

Andrea spent the greater part of the 1920s monitoring the activities of that country from afar.

The death of King Constantine in January 1923 did little to lessen the bitterness of Greek factions.[22] It was soon clear that the Greek government would not rest until it had removed George II. Colonel Plastiras, leader of the Revolutionary Committee, became the vociferous scourge of the Greek royal family. In December 1923, he accused them of having created a gulf between the Greek people and the government, of preventing Greece from joining the Allies in 1915, and of causing the death of 80,000 men by violating the Treaty of Serbia and surrendering Fort Rupel to the Germans and Bulgars. And then there was the Asia Minor campaign. Plastiras declared that 'the forfeiture of the Crown by this Dynasty is a national necessity'.[23]

The Greek Cabinet decided that the King should leave Greece until a definite decision had been reached. George II thus departed for Romania on 19 December and, having departed, was unable to return. Following this, he would say that one of the requisites of a king of Greece was to have a Revelation suitcase packed and ready at all times.

With the departure of her nephew, Alice's hopes of returning to Corfu were dashed. On 18 February General Pangalos made a violent attack on the Greek royal family in a National Assembly debate. In particular, he attacked Andrea *in absentia*, declaring that his trial had proved his responsibility for the defeat of the Greeks at Sakharia. He said that the Prince should have been executed, but had been rescued by what he called a semi-official British envoy who had come to Greece with 'a sackful of promises, one of which was the payment of the unused credits'.[24]

The attack hardly helped the King's cause in the plebiscite on the monarchy that was held on 25 March. The Greeks voted for a republic. The new Constituent Assembly then authorized the 'forcible expropriation of the property belonging to all members of the deposed Dynasty',[25] igniting complicated negotiations concerning the fate of Mon Repos.

*

Since their precipitate departure from Mon Repos, when Alice had taken with her only what she needed for the journey, the villa had been empty, but for the butler, Mr Blower and his wife, Agnes, who served as caretakers. There were arguments as to who owned it, since the villa was originally presented to George I by the municipality of Corfu, though the King had then bought more land with his own money.

In January 1926, Sir Gerald Talbot was sent out to investigate and concluded that the house and furniture were safe. In May that year, Andrea leased it to Dickie for twenty-one years. Meanwhile George V said he would help if he could, but the British Foreign Office consistently refused to intervene.

Throughout the late 1920s, the political situation in Greece remained volatile and the threats to Mon Repos loomed and retreated accordingly. Pangalos had seized control of the government of Greece in April 1926, but by that August he had fallen, fulfilling Andrea's conviction that by having 'a free hand to play the dictator', he was 'likely to break his neck over the job'.[26] It was feared that his successor, General Kondylis, being 'a much stronger republican', was 'less likely to deal leniently with the property', nor would he be inclined to honour any undertakings given by Pangalos 'if it does not suit him to do so'.[27]

It seemed, however, that the elections of 7 November might lead to the return of the monarchy to Greece, in which case Alice and Andrea might be able to return to Greece. Alice and her mother waited anxiously at Kensington Palace for the results, methodically tackling the crossword puzzle in the *Sunday Chronicle* to steady their nerves. But the republicans won and Kondylis remained in power.

Another fracas between the Greek royal family in exile and the government occurred when on 18 June 1926, Andrea's mother, Queen Olga, died at Christo's home in Rome, Villa Anastasia. The various Greek governments that came and went with startling rapidity during those years were divided in their opinions of the Greek royal family, but on the subject of Queen Olga they were united – they held her in high esteem. The republican government therefore offered to pay for the funeral and to allow her return to

Greece for burial. The offer was declined in peremptory manner by the royal family, all of whom, including Alice and Andrea, gathered at the Orthodox church in Rome for the funeral on 22 June. Thus, even at this time of mourning, offence was caused on all sides.

Alice's most earnest involvement with Greek politics burgeoned into a bizarre idea that Andrea should become President of Greece. Before long, George V, various Cabinet ministers and the League of Nations were embroiled in the scheme.

In the summer of 1927 Alice went to a dinner party where she met the American banker, Norman Davis,* a man dedicated to encouraging American support of the League of Nations. Alice told him that the political situation in Greece was unstable, equally divided between royalists and republicans. Davis told her that the League of Nations was discussing the possibility of giving Greece a loan. He said that stability was essential if the bankers were to take up the loan and promoted the idea that Prince Andrew should be elected President. Alice talked to Andrea about it and adopted the presidential scheme with enthusiasm.

Alice asked Davis if she might mention the matter to Sir Eric Drummond at the League of Nations in Geneva. Davis agreed. So Alice suggested to Drummond that they meet secretly either in Geneva or Paris. Sir Eric thought that there were too many journalists in Geneva who would certainly recognize her. A meeting was arranged at 5 rue Washington in Paris at 11.00 a.m. on 1 July.

Alice told Sir Eric that Andrea would need the full consent of both parties to stand and that he would 'undertake to remain a loyal republican during his four years' term of office. After the four years there would be elections and people could then decide whether or not they wished for a monarchy or a republic; but during the four

* Norman Davis (1878–1944), banker and diplomat. He began life as a farmer in Tennessee. A lifelong democrat, he believed that international problems could invariably be settled by a business approach. In 1927 he was a delegate to the Geneva Economic Conference.

years Prince Andrew would not encourage any royalist movement.'[28]

Alice also said that the exiled George II would approve because of the loan, and that since a newspaper in Athens had mooted the idea, both political parties were canvassing the idea of adopting Prince Andrew. 'Therefore,' concluded Drummond, 'the situation was somewhat dangerous.'[29]

Drummond gave the standard reply that the League did not interfere in the internal affairs of another country, but Alice was undeterred, pointing out that Andrea's election would suit both the moderate republicans and the royalists. She said that the army officers were tired of army interference in politics and that Andrea would see that there was no political influence in the army. Sir Eric then told Alice that he could make no official comment on this. Alice quickly replied that she expected none, but wanted him to be fully informed of the situation.

The next day Alice made a hurried visit to London to see George V at Buckingham Palace. Her scheme horrified him and he told her that only if Andrea were unanimously invited by Greece to stand should he do so. By way of diverting her, he suggested she might go and see the British Ambassador in Paris, Lord Crewe.

On 4 July, back in Paris, Andrea and Alice called on Lord Crewe at the British Embassy. Alice told him of her conversation with the King and widened the suggestion to 'the possible nomination of Prince Andrew or one of his brothers as President of the Greek Republic'.[30] Lord Crewe reported back to Lord Stamfordham:

> I do not know how it may strike the King, but I see a certain attractiveness in the scheme, on the rather large assumption that a sufficient majority of the Greek people may be convinced that this regime offers the only hope of obtaining a large loan, and the equally large assumption that the bankers will be thereby induced to offer it on reasonable terms. I do not see how the British or French Governments can take any active part, except by encouraging the League of Nations to endorse the loan if the conditions admit of it.[31]

In September, after a holiday on the Lido in Venice, Alice and Andrea went to stay with the 'absurd'[32] Prince Theodore Ypsilanti, former Master of the Horse to the Greek royal family, at Gmunden, near Vienna. Alice told him about the Davis plan, adding that George V 'had approved of it'.[33] The former Greek Minister, Sp. Mercouris, a close wartime ally of King Constantine's, visited them there and told Andrea how unhappy he was with the situation in Greece, so Ypsilanti briefed Mercouris about the Davis plan, claiming that Davis had spoken to him, so as not to involve Alice or Andrea in anything resembling a plot against the exiled George II of Greece. Alice explained all this to Sir Eric Drummond:

I would beg you as a personal favour to be kind enough not to deny all knowledge of Prince Ypsilanti and his doings in a definite manner so as not to ruin his efforts of finding a peaceable solution for the present great difficulties in Greece. I will write a few lines to Norman Davis himself also to explain how matters stand. Strictly in confidence, I would like to add that the popular party are extremely dissatisfied with the present government in Athens, intending to accept all the conditions demanded by the League of Nations and have the intention of protesting against these conditions in the Chamber when it reopens on the 15th October. If they have Norman Davis's proposal in hand, they hope that the conditions will be less severe than the others and more acceptable to the Greek people at large, as well as having a hope of finding political stability for four years to come.[34]

Exasperated by Alice's persistence, Sir Eric replied with deferential politeness that neither the League of Nations nor he himself could take any action in the matter. He had listened before, and he could do no more now. He promised to keep the contents of her letter 'entirely secret', which was tantamount to saying he would ignore them. He concluded:

I ought perhaps, however, to add that Mr Norman Davis informed me of his conversation with Your Royal Highness. From his account, it would appear that the meaning of what he said must have been misunderstood. He did indeed (so he informs me) express the personal opinion that political stability was needed for the successful floating of a loan, but added that he could not believe that any intelligent or reputable bankers would attempt to interfere in such matters as the choice of a Government, and stated, further, that in his opinion, any such interference by outsiders would be unwise and harmful. If, however, as I understand, Your Royal Highness intends to write to Mr Norman Davis, he will doubtless in his reply make his position clear.[35]

Drummond did not entirely keep his word. He sent copies of the correspondence, in strict confidence, to Sir Austen Chamberlain. He in turn sent them to the King, calling his attention to Alice's misinterpretation of friendly advice as approval to her scheme. 'The Princess is evidently carried away by her hopes & reads her own thoughts into the guarded language of others,' wrote the Secretary of State. 'Sir Austen confesses that he thinks the project chimerical & the raising of the question in any form at the present time unwise.'[36]

The final word went to the King, who was yet more aghast that Alice was going to take her scheme to the League of Nations, a fact she had omitted to tell him. 'Ladies get carried away. At the present moment with Pangalos plots & intrigues going on,' observed the bearded monarch, 'I should think it would be most unwise for Prince A. to go near Greece.'[37] No doubt he told Andrea so, when he lunched at Buckingham Palace on 23 November.

18. Family Life

The circumstances of exile dictated that Alice should now depend on both her Greek family and her English one, the German relations falling somewhat into the background. These years of exile brought her more into contact with her mother again.

Since her widowhood, Victoria had lived permanently in her apartment on the north-west corner of Kensington Palace. Louise lived contentedly with her. Also living in the palace were her two surviving aunts, Princess Louise, Duchess of Argyll, and Princess Beatrice, over both of whose welfare Victoria maintained a caring vigil.

The mainstays of Victoria's life were her maid, Edith Pye, and Baroness Buxhoeveden, the former lady-in-waiting to the Tsarina. The Pye-Crust had been with her for years and was virtually a member of the family. Sophie (Isa) Buxhoeveden was a newer recruit to the team, having escaped execution in Russia and now settled at Albert Mansions, near the Albert Hall. She helped Victoria with her correspondence and later with her memoirs, which were written, though not published.

Isa Buxhoeveden had accompanied the Tsarina as far as Ekaterinburg and later wrote a good biography of her and also wrote her memoirs called *Left Behind*, which, with characteristic royal humour, the grandchildren referred to as 'Baroness Buxhoeveden's left behind'.[1] Her life was chaotic, and many are the anecdotes of her misadventures. In Belgium, on a tram, her floral hat had caught fire and a man then stamped on it. Arriving on board the imperial yacht, the companionway had dipped and soaked her red train in the sea. A sailor followed after her, mopping up the dye as it stained the deck. A boy once hit her on the leg with a cricket bat, and she endured disagreeable maladies, Victoria referring to Isa suffering from 'boils at the opening of her "sit-upon" '.[2]

Victoria's team was completed by the ever faithful Nona and Dick Crichton, now living in straitened circumstances. Victoria loved to visit them at Fishponds. It was, she wrote, 'the last real home I had, for without Louis I don't think any place will feel like home again.'[3] There the Crichtons kept chickens with varying success, and endured the hovering presence of Dick's fierce stepmother, Lady Emma Crichton, at nearby Netley Castle on the seafront.

When not coping with her extended family, Victoria was preoccupied with the drama of the possible survival of her niece Anastasia and a string of impostors claiming to be her. She dismissed the predominant one, Frau Tchaikovsky (later called Anna Anderson), because her ears did not match Anastasia's. These had impressed her, being 'the counterpart almost of those of my father's brother, Henry of Hesse, whose ears always drew our attention'.[4]

After her mother's death, Alice supported Dickie, Louise, Lu of Hesse and others in continued litigation against Anna Anderson, contributing funds to a court case as late as 1961. Eventually DNA testing proved that Anna Anderson could not have been the Grand Duchess.

During these years Alice frequently consigned her elder girls into the care of her mother, who sometimes sent them to parties with Louise, with whom they had remained friends, or with their new aunt Edwina, who generously passed on her clothes to them.* This was normal procedure within an extended family, and living in a small house at St Cloud they could not afford their own. As others took responsibility for them, so the seeds were sown for Margarita and Theodora to veer away from Alice and confide more in Louise.

Both girls were of an age when entry into society was their main concern. Alice encouraged this without doing a great deal to help them. From the social pages of the time, it is possible to assess their progress.

* Edwina ordered clothes with extra-large turnings and hems in order to pass them on to others of more generous build.

The highlight of their social life in May 1923 was a *thé dansant* given by Princess Troubetskoy, though the July dance given by Mr and Mrs Cornelius Vanderbilt at Brook House, attended by the Prince of Wales, the Duke of York and his new Duchess, was spectacular. Alice then came specially to England to take them to the King's garden party at Buckingham Palace in July.

A memorable occasion, long remembered, was Queen Alexandra's birthday party for Princess Victoria, also in July 1923. The beautiful old Queen habitually entertained the children of Princess Victoria's married friends on her daughter's birthday each year, a rather heartless reminder of her unmarried state. Approaching eighty, enamelled and bird-like, Queen Alexandra was showing signs of being confused. Dressed that afternoon in sequins, she saw Alice and Andrea, and asked who Alice was. When told, she began to laugh. 'Andrea says he's married to this woman!' – forgetting that twenty years before she had attended their wedding.[5]

Alice was forever hopeful that Margarita and Theodora would find themselves suitable husbands. Thus Margarita and Theodora spent much of the autumn of 1923 at Kensington Palace. They passed Christmas at Holkham with the Leicesters, and saw in the new year of 1924 at Sandringham. Once a week their other grandmother, Queen Olga, spent the evening with them.

In January 1924 they attended the state opening of Parliament and Victoria chaperoned them to a number of charity balls, taking their youthful enthusiasm in her stride. The girls were evidently 'happy & contented'.[6]

The summer season of 1924 provided more glamorous social activity than the previous year. In May Alice and Andrea took Margarita to a dance given by Lord Iveagh for his granddaughter, Aileen Guinness. Similar parties punctuated the month of June. Alice took Margarita to the Gold Cup at Ascot, in the royal party. In July she took Margarita and Theodora to the Prince of Wales's thirtieth birthday party at Spencer House, then rented by Mrs Cornelius Vanderbilt. That quirky American invention, the cocktail bar, was a noted feature of the evening.

The family attended a view of de László's work at the French

Gallery in Pall Mall on 25 June. The following week Alice took the girls to Lady Beauchamp's ball for the coming-out of Lord Emley at Grosvenor House. In July they attended the Buckingham Palace garden party, Alice 'in white crêpe marocain and georgette, with a small white hat',[7] and the Eton and Harrow cricket match in oppressive heat. At the end of July Margarita (in a scarlet hat) and Theodora (in a green one) were thrilled to see George V's horse, *London Cry*, win the Goodwood Stakes.

At the end of the season the girls had certainly had more sophisticated fun than they could have hoped for in Athens, though for neither of them was the season capped by a proposal of marriage. The truth was that exiled Greek princesses with no fortunes of their own were not deemed good catches in London society. This did not stop Alice from conspiring, however.

In the 1925 season, the girls were scarcely noticed at all in the social pages. Only when they accompanied Edwina to the Grosvenor House Bazaar did they earn the sobriquet of 'those pretty young princesses'.[8]

In February 1927 it began to look as though Margarita had found a husband. She had met Prince Franz Ferdinand, the 25-year-old heir to the Isembourg-Birstein family, on her visit to Uncle Ernie at Tarasp the previous summer. Both she and Theodora had liked him very much. They liked Birstein itself, a small town north-west of Frankfurt. They liked the family and the way the young man got on with his parents, and his approach to both the property and the people of Birstein. Alice met him and was 'delighted with him'.[9]

Religion was a problem, the Isembourg-Birsteins being Roman Catholics, though only for five generations. Margarita made it clear that she would not change her religion. At this time the young man was waiting to get to know Margarita better before proposing. 'I must say I feel really pleased for Margarita from all I have heard,' wrote Louise. 'So I hope the engagement will come off when next they meet.'[10] Meanwhile, according to Louise, Theodora had indulged in 'a violent flirtation with the old Furst which must have been very funny'. She added cryptically: 'Repetition of Alice in the old days.'[11]

Nothing came of the Isembourg-Birstein romance,* due to 'mutual disagreement',[12] and by the end of the decade, neither Margarita nor Theodora were any nearer finding a husband.

In June 1923 Alice was thrilled to hear that Louise was to marry. She wrote to Dickie: 'What a relief & a happiness to know she will marry such, such a nice person, who is everything she deserves to have for such a wonderful, unselfish, sweet nature as hers. How happy poor Papa would have been.'[13]

Louise's engagement took everyone by surprise, not least Louise herself. Ever since her traumatic engagement to Stuart-Hill, she had resigned herself to staying at home. Indeed, she enjoyed the role of being maiden aunt to Margarita and Theodora, aware that she was expected to seek out husbands for them. Suddenly, to her intense surprise, she found herself the object of romantic attention. She panicked.

Louise confided only in her mother, Alice and her brothers. As ever it is her version to Nona that has survived: 'I am a very agitated, fussed & worried woman,' she began before pouring out her heart:

> You know that Gustaf of Sweden is over here. I met him to talk to for the 1st time three weeks ago. Before that I had only met him just to shake hands with, the various times he has been over here. I thought him awfully nice & we got on rather well together. He came to see us a few times, tea time as he had nothing much to do. Then last Sunday he took Mama & me for a drive to Hampton Court, it suddenly dawned on me that naturally everybody hoped he would marry again & that I was a suitable person. I saw that he liked me & was taking a lot of trouble to get to know me. You can imagine my agitation & worry not knowing what to do or think.[14]

Louise expressed her concerns about her own age, thirty-four, the need to marry before getting too old, the fear of uprooting

* Prince Franz Ferdinand (1901–56). Married 1939, Irina von Tolstoy (1917–98).

herself from her country, his position – 'my one nightmare is anything to do with a court' – and Gustaf being a widower with a large family. 'Of course,' she wrote, 'I would love to have the companionship of a husband & children of my own but one must care for the man sufficiently.'[15]

Louise had found a rare man. The Crown Prince of Sweden was born in 1882 and had married Princess Margaret, daughter of the Duke of Connaught, in 1905. They had four sons and a daughter, but in May 1920 the Crown Princess had died.

The Crown Prince was by nature a scholar. As a young man he had been given a Chinese pot which had inspired a love of Chinese artefacts. All his knowledge was acquired from books and he became a considerable expert long before he visited China. He was a dedicated archaeologist and a firm friend of the art connoisseur, Bernard Berenson, who described him as 'a work of art in himself'.[16] He was a good cook and he drank no alcohol, aware that the Swedes were inclined to drink too much. He had an enviable zest for life, and enjoyed everything he did, be it attending a parade, giving a banquet, digging a hole or discovering a new picture. Unlike Louise, who had picked up some raw language in her nursing days, Gustaf never swore. Once, at Broadlands some years later, he nudged an electric fence. All he said was 'Bother.'[17]

Victoria encouraged Gustaf to court Louise discreetly, believing that marriage to the lonely widower would be good for her, given 'her diffident nature & mistrust of her capacities'.[18] Louise saw some irony in her situation.

It has all burst on me like a bomb. I think of myself a fortnight ago & now & really wonder where I am. Everything has its funny side. There am I who thought my great interest & occupation was looking after M. & D. & trying to get them married & now they are as keen as anything to do the same thing for me. They have been so sweet & discreet about it.[19]

When she made up her mind ten days later, she relaxed, writing to Dickie: 'Well, Dickie, I have accepted Gustaf. I am sure you will be delighted. I must say it is rather marvellous.'[20] Thereafter, new problems arose: Gustaf breaking the news to his children, and in particular to his daughter, Ingrid, who held her mother's memory sacred, seeking approval from George V, and in due course, overcoming complicated negotiations of protocol as to whether or not Louise was a member of the British royal family and thus able to marry Gustaf without him surrendering his rights to the throne of Sweden.

Alice thought the couple should have the chance to get to know each other better and thus invited them to join her family for their summer holiday. Most places were booked, but they found rooms at Arcachon in the Gironde. Louise found Alice and Andrea 'in good spirits', and less isolated than in Switzerland. She also observed Philip, now two, reporting to Nona: 'Philip is quite too adorable for words, a perfect pet, so grown up & speaks quite a lot & uses grand phrases. He is the sturdiest little boy I have ever seen & I can't say that he is spoilt.'[21]

Gustaf arrived with his children. Louise became devoted to Bertil with his passion for motor cars and aeroplanes, but remained shy of Ingrid, who was 'terribly upset & *unhappy* poor little thing'.[22]

Louise married Gustaf at the Chapel Royal in London on 3 November 1923 with Alice's daughters as bridesmaids. She then settled in Sweden, where the Swedish people were pleasantly surprised when they saw her in the flesh. The British Ambassador reported: 'On all sides one hears flattering remarks about her refined and noble bearing, her gentle manners and sweet expression, which much exceed the most optimistic expectations formed by the public from inferior photographs published in the Swedish press.'[23]

Louise was to face one tragedy early in her married life. In 1925 she became pregnant. She hoped to give birth to the baby at Ulricksdal Slot, a 1640 Renaissance palace close to Stockholm, which Louise and Gustaf decorated themselves. But the child, a girl, was stillborn on 30 May, not sufficiently developed to live, because Louise's placenta had shrivelled. Unselfish as ever, she confided to Nona: 'If possible I appreciate all the more now what it is to have Gustaf & now how lucky I am to have him. He has my love now more than ever, all that I had for my baby I feel I have now also given him.'[24] They had no further children.

During the 1920s, a great many of the older members of the family died: Alice's aunt, Marie Erbach, and Christo's wife, Nancy, in the summer of 1923, and her last Battenberg uncle, Franzjos, in 1924. The death of Franzjos highlights the generosity of Dickie's wife, Edwina, who, though she never met him, had been sending him an allowance and continued to send money to his widow Anna until her own death in 1960.

Edwina also gave thought to Philip. In the summer of 1924 she took out an insurance policy for her three-year-old nephew. 'It was too dear of you & Edwina to think of it,' Alice wrote to Dickie, '& I can't find words to thank you for your extreme generosity. Such a possibility never entered my head & makes the pleasure all the greater.'[25]

On 20 November 1925, Andrea's aunt, Queen Alexandra, died at Sandringham, having already ordered her Christmas card for 1925. When she began to sink, Alice warned Dickie: 'Minny has telegraphed to Aunt Beatrice from Sandringham that Aunt Alix was conscious but not expected to live through the night.'[26] Alice, Andrea and Victoria played a full part in the funeral.

On Sunday 29 November Victoria and Alice dined at Buckingham Palace with the King and Queen. The King naturally minded that his beautiful mother had passed away, but at dinner Alice made him laugh. She told him that a Swedish official had made a great business of showing Louise some important Swedish jewels. This had involved conducting her into a great vault, with the unlocking of many heavy doors. Once within the inner sanctum the custodian locked the door and announced grandly: 'And now I am going to open my drawers and show you my treasure!'

This became one of George V's favourite stories. That evening Queen Mary heard the great laughter and asked what it was about. Likewise, that severe consort saw the funny side, and, on hearing the punchline, enquired: 'And did he?'[27]

*

Alice and Andrea spent most of their time at St Cloud, and Cécile, Sophie and Philip were there with them. There is no evidence as to how much Andrea had been affected by the Greek débâcle, but though he professed to wish to return to Greece, in essence he slipped into a life of relative idleness.

When at St Cloud, Andrea took his youngsters for expeditions into Paris in his motor, or for walks around the Bois de Boulogne. They played tennis on the court between their little house and Big George's villa. Big George and Marie gave a family lunch party at St Cloud every Sunday. Otherwise, Marie spent much of her time living in Paris with her father, pursuing her career as a psychoanalyst, while Big George lived next door quietly. Big George had a town house in Paris in the rue Adolph Yvan, and frequently visited his Uncle Valdemar in Denmark.

Other members of the Greek royal family, such as Nicholas and Ellen, were living at St Cloud with their daughters, and close neighbours of Alice and Andrea were his cousin, Meg Bourbon,* and her family.

There is no evidence of any disharmony between Alice and Andrea, who were more often together than not. Sometimes Alice travelled to England alone, and in the summer of 1924, the children were all sent to the seaside, while she stayed at St Cloud, laid up with a treatment for varicose veins, which kept her in bed for four weeks. 'I feel very shaky,' she told Dickie, 'but I think they will be permanently cured.'[28]

The same summer, Andrea went alone to Florence with Christo to a family gathering which included Queen Sophie, her daughter Katherine, and George II and his wife, Elisabeth.

Two years later, in the summer of 1926, Alice and Andrea took a summer holiday in Cannes, while Cécile, Sophie and Philip were sent to England, the two girls to Kensington Palace with Virginie

*Princess Margrethe of Denmark (1895–1992), married Prince René of Bourbon-Parma (1894–1962). Their two children were Jacques (1922–64) and Anne (b. 1923), who married King Michael of Romania. There was a baby, Michel, born that year.

Simopoulos,* and Philip to Adsdean† with his nanny, Emily Roose.

The family's attitude to the five-year-old is well demonstrated in a letter from Victoria to Nona: 'Philip goes to Adsdean where they can keep him till autumn if desired, only for Goodwood week his room will be needed for guests, so if you still would like & could have him & Roose, that would be the time for his visit to you.'[29] Philip was sent to Fishponds, which he enjoyed, describing Nona to his grandmother as 'Mrs Good' and explaining the nickname – 'because she is good & that is the right name'.[30]

The prospect of the Greek royal family returning to Greece became no more likely. Family life continued in its set mould. And no doubt the lives of Alice and her family would have drifted on in much the same way, had she not begun to manifest signs of collapse in health and spirit.

* Virginie Simopoulos, Alice's lady-in-waiting 1913–55.

† The home of Dickie and Edwina Mountbatten, near Chichester.

19. Descent into Crisis

Alice still felt deep suffering over the loss of her two aunts in Russia, and wished to emulate her aunt's example and to found her own sisterhood. Only recently, Andrea himself had nearly lost his life. Exile in Paris was neither stimulating nor directed, and despite the financial help given by Marie and Edwina, the circumstances of bringing up a family of five were never easy. Andrea still took a distant interest in what was happening in Greece, without intriguing in any way, but beyond that, he veered towards an easier existence. Alice and Andrea were still on good terms, but it is hard to assess how good. As a result of all these things, Alice's interests again became more spiritual.

Previously sealed medical reports reveal that in 1925 Alice fell in love with a married Englishman. We do not know who he was.* But her lady-in-waiting, Virginie Simopoulos, later told Alice's doctor at Kreuzlingen that Alice had fallen in love, and pursued the possibility with great energy, but that it had not been an actual affair and finally she had given up, realizing there was no future in it. In one of her more distant moods she had written to him that they would 'meet again in another world'.[1]

Everything in Alice's background was strictly conventional. She herself had high moral principles and nothing in her character was flighty or flippant. She was no Edwina Mountbatten or Nada Milford Haven. The fact of falling in love and resisting temptation almost certainly needed an outlet of some kind. Without even knowing why, Alice turned towards religion as a safe outlet for these repressed feelings.

Alice veered towards a more spiritual life quietly, and at first

* There is no mention of him in any of the family letters, either at this time or later. He is mentioned only in the medical report.

imperceptibly. In the spring of 1926, she paid a visit to Darmstadt. Her reading of the Schuré book drew her to the philosophical work being overseen by her Uncle Ernie in the years following the First World War.

She became a student of the works of the Baltic philosopher, Hermann von Keyserling, who had founded the School of Wisdom and Thought in Darmstadt in 1920, under the 'particular and unusual personality' of Ernie, as Keyserling described him, 'whose magnanimous initiative made possible the material founding of the school'.[2] In 1921 the Indian philosopher Rabindranath Tagore had joined them for a symposium. The president of the school was Ernie's Hofmarschall, Count Kuno von Hardenberg, who was later to play an important part in Alice's life.

Keyserling is not well remembered these days, but in his time he was a great traveller and described his world voyage of 1911 in his book, *The Travel Diary of a Philosopher*. In Darmstadt his ambitions were high – to regenerate mankind on the new basis created by the war, and to head a large movement of spiritual renewal. Though always described as a philosopher, Keyserling defined his role at Darmstadt rather differently.[3] He explained:

> The School of Wisdom should much rather be called a strategic headquarters than a centre of study; it is exactly for this reason that it evokes so much enmity. It undertakes, by means of the proper psychological methods, to in-build the impulse of life-renewal on the basis of the spirit, which I stand for, into the broad body of historical reality. But primarily I feel myself to be, in sharp contradiction to the man of the *Travel Diary*, a statesman and field-marshal. Aiming at sense-realization, I must be a *Realpolitiker* before all; my purpose being to thrust the world one stage farther ahead, my first thought must be to set things in motion.[4]

Still an earnest traveller, Keyserling concluded that Darmstadt did not represent a fixed programme for him, but it was 'nothing more or less than the living centre of a new manner of life which issues from the spirit'.[5] All this appealed enormously to Alice, who studied Keyserling's methods privately without ever imposing her thoughts on friends or family.

Towards the end of June 1928, Alice arrived in London to stay with her mother and to launch Cécile, now seventeen, into English society. Early in July Alice took Cécile to the Countess of Ellesmere's ball at Bridgewater House* and at the beginning of August, they spent the weekend with Dickie and Edwina at Adsdean. They went to Cowes for the Regatta, watching the great yachts race past the house where they were staying, and then they went to Holkham. Later Cécile went to Scotland and spent some time at Balmoral '& got spoilt by the King & Queen',[6] as Alice put it.

Andrea was not part of this London season, but he and Alice took a motor trip together, returning to St Cloud on 8 September. Alice then went to Ulriksdal to stay with Louise, who had been unwell earlier in the year.† The rest of the family were farmed out elsewhere. Margarita, Theodora and Philip went to Sinaia in the Carpathians to stay with Queen Helen. Andrea elected to go off by himself, evidently in need of a break from family life. He went to Marienbad for a cure and came back feeling 'at least ten years younger',[7] Louise said.

Alice and Andrea were due to celebrate their silver wedding in October. In advance of this, the family put their heads together and elected to pay for sketches of the heads of Margarita and Theodora by de László, already commissioned by Alice at a special price.

Alice's family were back at St Cloud at the beginning of October in time for the celebrations. Emily Roose, Philip's nanny, was still away, and so Alice slept with Philip in his nursery. 'Philip is always very good with me,'[8] she wrote to another of his carers. She prepared to knit him some woollen jerseys.

The silver wedding was celebrated at St Cloud on Wednesday 3 October. A group photograph of the family was taken in the garden in beautiful autumn weather. A few days later there was a dinner

* This party became notorious when Lady Ellesmere evicted some gatecrashers.
† Louise had undergone an operation for the removal of a lump in her left breast.

for seventeen guests at 5 rue de Mont Valérien. The dining room only seated ten, so the others were fed in the drawing room. Andrea's ADC, Menelaos Metaxas, came specially from Athens with his wife, and Georgina von Rotsmann, Onor's lady-in-waiting, sent a cushion from Wolfsgarten.

When it was all over, Alice wrote to Dickie to thank him for remembering the anniversary and for his share of the de Lászlós. 'I can't tell you what pleasure your joint gift of pictures of the girls has given Andrea & me. Dolla's is ready & perfectly charming & Margarita is being done this week, as László delayed his arrival here . . . My thoughts are often with you. I feel sure everything will be alright.'[9]

With hindsight, it appears that the silver wedding was something of a goal that Alice needed to attain, after which she let go of certain reins and descended sharply into crisis. It is certainly true that after that occasion Alice and Andrea were never happy together.

On 20 October, just a fortnight after the wedding anniversary, Alice was quietly received into the Greek Orthodox church. Her change in religion may have triggered her illness, or maybe her illness triggered her need to adopt the faith.

Either way, this was not a step lightly taken. Alice risked causing disharmony in the family, as had happened when Ella took the same step in 1891.* Victoria felt the need to explain it carefully to Alice's brothers. She wrote to Georgie:

Alice, when she was with me this summer, told me that she had long considered joining the church to which her husband & children belong, & whose services she has attended for so many years. On the 20th she has definitely taken the step & was received into the Orthodox church, privately in the little private chapel at St Cloud. I think it will be a help & comfort to her, & you know I have always thought that everyone

*Ella's father, the Grand Duke, had written to her: 'Your news grieved me deeply . . . My God, what can one say!. . . It torments me to such an extent.' [Louis IV to Ella, 14 January 1891, quoted in Lubov Millar, *Grand Duchess Elizabeth of Russia* (NOPS, California, 1991), pp. 59–60.]

should be free to believe as much or as little as they wish & if there is a church that they wish to join, they should do so, as long as they justify it to their own conscience. As Alice wishes her change should not be talked about all over the place, I only inform you, her brothers & sister about it.[10]

When he heard the news at the same time, Dickie responded to his mother's letter from Malta: 'Georgie & I feel identically about religion as far as Alice is concerned and would willingly see her adopt the Shinto religion if she felt that way.'[11]

Nobody noticed anything strange in Alice's change in religion. Far from becoming in any way ascetic, Alice became more worldly than ever before, attaching more importance to material things, such as clothes and jewellery.

During the winter of 1928–9 Alice was occupied with another project, which both exhausted her and sharpened her memory of the biggest crisis in Andrea's life. She translated the book that he had written about the Asia Minor campaign from Greek into English. It was a labour of love. While the book contains passages that are stylishly written, much of it is an apologia, supported by copies of letters exchanged. Another feature is the relentless movement of one division here, one there, limiting the book's interest to those with a penchant for detailed analysis of battles.

To achieve a professional translation, Alice worked for three consecutive hours every day for four months, and her lady-in-waiting, Virginie Simopoulos, wondered if the work had not created too much of a strain for her. The book, *Towards Disaster*, was submitted to John Murray for publication. About a thousand copies were published in 1930, and it was not deemed a success as a publishing venture.*

* Now it is a collector's piece of some rarity. Some authors take the view that it should never have been written; others (Basil Boothroyd for example) have commended its literary style, while noting: 'It contained absolutely no jokes' [Basil Boothroyd, *Philip* (Longman, 1971), p.70]. There are some nicely turned descriptions of disliked Greeks.

Alice returned from a two-week visit to her mother with Andrea, in May 1929, having bought a great number of philosophical and mystical books in London. Only then did the deterioration in her state of health begin to cause concern. She became intensely mystical and would lie on the floor in order that she could develop 'the power conveyed to her from above'.[12] She believed that she had developed the power to heal in her hands and she used this effectively on the rheumatism of the children's nanny, which encouraged this belief. By June she was claiming that she could stop her thoughts like a Buddhist.

In the summer of 1929, most of the family departed in different directions, though Alice stayed in Paris with Margarita and Sophie. Dickie noticed nothing untoward in her state of health when he and Edwina lunched with her on Saturday 30 June.

Andrea was again away and did not reappear until September. Alice spent part of her holiday at Wolfsgarten, taking Nona and Dick Crichton with her. It was a depressing summer, not helped by a visit to their former home, the Heiligenberg, which they found in a dilapidated state. The reassuring presence of Nona suggests that Victoria may have felt that Alice needed sympathetic protection. At Wolfsgarten, Alice talked to Nona a great deal about the healing power in her hands and how she had received divine messages about potential husbands for her girls. Nona passed this disturbing news to Louise. That letter does not survive,* but Louise's reply to Nona does:

It is rather worrying & upsetting what you write about Alice. One can only hope that this phase will pass quickly. Alice always had had a tendence [*sic*] for the supernatural . . .

I do wish she would take up Christian Science, which she has been

* In the 1950s Louise consigned most of her family papers to Dickie at Broadlands. Before doing so, she asked his advice and he suggested that any papers that hinted that Alice's illness was in any sense mental should be destroyed. Louise tore up some letters written to her by Andrea, and certain other papers. On the other hand, Dickie filed much about Alice's illness in his archives, notably in the papers of Nona Crichton, with no evidence of any censoring.

interested in, that is [a] much more balanced thing to believe in. There she can use her newly discovered gift of healing without doing harm. I wish to goodness Alice would not have these mad presentiments about the girls' marriages.[13]

Louise, who had recently suggested to Alice the Crown Prince of Denmark as a possible suitor for Cécile, now began to regret her attempts at matchmaking.

In September Alice applied to work in a small clinic, employing her hand-healing. She continued to train herself in hand-healing as best she could and in the process became strained by overwork.

In October she wrote to her mother about her philosophical studies and told her that she would soon be in a position to communicate her findings to the world. She said that many would not believe her, but she was sure that she could help some people.

By November her mental state was giving such cause for anxiety that Andrea appealed to Victoria for help. He said that Alice was not attending to any of the normal domestic duties in the house, nor would she talk to her family. In the middle of December Alice herself admitted that she was in bad health. She wrote to Louise to say that she was 'so run down & had been much worse with the flu in her head than the others had guessed'.[14] She left for an hotel in Grasse with a maid in order to have a complete rest. She arranged Christmas for Andrea and the children before her departure and then stayed away. She suffered strong headaches, felt miserable and exhausted, and talked and laughed a great deal. Christmas Day itself was a particularly low point. Alice lay in a hot bath for hours on end and ate almost nothing.

Then on a sudden whim Alice returned to St Cloud. Though still tending to be uncommunicative, she announced that she was 'a saint'[15] to Meg Bourbon, Andrea's cousin. She lay on her *chaise-longue* in a state of ecstasy, talked darkly of evil influences in the house and tried to banish these by carrying a sacred object with her. She wrote to her English friend, telling him that she could not marry him as she was now 'the bride of Christ'.[16] And her presence in the home became disturbing when she called the priest and arrived downstairs in a confused state, announcing that she was 'having dinner with Jesus Christ'.[17]

As the crisis in Alice's health developed, the family became yet more anxious and both Andrea and Margarita wrote to Victoria, asking her to come over. As ever, Victoria proved a stalwart help, arriving in St Cloud early in January 1930. She confided her concerns to Nona, telling her that she might need her help and would not hesitate to ask for it:

I think it was very necessary I came. The whole family are frightfully worried & with reason alas! My poor Alice is in a quite abnormal state mentally & bodily. She looks frail & exhausted. She received me with a sweet smile & showed me my room, but hardly spoke & was so tired that she retired to bed. She was a little better this morning & actually came into the garden where I was with Margarita before lunch & assisted at lunch – hers consisting of a couple of mouthfuls of vegetables & an orange. I talked a little after lunch alone with her. She tried to be interested in what I said, but was reserved about her religious experiences. Nobody knows why she came back, but she is inspired, she thinks, in all her actions. She has visions of Christ & has told Meg Bourbon, with whom she actually has had a conversation, that in a few weeks time she will have a message to deliver to the world. She wanders praying about the house at times. She told Meg she was in bliss & to me too she said she is happy. I think she has anaemia of the brain from too much contemplation & starvation & is in a critical state.[18]

Louise was relieved to hear that her mother was with Alice, hoping that now she would 'pick up her bodily health quicker than perhaps she thinks & then she will get her mental balance again'.[19] Victoria and Andrea went to see the doctor in whose small clinic Alice had been working as a hand-healer. He was unable to help, having not seen much of her, but he recommended Dr Chignon, a 'mental specialist',[20] who was also a deeply religious man, to advise them. Andrea wanted his mother-in-law to take Alice back to London with her, but Alice said she was content to be where she was. Equally, she was content for her mother to remain a while longer.

On 11 January 1930, Victoria wrote to Nona:

> Poor Alice seemed better for a couple of days & actually wrote & addressed a few cards of thanks for New Year greetings, but she spent yesterday again in bed, apparently absorbed in contemplation etc. Andrea returns this afternoon. It is hard to see one one loves so altered physically & mentally & to be powerless to help . . . My comfort is that she seems contented, often even happy, & does not in the least realize what we think & feel about her.[21]

Anxious for further advice, Andrea and Victoria summoned Alice's gynaecologist, Dr Louros, to come to Paris from Athens. When he arrived, she told him that Christ was always with her and that Christ had to be consulted about whatever the doctor advised. Dr Louros diagnosed Alice's psychosis immediately, but she would not take his advice or do as he requested.

Help then came from Alice's sister-in-law, Marie (Princess George of Greece), by this time a distinguished psychoanalyst in her own right.[22] She recommended that Alice should go for psychoanalysis to the clinic of Dr Ernst Simmel at Tegel, just outside Berlin. Dr Louros told Alice that Christ advised this. Alice consented and in February 1930 Dr Louros took her to Berlin. She was admitted to Simmel's clinic.

20. Tegel and Kreuzlingen, 1930

Anyone who has ever read a medical report will know that every move the patient makes and every observation of doctor or nurse is faithfully recorded. This stage of Alice's story subjects her to the harsh light of examination in close detail, going further than the observations of her mother and others that have survived the years.

Psychoanalysis was developing at speed at that time, yet the general approach to mental ill-health was hardly enlightened. Every generation has its 'fashionable' illness, and the religious crisis, with its undercurrent of mysticism, was prevalent at that time. R. D. Laing, writing from the stance of the anti-psychiatrist, argued that doctors invented descriptions of illnesses which did not in themselves exist. Just as manic depression is better understood and treated differently today, so Alice's particular crisis might have been approached very differently sixty years later. However, despite all the tests and examinations, the theories and conclusions, it is impossible not to believe that when a breakdown was suffered in a family of Alice's social standing, the prime concern of doctors and family was to take the patient to a safe place, keep him or her well looked after, and to make sure that whatever the patient did was done neither in public nor in the drawing room at home.

Alice's brief stay at Tegel was no more than a staging-post. She was placed in the care of Dr Ernst Simmel.* He was a psychoanalyst and one of Sigmund Freud's early co-workers. Born at Breslau in 1882, he had published a book called *War Neurosis in Psychic Trauma* in 1918, and then various essays on psychiatry, concerning addictions, organic disease and applied psychoanalysis. Simmel opened

* Dr Ernst Simmel (1882–1947). He was forced to leave Germany in 1934, being Jewish. He settled in Los Angeles, where he established a medical centre to train psychiatrists in psychoanalysis.

his clinic, the first ever psychoanalytic sanatorium, in 1927, about half an hour's drive north-west from Berlin. Sigmund Freud, a frequent visitor, described it as 'beautiful and quiet, situated in a park a few minutes from Lake Tegel'.[1]

Alice began by welcoming the psychoanalysis imposed upon her, having always taken an intelligent approach to the working of the mind. She felt liberated to talk about matters such as sexual love, which greatly shocked Andrea when she addressed him on the topic. There followed a number of medical tests. Her gynaecologist from Athens, Dr Louros, examined her again, gave a positive report, and thus concluded that contrary to what many may have supposed, the illness was not caused by menopause.

After several discussions with Alice and further examinations, Dr Simmel diagnosed Alice as 'paranoid schizophrenic'. In the centre of her fantasy was Christ. She believed herself to be the only woman on earth and to be married to Christ.* She was 'physically' involved not only with Christ, but through him with the other great religious leaders such as Buddha. She felt that she should be the link between these various gods and people on earth. When admitted to the clinic, she was very low physically because she had been fasting for several weeks. Dr Simmel talked to her, establishing a good rapport, and he liked her. He was able to persuade her logically that 'her inner experiences seemed abnormal to the outside world, and that therefore she had to be reserved as far as communicating about these'.[2]

Simmel believed that Alice was suffering from a 'neurotic-pre-psychotic libidinous condition', and he consulted his old friend Sigmund Freud about it. This condition was not menopausal, but the doctors were told that her marriage to Andrea was now one of companionship. Freud advised 'an exposure of the gonads to X-rays, in order to accelerate the menopause',[3] presumably with the intention that Alice would then become calmer. Dr Louros was consulted again, as were other doctors. The treatment was agreed

* Her lady-in-waiting, Virginie Simopoulos, believed that Christ represented the Englishman rather than Andrea [VS to B, 27 June 1930 [UT]].

and carried out by Dr von Schubert, the aim being not to trigger the menopause but to accelerate the general process. There is no evidence that Alice was consulted about this.

Simmel's sanatorium was not a closed institution. Once Alice had put on weight, some twelve pounds, he felt able to permit her to move about freely. She went to the theatre in Berlin by herself and on other excursions. While at Tegel, Alice heard the news that the first of her four daughters had got engaged. Cécile was only eighteen when she agreed to marry her 23-year-old cousin Don (Prince George Donatus of Hesse), Ernie's son. Cécile wrote to tell her mother that she was happy in Darmstadt, and Alice replied with perfect coherence:

> Don is such a sensible, dear boy & you also have so much sense & judgement that the latter will always be able to help you with your rather sensitive & capricious temperament, sometimes in very high spirits & sometimes low & depressed, & so I think you too will not allow misunderstandings ever to disturb your married happiness seriously. For you know, dear child, each woman manages & directs her married life herself, just as she would control herself in a profession if she had one & so you see when a girl marries a decent boy, she makes her *own* happiness with her *own* judgement & self-control. No marriage entered into, in that spirit, with the most dissimilar characters even, ought ever to be a failure. A little patience in the first years & one has an enduring happy love & friendship for life & which unlike ordinary friendships will be just as fresh when you are old.[4]

The letter says much about Alice's view of her own marriage at this time of crisis. Not only was she articulate on the subject, but she showed a strong sense of independence.

Alice wrote to Cécile that she did not think she would need to remain at Tegel much longer. As she became fitter, so she began to declare herself better, which she was not. Then she caught mumps. Alice became suspicious that the doctors were trying to lock her up; she wanted to go home to her children and got particularly annoyed with Simmel when he urged her to stay. But

Simmel did not have the authority to detain Alice against her will, and so, after a mere eight weeks, she discharged herself. She returned to St Cloud on 7 April.

'I found everybody looking very well indeed and the season far more advanced than in Berlin,' Alice wrote to Cécile on her return home. 'The fruit trees are blossoming & the leaves beginning to come out, & the air is very mild & I must say I am truly delighted to be back after 8 weeks absence.'[5] In the top left-hand corner of this otherwise normal letter, Alice put a small cross, a symbol often used by those who engage in automatic writing. With hindsight, this was sure indication that Alice was far from well. Invariably, when the little cross was there, Alice was at a low ebb in her volatile condition.

It was not long before the children were finding their mother strange, and complaining that she talked perpetually about Christ. Andrea became alarmed. He felt unable – perhaps also unwilling – to cope, and he was convinced that internment was inevitable. He crossed to London to talk to Victoria, to whom, as ever, the family turned in times of crisis. Together they consulted two more doctors, one of whom was the famous Dr Thomas Ross,* director of Swaylands, the 'nerve' hospital founded by Edwina's grandfather, Sir Ernest Cassel, which had treated many shell-shocked cases from the First World War. Victoria related her discussions with Andrea to Nona:

He & I have had long talks. I saw Dr Robertson yesterday, as he luckily had come to London. He confirmed Dr Ross's opinion & advice of internment. Andrea & I feel that it is the only right thing to do, both for Alice & her family. How hard it has been to come to this decision & what we feel about it you know. This Easter will be a miserable one.[6]

*Dr T. A. Ross (1875–1941), Edinburgh-born doctor. Physician at the Royal National Hospital for Consumption, Ventnor, 1901–17. Director of Swaylands, the Cassel Hospital for Functional Nervous Disorders 1919–34. Author of *The Common Neuroses* (1923) and *An Enquiry into Prognosis in the Neuroses* (1936). The aesthete, Stephen Tennant, was one of his patients.

Easter was meant to mark the official engagement of the heir to the Hesse-Darmstadt family to Cécile and in honour of this Ernie had invited the whole family to gather at the Neue Palais in Darmstadt. Victoria set off for Germany from London on 12 April. Andrea returned to St Cloud from London on Monday 13 April. The same day Alice took the train to Darmstadt with Philip. Andrea joined them with two of the girls by car on the day after. Easter fell at the end of that week.

Alice clearly enjoyed her visit and when all the family were together, she joined naturally in the general conversation. Her treatment at Tegel seemed to have done her good. Yet all was not well, and Alice's mother suffered an agony of dilemma over the plan mapped out for her, which would presently grind into effect:

When alone with Ernie, Onor & me, she has spoken of her ideas & to Andrea she has said some very distressing things. Her illusions are still firmly rooted & it is an effort to lay them aside for a while. She looks fatter & stronger & eats & drinks everything, but her face has altered & when not talking, her expression, especially in the eyes which seem duller, is altered too. I have spoken with an excellent & very nice Heidelberg professor,* who has recommended a private sanatorium near Konstanz, on Lake Constance, which seems in every way suitable. It is run by a very good specialist, lies in a fine park of its own, & has 3 separate establishments for closely interned patients, semi-interned & a so-called free section where the patients can go into town etc. with a nurse. The patients are all higher class, educated people, so that if Alice likes to make the acquaintance of any of them, she will find suitable companionship.

We hope Dr Simmel, whom she now praises & seems to like, will come here some time next week & manage to influence her to leave with him. Andrea & Marg. return to Paris on Wednesday [23 April] . . .

I hope & think Alice will like the new place, once she has settled down. She seems to have liked Tegel, only she felt bored after a while & restless there.

When she is enjoying being amongst us, I feel a brute & then again

* Professor Dr Karl Wilmanns.

come moments when I clearly realize the need of her going away. My brother & Onor are a help & comfort to me.[7]

Andrea and Margarita duly left and Sophie went to Friedrichshof to her future mother-in-law. The others stayed on.

The transfer took place on 2 May, less than a month since Alice had discharged herself from Tegel. The process was a brutal one, involving the suspension of normal concerns for civil rights. Guile and then force were used to achieve the goal.

The Heidelberg professor, Karl Wilmanns, arrived in Darmstadt without having yet met Alice, to secure her transfer. Victoria liked him, describing him as 'not only a great medical authority on insanity, but also an honest & very kind-hearted man'.[8] Alice met him with her customary politeness and with no suspicion of his motives. Wilmanns found himself alone with her. As he put it, 'her relations had decamped for understandable reasons and left the rest to me'.[9]

Theodora, Cécile and Philip went out for the day with Victoria, Ernie and Onor. When they returned, Alice had gone. The next day they returned to Andrea at St Cloud, leaving their grandmother behind. Upon her fell the onus of visiting Alice and talking to the doctors.

Victoria's account of the transfer suggested that Professor Wilmanns explained Alice's predicament to her, that 'her head was ill as well as her body',[10] after which she withdrew for a short prayer, agreed to a sedative to alleviate the strain of a seven-hour car journey and left in Ernie's car for Switzerland.

The truth was less palatable. Professor Wilmanns was, in his own words, 'hard-boiled'[11] in the business of difficult transfers, but even so, the process of moving Alice disturbed him. She met him, full of confidence, but when he began by trying to persuade her to accompany him, she refused and tried to delay the decision. When she realized the gravity of his intent, she tried to slip away. At this point force was used and an injection of morphium-scopolamine administered to sedate her. Alice was removed from Darmstadt and kept sedated with a few drops of hyoscine concealed in an orange on the journey south through the Black Forest. She arrived at Kreuzlingen at 11.00 p.m. the same day.

The transfer was accomplished against Alice's will on the instructions of her mother and with the acquiescence of Andrea. She was not certified, but this time the doctors did not have the authority to release her. They depended on permission being granted by her mother.

Alice's precipitate departure from Darmstadt was effectively the last time the family unit lived together. Andrea would see his wife but a handful of times over the ensuing years. From then on, he relinquished his role as husband and presently he closed down the family home in Paris. Mythology has it, unfairly, that in his later years he became something of a playboy. This is too simplistic. It is true that he resigned himself to an easy social life, punctuated by an occasional political stand. He swam with the flow, taking his meals and holidays where they were offered. He could perhaps be described as a *boulevardier*, but he was no playboy. He became a lonely man, moving between Paris, Germany and the south of France.

The daughters were soon to be married, making new homes in Germany. The real loser was Philip, who was consigned to the care of his grandmother, Victoria, with occasional help from uncles and aunts. 'I was at school in England, and George and Nada Milford Haven were very kind to me,' recalled Prince Philip.[12]

Victoria rose to this new challenge in her customary redoubtable manner. Many years later, Alice herself paid tribute to what she achieved in a letter to Philip. She told him that she 'looked after you quite as if you were her youngest son'.[13]

Alice found herself in the Bellevue Clinic at Kreuzlingen in Switzerland, the sanatorium of Dr Ludwig Binswanger.* It was a famous institution run by a well-known doctor. Binswanger was a Swiss

* Dr Ludwig Binswanger (1881–1966), son of Robert Binswanger, psychiatrist. His uncle was also a psychiatrist.

psychiatrist and psychotherapist, and the founder of the analysis of existence. Born in 1881, he had studied with C. G. Jung, under whose tutelage he had learnt about psychoanalysis. He had been a friend of Sigmund Freud since 1907, without being a Freudian himself. Freud considered Binswanger to be 'highly respectable, serious and sincere',[14] but questioned his talent. Conversely, Binswanger admired Freud as a kind of father-figure, while occasionally criticizing his methods. The other strong influence in his life was Martin Heidegger.

After his studies Binswanger had joined his father and uncle at the Bellevue Clinic and served as its Medical Director from 1911 to 1956. Binswanger believed in man not as a trouble-prone apparatus but as an holistic person. He took particular note of a patient's social relationships and surroundings. He was a great believer in the ability to love as the basis of self-knowledge and understanding of others. He formed his therapy from coming to an awareness of how and why the patient had failed in his existence. He disapproved of electric shock therapy and the use of straitjackets.

Victoria had mentioned to Nona that the patients tended to be well born. There were also some famous inmates, who had found their way to the Bellevue for a variety of reasons. Writers were drawn there, either to 'iron up their nerves',[15] as Norbert Jacques put it, or to take sanctuary, as happened in both World Wars. In the 1914–18 war, Binswanger sheltered the novelists René Schickele,* Leonhard Frank† and Otto Flake.‡ The writer Robert Faesi rowed the poet Albert Ehrenstein¶ across Lake Constance to safety after he had published his views on the misery of war. In 1933 the Jewish novelist Alfred Döblin§ would take refuge there

* René Schickele wrote about Binswanger in his novel, *Symphony for Jazz.*

† Leonhard Frank (1882–1961), novelist who wrote touchingly of unconventional love affairs in books such as *Karl and Anna* (1927) and *Brother and Sister* (1929). A revolutionary pacifist in Switzerland in the First World War, he left Germany in 1933 for the US, but returned to Munich in 1952.

‡ Otto Flake, member of the Dada movement.

¶ Albert Ehrenstein, author of *Tabutsch* and *Robbers and Soldiers.*

§ Alfred Döblin (1878–1957), author of *Berlin Alexanderplatz.* He was fleeing from the Nazis.

from Berlin, Binswanger granting him sanctuary and saying he thought 'foresight preferable to hindsight'.[16] In the Second World War Binswanger would offer the clinic's facilities to the novelist Thomas Mann and his Jewish wife, Katia, for a last meeting with her German parents, only to find them forbidden to cross the nearby German border.

There were the genuine inmates too, described by Faesi as the 'many physically stranded and mentally ill'.[17] It is hard not to sympathize with Joseph Roth's* description of the Bellevue in his novel, *The Radetzky March*,† as 'that institution on Lake Constance, where spoiled, wealthy madmen underwent careful and expensive treatments, and the attendants were as nurturing as midwives'.[18]

Amongst the patients were the handsome German actor Gustav Gründgens,‡ the famous German Expressionist painter Ernst Ludwig Kirchner,¶ who painted woodcuts of the doctors and staff while there in 1917–18, and the playwright, Carl Sternheim.§ Elisabeth Bergner,|| the Viennese-born actress, rested there, exhausted after stage triumphs in hysterical and Expressionist parts

*Joseph Roth (1894–1939), Austrian writer, currently enjoying a deserved revival. A chronicler of the Jazz Age, and in the words of Michael Hofmann 'one of the great poets of alcoholic decline' [Roth, *The String of Pearls* (Granta, 1998), Introduction, p. vii].

† First published as *Radetzky-Marsch*, Berlin, 1932.

‡ Gustav Gründgens (1899–1963), actor and director. Intendant of the Berlin State Theatre. Born in Hamburg, he acted in Germany until the end of the Second World War. Famous for his portrayal of Mephisto in Goethe's *Faust*, on which Klaus Mann based his famous novel, *Mephisto*. Instrumental in turning Düsseldorf into a thriving theatrical centre. Director of the Hamburg State Theatre. He died, apparently by his own hand, in Manila.

¶ Ernst Ludwig Kirchner (1880–1938), original member of die Brücke in Dresden. Suffered from tuberculosis. Committed suicide 1938.

§ Carl Sternheim (1878–1942), satirical German dramatist, popular in the 1920s. His work was later banned by the Nazis.

|| Elisabeth Bergner (1897–1986), heroine of the German theatre, who left Germany for London in 1933.

in Zurich in 1920. The art historian Aby Warburg* had suffered a grave nervous breakdown at the end of the First World War and his condition was deemed hopeless. Eventually he asked Dr Binswanger if he could test his self-control by giving a lecture to the patients. In April 1923 he surprised them by delivering a well-researched paper on serpent rituals and was released.

The most famous inmate of all was the Russian dancer Nijinski.† He was an incurable schizophrenic, who had been a patient there some years before. In 1929 he began a further ten-year sojourn, and was thus in the clinic throughout Alice's stay. Sometimes he could be seen sitting on the lawn with other patients, 'a slim, middle-aged man resting in a chair, looking ahead with wandering but far from vacant eyes',[19] as his friend, the dancer Anton Dolin, put it.

The sanatorium complex‡ was set in a small, attractive park in Kreuzlingen, within sight of the German frontier, on the borders of Lake Constance. It was close to the railway station, a temptation, from time to time, for disenchanted patients. The grounds contained a variety of villas, more like small private mansions, in which the patients lived. There was an orangery, a bowling alley, a kitchen garden, tennis courts, extensive halls such as might be found in a residential hotel with chairs and tables set about the room, writing tables and large communal dining rooms for certain patients. There was a music room, a billiard room and a bath house for therapeutic bathing, and some of the bedrooms had well-equipped private bathrooms.

Alice was placed in Villa Maria, built in 1899, secluded amongst trees, with rooms for ten ladies. On her arrival she was met by the doctors, who noted her imposing appearance and her slight deafness.

* Aby Warburg (1866–1929), art historian and founder of the Warburg Institute. See *Aby Warburg – an Intellectual Biography*, by Professor E. H. Gombrich (Phaidon, 1970).

† Vaslav Nijinski (1888–1950), Diaghilev's leading dancer with the Ballet Russe, 1909–13.

‡ In 1929 the interior was redesigned by the writer and architect Rudolf Alexander Schröder, who considered the Bellevue his home from home.

'At first sight,' they noted, 'with her slightly stereotype smile, she makes a rather pensive, but not directly psychotic appearance.'[20]

The following day Alice was visited by Dr Binswanger and his colleagues, Dr Beringer and Dr Wenger. She told them that neither was she ill, nor were her nerves exhausted or overstrained. She told them she was in direct contact with Christ and that when she prayed she felt intimately connected to him. She was critical of the behaviour of the doctors in bringing her there, describing the way they proceeded as 'inconceivable to her, completely unpsychological'.[21] She wrote at length to her mother to complain. She was especially angry with Professor Wilmanns, because she had been brought there against her will, and later expressed the hope that other women would not be treated as she had been.

But her chances of being released were slim. Wilmanns, the man responsible for Alice being there, wrote to Dr Binswanger:

> I am afraid that an improvement in the princess is not to be expected in the foreseeable future. Her relations reckon on an extended stay at Kreuzlingen. It will be a relief to you, as I know your attitude to sensible patients requesting to leave, if the responsibility for a prolonged restraint against the patient's will is taken from you – at least as a matter of form.[22]

Alice explained to Dr Binswanger that she heard voices, defining this: 'You see, it is as if you were reading aloud and at the same time hearing your own voice.'[23] Alice told him that she had been given the gift of Christ by God, and that she heard the voice of Christ and had a special religious mission.

On 8 May 1930 Victoria came to visit Alice and to talk to the doctors. She stressed that sexuality was playing a big part in the illness. Alice spoke frequently of prostitutes and claimed that Christ teased her in the way that Andrea had in happier times. Victoria had tea with Alice and explained to her that her stay at Kreuzlingen was likely to be lengthy. Alice seemed to accept that Dr Binswanger would know when the time was right for her to be discharged. However, she refused to have anything to do with Professor Wilmanns. At this time she was unaware of her mother's role in sending her to Kreuzlingen. She complained about nothing, but asked for keys to her cupboards and some small nail scissors.

During the next few days Alice often remained in bed, interested only in her private concerns. She requested her freedom and believed that while the doctor was capable of dealing with physical ailments, he was inadequately qualified to tackle the mind. She was frustrated by her plight, and aware that one of the prime motives in detaining her was to prevent her from disseminating her religious theories to a wider audience. She was right.

Alice was much observed while at Kreuzlingen. At certain times she was fidgety, and pulled faces when she thought she was alone. The nervousness could produce twitches in her face and hands, and at worst, she appeared to be shivering all over. Her face showed evidence of suffering. There were days when she just stared into space, lost in thought. When she walked in the park, she might suddenly stop, look up at the trees and then move on. Sometimes the voices that had obsessed her earlier returned to her. She told the doctors about the philosophers she had studied, Socrates, Plotin and her favourite, Plato.

At the beginning of her stay she read long, difficult books, but gradually she read less. There were times when she was reserved and uncommunicative. She liked to walk, and occupied herself with painting, showing a 'distinctly decorative talent'.[24] Above all, the doctors recorded, Alice made no demands. She required no visits, nor other diversions.

In company Alice was never other than composed. She loved to see children in the street and said she longed for grandchildren, especially since she could not have any more children herself. One day she was out in the town with a nurse and recognized a lady she had known while in exile from Greece, in Baur au Lac in 1917. Alice immediately went over to her and they had a brief conversation. She liked to make excursions to Mainau,* the beautiful island in the

* Mainau was owned and run by Count Lennart Bernadotte (b. 1909), son of Prince William of Sweden and Grand Duchess Marie of Russia, whose wedding Alice had attended in 1908.

lake, famed for its variety of botanical plants. No stranger would have entertained the smallest suspicion that she was ill.

On 17 May 1930 Alice sent Cécile a postcard, saying that now she could sit in the garden, and adding with a hint of disapproval: 'Saw your name in the papers at Mrs Corrigan's* dinner.'[25] From St Cloud, Cécile replied: 'The Corrigan party is the only one I've been to, as we have been so busy getting clothes and shopping that usually we have been too dead to move in the evening.' She passed on family news and revealed that Philip would be going to school at Cheam in England and that he was 'thrilled at the idea'.[26]

On 1 June Alice wrote a card to Philip, apologizing for missing his ninth birthday at Wolfsgarten,† where the family were gathering for joint celebrations of the engagements of Cécile to Don of Hesse, and Sophie, not quite sixteen, to her second cousin once removed, Prince Christoph of Hesse,‡ a grandson of Empress Frederick.

On 8 June a mass of flowers arrived for Alice from her two daughters and their future husbands, to mark their official engagements. As the hospital report stated, the patient 'cried much yesterday'.[27] Cécile wrote to her mother, telling her of the excitement of the day, with all the telegrams and letters to answer. Andrea had arrived in Darmstadt looking tired, but had now left for Marienbad, looking 'much fatter and browner'. And there was more news of Philip:

* Laura Corrigan (1879–1948), Wisconsin-born hostess, who deployed her late husband's fortune to entertain the upper classes with excessive generosity. Famed for her malapropisms. After a trip to Agra in India, she declared: 'It was wonderful to see the Aga Khan by moonlight.'

† A former nanny, Nana Bell, wrote to him urging him: 'I know how difficult it is to write letters on holiday, and you must write to your dear Mama often' [Nana Bell to Philip, Simons Town, South Africa, 24 July 1930, BP]. On 28 July Alice wrote to Philip: 'You might write me a postcard and tell me what you are doing' [Alice to Philip, Kreuzlingen, 28 July 1930, BP].

‡ Prince Christoph of Hesse (1901–43), sixth son of Friedrich Karl, Landgrave of Hesse-Kassel ('Fischy') and his wife, Princess Margarethe of Prussia ('Mossy'). Twin brother of Richard.

As for Philipp [*sic*] he is quite blissful. U. Ernie and A. Onor gave him a new bicycle for his birthday. And he rushes about on it all day. In the evening from the moment he has finished his bath till he goes to bed he plays his beloved gramophone which you gave him. He got really lovely presents this year. Dolla and Tiny gave him pen-knives, and Don a big coloured ball for the swimming pool and I gave him a rug to lie about on in the garden.

He is very good and does just what A. Onor tells him.[28]

Alice was particularly glad to have had Philip's birthday described, 'as no one else has done so'.[29] Alice sent Cécile a brooch. Her recent letters all bore the little '+'.

On 25 June Prince Christoph, Alice's prospective son-in-law, visited her. Then Virginie Simopoulos came to see her, finding her changed: 'Much calmer, more depressed, introverted.'[30] Her mother, who visited her for a week at the beginning of July, was sufficiently pleased with her progress to agree that she should go to Braunwald, in the mountains of Glarus (between Lucerne and Davos) in August.

Alice was still undertaking exercises to classify her thoughts, dividing them as to their origins, whether from the lower subconscious or the upper. She tried to clear all thoughts before sleeping, except the word 'search', convinced that her first waking thought would produce the thought she was seeking. Whereas earlier she had been observed through the night by a nurse, by July, she was sleeping whole nights without one.

Towards the end of July Alice began to set aside some time each day for writing. She wrote a short article, filled with superficial and religious phrases, which she intended to send to the *Daily Mail*. The hospital authorities alerted Victoria, who wrote that Alice had already made a fool of herself and Andrea by sending her views to a Greek newspaper. Victoria wrote to the editor of the *Daily Mail*, warning him that her daughter had had a nervous breakdown and that no articles by her were to be published. Victoria was concerned that the 'mania' that had a hold on her mind had directed itself from religion to politics in its quest to convert the world. She urged

Binswanger to 'supervise her writings at your discretion and if necessary intercept them'.[31] This was done.

Alice's Aunt Anna, who was living at Stein-am-Rhein, came to see her in July. Alice then absorbed herself in drawing up a potential new constitution for Greece, working daily at this from two to four each afternoon. The resulting seven-page document was written in measured tone, and gave evidence of considerable thought and organization, considering in turn how the President and Prime Minister might be elected, how each province be ruled, aspects of taxation, and the role of the monarch or president, judges and senate. Alice also considered recommendations for the working of the constitution:

> It should not lay down too rigid and uniform a plan, but should allow for natural growth and diversity. Unless some latitude is provided, so that within a given framework, adjustments are possible, the legislative machine has to go on working under the handicap of faults of structure which experience makes manifest: Constitutional progress should be the outcome of practical experience.'[32]

Binswanger asked Alice to write an exposé on the soul, God and spirits. Evidently the result of this was 'humbug'.[33] One day Alice asked the doctor: 'What holds the waves of the radio together between transmitter and receiver, after the sounds have died away?' She answered her own question: 'Certainly the ether which entertains the unity.'[34]

On 2 August, Queen Sophie came to see Alice and concluded that it was practically impossible to hold a coherent conversation with her. Alice's youngest daughter, Sophie, came on the same day, after which Alice was much more cheerful and less inclined to dwell on gloomy theories about the soul and spirit.

Although Alice continued to appear absorbed in thought, her expression either pensive or radiant, she remained friendly and composed when in the presence of the doctors. In advance of her holiday, she ordered the first of the severe habits that she would adopt in later life, high-necked, long-sleeved and made of rough linen. She also obtained a picture of Christ, with what was presented as a loving dedication from Christ to Alice.

On 15 August Alice left Kreuzlingen for an hotel in Braunwald for a fortnight's stay. She wanted to take her worldly possessions with her, in particular a large photograph album and her copy of Schuré's book of 'philosophies', *Les Grands Initiés*. From her new mountain-top base, she wrote cards to Philip and his sisters, describing the mountains as 'marvellously beautiful'.[35] She travelled with a nurse, Schwester Lina, and a maid, Miss Hoch. The nurse reported that the stay was passing pleasantly and Alice only became upset when she was not allowed to hang up a picture of Christ in her bedroom. The nurse tried to explain that it might cause profanations.

By 23 August the situation had deteriorated. Schwester Lina wrote to Dr Wenger, complaining that Alice was puzzling, kept them on their toes and was unpredictable. In conversation she implied that she would not be going back to Kreuzlingen. She said to the maid: 'I told you I am completely healthy and that I went to the sanatorium completely voluntarily to stay there on my own free will in order to sort some things out and to help unhappy patients so that they could recover and go back to their families again.' Schwester Lina continued:

On Monday we had great excitement about the picture she gave the maid as a souvenir of herself, saying she no longer needed it. Alice asked: 'Who decided that that picture was not to be taken with us?' I told her that it was the doctor and explained why. Then she made a long speech in which she said: 'The doctor shouldn't forget that at some time he will have to appear in front of God's throne and give an account of his actions. If he wants to help ill people, he has to ask the dear Lord to help him first because, with his human instinct he can't do it. Go to Kreuzlingen and tell the doctor that.' I told her: 'No, I am not going to leave you.' She then kissed me and said: 'I like you, you can stay with me until I go home to my Heavenly Father.' Then she gave me back her passport and told me: 'Keep it as a memento. There's a nice picture in it, and I don't need it any more.'[36]

Alice wrote to Louise putting off her proposed visit of 24 September, on the grounds that she did not know where she would be. She wrote to Count Hardenberg,* one of the few men she trusted, asking him to visit her in Lucerne. As to Alice's routine, the nurse described it:

Up until now she has come regularly to the table for meals, lies down outside from 11 a.m. onwards and then after meals and after tea takes a walk which she finds very exhausting. She doesn't stick to her writing times any more, mostly taking her writing materials to the reclining chair outside, but as you know, she always has an excuse. I watch her all day as best I can. I don't disturb her as she is mostly absent-minded anyway, but I don't think we have anything to be afraid of yet – she still has all sorts of things going on, but something is keeping her mind well occupied. For the last two days she only spoke when she had to or about unimportant things and she is always laughing. For the time being, one still can't get any closer to her. What do you think, doctor? I do my utmost as does the maid . . . I hope that she is not going to change her plans again in order to make no problems for us.[37]

Next, Alice wrote to Dr Wenger that she had assumed responsibility for her plans, that Andrea and her mother were in agreement with these and that she would be going to Lucerne. Wenger replied that she would have to comply with the agreement made with Dr Binswanger (who was away) to return on 1 or 2 September.

There were worrying developments. Alice gave her maid, Miss Hoch, all her jewellery, clothes, books and other possessions with instructions as to how these should be distributed. She told her nurse that she would not return to Kreuzlingen. 'You will return without the princess,' she said, 'for he has to set me free, if he wants to or not, it shall be conveyed to him by a higher authority.'[38] Alice talked darkly: 'Soon I will have a long and beautiful journey ahead of me,

* Graf Kuno von Hardenberg (1871–1938), an art expert in Dresden, and court chamberlain to the Grand Duke of Hesse from 1916. President of the Society for Free Philosophy. Director of the grand Ducal property administration.

to which I am looking forward very much.'[39] In despair her maid, similarly addressed, tried to get her to take an interest in the weddings of her daughters. She said: 'I will assist at every wedding, even though no one will be able to see me. I shall be able to see everything.'[40]

At the end of August they moved to Lucerne. Alice wrote a note in her bible indicating that 8 September would be the day of her departure. She then wrote a number of farewell letters, including one to Dickie, adorned with the worrying little '+'. Some of these farewell letters were intercepted, but Dickie received his (then or later) and filed it in his archives:

I do not know when we shall meet again, so I would like you to get something to remember me by & enclose a cheque for £25. Mama told me that just after your terrible anxiety for Edwina you broke your collar-bone & poor Patricia [his daughter] her arm. I hope you have all recovered from your misfortunes & especially Edwina. Give her my love & ask her to take care of herself. Kiss the chicks from me, good-bye dear Dickie, with fondest love ever from your loving sister, Alice.[41]

Alice then distributed all her possessions and finally became so 'agitated' that she was about to 'plunge from the balcony of the second floor of the Hotel National'. As soon as he heard this, at the beginning of September, Dr Wenger drove in haste to Lucerne and took her back to Kreuzlingen against her will.

Alice returned to the Villa Maria, which was not as bad a fate as being completely incarcerated. But in this new phase of detention Alice became morbid and preoccupied with settling her affairs. She announced that she would not live much longer, and took to her bed. She berated Dr Binswanger for not delivering her farewell letters and told him that her orders had reached their destination by means of ether waves.

On 18 September Alice wrote a letter to Dr Binswanger, which in his opinion represented 'the best achievement of the patient intellectually during her entire stay here'.[42] Interestingly, her handwriting also retained its usual free-flowing style:

I want to describe to you my attitude in the religious-philosophical field with the following words: Once upon a time, there was a young man whose mother enjoyed a great reputation thanks to her healings which she carried out by means of herbs. Her son was a bright man who wanted to become a doctor. After he had finished his medical studies and became a practising doctor, his mother paid him a visit and showed him a new plant which she had discovered. She told him about the power this plant possessed to heal a newly emerged disease, and she suggested to her son that he use this plant. But he answered her: 'But I see that this plant has a disease, and it cannot be useful. First I want to keep it and take care of it, and when it is healthy again, I can try it out.' To this his mother answered: 'If you deprive this plant of its disease, it will lose its healing power. What appears as sickness to you, is precisely the means by which I am healing the new disease, which you are unable to cure with instruments or serum.' Well, dear Doctor, I have presented you with this problem in order to see how you will solve it. Are you going to keep this plant, in order to cure it, or are you going to use it for the welfare of mankind? So *Aufwiedersihen* this afternoon, your devoted Alice.[43]

Alice remained in a low condition for some time, believing that she was on the point of dying. This belief sometimes frightened her. On 22 September, she handed in three more farewell letters, one for her mother and two for servants, containing cheques, which she asked be delivered after her death. Then she demanded to see her sister Louise, but this was forbidden until the winter. Her condition deteriorated, she suffered various attacks, her heart becoming unsteady, and she was administered digitalen in the morning and coramin in the afternoon.

When Alice was better, the doctors surmised that her recent attacks resulted from the conviction that she was dying, to which she appeared to submit, her overall state weakening, leaving her unable to speak. In October Louise came to see her. When Margarita and Theodora came to see her for three days in the same month, Alice told them that both Binswanger and Louise thought she was mad.

Meanwhile the wedding plans were progressing, Cécile dealing with Sophie's trousseau in Paris and her own. 'Tiny's clothes are nearly ready,' Cécile wrote to Alice. 'I saw her trying them on the other day. They are lovely and her wedding dress is too beautiful for words. Satin and quite simple with a lace and tulle veil. They have not started mine yet.'[44]

Louise came to see Alice again before going to Kronberg for Sophie's wedding to Prince Christoph of Hesse. She stayed with Alice at Villa Maria and found her much better. Her weight was improving, she was sleeping and eating well, and her pulse was better, though still slow.

There was no question of Alice attending Sophie's wedding on 15 December. 'She felt not strong enough & too shy of strangers to want to assist at the wedding,'[45] explained Victoria. For the occasion, old servants came out of retirement and put on their old liveries, and Kronberg was made festive. Andrea arrived from Paris with the Greek priest and Theodora. At the wedding itself, Theodora, Cécile and Philip helped Sophie dress in her room at Friedrichshof. Prince Friedrich Karl of Hesse-Kassel, her future father-in-law, loaned her the Empress Frederick's diamond tiara as a final adornment to her bridal gown.

The Greek priest conducted the Orthodox wedding service in a fine voice in the drawing-room at Friedrichshof, and Philip carried Sophie's train with dignity. The bride was then accompanied to the church at Kronberg by her father, Philip and her grandmother. Here the Protestant service was held. 'Tiny was like a child at a party in her enjoyment & excitement over her wedding,'[46] wrote Louise. Early in their honeymoon, they paid a visit to Alice, which was deemed a success.

The one person whom everyone felt sorry for on Sophie's wedding day was the bride's father. 'I can't tell you how sorry I felt for Andrea,' wrote Louise. 'He behaved splendidly but had the greatest difficulty not to break down. We did our best to keep him cheerful & his girls were touching in looking after him.'[47] The evening after the wedding, Andrea returned to Paris with his brother, Big George, on some business connected with fire insurance.

As Christmas came, Alice joined in celebrations at Bellevue House, watching the Christmas play and staying up until 10.00 p.m. After this, she asked one of the hospital helpers if she could stay with her as she found the Villa Maria too lonely and the Bellevue too full of people. But the consensus was that Christmas had done her good.

On Boxing Day Victoria arrived from Darmstadt, bringing Philip with her. They stayed for a few days at the Hotel Helvetia in Kreuzlingen, close to the clinic. Alice had longed to see her son. The visit passed off well, though Alice told her mother that she did not believe she would live long and that what small amount of money remained to her should be passed to Andrea.

21. Kreuzlingen, 1931

At the end of January 1931 Alice handed her nurse her copy of *Les Grands Initiés*, tied with a white ribbon, and told her to burn it immediately. The book was inspected by Dr Binswanger and found to contain various passages, underlined by Alice, and pencil inscriptions indicating that Christ loved her and that she was a saint, one such reading: 'Saint Alice has been initiated five times, 1. Christ, 2. Moses, 3. Krishna, 4. Mohamed, 5. Buddha.'[1] Alice declared that she had finished her teachings, but wished to continue her exercises. For this reason, she wished her favourite book burned.

Cécile was married on 2 February, another ceremony which Alice missed. Men and women lined the streets of Darmstadt, and the car taking Andrea and Cécile to the Alte Schloss *kirche* was so surrounded that it could not move. They made their way into the courtyard of the Alte Schloss on foot, with much hand-shaking, while Andrea was greeted with cries of '*Hoch der Herr Papa*'. 'It seemed very funny in a "republic" but was a nice sign of the affection of the people for Uncle Ernie & his family,'[2] wrote Victoria to her son Georgie.

On 10 February Victoria went to Kreuzlingen to see Alice. Shortly afterwards, Alice became very weak. The doctors were not sure whether this was due to a physical cause or on account of her psychic condition. At one point she had to be supported while standing up, and then stood for ten minutes at the table, saying nothing and just staring with half-closed eyes or a rigid, glazed stare. When she walked she used two sticks to support her, and she was often out of breath.

When this crisis passed, Alice told Dr Binswanger that her stay at Kreuzlingen was proving too hard for her. She said that this was affecting her physically and manifesting itself in her subconscious. Alice demanded that she be allowed a two-week holiday with

Georgina von Rotsmann, Aunt Onor's lady-in-waiting and an old family friend from Darmstadt, who was due to visit her in March. This was refused on the grounds of 'the bad experiences of Braunwald',[3] which Alice attributed to the nurse's inability to cope with caring for her. This confrontation ended unsatisfactorily, as a result of which, on 23 February, Alice wrote a letter to Binswanger:

> Dear Doctor,
>
> You suggested that I should give you my opinion in writing. I am taking this opportunity to repeat to you that I find my stay here has affected my nerves. I realise that I cannot explain to you the real reason for this nervous strain. I can only hope that you won't refuse my request, which I hereby submit to you, that you now give me back my freedom.
>
> If you want to know how I will use it, I would first drive with Frl. v. Rotsmann to a quiet little place in the Tessin valley, take an air and sun cure, and at the end of March drive with her to Darmstadt . . . and at the beginning of April would take a cure at Nauheim. My mother and my little boy could visit me there.
>
> In all friendship, Alice.[4]

One of Alice's problems at Kreuzlingen was not knowing when or if she would ever escape. Perhaps her worst day was her forty-sixth birthday on 25 February, when she lost her composure before the doctor, refusing to speak to him and pulling faces. Yet a few days later she had recovered. Hearing that Dr Binswanger was ill, she went into town to get him some flowers and wrote him a note to say that she knew how to separate official dealings with him from personal ones, but adding that she did not agree with his methods and would soon have to leave his clinic.

The mood swings continued, yet better communication was resumed. However, on 4 March, Alice questioned Dr Binswanger about her rights. For the first time he explained to her that he had no legal right to discharge her, nor indeed to retain her. This depended, he told her, entirely on her family. When she heard this, she froze 'like a pillar'.[5] He explained that she could either write to her mother about this or wait until her next visit in April. Alice neither replied, nor then permitted her pulse to be taken. From this moment of realization, Alice became resentful of her mother and never wholly forgave her.

Alice conceived an idea which, even late in life, she never surrendered, that she was suffering from a serious heart condition. She maintained that this was confirmed by Dr Hämmaerli, a heart specialist in Zurich, who came to see her in mid-March. On 24 March Alice wrote:

I feel that I owe you an explanation about the state of my heart. In December 1929 I seriously strained my heart by my studies to obtain the wisdom of God in the world beyond. Before having recovered, it received a new blow from the violent manner in which I was brought here. The height of Braunwald further disagreed with my heart, even more so on the way down from the mountains. As I arrived in Lucerne, I felt rather ill and weak. In this state my heart received a second strong blow in my abrupt transfer here. In this manner, psychotherapy has seriously, although unwittingly, impaired my health.

I trust that you will now give me up entirely to the doctor in Zurich for further treatment. Also I believe that the change of air will do me good.

In the hope that you will now have become aware of a few things, I remain, your devoted Alice.[6]

This was not the case, however. Though Alice had certainly suffered minor problems with her breathing, Dr Hämmaerli had found nothing wrong with Alice's heart. Dr Binswanger informed Alice of this and told her that she must undertake new walking exercises. By April Alice had stopped using her two sticks, and though still needing assistance, was somewhat better. Nevertheless she made no attempt to walk on her own. Binswanger informed Victoria of these developments and, in a letter dated 29 March, she gave him her diagnosis of the situation:

The lack of love of life, especially since the princess believes that she conveyed her mission by means of telepathy from Braunwald to the society in England,* is probably the hidden reason for her physical feebleness. I also think it is not to be excluded that she is still pre-occupied, by means of auto-suggestion, in inducing her body to die off, and I am quite convinced that part of her desire for freedom is to be attributed to the fact that the care and supervision she is receiving in the sanatorium is perceived by her as a check on her endeavours.[7]

Alice also addressed the auto-suggestion claims. She claimed that she had been obliged to use this to overcome her paralysis and the weakness of her heart.

But just as I used auto-suggestion to be able to live and walk again, my subconscious put up resistance to your suggestions so that I did not want to live, get up or walk. I had to use strong auto-suggestion for my rest and nerves . . . Even if I did not have confidence in you, nevertheless I found hope and love, and as the apostle Paul says 'the greatest of these is love'.[8]

Victoria came to Kreuzlingen in April with Philip on their way to Margarita's wedding. Victoria was pleased with Alice's health the first two days, but then dismayed that Alice launched into accusations concerning the method of her transferral to Kreuzlingen.

On 20 April Margarita was married at Langenburg to Prince Gottfried (Friedel) of Hohenlohe-Langenburg, like Margarita, a descendant of Queen Victoria. Following the wedding, Alice was visited by Andrea for the first time in almost a year (his only visit to the Bellevue), and also by Sophie. Hearing of this, Louise's concerns were for Andrea rather than for her sister. She hoped that 'it did not upset him too much',[9] and worried that he lived too far away for her to help him.

At Kreuzlingen Alice had not been idle. On a walk in the town, her nurse spotted her drop a letter into the letterbox in the wall of

* The Panacea Society, whose offices were at 19 Rothsay Road, Bedford, in England.

the nearby Hotel Helvetia. She had written to Mr Erskine, the British Consul-General in Zurich, informing him that she was being detained against her will. The Consul-General got in touch with Dr Binswanger, who advised him to send the letter to Alice's mother, while politely acknowledging it.

On 23 May Alice wrote another letter to Binswanger, informing him that she had investigated her right to freedom, and was of the opinion that 'the means at your disposal are insufficient to make a correct diagnosis of my case'. Unfortunately, Alice somewhat ruined her case by suggesting he send a telegram to the offices of the Panacea Society in Bedford, where her disciples were about to hold a conference on the 'new science of the soul and the art of healing',[10] at which her presence was required.

After Whitsun, Binswanger confronted Alice about her letter to the Consul-General. She told him that she was quite within her rights to contact him, since she did not believe it was necessary for her to continue staying at Kreuzlingen. Furthermore she told him she would do so again if necessary, to which he rejoined that he would then place a nurse permanently at her side. He used the traditional ploy of suggesting that she was breaking the trust that they had established in their talks and that she had acted disloyally. This conversation was perfectly civil, and ended with Alice asking him to consider the possibility that she was not ill, or that he bring her to a state where she was 'sane'. She said: 'Personally I have nothing against you, since you are actually progressive.'[11] Soon after this, she resumed painting after a long lapse.

Alice told her nurse that they had declared her ill and locked her up because they did not like her ideas. She said that this often happened and cited Count Zeppelin,* who was considered mad but stuck rigidly to his cause. Showing that even in the face of this seemingly hopeless struggle she retained her spirits, she said: 'Well, nurse, if I don't catch 'flu or some other disease, we shall still be

* Count Ferdinand Zeppelin (1838–1917), German soldier and inventor. He retired from the army as a general in 1890 and devoted himself to aeronautics. In 1899 he built the first of his floating airships. These played a memorable part in the First World War.

staggering through the park together in thirty years' time, by which time our hair will be grey. We will then have our photographs taken and give one to Herr Doktor. The main thing is not to lose one's humour.'[12]

Dr Binswanger consulted Victoria about the letter to the Consul-General. Victoria wrote to Alice to say that neither she nor Andrea believed her sufficiently recovered from the after-effects of her intense studies to be able to lead a free and independent life. She persuaded Georgie to write in similar vein. Turning to the question of Alice going elsewhere for treatment, Victoria asked Binswanger:

> Do you not think, dear Doctor, that such a change of environment would be harmful for her? In any event, it could not help her much. We have so much confidence in you & are so content with all the care etc. at Bellevue that we would regret very much, if one could not leave her there. I only fear that in her discontent at not regaining her freedom, my daughter might try something unreasonable and wouldn't obey you any more. It would be dreadful for us if she had to be transferred to the closed ward. In my eyes it is the lesser evil if she were to write to the authorities again.[13]

In June Alice's moods swung dramatically, but she was pleased to hear of the engagement of her last daughter, Theodora, to the Margrave of Baden. He and Theodora visited her, as did Cécile and Don, visits that she enjoyed, though found tiring. Not long afterwards, however, she veered away from her family, tearing up a letter from her mother, whom she now saw as her gaoler, and telling Dr Binswanger that she did not wish her mother to visit her since she no longer understood her. She continued to see Georgina von Rotsmann, but presently fell out with her since she appeared to be supporting the views of the doctor. Dr Binswanger felt particularly sorry for the lady-in-waiting as she was so attached to Alice.

In July Alice was again preoccupied with her family detaining her. She told Binswanger that he could not possibly form a judgement on her when he only saw her for five minutes a day, and suggested that she go to a more progressive place, where they could screen her brain or try other methods. She preferred to be released altogether and told him with confidence that she could provide for herself, being able to sew, make her own clothes or undertake translations.

It is clear that by this time Alice's stay was having a detrimental effect. Binswanger was forced to report to Victoria that there was now 'an actual state of slight confusion',[14] and that the religious ideas now predominated and there were states of religious ecstasy. Binswanger had a nurse sleeping in the room next door to her. Presently, Alice's relations with Binswanger became less cordial. One day she suddenly smacked him across the face, and thereafter, in the month of August, probably on account of her despair, her behavioural patterns became eccentric and exaggerated.

Theodora was married to the Margrave of Baden in Baden-Baden on 17 August. Her wedding was the fourth family wedding missed by Alice. Berthold was the son of the famous Max of Baden, former Chancellor of the German Empire, and had succeeded as Margrave in November 1929. He was related to Theodora in numerous ways, including being a descendant of George III. Louise liked Berthold, but was slightly concerned about Theodora. 'I think he is very nice,' she wrote to Nona. 'I do hope Dolla will have a very happy life with Berthold because I think in some ways she expects more than her sisters.'[15]

Andrea had left for Paris immediately after the other three weddings, but this time he came to Wolfsgarten with Sophie and Christoph to join Victoria, Louise and Philip. Sophie succeeded in making her father laugh. 'I have long not seen him so cheerful,'[16] wrote Louise.

On 24 August Theodora and Berthold went to visit Alice on their way to honeymoon in the poet Axel Munthe's villa on Capri. In her discontented state, Alice received her daughter outside her room, and though amiable and pleasant, did not let Theodora take off her coat and dismissed her after two minutes.

As August moved into September, Alice's general condition deteriorated further. She told her nurse that it was lucky they all assumed she was mad as she could thus continue her work inconspicuously. She walked about barefoot and held her hands in blessing over her teacup. She became obsessed with the power of electricity and continued to say that she would do more strange things so that they thought her mad, and she would always stay there working away. She began to hide things in her room, cutting objects up and putting them in parcels.

On 17 September Margarita came to see her. Alice was on the balcony of Villa Maria when she arrived and went to meet her on the stairs. They kissed several times but hardly exchanged ten words. Margarita left in tears, and after she had gone, Alice went to have a bath and was heard to be crying hard. Later she had lunch and dinner at the common table, pinning a flower to her dress. As usual her mother was informed and agreed that for the time being visits from members of the family were 'not only unwelcome . . . but also harmful to her momentary state of health'.[17]

In mid-October Alice felt well enough to attend a concert in the hospital and to go to Bellevue for a meal. She then wrote to her mother announcing that she wished to be naturalized in Switzerland under the name of Mrs Alice Battenberg, 'since it must be obvious to you and the whole family as well as to myself that it is better that I shouldn't take up my former life'.[18] She asked that Count Hardenberg come and visit her to organize this and threatened to involve the cantonal authorities in Switzerland if this did not happen.

Aware that she had probably lost her daughter's confidence, Victoria was keen that Hardenberg, a man she judged basically 'normal' if a little 'bizarre' in certain aspects, should call on Alice, since she trusted him and had discussed her ideas with him in the past. She concluded: 'Should he succeed to induce her to stay for a while longer at Bellevue, it seems to me to be good for general health; if this urge for freedom would get thereby somewhat satiated, all the more so, since dull days are impending.'[19]

Count Hardenberg played a strong role in Alice's life from now until his death. He combined several elements. Not only was he Ernie's court chamberlain, but he was keenly involved with

Keyserling at the School of Wisdom and Thought, Keyserling paying tribute to his 'fine spirit of understanding and of co-operation'.[20] He was noted in Darmstadt as an old-fashioned man who eschewed the motor car in favour of a smart, shining brake pulled by an elegant team of horses. From now on he took responsibility for Alice's finances, full payment for her treatment coming, with no interference in how this was administered, from her ever-generous sister-in-law, Edwina.

During her stay at Kreuzlingen, Alice wrote to her Uncle Ernie, appealing for his help, and reminding him:

> In the old days you were considered mad when you did up your rooms in the new style and although I did not admire them, I said: 'He is right to pave the way for the future.' Now it is my turn to be criticized by people who do not like the idea of the RED FLAG being used as the standard of the Kingdom of GOD for the work of conciliation and love allowing all classes all nations and the 5 religions. Please defend me.[21]

Uncle Ernie did not come to see her.

At the end of November an Indian prince and his wife came to tea with her, which she enjoyed. The prince brought her a flat stone and sometimes she moved her hand strangely over it. But each day her moods were different. When brought a photograph of Cécile and her baby, Ludwig,* she tore it up angrily. Later, though, she again cried a lot.

Louise wanted to come to see Alice, but when consulted, Alice replied: 'No, better not. It's still too early for my sister. It would only upset her unnecessarily.'[22] When reporting this to Louise, Dr Binswanger added that Alice was taking an interest in many things, and often spent time with the other patients.

Binswanger was in touch with Andrea at this time, forwarding a letter to him on 26 November, and suggesting that he recommend Hardenberg as a representative of the whole family. He told Andrea that Alice was not in poor health, though the 'fixed religious idea'

* Prince Ludwig of Hesse, born 25 October 1931.

prevailed. While in general company, she appeared entirely correct in all aspects of behaviour. Only when in her own room did she sometimes display 'how confused and ill she still is, alas'.[23] Andrea replied a little dismissively from Paris: 'I am sorry to see by my wife's letter that her ideas have not changed or altered for the better. On the contrary, I fancy I perceive her ideas and fancies have crystallized into a kind of foundation upon which the rest of her spirit is now based.'[24]

In December Alice took an interest in the work of the Salvation Army, forever packing up parcels for them. But an intercepted letter in one of the parcels revealed that she had ordered a taxi and planned to escape when she attended a service in the Protestant church. She was therefore forbidden to go to church on Sunday 13 December. She took the news calmly, but told her nurse that she would continue to try to escape until she succeeded. Theodora then came to see her and this meeting passed off well.

Theodora was now living at Salem with Berthold. Their castle, a former Cistercian monastery, was ten miles north of Lake Constance and thus an easy journey to Kreuzlingen. On 16 December Theodora wrote at length to Dr Binswanger, telling him about her visit. Alice had not appeared so well for two years, she showed Theodora her weaving work and spoke calmly about the family. In the expounding of her views, some were 'completely healthy', others 'naïve to a degree of total infantility'. Theodora found herself in the position of having regained her mother's confidence, and this led Alice to confide her long-held wish to leave the clinic at any cost. Her latest plan was to work quietly, out of the public eye, with the help of a secretary to alleviate the strain on her heart. Alice explained some of her actions, how she had hidden notes in parcels in the sure knowledge that the doctor would find them and sometimes behaved in a shocking manner to see for herself if the doctor could tell the difference between 'an hysterical act' or 'an act of great discipline'. Finally Alice asked Theodora if she could come to Salem for Christmas. Theodora's letter to Dr Binswanger was to ask if indeed it might be possible to have her for two days.[25]

Dr Wenger replied because Dr Binswanger was ill. His point

was that though Alice appeared well in company, which gave cause for optimism in the future, 'our medical observations oblige us to form a different judgement'. He continued:

> However, the mental activity of the princess is dominated by a complex of ideas and sensations which are clearly unhealthy. Despite her often correct external behaviour, her attitude towards life and people is abnormal. This pathological core has occasioned a delusive system [to develop]. Its content is certainly dictated by the fund of generosity which the princess has in her; but its details and manifestations lack any critical sense to a degree that one must at all costs prevent our patient from publishing her projects or to attempt their realization. We will be happy to show your Royal Highness some writings to prove this point. The princess is convinced that she has been entrusted with a mission by providence, she believes herself to be gifted with magnetic powers. We have recently noticed an increase in her unhealthy ideas with a tendency above all to bring them to life, to communicate them to other people. She ardently wishes to leave the sanatorium in order to regain her freedom of action and to realize her projects. The strong influence exerted by her ideas on her whole person does not prevent her eventually from being very skilled in the pursuit of her object. It is thus that the princess tends to make use of your R.H. in order to achieve her purpose.[26]

Wenger concluded that any proposed holiday would 'constitute a danger for the patient and her entourage, a danger for which we could not take responsibility'.[27] But he encouraged visits from Theodora, particularly since it was not long since Alice had refused any contact with her family whatsoever.

Again in December Alice pressed Binswanger to allow her to leave, stating that in this sanatorium only the body was being treated, not the mind. Everything worked as in a barracks. Alice said she needed philosophers about her with whom she could discuss her ideas. She said her heart was suffering from 'lack of spiritual understanding and getting more and more ill, though not organically ill'.[28]

On 20 December, while looking far from well, Alice put forward the theory that she needed an obstetrician of the mind who could deliver her thoughts in the way that babies are delivered.* She resented being continually told to rest. Dr Sträuli then examined the patient and found her heart slightly enlarged. Alice requested that she be cared for by an Indian doctor, but the Swiss doctor merely urged her to rest. The report for the day records a sad scene:

> Instead of doing this, she dressed in expectation of the visit of the Margrave of Baden and his wife, had lunch with them, and ordered the nurse to pack her things, since she then wanted to leave. When the children wanted to take leave, she put on her hat and coat, declaring she was going with them, clung to her son-in-law and daughter, got more and more agitated. If she couldn't get out of there then, she would never get out any more. She had to be detained by force. When she realized that resistance was useless, she yielded, and seemed to be complying with the reasoning of her son-in-law who repeated to her that he couldn't do anything against the doctors. Finally she parted in a friendly way from the children. She looked quite worn, exhausted, cyanotic. She lay down on the chaise-longue, said to the nurse, since they thought her mad, she was going to conduct herself accordingly henceforth, neither eat, nor wash, nor go to bed any more. She wanted to see what kind of force they would then employ.[29]

Even in the face of this latest disappointment, Alice told Dr Binswanger: 'I want to learn how to transform all the evil here into good, in order to apply it in a sanatorium of my own for criminals who will all be cured. Materially speaking this sanatorium is a first rate one. Only the medical method is mediocre.'[30]

On Christmas Eve, Alice was examined by three doctors. They

* Alice's grandson, Rainer von Hessen, points out that Alice was ahead of her time in presenting this view. In 1988 the German philosopher Peter Sloterdijk gave a lecture explaining that Socrates saw himself as a 'midwife' to his pupils. Sloterdijk concluded that 'the European arch-philosopher in decisive matters, did not believe in argument but in initiation'. Argument led to one party falling for the opinion of the other. He preferred the idea of implanting an idea, letting it grow until it was developed enough to appear.

found that her general condition had weakened. She was pale and tired. She told them she felt feeble in the region of the heart, and had a general feeling of heaviness in the arms and legs and of blood congestion. They noted a slight dilation on the right side of the heart. What was especially significant was Alice's general physical collapse, compared to the relatively favourable conditions of her heart. They made various recommendations regarding drugs and resting. They made none concerning her psychotherapeutic treatment.

After Christmas Alice wrote some letters to her relations, thanking them for their attention. So too did Dr Wenger, painting a rather dismal picture. Manic activities were increasing, with Alice at work on her theories and attempting to promulgate her ideas by notes written inside Salvation Army parcels. She would not rest. She had had two visits from Theodora and Berthold, the first a success, the second the cause of 'great exasperation'. He thought her main aim at the turn of the year was to stay in the clinic and continue her work. He was wrong.

22. Escape

Alice began the new year by complying with the orders of the Zurich physician, Dr Hämmaerli, to remain in bed each morning. In the early part of the year, she was often irritated. Again she tore up a photograph of her grandson, Ludwig, 'showing a certain satisfaction when a rip went across the head',[1] and she was often tired and showed suffering on her face. She was delighted when Dr Binswanger remembered her interest in Count Zeppelin and gave her a book on him. She was so pleased that she pressed it to her lips. She searched the contents page and found a chapter called 'Candidate for the Madhouse'. This she showed to her nurse, nodding meaningfully. Then she burst into tears.

Alice's heart was more of a problem this year. It could be that the despair induced by her prolonged stay lowered her spirit and the varying states of agitation and depression caused genuine ailments to take over. On 19 January, while being massaged, she suffered a fit of cardiac faintness, during which her pulse rate declined, her complexion and lips went slightly blue and she gasped for breath. Various drugs were administered, and there was a further attack later in the day. Her condition was pronounced to be serious and she had to lie quietly for some days.

From this Alice recovered and was pleased to have two visits from Count Hardenberg at the end of January, during which she talked with him about the family and life at Darmstadt. On 30 January she saw Theodora again and sent a telegram to Louise in Sweden, which read: 'If can get permission go Lugano, could you accompany me, Alice.'[2] At no point did she swerve from her wish to leave the clinic.

As her heart condition resolved itself, she created a panic about her wish to celebrate Andrea's birthday on 2 February, and then she rearranged her room. In the second week of February she began to read the newspapers after a lapse. She resumed her painting, and pronounced her first effort modern. 'The people who invented modern painting must all have been sick,'[3] she said. Then she pointed at her head.

Victoria hoped to see Alice on her birthday on 25 February, but was delayed leaving Malta where she had spent part of the winter with Dickie. She stayed with Theodora at Salem and paid short visits to the clinic. She found Alice feeble, pale, but not thin. 'Her heart has been really very bad, but is better now, the pulse stronger,' she told Nona. Victoria found Alice resigned to staying at Kreuzlingen because she was so weak. She could only take a visit of half an hour before being exhausted. But Victoria hoped to 'arrange for a change of air & surroundings for her in summer',[4] at last a ray of hope. To Dickie she was more forthcoming:

> I saw Alice twice when I was at Salem with Dolla. It takes only 1¼ hour to motor from there to Bellevue, Kreuzlingen. Her heart was really very bad this winter & needs great care & quiet still, though better. She got dilatation of it & it will take a long time to get stronger again. Luckily a physical malady is quite comprehensible to her & as she likes the doctor who treats her heart, she is willing to keep quiet & has given up the hopes of leaving the sanatorium till she is stronger. Mentally there is not much change. She was pleased to see me & hear about you all.[5]

Victoria urged Dr Binswanger to arrange another visit from Count Hardenberg, with whom she was in such sympathy, 'because any slight diversion and joy in her sad life has to be granted to her'. She felt that her own presence was a nuisance to Alice 'for I am conscious that in her eyes I bear the responsibility of her being deprived of her freedom'.[6] Victoria hoped that by remaining absent now, she would retain some of Alice's affection for her.

At the end of April 1932, Alice complained that it had been difficult for her to be at Kreuzlingen since the first day. She said that only people without a mind of their own could stand it. Some of the patients had told her that they did not mind the keys being taken away. She, on the other hand, had a certain standard to maintain and had to do so without the help of a maid. At the end of this outburst she started to cry and said: 'The day after tomorrow I shall have already been here for two years.'[7]

Throughout the summer Alice's state fluctuated as before. Sometimes she was too tired to get out of bed, at others she allowed herself to be wheeled about in her wheelchair. Dr Binswanger thought the origin of this was psychic rather than physical. In July Professor Wilmanns came to see her but got a frosty reception. Then, on 7 July, a new doctor called on her, identified only as Dr Kr. in the case history. Alice asked this new doctor if he had undertaken any war work in hospitals and was disappointed that he had not. She said that she was trying to combine the principles of Coué with those of Freud, and establishing through her work 'a parallel between the mind and the body, the mind digesting various thoughts like the stomach, generating ideas as a mother generated her child'.[8]

Alice had various complaints to make about Dr Binswanger. He worked too hard, had too many patients and wrote too much. He did not have enough time to talk to his patients. Besides he was only there because he had inherited the sanatorium (from his father and uncle). The new doctor pointed out that Binswanger had learned his knowledge and skill. Alice riposted that she was saying not that he was a bad doctor, but that he refused to believe her to be mentally normal. In conclusion she felt that Dr Binswanger should confine himself to giving lectures.

Her first conversation with Dr Kr. had lasted nearly five hours. Two days later, at her request, he visited her for the second of three talks. He asked if their first talk had not tired her unduly and she replied: 'It has refreshed me mentally.'[9] On this occasion, Alice expounded her theory. He recorded:

With a solemn air she then initiates me in her system. Previously she had claimed she was the sole bride of God; but now she realized that every woman, by bodily and mental self-education, could achieve this position. At the same time she was able to remain quite worldly and even wear a low-necked dress. Presently I was asking her: how was it with men who had gone through the same self-education? She then informed me that

God was actually a bi-sexual being; the corresponding man simply becomes the bridegroom of the female part of God. Christ had become God in the shape of a man. When I asked why God had not also appeared in the shape of a woman, the patient was startled for a moment, and then admitted that this point was certainly lacking in the Christian religion, but not in the Indian one. The prolonged discussion which followed proved that the patient colours most religious terms in a sexual way. When I pronounced the word 'jealousy', she replied that I would not talk about this without a reason, that I was certainly alluding to the jealousy of Dr L.B.[10]

After fifty minutes, Alice asked Dr Kr. not to communicate what she had told him until he had undergone a divine inspiration. What she meant by this was unclear, but she said that the divine intervention had to follow a holiday on which he had been able to commune with himself.

The third meeting took place on 18 July. Dr Kr. told her that he could not imagine a bisexual God, since he did not impose the human form on his idea of God. Alice listened with some gravity, thought for a while and then said that there existed certain people who could enlighten him. For the rest of the visit Dr Kr. was left talking on his own. The next day she told Dr Binswanger that Dr Kr. was too analytical for her. She explained that when she had tried to talk of astronomy and astrology, he had 'shown great modesty in saying that [he] understood but little of these things'.[11]

From these reports it appears that little progress was being made with what the doctors would consider to be Alice's recovery to a point of mental stability, or to her own attempts to persuade them to let her go free or go elsewhere.

By now Alice was thoroughly fed up and decided to make a bid for freedom. On 27 July, while her nurse was having lunch, Alice seized the opportunity of the moment, jumped from a window of Villa Maria into a flowerbed and made off in the direction of the nearby railway line.

On discovering that Alice had gone, the hospital authorities alerted the customs at the various border crossings. Meanwhile Alice had made the briefest of journeys to the station, and succeeded in slipping into a waiting railway carriage, carrying a bundle of laundry and shoes. Here she was arrested.

Returned to the Bellevue, she was in a surprisingly good mood. She was interviewed by Professor Wilmanns, whom she told that she was fed up with being a princess and wanted to lead the life of an artist. She congratulated the professor on capturing her, but warned him she would try again. She did not wish to go to another sanatorium, where she would have less freedom than at present. Dr Binswanger was away for a few days so she would talk to him on his return.

When he heard about the escape attempt, Binswanger pronounced it 'all the more absurd' since the very day before, following Alice's express instructions, new plans had been made for her, and her Kreuzlingen phase was to come to an end.

Andrea and Alice's mother were both at Salem for the christening of Theodora's daughter, Margarita.* They had approved the plan that Alice should go to a different sanatorium, and to this plan Alice had seemingly agreed. Philip stayed with Theodora for part of that summer and she took him to see his mother. Unfortunately they found her so depressed that she hardly talked at all. When Victoria went over to tea with Alice, she found her physically better, in a good frame of mind and interested in family news:

> She has now been nearly 2½ years at Kreuzlingen & as she is 'fed up' with the place (though friendly with Dr Binswanger) & quite convinced that another winter there will be bad for her heart, B. & we are agreed it is time she should have a change, though alas not fit for freedom yet.[12]

Binswanger had recommended Dr Oscar Forel's luxurious sanatorium, Les Rives de Prangins, on the shores of Lake Geneva near

* Princess Margarita of Baden, born at Salem, 14 July 1932, after a twelve-hour labour. At first it was thought she would be called Alice. Dickie wrote: '[Dolla] has plenty of time yet to have a son' [MtB to VMH, KP, 18 July 1932, MB/M65 – HL]. Married 1957, Prince Tomislav of Yugoslavia. Divorced 1981.

Nyon, to which he had sent patients before. Its most famous inmate was Zelda Fitzgerald, the novelist Scott Fitzgerald's schizophrenic wife. Prangins cost about the same as the Bellevue and Edwina would continue to pay the bills. This plan would be implemented as soon as possible.

Dr Forel was summoned to see Alice. But Alice was now obdurate, refusing to go to another sanatorium and suggesting various alternatives. On 1 August Victoria came to visit her again and decided that a change of sanatorium made no sense. At this point, in Binswanger's words, 'the patient feigns shortness of breath again, lies in bed & asks for Dr Sträuli on behalf of her heart'.[13]

As ever, Victoria was sensitive to the problems that such a move involved. She was aware that if Alice thought Dr Binswanger approved of the new clinic, she would refuse it, believing that Binswanger would still have influence over her. Victoria believed this was the reason behind her rejection of Dr Forel.

Professor Wilmanns raised the strongest objections to any plan to move Alice. He was convinced that she was getting the best treatment possible at Bellevue and that a different institution would offer no advantage. 'After the patient's recent attempt to escape, one should dissuade her mother most seriously from sending her to another place. I am afraid that at Prangins, she will have even more chances to run away.'[14]

Victoria disagreed. She saw the importance of a change of scene to build up Alice's morale, though personally she retained the greatest confidence in Dr Binswanger. She explained:

> It is hard for me to ignore the re-iterated wish of my daughter. Her freedom which is of course playing the dominant role for her is as yet quite out of the question. But I hope to be able to persuade her eventually to submit herself to a psychiatrist, since she can always entertain the hope that a new doctor won't share our opinion of her complaint . . .
>
> There are so many psychical and physical reasons to be considered with mental patients that a complete environmental change could even have perhaps a beneficial effect. I beg your pardon that I, as an amateur, dare pronounce this thought, at which you will probably simply smile.

However, I cannot regard the question of my daughter's general state of health, other than in a prejudicial way, and you will certainly understand my desire to fulfil her wishes as far as possible.[15]

Alice's persistence had finally won Victoria over. Victoria consulted the Queen of Italy,* who recommended the Martinsbrunn Sanatorium in Merano, in the south Tyrol. This establishment, a much freer place, was known to be good for heart ailments,† and most specifically did not take 'any bad forms of lunacy'.[16] It was run by Dr Norbert von Kaan, who agreed to take Alice.

In the meantime Alice took exercises in order to walk better. Otherwise she lay about, was physically calm and composed, happy to go to Merano, and her pulse stayed regular without medication.

On 23 September Schwester Lina accompanied Alice to Merano. She was dismissed from Kreuzlingen, 'improved', as Dr Binswanger put it.[17]

It is as well that Victoria did not follow the advice of the doctors, and in particular that of Professor Wilmanns. It is a shocking thought that had she done so, Alice might have remained in the Bellevue for the rest of her life.

* Queen Elena (1873–1952), fifth daughter of Prince Nikola of Montenegro, and elder sister of Princess Anna of Battenberg.

† Mussolini's wife was cured of incipient lung trouble there in 1926.

23. Alice Itinerant

Alice brightened considerably after her transfer to Merano. In October 1932, Louise was relieved to hear that Alice liked being there, and Victoria told Dr Binswanger that she thought it a worthwhile risk, though 'would have preferred it had she submitted patiently to her constant sojourn at Bellevue and remained in your care'.[1]

Alice now began an extraordinary nomadic existence which lasted until 1937. Her mother knew where she was, but other members of the family did not. Over time these years have become obscured. Only now, as previously sealed papers are opened, has it been possible to trace her whereabouts.

At the end of 1932 Alice was still at Merano. At the beginning of December Victoria visited her on her way to another stay with Dickie in Malta. Victoria found Alice much improved. The Martinsbrunn Sanatorium afforded her greater freedom. She lived simply, having dispensed with the services of a maid, and looked after her own clothes. Victoria was pleased that Alice asked after Nona for the first time in two years. The Pye-Crust, in attendance on Victoria, commented that Alice seemed improved in spirits and was taking an interest in everyday things.

Alice had made friends with a Swedish lady, called Miss Heilskov, who acted as her secretary and was happy to discuss philosophical ideas with her. Miss Heilskov was a masseuse and physiotherapist of late middle age, who had been employed at the sanatorium for nine years and whom Dr von Kaan recommended highly for 'kindness and honesty'. Before that she had worked in a large asylum for the insane in America and was thus trained to deal with mood swings.

The greatest shock for Victoria was when Alice told her that she did not wish to return to her family or to resume former ties. There is no doubt that Alice still felt betrayed by her family in the matter of her two and a half years' stay at Kreuzlingen. Her mother had put her there; Andrea had sanctioned this. Thus she now decided to pursue her own life quietly without any of them. But although it was clear that she needed time to herself in order to regain her physical and spiritual strength, total severance from her family was a serious step with wide implications. Before her illness Alice had been the mainstay of a close-knit family. Her daughters were married, but Philip was only eleven, an age when a mother might well have expected to look after him. Alice's decision was tantamount to a renunciation of her role as mother.

Victoria talked to Dr von Kaan, whom she found a 'very clever man', with a 'high reputation',[2] and between them they agreed that Alice should be allowed freedom under surveillance. Thus, shortly after Victoria left, Alice moved into a modest pensione in Merano, still accompanied by Miss Heilskov. 'I feel at last one dares hope again,'[3] commented Louise, when she heard the news. Just before Christmas, Dr von Kaan reported that Alice was feeling well in her new home, and enjoying her freedom on probation.[4]

On 2 January 1933 Alice left Merano with Miss Heilskov and settled in Nervi, a quiet seaside resort on the Italian Riviera between Genoa and Portofino, recommended by Dr von Kaan. They rented a tiny cottage, called the Villino Etter, which belonged to an hotel. Situated on the via della Marina, it nestled in the rocks just above the promenade by the sea. Alice became preoccupied with setting up home and thus had no time to dwell on philosophy.

Victoria spent four days with Alice on her return from Malta in February. She found her daughter in bed with a chill, and a little tired when talking. She had put on weight. Victoria reported to Nona:

She was nice & friendly, but had hinted to her companion that a longer visit from me would be tiring. She has got so out of the way of needing her family that though she likes to hear all the news & sends her love, visits upset her routine life. It was nice to see her calm & contented with her freer life. Her heart was in a satisfactory condition, but she is nervous about fatiguing it, unless she gets keen about something such as organizing her house, when she can do a lot apparently without harm & because she does not like passing strangers, she gets no exercise except doing her room & a quarter-deck walk behind the Villino & as a result is getting too fat.[5]

Victoria thought Alice was set to remain there until May. Meanwhile she stayed at Darmstadt and was on the point of leaving for Sweden to see Louise when she heard disturbing news:

Alice suddenly decided she would leave Nervi & go to Basel to be in touch there with the publisher of a magazine we know nothing about. As Hardenberg happened to be in Switzerland we sent him straight to Nervi to see Alice, who agreed to wait a short time & he goes to Basel today to see about arrangements there for her. (He has just telegraphed she is going with him.) She has evidently got into one of her excitable states, which from former experiences I conclude won't last long & be followed by a time of apathy. So she may still possibly remain at Nervi. Anyhow I have put off my journey to Sweden until the situation is cleared up & I can feel more reassured for a while. It is disappointing to find that there is no real improvement in the symptoms of her malady.[6]

Miss Heilskov had returned to Merano to be replaced by a young Swiss secretary called Miss Nussbaum. Alice told the Danish Consul at Genoa that she wanted to leave Nervi on 18 March to go to Basle, stopping at Turin. Her plan was to relinquish the services of Miss Nussbaum in Turin, but the secretary left her employ while they were still in Nervi. Alice had dictated a letter to *Die Weisse Fahne** at a small place called Villingen in the Black Forest, enclosing an article for publication and asking that a representative meet her in Basle on 22 March.

From the start, one of the great concerns of Alice's family was that she should not make a fool of herself by publishing articles in

* *The White Banner*, described by Victoria as 'some unknown mystical society' [VMH to NK, Darmstadt, 24 March 1933, BA].

the paper. Victoria told the Danis Consul not to let Alice have any money for the journey. The family awaited developments in some trepidation, particularly hoping that it would not be necessary for Alice to return to a sanatorium.

Count Hardenberg proved masterly in his dealings with Alice. He met her in Basle, where fortunately the representative of *Die Weisse Fahne* did not materialize. Alice then remembered someone who lived in the Eifel, a little south of Bonn. She and Hardenberg made the journey as far as Mainz, when he was able to tell her that the Eifel person had left a year before.

Victoria came to Mainz to see Hardenberg, without seeing her daughter. By this time Alice was worn out and ready to accept any plan proposed by the long-suffering Count. He steered her to a pension at Bad Kreuznach, the spa in the Palatinate where the Hesse and Battenberg families had gone regularly in earlier days. A nurse was found to look after her. The best doctor at Kreuznach was briefed about her condition. Confident that the crisis was over, Victoria left for Sweden, happy in the knowledge that Uncle Ernie and Hardenberg were a mere two hours away by car and that Alice was likely to be subdued for a while.

Alice did indeed settle, and chose to take the baths there of her own accord. Her mother hoped that these, 'being good for ordinary glands, may I hope also have a salutary effect on those unknown ones, which probably by wrongly functioning are one of the causes of brain-trouble'.[7]

In the summer Victoria wrote to Dr Binswanger giving him a report of Alice's progress and of what she called her slight relapse. He replied that he was vividly interested in her case, adding: 'Had her human concern not adopted such unhealthy forms, she would indeed have become an exceptionally kind and outstanding spiritual personality.' The doctor thought that Alice had conducted herself better than he had dared to predict, a small admission that he had misjudged her. Victoria asked him if the illness was likely to take a turn towards the dangerous. He believed that, while there might be some problems, it seemed that the cycles of relapse were diminishing in intensity:

On a practical level the main danger seems to me that the princess might fall into wrong hands and be exploited financially. This danger could best be met with a legal incapacitation, of which, if my memory does not fail me, we have already talked. The difficulty with this would be to find an authority that could proceed with the matter. In any case it is important to inform anyone that she employs that she is a mental patient, and that consequently one takes a closer look at these persons. Therefore one has to, as your R. H. has realized yourself, maintain a certain contact with her. It would be advisable, if the princess were settled at one place for a longish period, to find a trustworthy person who would inform the family as soon as anything worrying happened in the internal or external condition of the princess.[8]

Binswanger further advised Victoria that Alice should be told that she was not fully cured, and that her freedom depended on her future conduct: 'I consider it to be very important that the "phantom" of a new institutional treatment and the memory of the "deprivation of liberty" in this place should not completely vanish from her mind and continue to act as a curative inhibition.'[9] What Binswanger was suggesting was that Alice would behave better if she lived under the threat of being returned to an institution.

It was natural that Alice's family should continue to worry about her, especially when her earlier illness was taken into account. Alice was heading towards recovery. That she was still inclined to be eccentric and that she pursued an unconventional path is without doubt. As it turned out, her family were being over-cautious. Above all, they were keen that she should not have to return to a sanatorium. 'Poor Alice seems to be quite content,' observed Louise in September, '& that is the chief thing.'[10]

At some time that summer Alice made her way to Cologne, and booked in to the Excelsior Hotel. She cast about for somewhere to live and found rooms let out by Frau Reuter* at Bachemer strasse,

* Frau Reuter, wife of a shareholder in the Bols liquor company, who was often away hunting.

26. Alice surprised her landlady by arriving in a taxi, wearing a silver-grey robe, and only when she showed Frau Reuter her impressive diplomatic passport would she believe she had a real princess on the doorstep. Alice took three rooms: a large sitting room, a bedroom for herself and a former guestroom for a companion, an educated girl whom she described as her 'pupil', who undertook household chores for a monthly wage. Frau Reuter's daughter, Almuth, helped Alice unpack and was much impressed, at the age of eleven, by the large collection of silk shoes that Alice brought with her. Rent was agreed, but nothing paid. Later Count Hardenberg arrived and settled that.

Almuth Reuter recalled that Alice used to sit on their terrace in the afternoons, just staring into space. She once mentioned that she had had a vision and seen St Barbara, probably a reference to Sister Barbara, Ella's faithful companion. She was visited by Count Hardenberg from time to time, and then they would be ensconced in a room together, and sometimes, as he left, he gave the impression of having failed in some specific mission.

This was Alice's period of self-imposed exile. Almuth got the feeling that Alice did nothing, and that she was very lonely, but always dignified. She recalled: 'She was always glad when my mother invited her, and would talk about past times, her childhood, the Battenbergs, and, by the way, she excelled in the art of dealing with a little piece of cake for an hour.'[11]

By September Alice had settled at Brück, just outside the city. She was to remain in the Cologne area for more than four years. Somehow she found a couple called the Dilmits and they became her loyal friends. Herr Dilmit was a German-Russian who wrote and lectured on political economy. Both he and his wife, a Caucasian, had been in a Russian prison in 1927, and he had written a play about this. Frau Dilmit was also a writer, reviewing books for various German newspapers. The Dilmits were not rich, but comfortably well off. Alice was drawn to them by the idea that they could help her write a book on a religious theme.

Victoria had never heard of the Dilmits and flew out to Cologne on 9 September to meet them. She described them to Dickie:

I saw Alice one afternoon at her friends the Dilmits' house, first alone, & then together with them for tea. I found her very well & very contented. She likes her flat at Brück, which is more or less a village still & surrounded by fields & woods, though a suburb of Cologne. Also she told me she had at last found the right people to help her & to be interested in her work. They make notes of what she tells them & put her ideas (those that are clever & sensible) into proper shape.[12]

The Dilmits impressed Victoria as kindly people, who admired Alice's originality and brains, while being aware that her mind was not quite right. The Dilmits visited her about three or four times a week. Victoria was satisfied that their motives were not financial and that Hardenberg controlled the expenses carefully.* She thought: 'Their vanity is a bit flattered by looking after a Princess & they flatter themselves that they can help to cure her & they seem to want her to see her relations. Certainly for the present all is going well & it was nice to find Alice cheerful & enjoying what she thinks is her complete freedom & independence.'[13]

Alice remained at Brück, working with the Dilmits on her proposed religious book throughout 1934. At the end of February the Dilmits took her to Aachen for a few days, duly reporting this move to Count Hardenberg. Otherwise the year went by with little news of her reaching her family, though in June she was described as 'keeping well'.[14]

Most of what can be known of Alice at this time is recorded in a report that Victoria gave to Dr Binswanger when she went to tea with him at Kreuzlingen in July 1934. She told him that Alice now lived in complete privacy. Binswanger noted:

Conception of ideas entirely unchanged. Has once slapped a maid – who refused to get into a cold bath, ordered by the patient, it being winter and she having a strong cold – so badly that she had to see an ear-specialist.

* Alice's allowance of about £110 a month, previously handled by Count Hardenberg, was now sent direct from Edwina to an account in Herr Dilmit's name in Cologne. Dilmit was directly responsible to Edwina's secretary, Miss Underhill.

From time to time she throws objects on the floor. Talks constantly about writing a book.[15]

When occasionally she behaved badly, the Dilmits usually succeeded in mollifying her, Victoria told the doctor. Alice now lived in total privacy and would only see her mother at the Dilmits' house. There she was friendly, though never asked after her children, with whom she now had very little contact. She never spoke of Kreuzlingen, and she had grown older in appearance. Although it was clear that Alice was still not fully cured, Victoria's meeting with Dr Binswanger reassured her that the present arrangement was 'quite the right thing'.[16]

Alice was still at Brück at the beginning of 1935. Victoria hoped to arrange a visit to her on her annual visit to Malta in February, but this did not happen. However, she was able to call on Alice on her return, coming from Wolfsgarten on 26 May.

The meeting was unsatisfactory to say the least. Victoria found her fifty-year-old daughter 'not particularly pleased at my coming. Bodily she is well, mentally no better . . . The great thing is that she continues to like & trust the Dilmit couple, with whom I had a long, satisfactory talk.'[17]

Later in the summer Alice went for a holiday in Bohemia with Herr Dilmit. 'She went through an excited stage afterwards,' Victoria told Dickie in November, 'but is in a calm period at present.'[18] At the end of the year, she added: 'Poor Alice, alas, has not yet ever had a period of normality, though I don't think she is worse.'[19]

Not until August 1936 did Alice agree to see her mother again. This time Victoria came from a large family gathering at Hemmelmark for her sister Irène's seventieth birthday. For moral support, she took Aunt Onor with her. Together they had tea with Alice in Cologne. Victoria found Alice 'well, sensible & friendly', but did not see her alone as Alice was still feeling guilty about their ten-minute meeting a year before. Afterwards Victoria talked to the Dilmits:

> They find no change in her condition with its ups & downs of quieter more reasonable periods & the contrary. She is still full of her grand & fanciful notions, but can talk & argue well & there is no deterioration in her mental faculties, only the guiding screw loose in her brain.[20]

Moral support came from old Princess Louise, Victoria's 88-year-old aunt and neighbour at Kensington Palace: 'I do feel *so for you* & *your* pluck & patience is wonderful & surely you will be rewarded.'[21]

At the end of August Alice took a holiday with Herr Dilmit in the Carinthian Alps. They stayed at Platten See, not far from Budapest. By chance her sister Louise was in the vicinity on her summer holiday, travelling under the name of Countess Gripsholm, and on 1 September Herr Dilmit made a point of meeting her for the first time. Louise reported her thoughts:

> He made a good impression & I thought him straight-forward, simple & very kind & good hearted. Alice is well & calm, the trouble always is for him that Alice is so restless when they travel, always wanting to move on after a while. He would prefer to rest quietly at one place.
>
> What I liked about him is that he seems really fond of Alice in spite of all the trouble. When I said how more than grateful I was to him & his wife, he pushed it aside & said one has ones duty & ones neighbour & what one undertakes one carries out & they have no children so they look after Alice instead.[22]

Louise hatched a plan with him so that she and Alice did not meet by chance. Dilmit avoided the centre of town and he telephoned Louise in advance if they were making an expedition somewhere where Louise might be. She thought it tragic that they were almost in the same place but must avoid a meeting that might disturb Alice. Louise was resigned to this: 'It would only upset her & make things difficult for Dilmit.'[23]

Alice was still in the Cologne area at the end of 1936, but presently she left the Dilmits. Why she did this is unclear. There is no evidence of a disagreement, yet equally no evidence of further contact between them. There is every chance that the move was part of the process towards full recovery.

The move came about because Alice's companion met an architect in Italy, who showed her a prospectus for what she thought was his estate, Breibach, near Kürten, in the Bergische Land, about fifty kilometres east of Cologne. Having liked the architect, she recommended that Alice visit the estate. When she arrived there, Alice discovered it was run by his brother, Reinhold Markwitz, but as she took a liking to him, his wife Hedwig and his sister Berta, it did not matter. Reinhold Markwitz was a lawyer and member of the Social Democratic Party. A year before he had been forced to renounce his profession and give up his notary's office in Duisberg in the Rhineland, which he had run with a Jewish partner.

Towards the end of November,[24] Alice moved to Breibach. She stayed in a farmhouse turned boarding house, a rural retreat, with a large open fire, ultraviolet light treatment, its own trout, organic wines and cream waffles for tea. Breibach was a modest establishment, housing about twenty-eight guests. Alice checked in as 'Countess Hohenstein', a name that she tried to adopt on an interim-passport.*

Alice passed her stay in her traditional seclusion, often sitting on the floor of the communal sitting room near the fire, and helping peel potatoes in the kitchen. A fellow guest was Käthe Lindlar, who was recuperating from an illness. She was told that the princess did not like being talked to. But Alice spotted Käthe reading a book by Rabindranath Tagore, the Indian philosopher, who had visited Darmstadt in 1921. They struck up an animated conversation in which Alice expounded her views on girls' education and the theories of Montessori and Fröbel. Käthe described Alice as 'a very modern woman with incredible vision. She clarified much about

* Neither Alice's Uncle Ernie nor Count Hardenberg objected to her changing her name, though Hardenberg could not let her choose 'Hohenstein', as there was already a family of that name. He advised Princess, Countess or Mrs von Battenberg [Count Hardenberg to Reinhold Markwitz, Darmstadt, 22 January 1937, private collection].

world politics for me.' She was also impressed by Alice's 'very expressive hands'.[25]

During her stay, Alice urged Markwitz to adorn his woods with small panels naming the trees so that children could learn as they went for walks, but this was not done in his lifetime. When children went out, Alice was solicitous in clearing broken glass and stinging nettles that might harm them.

Alice was soon inspiring Markwitz in his writing. 'Reinhold, you must do good,' she would say to him, 'even if you believe our present mankind to be undeserving of it.'[26] In him she found a man who could be both a spiritual and intellectual adviser. He was a contrast to the ambitions of her own family, living a simple and contented life. He was perhaps eccentric, but he was also a man of moral integrity, with humanitarian views, ready to shelter people in trouble, and he saw through the ideology being promulgated by the Nazis.

Some years later, Markwitz wrote a book in which he paid tribute to the influence which Alice had on him:

> I owe her the conviction that every person has the duty to contribute to the progress of mankind, according to his abilities, even if he thinks it is useless, or believes he has a reason to despise the respective present-day mankind. It was only this conviction which enabled the beginning of this work at a time when the bad spirit of National Socialism was celebrating its greatest triumphs before the war, apparently favoured, or at least tolerated benevolently, by almost all civilized nations.[27]

In the soothing company of the Markwitz family, Alice achieved what many of her fellow patients at the Bellevue had failed to achieve. She began to get better. She regained a more conventional composure that allowed her to cope with the outside world. In so doing she did not renounce either her independence or her private, inner beliefs. She regained her health once she was out of the care of the doctors. As far as her family was concerned, she came into focus again after her long sojourn in self-imposed exile. She made tentative steps towards resuming the reins of normal life.

As 1936 closed, so Alice wrote to Cécile, thanking her for sending photographs of her new daughter* and of Philip. Alice also wrote a letter to Philip. This was an important development. 'Your little daughter is so sweet and chubby,' she wrote to Cécile. 'Philip I barely recognized, he is so changed. Give him my love please.'[28]

* Cécile gave birth to her third child and only daughter, Johanna, on 20 September 1936.

24. Philip and Andrea

Alice was happy at Breibach and stayed there well into 1937. Her mother visited her in April, eager to meet Reinhold Markwitz, this new influence in her daughter's life. Victoria judged the Markwitzes 'sensible people', finding the atmosphere at Breibach 'somewhat prosaic, though not unintellectual & seems to have done Alice good'.[1]

During the visit, Alice lunched with Victoria at her hotel and they walked round the town together. This was so encouraging that presently Cécile and Don took Philip to lunch with her in Bonn. They returned to Darmstadt 'delighted with their meeting', having found Alice 'affectionate, bright & cheerful'.[2]

This was the first time that Alice had seen any of her children since August 1932. In the intervening five years much had happened. It must have been a poignant moment for Alice seeing Philip again. He was no longer the 'little boy' who might have come and spent some time with her on a cure. He was now fifteen.

After Alice's removal to Kreuzlingen, Philip had been in the care of his grandmother, though his official guardian was his uncle, Georgie Milford Haven, an arrangement that suited everyone including Andrea. He never heard a word from his mother, not even a birthday card, but every summer he joined his father for part of his holiday. Philip was sent to Cheam School in England. Victoria and Georgie attended to the business of sorting out his school clothes, which were frequently 'in great disorder'.[3]

Of Alice's children, Philip was the one most neglected. Inevitably he was sent from one household to another. When his grandmother was in Sweden in 1933, she arranged that he spent his Easter holidays partly with Georgie and Nada (their son, David, a bit older than Philip, was at Cheam School with him), and partly with Nona.

She hoped it would not be too long for Nona, but added 'as he is one of those lucky people, who can take an interest in any job & you have a talent to occupy children, I am sure he will be happy at Fishponds'.[4]

In the same year Philip's summer holiday plans were disorganized. Victoria sent him to Wolfsgarten rather suddenly so that he could join his father there and travel with him, first to stay with Theodora at Salem and later to enter one of the preparatory schools there, Spetzgart. On 9 August his old nanny Emily Roose died in South Africa, having served the family for twenty-five years.

The following summer, 1934, it was the same story. Victoria and Philip were at Wolfsgarten. Victoria did not know what to do with Philip, since she felt honour bound to defer to his father, who failed to materialize. She wrote to Georgie, explaining the predicament:

Philip may go there (Hemmelmark) with us & back to England with me via Hamburg & Southampton but we can settle nothing about his movements until having discussed them with Andrea, who after a delay of 4 weeks turns up this evening, we suppose en route for a cure in Marienbad. I hope it is not too inconvenient to leave you without definite news of Philip's movements, but it has been unavoidable.[5]

In the end Philip was left in Germany and returned to Salem with his father. Altogether he spent two terms at Spetzgart and one at Salem itself, the school founded by Berthold of Baden's father, Prince Max, and the legendary headmaster Kurt Hahn. Philip remained at Salem for just one more term. Owing to the political situation in Germany and Kurt Hahn's move to Gordonstoun, Philip was sent to the Scottish school in the autumn of 1934.

In November 1935 Andrea stayed with Victoria and outlined his plans for Philip to her. She reported these to Dickie:

He has decided that Philip is to finish his schooling at Gordonstoun & hopes it can be arranged after that, for him to pass the public school exam for entrance in our navy & be allowed to serve for a few years, as Juan* was. It will be the best training for the boy & Philip is quite keen about it. The naval officer, who is sports master etc. at the school will work him up.[6]

His grandmother was good to him, and he was in some awe of her. She coped well, though when Philip returned to her from Wolfsgarten in January 1936 after a stint in bed with inflamed kidneys, she allowed herself a rare moment of self-pity: 'Children & grandchildren, though a pleasure, are decidedly a worry at times,'[7] she wrote to Dickie.

Nor was there a hint that Philip was unhappy with his lot. He explained: 'I was at school in England, and suddenly my family had gone. My father was in the South of France and my mother was just ill. I had to get on with it.'[8]

Only once was there the suggestion that the grown-ups were worried about him. Kurt Hahn wanted him to see the Naval Review at Spithead, after the coronation in 1937, but the family decided that 'the life here now, amongst grown-up relations & with hours of idling are not good for him & the sooner he gets out of it & back to school the better'.[9] His grandmother dispatched him back to Gordonstoun.

Presently Andrea would reappear briefly in Alice's life. His had been a peripatetic existence since she was taken from Darmstadt in May 1930.

After closing down the family home in Paris soon after Alice went to Kreuzlingen, Andrea either lodged with his brother, Big George, in his Paris home at 7 rue Adolph Yvon, or stayed at the Travellers Club.

For several years, the fate of Mon Repos was an irritant, with constant threats of confiscation by the Greek government. Though

* Prince Juan, Count of Barcelona (1913–93), son of King Alfonso and Queen Ena, and father of the present King of Spain. Served as a Midshipman, RN, 1933–5.

Venizelos was keen that Andrea be left alone, the British envoys feared a change of heart in 1931 following the publication of recent memoirs by the princes, 'of which there appears to be an unfortunate recrudescence of late, not to mention the publication in English last year by Prince Andrew himself of his personal experiences entitled *Towards Disaster*. . . Many anti-Venizelist quotations from it were published in the press here.'[10]

In 1932 Dickie and Edwina removed thirty-two cases of possessions from the house, and Louise organized a steamer to convey them to Stockholm. On one such expedition, the Prince of Wales was with Dickie and took a fancy to a pair of Andrea's binoculars. Dickie bought them for him for £25, and when he told Andrea this, Andrea commented: 'He's very welcome to them. What shall I do with the beastly things anyway?'[11]

Andrea won a lawsuit over his ownership of Mon Repos in 1934, but behaved in cavalier fashion with his lawyers and the caretaker, Blower. 'Everyone connected with the case is driven mad by Andrea who will never answer or acknowledge any form of communication,' reported Dickie. 'It appears that Blower & the lawyers have been more or less acting on my instructions but luckily I told Andrea all I had said when I saw him a few months ago in Paris & he seemed to agree with all I had done.'[12]

The Greeks handed Mon Repos back to Andrea, but it became a white elephant. Andrea finally sold the villa to George II, buying himself an annuity with the proceeds.*

Understandably, Andrea found it hard to conceal his bitterness over his exile and from time to time his public utterances upset the Greek politicians. In May 1932, he attacked Venizelos in the Greek press for making disparaging remarks about the exiled royal family in the Chamber. Andrea described his family as 'wandering in foreign parts in poverty, deprived by Monsieur Venizelos of fatherland and nationality at a moment when he, now an extremely

*Mon Repos was used as a summer home by King Paul and Queen Frederika in the 1950s and 1960s, and inherited by King Constantine. The fate of the house is still a matter of dispute between King Constantine and the Greeks.

wealthy man, abandons an unhappy and exhausted Greece whose people are poverty stricken and miserable'. The ministers shot in 1922, he added, were 'national Martyrs, assassinated by Monsieur Venizelos'. The British Minister reported the reaction to this in Athens:

Eleftheron Vema reprints the letter and expresses the hope that every Greek will read it as it is quite sufficient in itself to explain the history of the past ten years. Perhaps, too, it adds, if Prince Andrew will read it through, coolly, he will understand how it has come about that he and his family are not in Greece . . .

It is clear that so long as members of the former royal family persist in taking up a party political line, they could only return to this country identified as political partisans, and they would have to go out of office with the party that brought them back.[13]

Andrea remained unmoved. 'I spent quite an agreeable, though rather lonely summer down here,' he wrote to Dickie from Monte Carlo. 'Happily, Dimitri and Audrey* were there part of the time.'[14] Andrea returned to Paris in the autumn before joining Ernie, Onor and Philip in Darmstadt for Christmas. Then he went back to what he called 'gay Paree', before setting off again for Monaco.

Andrea spent his summers drifting between Cannes and Monte Carlo. He made friends with an intriguing character called Gilbert Beale, whose fortune derived from Carter's Tested Seeds, a company which prospered because of the innovative idea of depicting the flowers-to-be on the seed packets. Beale was responsible for the grass on the tennis courts at Wimbledon. He dabbled in property, he and his brothers laying out golf courses a suitable distance from London. They would get into a train, drop off for a short nap, and at whatever point they awoke, leave the train and look for an

* Prince Dimitri of Russia (1891–1942), Ella's ward, had married Audrey Emery (1904–71), from Ohio, in 1926. They were divorced in 1937. He was Andrea's nephew. Their son, Paul R. Ilyinsky, became Mayor of Palm Beach, Florida.

appropriate site to lay down a golf course. They designed the first courses in Russia and Egypt and one for the Kaiser.

Beale lived to be almost a hundred and is remembered today for the Child-Beale Wildlife Trust at Lower Basildon, near Reading. Though this was his base, he spent most of his time on his yacht in the south of France, where Andrea was a welcome guest.

Beale was a dapper figure and in France he was invariably clad in yachting clothes. He was something of a lady's man, and there was no shortage of female company aboard *Angela* and later *Susannah Jane*. Beale was a life-long bachelor, saved from a number of unsuitable marriages by the vigilance of stern sisters, who occasionally materialized in the south of France, if Beale was not careful.

It is from his association with Beale that Andrea acquired the reputation of philanderer. It is more likely that what he enjoyed was the free hospitality and the easy life.

Margot Hambling met him in the south of France in the summer of 1936. She recalled that their days were spent at leisure on Beale's yacht, invariably moored in Cannes harbour, where the drinks arrived at eleven. 'Sometimes they went on to lunch, sometimes they just went on drinking,' she said. Following a siesta, the party foregathered for more drinks in the evening. Some went sightseeing, others played bridge; Andrea enjoyed the casino.

Margot Hambling concluded that Andrea was fun-loving, but though he enjoyed the so-called good life, she saw in him an element of sadness. He lived a 'hand-to-mouth existence', and missed living in Greece. So far as Alice was concerned, he sought no further involvement.[15]

Every now and again Andrea's nomadic life was punctuated by a political intervention. In January 1935, an interview with Andrea was published in one of the Greek newspapers. He declared that a strong movement towards the restoration of the monarchy was spreading in Greece. He claimed that he received a hundred letters and telegrams a day denouncing the republican regime. 'We shall not return as avengers,' he said, 'but as symbols of the love of the people on whose will alone the restoration will be founded; we shall return as restorers of the majesty of Greece, not as invaders. The Royal Family will bear no malice towards anybody, as we saw on another occasion.'[16] Unfortunately this article appeared in a paper edited by a man called Polychronopoulos, whose father was on trial for the attempted murder of Venizelos in 1933. However, the monarchy was restored in Greece in November 1935, and Andrea had more reasons for optimism.

There had been twenty-three changes of government in Greece between 1924 and 1935, one dictatorship and thirteen coups. Greece was in a state of chaos, both political and financial.[17] Meanwhile, George II had lived first in Bucharest and latterly in London. His childless marriage to Elisabeth of Romania had floundered as she took to the gaming tables, grew fat and presently settled down with a lover called Alexander Scanavi, her husband's banker, who served as her chamberlain.[18] In July 1935 a quick divorce was granted in Bucharest on the grounds of 'desertion'.[19]

The exiled King spent long periods visiting his mother, Queen Sophie, until her death in January 1932. Thereafter he lived in a small suite at Brown's Hotel in London and became a dedicated Anglophile. He made friends with the Duke and Duchess of York, and acquired a discreet mistress called Joyce Britten-Jones, a good-looking, well-dressed widow, once described as 'the Mrs Simpson of Greece'.[20]

On a visit to ex-King George in London in October 1935, Andrea stayed with Victoria at Kensington Palace and explained what was happening in Greece. Victoria reported to Dickie:

George of Greece (King) is not looking forward with any real pleasure to his return. He had a sort of family meeting here a little while ago to which Andrea came over & stopped 3 days with me. He was pleased with his nephew's sensible views, & his friendliness to the older generation & that he does not wish to have them dancing attendance or settling in Athens. Andrea is to go out there as soon as convenient to show himself & to be received well, to wipe out the shameful departure after the mock court martial.

The whole family will later on go to Athens for the translation of the remains of Aunt Olga, Tino & Sophie to Tatoï,* but won't remain long. It is such a tragedy that our poor Alice can't go too & I fear these Greek events will excite her again . . .

Andrea nearly broke down speaking about her & his lonely return to Greece.[21]

British affairs in Greece were looked after by Sir Sydney Waterlow,† nicknamed 'The Water Buffalo' on account of his magnificent walrus moustache, which he curled upwards at each end. As a young man he had been turned down by Virginia Woolf, written a life of Shelley and been cited as co-respondent in a divorce case by an impotent husband. A *ceinture réglante* kept him puffed up like a pouter pigeon. He was both a 'great classicist' and 'a figure of fun'.[22]

Waterlow backed the restoration of the monarchy, but warned: 'To prevent failure . . . It is very important that Prince Nicholas should not come back here, and the King should not burden the country with any claim for money payments in arrear since his departure.'[23] Finally, after a sham plebiscite, in which the King received 95 per cent of the votes, because of multiple voting,‡ it was decided that the King should return.

* In November 1935, most of the Greek royal family gathered in Athens for the lying-in-state of Queen Olga, King Constantine and Queen Sophie. After a funeral service in the cathedral, there was a procession and the bodies were laid to rest at Tatoï. It was the occasion of Philip's first return to Greece, and he was sick in his top hat, passing it to an unsuspecting courtier on his way into the service.

† Sir Sydney Waterlow (1878–1944), British Ambassador to Greece 1933–9.

‡ A lorry of airforce men voted at one polling station in Athens. They then voted at three more stations. Infantrymen voted at the polling station near the old Parliament House. They then marched twice round the building, voting each time, before departing. Two ex-soldiers voted five times with seven voting cards. An electrician voted seventeen times. Blank certificates were issued by the Mayor of Athens and others to help this false electoral process. No checks were made at the polling booths, while at numerous stations there were no republican voting cards available. Intimidation and other means of cajoling were brought into play. At the end of the day the Minister of the Interior destroyed a quantity of royalist votes, saying 'No! No! I didn't mean them to go as far as that.' The final figure

On 5 November ex-King George issued a proclamation agreeing to return to Greece. He journeyed from London to Paris where he met Andrea. Awaiting the King's return in Athens, Waterlow again warned: 'Success of monarchy will be jeopardised if the King insists on installing Prince Nicholas and Prince Andrew in the country.'[24] He told the American Ambassador, Lincoln MacVeagh, that 'Princes Andrew and Nicholas "must not" remain long in the country or mix in affairs.'[25] The King arrived on Greek soil on 25 November 1935, and in March 1936 Venizelos died in Paris.

It was not long before Waterlow's worries about Andrea came to fruition. At the end of January 1936, the sentence of perpetual banishment from Greece imposed on him at his court martial was declared void. This permitted Andrea to return to Greece, and he wasted no time in so doing. He arrived in Greece in mid-May aboard the 167-ton yacht *Davida*, which belonged to a soi-disant Australian called David E. Townsend, whose registered address was the Société de Banque Suisse in Geneva. This bull-like man was remembered by Margot Hambling as 'a dodgy character',[26] and part of Gilbert Beale's circle.

Andrea attended a royalist meeting at Halandri, a village in the neighbourhood of Athens, which he publicly commended as 'always prominent in the struggle for legality'. At the same time he wrote to a royalist organization called 'Constitutional Youth', saying: 'I am acquainted with your magnificent efforts and I congratulate you from the bottom of my heart for your persistence and patience.'[27]

More or less all the Greek press seized on these innocuous words to declare that Andrea's attitude was damaging the reconciliation process and reintroducing old tactics that had twice cost King Constantine his throne, accusing him and Prince Nicholas of still being inspired by 'the same fanatical party spirit which, unless checked, will create a revulsion of feeling against the monarchy'.[28] *Hestia*, a moderate, non-party paper, described Andrea's visit as 'a

---

was 1,491,992 votes pro-restoration out of 1,527,714 votes cast. A mere 32,454 supported the Republic and 3,268 votes were invalidated.

serious blunder' and regretted that attempts to heal the feud between the major parties 'should be undermined by his ill-considered activities'.[29]

After spending part of the summer of 1936 in Cannes, Andrea returned to Athens in the autumn and lived at the palace as Principal ADC to the King.

The following April, Andrea sailed into another diplomatic incident by entering Cypriot waters, again on board Townsend's yacht, *Davida.* The Governor of Cyprus was soon preoccupied with whether or not Andrea intended to disembark. The Greek Consul, aptly named 'Scarpa', arrived in Larnaca, so the Governor of Cyprus sent his commissioner down to investigate. When the Commissioner boarded *Davida* at 8.00 a.m. the boat party were still in bed. A sleepy Townsend eventually appeared and a message was sent to Andrea to the effect that should he wish to land, he, the Commissioner, was at his disposal, largely, it seems, to annoy the Greek Consul.

Andrea decided to disembark, and the Greek Consul further stirred matters by telling the Commissioner in confidence that 'His Highness had stated that he would be sorry to think that he had received from the Italians, whom he hated, greater assistance in the matter of landing facilities than from the British Authorities.'[30]

The visit passed off harmlessly. A crowd of about a hundred people saluted Andrea, who then went on a tour. On their return to the yacht, a larger crowd had gathered, and there was some hand clapping and cheering. The Commissioner reported that Andrea had asked if Cyprus was not quite quiet at present and when told that the main problems were economic rather than political, had commented: 'All the trouble was due to the — fool of a Consul [the Greek Consul] we had here, a strong Republican incidentally.'[31]

Davida then sailed to Limassol, arriving there on 25 April. This time about seven hundred people turned out to see him. As he did not land, enthusiastic well-wishers sailed out in hired launches to greet him, asking: 'Are you landing, Your Highness?' to which Andrea replied: 'I shall think.'[32] But he did not land. The Governor of Cyprus summed up the business by writing: 'We were put in a rather awkward position and the Prince's visit had to be very carefully handled.'[33] The Governor made sure that Andrea received copies of his correspondence with the British Consul-General at Alexandria, the dual purpose being to prevent him from saying he had received 'inhospitable treatment from the Cyprus Government and because I wanted to discourage him politely from landing at Limassol'.[34]

These incidents showed how unwelcome Andrea still was in Greek national circles. Besides that, he remained alert and amusing, though under the surface, he was a bored, rather lonely man. In 1937 Victoria noticed a growing reliance on alcohol, and was pleased when Andrea told her that he felt better since confining himself to the occasional glass of white wine.

25. Recovery and Tragedy

On 15 April 1937 Alice went to Switzerland with Berta Markwitz, Reinhold's sister, dubbed 'an elderly, sensible person'[1] by the ever-vigilant Victoria. She continued to make good progress. In June she accepted Theodora's invitation to take a break at Schloss Kirchberg, a Baden house, perched on a hill above Lake Constance, opposite Kreuzlingen. This meant that she was twenty minutes by car from Salem. For the first time in many years, she remembered Philip's birthday, 'which I regret you are spending at school and not here'.[2]

Another sign that Alice was heading towards the resumption of her former life was her request to Cécile that Popoulo (Virginie Simopoulos) should come from Athens to resume her duties as lady-in-waiting, although this proved impossible. Alice told Cécile that she was enjoying Kirchberg, a charming place, 'but it is lonely – no intelligent people about'.[3] In a second letter she promised to come and see Cécile's children 'sometime'.[4]

Cécile went over to Salem in July and Alice joined her from Kirchberg. Cécile sent her grandmother a most enthusiastic report:

I must write and tell you how well I found Mama in Salem. She seemed to enjoy everything so much and is so interested in anything to do with the family. It was ideal for her living at Kirchberg as through that, it did not tire her so much having to be with people all day.

I saw her in Langenburg also, we went there for the day.

She was thinner, I thought, and much better in health. She actually climbed all those frightful steps up to Margarita's room with ease. But Marg. was worried about her plans, the latest is she wants to found an Orthodox convent in Greece. I should think she will realize that is not possible without money. But she also wishes to see Papa again and even hopes to live with him again.

I'm afraid she will be disappointed. Besides, she has built up an idealistic picture of Papa, which is quite wrong, I'm afraid.

But her summer is pretty well mapped out till she sees you and I'm sure you will be able to convince her that these things are difficult, if not impossible. She still varies a lot in her ideas. But her energy is greater than ever. If only one could find some occupation for her.

She was touchingly kind to Dolla and me in Salem. She actually made me a bed-jacket and Dolla a dressing gown. And she said to us another time: 'I think my grandchildren* are charming, but I prefer my own children.'

Also, what you say is true, she always refers to you when she wants to prove something.[5]

After Salem, Alice went to Berlin to see Sophie, where she visited the dentist and consulted a specialist about her kidneys. The latter diagnosed a sluggish liver, which caused gases to press on her heart so that she thought she was having small heart attacks. From Berlin she went to the Kuranstalt Hohenlohe und Haus Olga at Bad Mergentheim (in Franconia, south of Würzburg) to take a cure for her heart, arriving there, somewhat exhausted, on 25 July. She spent a few days in bed before starting the cure.

Meanwhile Victoria, who kept hearing optimistic reports about Alice from all sides, called on Dr Binswanger again. He noted their conversation:

Patient now talks of the time before and after her 'illness'. At one moment showed more pedagogic than religious inclinations. Also once wrote to a newspaper and wanted to establish connections as a correspondent to the *Bund* in Berne, but then declared that she wasn't capable of writing after all. At present she wants to found an order of nuns. Today's question

* Alice now had eleven grandchildren and more would follow in due course. Margarita had Kraft (b. 1935) and Beatrix (b. 1936). Theodora had Margarita (b. 1932), Maximilian (b. 1933) and Ludwig (b. 1937). Cécile had Ludwig (b. 1931), Alexander (b. 1933) and Johanna (b. 1936), while Sophie had Christina (b. 1933), Dorothea (b. 1934) and Karl (b. 1937).

[from the mother]: Whether the patient could pass the winter in a castle of the Margrave of Baden in Karlsruhe, which is answered in the affirmative.[6]

At Langenburg, Victoria heard from the maid, Elise Frauchiger, that Alice's daughters thought their mother completely cured and leading a normal life, but, as Victoria reported: 'She will always need to be discreetly watched over & guided, as Dr Binswanger told me.'[7]

Victoria joined Alice at the sanatorium at Mergentheim early in August and spent ten days with her, part of which coincided with a heatwave. This was a spa set in well-laid-out grounds, and a band played to the guests twice a day while they took the waters. It was reasonable in price and not fashionable, which suited Alice. On two days they made car trips and on another went to lunch at Rothenburg.

Alice was conscientious over her cure, having hot poultices applied twice a day in her room, lunching between 11.30 a.m. and 1.00 p.m. and taking supper in bed. She was free only in the afternoons from 4.00 to 6.00 p.m. She benefited from the cure, and Victoria found her interested in everything. By mid-September Alice was back with the Markwitzes at Breibach.

At Wolfsgarten Victoria found Uncle Ernie far from well. He was undergoing X-ray treatment on his lungs. She hoped he might be well enough to travel to England for the wedding of his son Lu to Margaret Geddes* on 23 October. As the apple trees of Darmstadt grew heavy with fruit and were propped up, the sands of time ran out for Ernie. And as autumn chills approached, it was harder for the family to maintain their customary optimism. Each afternoon he made his way to Onor's room, where he enjoyed listening to plays on the wireless. They set their hopes on a cure in Baden-Baden, but he deteriorated. He clung to life, waiting to see Lu and his fiancée, then slipped into a coma and died on 9 October. He was sixty-eight.

* Margaret Geddes (1913–97), daughter of Sir Auckland (later 1st Lord) Geddes.

Victoria was soon on her way back to Darmstadt to join the family for the funeral. Perhaps not wishing to upset her, no one told Alice of Ernie's death, but she read of it in the German newspapers. Unexpectedly she set off to Darmstadt and put herself up at an inn. She contacted Count Hardenberg to ask if she might join the family for the funeral. She was immediately invited to Wolfsgarten.

On 12 October Ernie's coffin, covered with the Grand Ducal flag of the House of Hesse and topped with Ernie's plumed hat, was conveyed on a horse-drawn gun carriage through lines of soldiers giving the Nazi salute. Hitler sent a message of sympathy.

Uncle Ernie himself had been too sophisticated to have dealings with the Nazis, and the Baden family had been warned about the Nazis by the Jewish headmaster of Salem, Kurt Hahn. But the Hesse-Kassel branch of the family had been won over and deployed by the Nazis to help Hitler gain votes in elections. Prince Philipp of Hesse-Kassel had been introduced to the NSDAP (National Socialist German Workers', or Nazi, Party) by his cousin, August Wilhelm of Prussia, the Kaiser's fourth son.

Sophie's husband, Christoph, had joined the party in 1931 and the SS the next year. There was therefore a strong Nazi presence at Ernie's funeral, and the contrast between the trappings of royalty and the display of Nazi uniforms presents a sinister image today.

Alice saw Louise for the first time in five years and Georgie for the first time in seven. Andrea, however, was not present.* Back in London, Victoria wrote to Philip to thank him for a letter of sympathy:

I don't know if any of the sisters have written to you to tell you about the funeral etc. & how Mama unexpectedly joined us for it & spent a

*Andrea was on his way to London with George II. On 28 October, he, the King, the Crown Prince and Prince Nicholas dined with Sir Sydney Waterlow at the British Legation in Athens. Andrea went with the King to a luncheon given by President Lebrun and other functions in Paris, and was with the King when he left by train for London on 7 November. Andrea and the King stayed on in London through November.

week with us all at Wolfsgarten. She was quite her old self again, like before she fell ill, and it was a great joy to Uncle Georgie & Aunt Louise to see her again after such a long time . . .

She hopes to visit Aunt O, Cécile etc. at Wolfsgarten after the new year, before Cécile's baby is expected. If you have any plans which are settled for your Xmas holidays, you might let her know. I am sure she would like to hear from you.[8]

Ernie's death meant that his son Lu's wedding to Margaret Geddes was rescheduled for 20 November. The family hoped this would be a happy event after the sadness of the last weeks, but a terrible tragedy was about to happen.

As the day of the wedding approached, the Hesse-Darmstadt family began to converge on London. On 12 November Cécile wrote a line to Dickie asking him to 'say a few words to the lustrous people at Croydon', explaining who they were and that they were just coming to England for a week for the wedding. In advance she thanked him and Edwina for putting up so many of them and added: 'I hope we won't be in the way.'[9]

The Grand Ducal family flew from Darmstadt on 16 November, the party consisting of Don and Cécile, Aunt Onor, and Cécile's two boys, Ludwig (six) and Alexander (four), who were to be pages. The best man was Baron (Joachim) von Riedesel and there was one lady-in-waiting, Aline Hahn. They flew in an air liner of the Belgian Sabena company and the early part of the journey was sunny. The plane was due at Steene aerodrome at Ostend to pick up two passengers. By 2.00 p.m., heavy fog had descended over the North Sea as the pilot headed towards Steene. He tried to land at the aerodrome. Rockets were fired by the aerodrome staff, but the pilot could not see them. An eye witness described what then happened:

I saw the aeroplane coming down out of the fog. It hit the chimney of the brickworks at a speed of about 100 miles an hour. One wing and one of the engines broke off, and both crashed through the roof of the works. The remainder of the aeroplane turned over and crashed to the ground in the brickfield about 50 yards farther on, where it at once burst into flames.[10]

Everyone aboard the aeroplane was killed.

The report into the crash established that the pilot had been trying to land 'blind', a method not known at Steene. Blame further attached to an official at Steene who should have transmitted a message to the pilot, telling him not to land there but to proceed to London. Of the rockets, the first worked, the second fizzled out and the third was fired too late.

In an instant the groom had lost his entire family, except for his small niece Johanna, who had been left at home.* The bride's father, Sir Auckland Geddes, asked the press to be solicitous to his daughter, and the wedding took place quietly, the very next day, at St Peter's, Eaton Square, the bride wearing a black suit and veil. Then Lu and Peg crossed to Ostend, were driven to an hotel in a German embassy car and later went to the local hospital where nuns had prepared a room and where the coffins lay, covered in flowers. What should have been a honeymoon voyage was spent in a funeral train.

Philip was told of the tragedy at school and never forgot 'the profound shock'[11] with which he heard the news. Louise wrote: 'My thoughts are hardly here at all & to think of Lu above all is more than one can bear. To lose one's entire nearest & dearest in just over a month is unbelievably awful.'[12]

The coffins were conveyed to the chapel of the mausoleum at the Rosenhöhe to await the funeral. Once again the streets of Darmstadt were lined with soldiers.

The funeral took place on 23 November. Alice came from Berlin with Sophie, and Andrea came from London with Philip. Alice and Andrea thus met for the first time since April 1931. And she saw her brother Dickie (representing George VI and Queen Elizabeth) for the first time since 1929. The funeral service was also attended by Victoria, Irène and Philip's three surviving sisters with their husbands. The Kaiser was represented. Hitler, Goering and Goebbels sent telegrams.

Whenever Andrea met Sophie's father-in-law, Landgraf

* On his return to Darmstadt, Lu immediately adopted her.

Friedrich Karl of Hesse-Kassel, he employed a humorous form of greeting by tradition. They would approach each other, turn their backs and bow back to back. 'Fischy' was rather surprised when, even on that tragic day, Andrea greeted him thus.[13]

Margarita wrote to Louise that Alice and Andrea got on well together. Louise commented: 'As poor Margarita said it is *hard* that Cécile had to die to bring them together.'[14] But too much time had passed for any hope of their living together again.

The tragedy hit Andrea particularly hard as Cécile was his favourite daughter. Her death overwhelmed him. A few weeks later he wrote to his mother-in-law: 'I'm keeping fit up to a point, but I cannot say that time has had any healing effect – it was a very, very hard blow and the weight of it becomes heavier as time passes.'[15]

While they were still together in Darmstadt, Alice spent much of her time sitting quietly with Georgina von Rotsmann, Onor's lady-in-waiting, who had been pensioned off following Ernie's death.

'I wonder how your poor Alice bears the loss of that lovely Cécile,' wrote Queen Mary to Victoria, 'or whether the shock has been too much for her.'[16] As it happened, Alice coped with the shock better than they had dared hope. Victoria reported to Dr Binswanger:

> Everybody found her exactly the way she was before her illness. She has cried bitterly, but showed a moving concern for all the surviving. Just before, she had been at her youngest daughter's, when she had her tonsils removed & was keeping her company by reading etc. Now she found it hard to return right away to the good people (with whom she intends to continue living), since they know so little of her former life & family, & so she travelled spontaneously & alone to Stockholm . . .
>
> Both the Crown Prince & his wife have written to me how nice & consoling it was for both sides that the sisters are together. A little 'kink' in the head she'll probably always have, but I think I am able to hope that it is not of a pathological kind.[17]

And so it proved to be. Some nine years later, Theodora called on Dr Binswanger on her return to Salem from Sweden and gave him a report on her mother. She told him that for almost a decade her mother had been 'completely cured'. The doctor recorded Theodora's impression: 'The first curative shock to her was brought about by the plane-crash causing the death of her third daughter, her husband and children. Contrary to what was expected, it apparently tore her out of everything.'[18]

26. Separate Ways

Alice had entertained some hopes of returning to Andrea, but she was to be disappointed. There were no scenes, no arguments. A few days after the funeral, each simply went their separate way, Andrea to France, Alice to a less certain future. There was never an official separation and their occasional meetings after this time were distantly amicable on both sides.

Andrea returned to Paris, and went south to Monaco for Christmas and then to Rome on New Year's Day 1938. Philip returned to England for Christmas but was summoned to Rome by his father, who wanted to take him to the wedding of Crown Prince Paul and Princess Frederika of Hanover in Athens. Andrea was also pleased that Margarita and Theodora were coming to Athens: 'bless them, it would have been very hard for me to be all alone.'[1]

Soon after the funeral, Alice went to Sweden, where she and Louise consoled each other. Louise pronounced Alice 'so balanced & so splendid about her sorrow'.[2] On 15 December Alice left to spend a week with Sophie in Berlin. On Christmas Day she went to the Rosenhöhe to her daughter's grave and stayed a night with Georgina von Rotsmann at the Neue Palais. Dickie sent her some money for Christmas. She was pleased and, as would now become a habit, promptly gave it away. She sent it to Cécile's nurses in her memory. From Darmstadt Alice went to Salem for the new year.

While she was in Sweden, Alice wrote to Dickie for the first time in over seven years. Her letter provides a striking example of how someone who was considered off-beam by her contemporaries none the less possessed a remarkable vision and prescience:

I would like to profit of the freedom of the post in this country and say a few words about Germany. You know there are many people there who would like to re-establish parliamentary régime. I am unaware if there is an organization as yet but their opinion is that it is too difficult to upset a powerful central government in Berlin, so they prefer to try and re-establish parliamentary régime in each German state again, trusting to the garrison forces everywhere to keep communism in order.

If you consider the advantage of a split-up Germany over a united militaristic German empire for the peace of Europe and of the world in general, it seems to me that it is in the interest of the Allies to encourage *secretly* the parliamentary tendencies separately in each state. Ultimately, of course, the ideal would be to unite all the German states with all the European states into a European federation with a common currency and no customs barriers.[3]

These ideas had been honed in discussion with Reinhold Markwitz. Alice's plan was nothing if not avant-garde two years before the Second World War, and even pre-dating Hitler's annexation of Austria and Czechoslovakia. She hoped that Dickie was influential enough to suggest the idea. There is no evidence that he pursued it. Later, of course, it was exactly the route taken by the Allies to create a decentralized, democratic Federal Republic in Germany, to prevent a future war and to integrate Germany into a united Europe.

In the new year Alice heard that Fräulein Markwitz had been invited to go to America and conceived the idea that she would accompany her. She wrote to the Greek Minister in Berlin asking for a visa. But her mother, Andrea and her surviving daughters were set against the idea. A fortuitous bout of flu laid Alice low again and the plan was forgotten.

The year 1938 was to give little relief to either Alice, her mother or Andrea. The deaths of Ernie and the five other members of the Hesse-Darmstadt family were followed early in the new year by that of Andrea's brother, Nicholas. He had been annoyed to have to order a new uniform for the Crown Prince's wedding in Athens on 9 January. He had little time to enjoy it. He fell ill at his villa at Psychico in Athens and died, aged sixty-six, on 8 February, muttering: 'I am happy to die in my beloved country.'[4] He was buried at Tatoï.

Also in 1938 Count Hardenberg died, having fulfilled his duties as Uncle Ernie's chamberlain. This was a particular sadness for Alice, since he had been her stalwart support during her illness, ever ready to come to her aid. Furthermore, she considered that he was one of the few people who believed in her.

Alice spent much of the early part of 1938 in Germany, recovering from a severe bout of inflammation of the lungs. But she was well enough to join her mother in London for her seventy-fifth birthday on 5 April.

All four of Victoria's children signed a card for her that day, but it was no time for celebration. These months had been further overshadowed by the painful illness of Alice's brother Georgie. Within days of the Hesse funeral, he had dined with Mr and Mrs Israel Sieff in their apartment at Brook House in London, and on his way out had turned and suddenly fallen, breaking his thigh. After numerous X-rays and examinations, it was discovered that he was gravely ill with cancer of the bone marrow. The family gathered in London, and a distraught Dickie wrote to his mother: 'You have us four children together this birthday & few mothers can have been loved so much by their children.'[5]

Georgie died three days after his mother's birthday, on 8 April. George VI walked in the funeral procession at Bray on 13 April and, reflecting the wide circle of Georgie's friends, one of the wreaths came from the film star Marlene Dietrich.

Alice had loved her brother, though there had been little contact between them for many years. While still in the navy, Georgie had become embroiled with a firm called P. G. Marr & Co, requiring Edwina to bail him out of a potentially serious financial disaster.* After the navy, Georgie had joined his brother-in-law, Sir Harold Wernher, as an English director of Electrolux, the Swedish company run by the dubious Axel Wenner-Gren, whose later associ-

* During his terminal illness, Georgie gave Edwina a cheque for £5,000 to repay her. With her characteristic consideration, she never cashed it.

ation with the Duke of Windsor in the Bahamas was to act to the Duke's discredit.

After Georgie's death Dickie was the natural candidate to assume Philip's guardianship, making himself responsible for dealing with the day-to-day expenses, guided by the family lawyer, Ernest Rehder.* Andrea gave Philip a pound a week when he joined the navy, but Alice herself lived on an allowance from Edwina. She received nothing from Andrea.

It is easy to appreciate why this was an unsettled phase for Alice. She was not yet sure how to realize her ideas. Within days of Georgie's death, Victoria was outlining Alice's latest plans. Alice was to maintain a base with her mother, but proposed to live incognito in a London hotel and to devote her time to studying welfare work. Her motive was to escape the endless rounds of family visits of which she had lately endured her full share, and to pursue some of the ideas that had developed while she was staying with the Markwitzes in Germany, 'subjects that really interest her'.[6]

Alice could not return to the Markwitzes because it seemed – wrongly as it turned out – that they were giving up their home for the same political reasons that had driven Herr Markwitz from his job. Nor did she wish to live with one of her daughters.

Victoria wrote to Nona, assessing Alice's position:

> One is inclined to forget that she is quite able now to look after herself, also that at her age she can do so. She has grown so much more tactful & considerate, fights against her impulsiveness & is all together a dear soul. That she is a bit touchy still is natural to her character . . .
>
> Her determination to live an independent life, studying the ways of mankind & its needs & being useful in her own way, I respect, also her firm resolve to spend as little as possible on herself.[7]

For the first time, Alice sought a positive way of emulating the

* The fees for Philip's Michaelmas term at Gordonstoun were paid from Theodora's fund (of which Georgie had been a trustee). The Baden Trust paid for a West Coast cruise undertaken by Philip at school.

example of Aunt Ella, though she still needed to explore the various alternatives. In May she moved to the Ladies International Club in Prince's Square, as part of her quest for independence. Then a friend called Miss Collin directed her to a number of institutions and rest homes which she visited incognito.

Alice went to see Grand Duchess Xenia of Russia, then living in exile at Hampton Court, and the Grand Duchess's young grandson, Prince Alexander Romanoff, remembered that Alice used to talk to her at great length and liked to help in the kitchen. More particularly she consulted the Grand Duchess's severe lady-in-waiting, Mother Martha, who told her of a rest home for Orthodox clergy, Reed House, at Plaxtol, near Sevenoaks in Kent.[8] In June Alice went to work there and made it her base for much of the rest of the year. Alice described it to the Markwitzes:

> I am living with a real Countess, a Danish woman who has converted her house into a recreation home for poor Russians. The house is small. Only five guests can be received & there is not much work.[9]

Thus Alice established a pattern that would continue into old age, opting for a more ascetic lifestyle, while continuing to play a limited part in family life.

These months in England were marked by a restlessness that remained with her for the rest of her life. But she looked upon her stay as only temporary. Her ultimate goal was to return to Greece. In June Andrea's former ADC, Menelaos Metaxas, came from Greece to discuss her developing plan. There was a difficult moment when Alice appeared to be acting on impulse again, announcing that she would join Louise, who was on an official visit to the United States with Gustaf. This was discouraged by Victoria, and Alice moved into the Mountbattens' London flat to await Philip's return from school at the end of the summer term.

Alice stayed in England until November. On the anniversary of the air crash, she visited the Rosenhöhe, observing the line of graves surrounded by begonias. Then she travelled to Greece for the first time since the precipitate departure in 1922.

27. Return to Greece

The previous two years had been more than unsettling and 1938 had found Alice living what her mother described as 'such a lonely, vagrant life'.[1] There were two thoughts behind Alice's determination to return to Greece – first that Philip was a Prince of Greece and ought to have a home there after leaving school and get to know his countrymen, and secondly that there were opportunities for welfare work in a country where such things had been neglected.

Soon after her arrival in Greece in November 1938 Alice found a flat in Athens at 8 rue Coumbari, in the same street as the Benaki Museum. On 5 December 1938 she wrote to Philip outlining her plan:

I have taken a small flat just for you and me. Two bedrooms, *each* with a bathroom and two sitting rooms, a little kitchen & pantry. I found some furniture stored away in various places from our rooms in the Old Palace, which I had not seen again since 1917, a most agreeable surprise & the family here are giving me things to complete it . . . * Dickie tells me there is a chance of you having a long holiday in Spring so I am looking forward to your living in our flat.[2]

After spending Christmas in England, Alice set off for her new life in Greece on 21 January 1939. It may well be that there was never a good time in the twentieth century to settle in Greece, but it is hard to think of a worse one than the beginning of 1939. There was a military dictatorship under General Metaxas and George II was tarnished by the association. A disturbing element was the Youth Movement, which had introduced a distinctly Germanic

* Louise sent the table silver from Mon Repos, which had been stored in Sweden.

political element into the life of the young, with organized rallies, uniforms, parades and flags, not to mention sexual scandals and even some fatal casualties at rallies. This had repercussions for the Greek royal family, as the British Ambassador, Sir Sydney Waterlow, pointed out:

A disquieting feature of this situation is its reaction on the Dynasty. The popularity of the Royal Family, never great apart from the high hopes aroused by the King in the early stages of his restoration, had already fallen to freezing point, and the action now being taken to enforce the youth movement has sunk it still lower. Although the Crown Prince is personally much liked for his natural and cheerful affability, when he and his sisters appear at theatre or cinema they are received in stony silence while a performance of Cretan dancers excites wild enthusiasm.[3]

The generally accepted conclusion was that the King and his family had 'now sunk definitely to the position of puppets in the hands of General Metaxas, and that they are tied to that position by financial interest'. Furthermore, it was felt, unfairly, that 'the King has now definitely belied his early promise and that the chances that he will save himself, even at the eleventh hour, by reacting strongly against General Metaxas, are rated as small.'[4]

Waterlow also reported that the Crown Prince had made a speech to the Youth Movement on the Champs de Mars, where the Fascist salute had been given. When the Crown Prince saw the Fascist salute, he took the outstretched hand and shook it, an ingenious way of avoiding the political implications.

Into this troubled atmosphere Alice returned. Louise hoped for the best: 'One is so happy for her starting again a simple, normal life on her own. I feel that none of us who have not gone through what Alice has can [know] what it must mean coming back after so many years & to fit in again to the average person's life.'[5] When Victoria sought Andrea's views, he seemed to agree that it was 'a good thing for Alice to live in Athens'.[6]

Alice settled better into her cosy flat than to life as a member of the Greek royal family. 'It is difficult to get accustomed again to court customs,'[7] she wrote to Frau Markwitz in March. A few weeks later, she wrote to Reinhold Markwitz to thank him for his support and friendship: 'You are still the only one who believes in me – especially since Hardenberg's death – and I would like you to stay close to me because here they only want me to perform *worldly* duties, & my poor soul often feels starving and thirsty.'[8]

Alice's other concern was the arrival of Philip, who took his final exams at Gordonstoun and left school at the end of the Easter term. It had been agreed that, when in Greece, Philip would make his home with Alice while continuing to use his various other family bases in London. Alice was pleased about this, while his headmaster, Kurt Hahn, and his Uncle Dickie were not convinced that living with his mother was an entirely happy arrangement.

Made aware of their concerns, Alice arranged for Captain Nicky Merlin* of the Greek navy to be seconded to look after Philip, accompanying him to social occasions and keeping what Alice told Dickie was 'a paternal eye on him'. She hoped this would 'satisfy you & Hahn'.[9] Presently Alice asked Dickie for another copy of his private code book, the last one having been packed amongst the books taken from Mon Repos, in order that he could communicate in secret with either her or Philip.

By May Philip was back in England and had entered the British Royal Navy as a cadet, 'consequent on a request from Buckingham Palace'.[10] The plan, presumably authorized by George VI, was that he should do the ordinary special entry cadets' training, one term at Dartmouth, then two in the training cruiser. It was not intended that he would stay in the Navy 'after he has reached the rank of Acting Sub-Lieutenant'.[11]

After some months in Greece, Alice returned to England to see her mother and Philip. Unbeknown to her, Cécile's two-year-old daughter, Johanna, then living with Lu and Peg at Darmstadt, had suffered a relapse in her meningitis after flu, which left her so weak that she could not lift her head when lying down. Alice had reached Paris from Marseilles on 6 June when her sister-in-law,

* Merlin was killed in action in 1942.

Marie, met her with a frantic message that Johanna was gravely ill.

Alice rushed to Frankfurt where Margarita and Friedel Hohenlohe met her and brought her to the Neue Palais. Johanna was being cared for in the Alice Hospital and though generally weak, had a strong heart. They knew she could not recover, but only in the last twenty-four hours did she fall unconscious. Alice was part of the family vigil, which she later described to Philip:

> As she never had very high fever, she had not fits or restlessness from the inflammation of the brain which is rare, but a godsend to us all. For we had such a sweet picture before our eyes of a lovely sleeping child with golden curls, looking for me so very like Cécile at that age that it was like losing my child a second time and I was thankful that Papa was away travelling and did not see that, for Papa adored Cécile when she was small and could never bear to be parted from her.[12]

The coffin was taken to the Byzantine mausoleum where Ernie had lain and the funeral was private. Johanna was buried next to her parents and brothers, who had died so tragically less than two years before.

'Margarita wrote that Alice was very brave & good,' reported Victoria, 'but her heart was rather affected by the shock & hurried journey. She has herself written to me & is now going for a rest to her friends, the Markwitzes, which I am sure is the best thing she could do under the circumstances. They like & understand her.'[13] From Breibach Alice wrote to Philip: 'I am quite exhausted by the strain and the sadness of it all.'[14]

On 16 July Alice joined Philip in London, staying at Kensington Palace with him until 11 August, with one weekend at Adsdean. Victoria found her 'so well & calm in her nerves, that we have enjoyed being together & I shall miss her'.[15] Alice took Philip to Paris for three days and they sailed to Greece together from Italy in *Cairo City*. Hardly had they arrived there than war was declared between Britain and Germany, on 3 September. For Alice this presented a problem concerning Philip's immediate future. She wrote to his guardian, Dickie:

[Philip] naturally would like best to go on training in England especially as he knows the language and people. But he feels quite rightly that as he is such an utter stranger to the language and people here, if he does not now remain here & try & re-establish contact with the people, it will be still more difficult for him to do so later on. This effort to try and feel at home here and know and understand everything in this country is more important even than his naval career, which will be modest in such a small navy.[16]

Philip's dilemma concerned where his loyalty lay. Was he to be a Prince of Greece or to serve in the British navy? Perhaps Greece needed him more? The King was childless, the Crown Prince had but one daughter, and in the line of succession there followed his uncle, Big George (who had lived in Paris for years), then his thirty-year-old bachelor son Peter, and after him Andrea and then Philip himself.

Philip's naval career was rescued by a sudden word from George II, instructing that he return to England and resume his training.* He left Athens on 21 September. Philip's grandmother was not sure that this was the right decision, as she told Dickie:

I still think it would have been better if he had stayed in Greece, where he belongs, but if, later on, he is appointed to some battle-ship he can get the training and schooling we all agreed he could get better in our Navy, & fairly safely, which for poor Alice's sake I hope you may be able to arrange for him. War is too serious a matter for boys of foreign countries to have to undergo the risks of & they can only be an encumbrance & of no real use to our country.[17]

This was one of the rare occasions when Victoria misjudged the calibre of the young man entering on a life of service, which, it has often been said, could have led him to the top of his profession.

Alice certainly felt that Philip belonged in Greece and should

* Victoria reported: '[Philip] said to Nada that his return to England was a surprise to him, but George his King suddenly decided he was to do so.' [VMH to NK, Lynden Manor, 26 September 1939 – BA]

take his place as one of the few princes of that country. His departure left her feeling lonely, and further isolated from her family.

There was a further complication, which Alice may have hoped was a reprieve. On 9 September, Big George's son, Peter, had disqualified himself from the line of succession by marrying a divorced Russian called Irène Outchinikova. The marriage took place in Madras and caused great distress to his parents, who only read of it in the newspapers weeks after the event. Peter's wife was never accepted as a member of the Greek royal house, nor allowed to enter Greece.

When news of the union eventually reached Athens in December, Alice wrote to Philip in England, warning him that he was now even closer in line to the Greek throne and would have to consider more than one aspect of his future:

> Before you go* I must tell you that there is a complication in the fact that Peter got married out in India. U. Georgie [Big George] is so upset & furious that he refuses ever to see him again. You know what that means, if Freddy [the Crown Princess] only produces daughters, I believe the constitution here demands that the queen should be born a princess. But penniless princesses don't matter if there is a civil list. On the other hand when Georgie [George II] discussed Peter's marriage with me, he said he did not expect the Princes to marry blue blood, provided the girl is decent & nice. Freddy is expecting in June, & we are hoping for an heir.[18]

Fortunately for Philip and for Alice, the Crown Princess produced a boy, Constantine,† on 2 June 1940, and the succession was assured.

In December 1939, following the funeral of Princess Louise, Duchess of Argyll,‡ at St George's Chapel, Windsor, Victoria

* Philip was on his way to spend Christmas with the Wernhers at Lubenham.

† Constantine, b. 1940. Succeeded to the throne 1964, married 1964, Princess Anne-Marie of Denmark. Left Greece following a coup in 1967.

‡ Princess Louise died aged ninety-one at Kensington Palace on 3 December 1939. Victoria kept an eye on the two remaining children of Queen Victoria. Uncle Arthur, at Bagshot Park, 'as bald as an egg now, but . . . alert of mind' [VMH to MtB, 5 November 1939 – HL], died in January 1942 aged ninety-two, while Princess Beatrice survived until October 1944.

approached George VI about plans for Philip. The King told her that he was to be appointed to *Ramillies*, which would undertake escort work in the Mediterranean and eastward. Dickie reported this to Alice, and she contacted Andrea in France. He liked the idea and gave his consent. Philip then won the King's Dirk at Dartmouth (as best all-round cadet), to the delight of the family, and joined *Ramillies* in Colombo on 1 January 1940.

The Second World War caused Alice the same problems that she and her family had endured in the First World War. Again, close members of the family found themselves fighting on opposite sides. It was a help that her cousin, Victor Erbach,* was German Ambassador in Greece, and thus a link back to her daughters, all of whose husbands later went to the front.

Alice contemplated going to Switzerland for the Christmas holidays to make sure that her German grandchildren had proper nourishment, wool clothing and boots. In the end she postponed her visit, but asked her mother to set up a small fund for this.

At the end of October, Andrea and his brother Christo turned up in Athens for their annual visit and stayed at the palace. Alice accepted that Andrea would not stay with her in her flat, which would have been too small. Andrea took a small flat of his own. Alice saw him occasionally during his visit. Then, after three weeks he left. She would never see him again.

Alice had hoped that Dickie might be in the Mediterranean at Christmas, but he was in Home Waters, and returned to Broadlands, which Edwina had inherited from her father in July. Therefore Alice spent Christmas alone in the flat, remembering her last Greek Christmas in 1921 when all the family (including the infant Philip) had been together. Even Popoulo, who had returned to act as lady-in-waiting, was away with her family.

★

* Prince Victor zu Erbach-Schönberg (1880–1967), son of Louis of Battenberg's sister, Marie.

Alice lost a rare ally in the Greek royal family with the death of Christo on 21 January, followed within the year by that of Andrea's sister, Minnie. Soon after his arrival in Athens, Christo had suffered an abscess to his lung, which later burst. Then he fell victim to flu.

Christo's death was an excuse for the acerbic American Ambassador, Lincoln MacVeagh, to express himself in particularly disagreeable tone about the prince and the Greek royal family: 'To bury this amiable cipher, the King mobilized once more the resources of the nation, as he did for the funerals of King Constantine and Prince Nicholas. Nothing becomes King George so much as his manner of taking leave of his deceased relatives, at public expense.'[19]

After describing the procession, MacVeagh turned to the onlookers. They expressed neither awe nor grief. At King Constantine's funeral, there had been large crowds marvelling and even weeping. This time they came 'to compare and criticise, and even to chatter and laugh'. Watchers in the windows even waved at their friends in the procession. 'The King has two more uncles to die,' observed MacVeagh, 'and of course hosts of cousins. If he continues handing them out these fine funerals, the people will end with dancing in the streets.'[20]

MacVeagh felt that this reaction demonstrated the lack of sympathy between the people and the royal house, emphasizing what a bad time it was for Alice to have returned to Greece. The Ambassador concluded his report:

> Prince Christopher told a royalist lady of my acquaintance only a short time before his death that he was sure his family would be 'kicked out' soon again. He possessed a certain shrewdness as morons often do, and a sour sense of humour which fed on realization of what others thought of him. If, as one of the spooks in which he believed, he was a witness to his own funeral, he can hardly have failed to hug his shadowy self with a phantom chuckle, remembering the sycophantic lady referred to murmuring telepathically 'Who's looney now?' For the 'Love of the people' which is the proverbial strength of the House of Glücksburg is all gone, and wherewithal shall it be strengthened when the crisis comes?[21]

Alice had other wartime problems, predominantly food and money. Back in England Dickie and Edwina turned their attention to new ways of paying her annual allowance of £552. A covenant that they had arranged met problems because, after Greece was invaded by Germany in April 1941, Alice was deemed to be residing 'in enemy occupied territory'.[22] A new deed was drawn up to last seven years, which paid the allowance in monthly instalments into the London account of George II, who then paid Alice the equivalent in drachmas.

It is traditionally supposed that Alice spent the entire war in Greece. But in August 1940 she escaped for a holiday at Tarasp, the Hesse castle near Vulpera, in Switzerland, loaned to her by Lu and Peg, where she hoped to see her daughters. Berthold Baden had been badly wounded in the leg in France and was at Giessen, while Friedel (a reserve officer) and Margarita were in Bohemia. Sophie was with her recently widowed mother-in-law, Mossy.

Alice's daughters were in a terrible position, suffering the traditional divided loyalties of being married to Germans, though there was some consolation for Theodora. Berthold had never got involved with the Nazis. Following his early wound, he almost lost his leg and was lame for life. He returned home a permanent convalescent. He and Theodora spent the rest of the war at Salem.

News of Andrea was uncertain until late in 1940 when Louise got a letter from him. He had been in Monaco and got stuck on the Riviera after the fall of France. He was still living on board *Davida*, but felt cut off as his radio had been taken away. He would rather have been in Greece, he confided in his letter: 'I would in any case not have been used, I am too old & not capable of much exertion & Georgie is a very careful man.'[23]

By August 1940, Italy became embroiled with Greece over allegations of Greek complicity with unrest in Albania. In October the Italian government declared war on Greece and invaded Greece from Albania. The British had promised to assist Greece and, with combined operations at sea, in the air and on land, expelled the invaders across Albania. Victoria worried about Alice 'so alone'[24] in Greece, and Andrea commented: 'To think it is going on round Yanina is a nightmare.'[25]

The Greek royal family were still in place, though George II was hardly seen in public. His remoteness worried Winston Churchill, now Prime Minister and directing the war activities from London. He asked Henry Hopkinson, then at the Foreign Office, to organize for the King's mistress, Mrs Joyce Britten-Jones, to be flown to Athens 'to stiffen the King of Greece',[26] as Churchill put it. Meanwhile the Crown Prince was active in the armed forces and his wife Frederika somewhat unpopular because of her German origins.

The socialite MP 'Chips' Channon arrived in Athens in January 1941 and, in a gossipy resumé on the Greek royal family, Lilia Ralli, Princess Marina's friend, told him that Alice was 'eccentric to say the least and lives in semi-retirement'. Andrea, she said, 'philanders on the Riviera'.[27] The King gave Chips a letter to take back to Victoria, confirming financial arrangements for Alice and adding:

> With Alice we talk and think of you so often. She is very busy looking after the needy families of soldiers and we only get to see her on Sundays. A few days ago Philip arrived here on leave [from *Valiant* in Alexandria], which naturally is a great source of joy for her. He is looking very well and happy.[28]

During Philip's visit, General Metaxas died, and on 31 January, he attended the funeral at the cathedral. Philip's cousin, Alexandra (the posthumous daughter of King Alexander), who was living in Alexandria, left a description of her great-aunt at this time. She recalled that in those days Alice lived in crowded rooms, filled with old-fashioned furniture and many Battenberg photographs. When Philip stayed, large meals were prepared, one of which included a compote of oranges. As Alexandra ate this politely, she found to her horror that it was frequently presented on future visits as her favourite dessert. Alice felt lonely again after Philip left Greece in mid-February.

Alice was delighted at the Greek victory in Albania in October, and moved to a villa nearer her charity work, returning to rue

Coumbari just three times a week to attend to business with Popoulo.

On 6 April 1941 the Germans invaded Yugoslavia and went to the aid of the defeated Italian forces. They then advanced into Greece. The Greeks were driven back but George II issued statements to the effect that he would never surrender. Alexander Koryzis, who had succeeded Metaxas on his death in January, told the King that Greece had no choice but to surrender. The King refused to countenance this. Already overwrought, the Prime Minister then returned home and, on 18 April, shot himself.

Four governments followed in four days, and rather more air alarms. It became clear to George II that to remain on the mainland would be to become a tool of the Nazis, and the royal family began to disperse. Frederika left without her husband, Princess Nicholas pressing a small cross into her hand, inscribed '*En touta Nika*'.*[29] With Frederika were Princess Katherine, and Princess Aspasia with her daughter, Alexandra. George II, Crown Prince Paul and the new Prime Minister, Emmanuel Tsouderos, left the next day, on 23 April, the King's name-day. Princess Nicholas refused to leave Athens, because her husband was buried at Tatoï.

Alice had no wish to accompany the royal family into exile. She stayed in Athens because she was committed to her charity work and knew that she could be useful there. Of the royal family, only she and Princess Nicholas stayed there. No news of Alice reached her mother, who wrote to Queen Mary: 'I am glad that at least Ellen is also still at Athens, so that she is not quite alone there. I am sure she has a lot of work to do looking after the poorest people.'[30]

* 'In this conquer', the words that the ancient Emperor Constantine was supposed to have heard during his vision of the cross, leading him to convert to Christianity.

28. Greece under Occupation

The Greek royal family remained in exile for the duration of the war. The Foreign Office in London was worried that some or all of them might descend on Britain. George VI made it clear that he would only wish George II 'to come to this country as a last resort & even then without his sister-in-law's mother [Princess Nicholas] if possible'.[1] Furthermore George VI did not want 'dynastic' children in Britain and therefore not the children of the Crown Prince. In the event the Greek King arrived in London, as did the Crown Prince, but most of the rest of the Greek royal family made their way to South Africa.

Back in Greece, Alice was now cut off from her family, but had work to keep her busy. 'I rely on her pluck & common sense to carry her through these times, which must be very painful to her,'[2] wrote her mother.

In the early days of the occupation, food supplies ran out. In May 1941 the American Ambassador, Lincoln MacVeagh, was reporting that 'food was almost unobtainable, and only procured with great difficulty'.[3] As the year wore on, conditions deteriorated drastically. The people of Greece existed in a state of 'unparalleled suffering', with 'mass starvation',[4] an undisputed fact. Five hundred to a thousand people, mostly children, died daily in Athens and the Piraeus. In December 1941 Tsouderos, Prime Minister of the Greek government in exile in London, wrote to President Roosevelt of the United States, explaining that 'the brutal Germans have long since discarded respect for any law and their only object is the reduction of the world by fire sword and famine'.[5]

Alice's cousin, Victor Erbach, the German Ambassador, had been recalled to Berlin in April, following the arrival of German forces, severing a vital link for her. Occasionally Alice was able to communicate with her family via Louise in Sweden. In July 1941 she gave up her flat in rue Coumbari and moved into Big George's three-storey house in Academy Road, in the centre of Athens. She had to start lighting fires as early as November and even so, almost froze. But she was able to minimize her expenses, and did not worry unduly about running out of food. The Athens Club, to which Andrea belonged, sent over meals and Louise succeeded in sending her the occasional food parcel. She knew that a time might come when she would have to borrow money to survive.

Alice organized and worked in one of the largest soup kitchens in Athens. Starving children were served dry bean soup or chickpea soup, with the occasional addition of some parsley, onions or oil, all of which was strictly measured and monitored, since starvation led to desperation and the provisions needed to be fairly shared. The soup was cooked in large cauldrons over wood fires. After the children had been fed, and if there was a surplus, the doors were opened to the hungry parents outside, who came pouring in to eat the leftovers.[6]

Alice was no threat to the Germans, politically or personally, and she moved about relatively unnoticed. She did her best to alleviate the suffering of the Greeks, but more as a nurse than as a princess.

Soon after the German occupation, Alice heard from Popoulo that the German general wished to call on her. She staged the meeting, so that she was in an inner room when he arrived, and Popoulo had to announce him. He advanced and attempted to shake hands, but she kept her hands behind her back. 'Is there anything I can do for you?' he asked. 'You can take your troops out of my country,'[7] she replied firmly. The German general may have been better received by Ellen, since it is recalled that she was treated more generously by the Germans.[8]

In that exceptionally bleak winter, Alice lost twenty-six kilos in weight, evidence that she shared the suffering of the Greek people. In December she wrote to Philip, having found 'a safe opportunity of writing':

Even in these anxious times I am full of hope and when I go for walks I look at all the houses to see if there is not a suitable one for us later on, as I am tired of flats and prefer a whole house. Uncle Georgie's house is very cold now as there is no means of working the central heating. Upstairs there is a room with a fire place, so happily I have one warm room in which to dress and sit and eat. Aunt Ellen is well and lunches with me very often. We are the only ones here and so we became very close friends . . .

I am still busy with my charities but do most of my work here, as I have so little benzine . . .

Don't worry about me. I am really and truly in good heart.[9]

However bleak her condition, Alice's messages home always maintained that she was in good health, even if she was not, and that nobody need worry about her.

Conditions in Greece were at their most desperate in December 1941, but as the weather improved, there were spring vegetables to eat. The Swedish government was helpful. Several Swedish ships brought flour, and the Turkish Red Crescent ship brought food for the soup kitchens, which was paid for by the Administrative Committee of American Relief (the Vanderbilt Committee)* in the United States.

Alice's old ally in constitutional matters, Norman Davis, was Chairman of the American Red Cross. Philanthropic as ever, he gave considerable attention to the plight of the Greeks.† Alice and Ellen were among those who began to receive food from the American Red Cross in 1942, and further to this they received provisions from Greek landowners of their acquaintance.

When not working in person in the soup kitchens, Alice sought ways of coming to the aid of Greece by using outside influence. Thus, rather to everyone's surprise, in May 1942 she obtained a visa from the Germans to leave Greece to visit Louise in Sweden.

*The Vanderbilt Committee, run by Harold Vanderbilt, placed 20 million drachmas in the hands of the Consul General for disbursement, of which 15 million were designated for Greek-Americans cut off from their usual sources of income, and 5 million for unspecified payments ordained by the Executive Committee.

†Norman Davis also urged that Turkey should be helped to send wheat to Greece.

On the way she saw her two elder daughters for three days in Berlin. 'I found Margarita and Dolla looking very well,' she wrote to Philip. 'Living in the country makes such a difference, where one can get butter, eggs, milk etc. You can imagine what joy it was to see them for 3 days & to get news of their husbands and children. They were looking so pretty and chic in haus clothes.'[10] From Berlin Alice flew to Sweden, arriving there on 23 May. To Louise she appeared to have weathered the recent crisis very well: 'Alice is so completely her old self, even more so than when I saw her last, so I have difficulty at times in realizing that those awful years were not a bad dream.'[11]

Alice would never have left Greece at that grave point in the war for a personal reason. A member of the Greek Red Cross in Athens had heard a broadcast from London by Dr Alexander Cawadias,* President of the Greek Red Cross. The Red Cross worker gave Alice a list of medical supplies which were urgently needed in Greece. This was then sent from Sweden to the Greek Legation in London and the British Minister in Stockholm asked Anthony Eden to pass on a message from Alice to stress the importance of receiving these supplies.

Soon after her arrival in Sweden, Alice wrote from Ulriksdal to Dickie, who had survived the sinking of his ship *Kelly* in May 1941 and had just been appointed Chief of Combined Operations:

At last I am able to send a few lines to say how overjoyed I am at your promotion and appointment. You have really and truly deserved them and that is the greatest satisfaction of all. I feel sure you must often have thought of Papa these past months and feel his guiding spirit in your work. How proud he would have been of you. By what a miracle from heaven you have been preserved through these dangers. Poor *Kelly*, why does it hurt so when a beloved ship goes but nothing can be gained without sacrifices. I know you must often have thought of me too and sometimes I dare say you were worried.

* Professor Alexander Cawadias (d. 1971), doctor to George II, senior physician, the Evangelismos Hospital, Athens 1914–24.

You need never worry about me. Mama says my character is like yours and ours the lucky characters that take us through many things more easily than most people. I am with friends who feed me amply. I am happy in my work which prospers in spite of tremendous odds. What more can I want? It is quite a job to feed 17,000 poor children from 1–6 years old, under the present circumstances, and to find money and food for a refuge for orphans. I am hoping to collect funds here, which is the object of my visit, and I return as soon as possible.[12]

A week later Alice replied to a letter from Philip, impressed by all that he was doing:

Dear boy, you must know me by now and how absolutely I share all your ideas and principles. Papa and I have never been for shirking sacrifices and dangers and consequently we take it for granted that our son is the same.

I see from U. Dickie's letter that you are serving in an English ship. I always thought that a foreign subject could not serve as an officer and so I and others at home thought you were in a Greek ship, especially as we heard that there were six new ones given to the Greek navy and supposed to be in England. Also we heard at home that there was a dearth of Greek officers for them and naturally thought that every available one like yourself (British Navy trained too) would be serving on board a Greek ship. How they could afford to spare you for an English ship puzzles me.[13]

Alice was careful not to write about anything political she may have heard when in Berlin, lest the Germans forbade her to return to Greece. She returned to Athens in September, managing to see Sophie on the journey back and finding her well and pretty 'in spite of worries and anxieties'.[14]

Back in Athens, Alice went to stay with Ellen at Psychico on several short visits. Ellen's son-in-law, the Duke of Kent, had been killed in an air crash on 25 August, and Alice went to keep her company. 'It was an awful shock and she looks pale and tired. But she is very brave and will not show any weakness.'[15]

The autumn was warmer in 1942. Queen Helen of Romania had been sending Alice food for the past six months and she was becoming 'quite plump, and not a scarecrow'.[16] It was possible to feel a little more optimistic.

Both Alice and Ellen were still engaged in social welfare work and drove in and out of Athens in their own cars, each obtaining some seventy-seven litres of petrol a month from the Swedish Relief Commission. Early in 1943, the matter was raised diplomatically between Stockholm and London as to whether or not there was an objection to this arrangement continuing. None was raised.

Besides the soup kitchens, Alice now took on two refuges for stray and orphan children, one for girls and one for boys. In some poor parishes of Athens she organized nursing sisters, who acted as district visitors, caring for the destitute sick in their own homes.

The summer was long and hot that year, and at one point Alice became run down and went to stay with friends at a small farm outside Kephissia. She enjoyed the farm products and was soon feeling better. In October she reported to Philip: 'I am quite my usual self again except for the 26 kilos I lost two years ago, which happily have not returned. You will be quite surprised to see me with a decent figure again, only my face is more wrinkled.'[17]

All Alice's letters that year give the impression that her life was routine and uneventful. She had 'little occupation',[18] she wrote, or: 'My life in this house is always the same.'[19] This was far from the truth.

When the Germans invaded Salonika in 1941, the entire Jewish community, some 60,000 Jews, or one-fifth of the entire population of Salonika, were exterminated. At that time, Salonika was entirely under German occupation, while Athens was under Italian occupation. A great number of Jews fled south to Athens, both from Salonika and from other parts of northern Greece. In 1941 the Nazis threatened to arrest any Jews they found in Macedonia and remove them to Auschwitz for extermination. The branch of the Gestapo charged with this task was called the Rosenborg Committee. With the fall of Mussolini in September 1943 this committee advanced its deadly endeavours to Athens, which had been something of a haven for the Jews.

Since the outbreak of war, the Jewish population in the city had expanded to nearly 6,000. The Greek Orthodox community did their best to help the Jews. By order of Archbishop Damaskinos, Angelos Evert, the Chief of Police in Athens, arranged for 18,500 false identity papers to be issued to assist the Jews to escape, and there was a campaign of concerted concealment. This was a considerable undertaking, as safe refuges were never that safe and there was always the danger of careless gossip. Even so this was a responsibility assumed by Alice at Prince George's house, where she was still living modestly, helped only by Popoulo and a small staff.

The family she took in were the Cohens, temporarily based in Athens. Haimaki Cohen was a property developer and former member of Parliament, who had housed George I, Constantine, Andrea and Alice at his comfortable mansion at Triccala, in the province of Thessaly, during a flood there a few months before the King's assassination in Salonika in 1913. George I had offered him a Greek decoration as reward for his services, but Cohen had modestly declined this. The King then told him that if ever he needed help from his family, he had but to ask. Haimaki Cohen would often visit Athens over the years, on which occasions he frequently saw the royal family.

At the outset of the invasion, Cohen had moved his family to Athens, where he had died early in 1943, before the situation became dangerous. He left a widow, Rachel, born an English subject, a daughter Tilde and four sons, Elie, Alfred (Freddy), Jacques and Michel. At first the whole family settled with three elderly Protestant ladies called Chrisaki, who lived in a farm on the outskirts of Athens, moving there in September 1943. They thought they had found the ideal refuge, but after about three weeks, a friend of Jacques Cohen told him that he had overheard a random conversation in which it was clear that their cover had been exposed.

Following their father's death, Freddy was the mainstay of the family. He was a lawyer and thus well placed to find solutions to difficult problems. He remembered the offer of the late King George and decided to seek out Alice, whom he knew to be living in Athens. To reach her, he appealed to a well-known society lady, Madame Nelly Eliasco, with whom Alice was known to take tea from time to time, asking her to approach Alice on their behalf.

Madame Eliasco did so, but Alice reserved her position. She told Madame Eliasco that she could not take the risk, while planning instead to contact the Cohens independently.

Coincidence now played its part. Freddy Cohen and his sister, veiled for safety's sake, were walking near Prince George's house when they met Madame Sophoulis, the wife of the former Prime Minister. They told her of their hopes, and were discussing this when a door opened by chance, and out came Madame Sophoulis's best friend, Madame Delgianni. Alice used Madame Delgianni as her conduit to reach the Cohens.

An hour later, Alice invited Rachel Cohen and her daughter, Tilde, to move in with her. On the very next evening, 15 October, they slipped into the house by a back door under cover of darkness. Here they occupied two rooms with a kitchen on the upper floor of the building. Alice enjoyed calling on them in the afternoon, and, recalling her interest in all the various religions, inspired by the Schuré book, enjoyed long conversations with them about Judaism.

Alice told the staff that Mrs Cohen was a former Swiss governess to the children and living in fear of Hitler. This was accepted and respected. A month later, the youngest of the four brothers, Michel, joined his mother and sister there, but remained secluded indoors.

Meanwhile the other brothers were able to escape across the Aegean, reassured that the ladies of the family were in safety. They reached the Turkish coast in a caïque and enlisted in the Greek Free Forces in Egypt.

There were periods when the Germans became suspicious. The front door of Prince George's house was opposite the residence of Archbishop Damaskinos, and there were always German guards on duty there. From time to time Alice was interviewed by the Gestapo. At these times, she made use of her deafness, feigning not to understand their questions and pretending to be less than bright. The Gestapo soon gave up pressing her.[20]

Characteristically, Alice never spoke of having hidden the Cohens. When Jacques Cohen tried to thank her in Rome some years later, she said sharply that she had only done what she believed to be her duty. The story became known much later through a friendship that developed between Freddy Cohen and Rear-Admiral C. D. Howard-Johnston, a friend of Dickie's, and thus Basil Boothroyd gave it a passing reference in his biography of Prince Philip.*

*'. . . Alice, who hung on stubbornly through the German occupation, her home filled with fugitives from the SS (it took courage to shelter, as she did at one time, a family of Cohens).' [Basil Boothroyd, *Philip* (Longman, 1971), p.97.]

29. Alice in Germany

At the end of January 1944 Alice arrived at Kronberg to visit her daughter Sophie, who had been widowed the previous October and was expecting a child. It had taken Alice three months to obtain a permit. She flew from Athens and took the train via Bucharest and Vienna to Germany.

Sophie's husband, Prince Christoph of Hesse, had been an early recruit to the Nazi party and a member of the SS. He had always sought to take part in active service and saw the best chance in Goering's newly created Luftwaffe in 1935. In March 1942, he was transferred to the staff of Jagdeschwader (fighter squadron) 53, stationed in Tunisia and Sicily, with missions to Malta. In time he became disenchanted with the activities of the SS. When Heydrich was assassinated in 1942, he told his mother: 'The death of a certain dangerous and cruel man is the best news I had in a long time.'[1]

With the Allied invasion of Italy, Christoph was driven back with his squadron to Castelgandolfo, near Rome, where he was suddenly recalled to Germany. On 7 October 1943 his aircraft, a Siebel 104, collided with a hill near Forli, and Christoph and his pilot were killed. The bodies were not found for two days. They were buried there.

'Poor dear Tiny,' wrote her grandmother. 'She loved her husband & had been so anxious about him ever since he was in Sicily . . . I am so sorry for Mossie too, this is the 3rd son she has lost in war, the two eldest in the last one & now her favourite in this one. This is now the 7th relation of mine who has lost his life flying.'[2]

Victoria was glad when Alice joined Sophie, but commented: 'Luckily they both have good nerves as they are so near Frankfurt, which has lately not been a pleasant neighbourhood.'[3] A few days later the wife of Wolfgang of Hesse* was killed there in a British air raid.

A British incendiary bomb had fallen on the chapel at Kronberg, where Sophie's father-in-law, 'Fischy', and Fischy's two elder boys lay buried. Sophie had retreated to her mother-in-law at Friedrichshof from Berlin some years before, with her four children and, with them, the four children of Christoph's brother, Philipp, after his arrest in 1943.

Sophie gave birth to a daughter, Clarissa, on 6 February 1944. Soon afterwards, when all was well, Alice returned to Greece. A little later, she was able to report to Philip:

As you know, I went to Tiny, who is *so* brave when she is with her children and us, being her usual self and making jokes but her hours in her room alone are hardly to be endured, and made all who love her, suffer so much for her that I realize now how much easier it is to bear one's own suffering than to share another's. I never suffered after 'the accident' [the 1937 Hesse air crash] as I did those three weeks with Tiny and I certainly will never forget them as long as I live. Her children are perfectly adorable, you would love them, and the new baby is too sweet for words.[4]

Alice could not see Margarita as there was no car and the changes of train to Langenburg were too complicated, but Margarita gave birth to twins on 7 April.

Alice returned to Greece in April 1944 and, in October that year, Greece was freed from German occupation. After that, she was unable to make contact with any of her daughters.

From 1941 until 1946 Alice and Ellen were the only princesses living in Athens, each in their respective ways engaged in charity work. During this time it was generally assumed that it was fortunate that they had each other to rely on. Certainly they saw each other

* Princess Wolfgang (1902–44). Marie Alexandra of Baden, married 1924. She was Theodora's sister-in-law.

often, and Alice was particularly solicitous to her sister-in-law when the Duke of Kent was killed. In the letters that Alice was able to write to Philip during the war years, she often spoke affectionately of Aunt Ellen and sent her love to him. It is clear too that news was frequently passed between the two princesses, when one or other heard something.

They were not always the best of friends. Alice was capable of being formidable at times, but fundamentally she had a more generous heart than Ellen. Nowhere in her correspondence does she speak other than warmly of her. Since her earliest days in Athens, she had been aware that Ellen looked down on her as a morganatic Battenberg princess.

Ellen had offended George V by insisting on being described as 'Imperial and Royal Highness' on the wedding invitation of Princess Marina, and in 1941 George VI had made it clear that of all the Greek royal family, she was the only one he refused to have in England.

Ellen could be less than generous in her judgements. She spread stories about the nature of Alice's illness in the 1930s. When a friend spoke of how wonderfully Alice had recovered from this, she replied with more malice than evidence: 'Up to a point!'[5] She was supposed to be pro-German, a rumour of which Harold Macmillan was aware* when he visited Athens in 1944, and which others have confirmed.

Macmillan came to Athens shortly after the liberation in October 1944 to preside over the return of the Greek government. Dickie had been worrying about Alice, so one of Macmillan's first tasks was to call on the two princesses. First he visited Ellen at Psychico.

He found her living in a large and comfortable villa with no material difficulties. She showed him her radio set, which she had been allowed to keep during the occupation, and served an excellent tea, which Macmillan did not want to eat. He noted:

* Macmillan noted that 'this old lady is regarded by us with some suspicion (she is said to have had Germanophile tendencies)' [Harold Macmillan, *War Diaries* (Macmillan, 1984), p. 558].

The Princess is a lady of fine presence. She must have been a beauty. The eyes, dark and lustrous, are remarkable. She reminded me of any Edwardian *grande dame*. Her conversation, though making the conventional references to the faults of the Germans, was more concerned with the dangers of revolution and Communism. EAM* is of course anathema: 'It must be stopped at once. It is the only chance. I know. It must be stopped'.[6]

After half an hour, Macmillan left, filled with the thoughts of those like Ellen who had seen a cultured and civilized age destroyed by two wars. Next he went to see Alice:

No doubt because of her English birth and unequivocal loyalties, Princess Andrew of Greece was living in humble, not to say somewhat squalid conditions . . .

She is a rather blowsy, lumpish and rather *Hausfrau* type. It would be hard to imagine anything more different from Princess Helen's character. I should imagine there were no – or only the most formal relations between the two Princesses. Hence the contrast between the palace and the flat.

Princess Andrew is not intelligent – and seemed very nervous and clumsy. She stayed in Greece and has been obviously working very hard and sincerely on relief, for children especially, with the Swedish Relief Scheme and the Swiss Red Cross. She made very little complaint, but when I pressed her to know if there was anything we could do for her, she admitted that she and her companion (an old lady-in-waiting who must, I think, have been the governess) needed food. They had enough bread; but they had no 'stores' of any kind – sugar, tea, coffee, rice or any tinned foods . . .†

This was a more agreeable interview and a more straightforward one than the last. But I rather enjoyed Princess Helen. She has the character![7]

*EAM, a left-wing party (the National Liberation Front).

†Macmillan arranged for some provisions to be delivered from army stores.

Macmillan did Alice an injustice, as confirmed by Major Gerald Green, who was to become a friend and confidante of Alice for the rest of her life. He was then Military Assistant to General Scobie, who arrived in Athens at the same time as Macmillan. Green recalled:

Mr Macmillan spoke with his mouth almost closed and had a heavy moustache. Princess Alice relied very much on lip reading. Therefore she wouldn't get a word of what he was saying and I think his comment was ungallant and boorish. He hadn't taken it into account that she had lived in Greece during the Italian and German occupation, where there was grinding poverty for everybody. She was not by any known means wealthy and she was wearing clothes she couldn't replace for years. It was all unfeeling of Macmillan.[8]

Gerald Green observed the contrast between the two princesses. 'Princess Nicholas loved jewels. She had a wooden travelling chest, containing precious jewels. She had four servants, an old butler and two maids. When she attended the liturgy in the Russian Orthodox Church, she sat on a throne.'[9]

The difference was confirmed by Jean Charles-Roux, in those days a French diplomat, now the incumbent of St Ethelreda's Place in Holborn, the oldest Catholic church in London. He arrived in Greece a little after the war and observed:

Princess Nicholas was very religious and mystical. She would have gone to the stake for her religion. She had an energy and a will that Princess Andrew didn't have. She thought Princess Andrew did not understand religion. But Princess Andrew later founded the only order of nuns in Greece to do social work. She said: 'It is all very well for Princess Nicholas forever attending the liturgy, but we must be practical.' Psychologically Princess Andrew's balance was frail, she had a German, dreamy philosophical approach to religion.[10]

Alice was still at Prince George's house when Charles-Roux found her, and 'glad to see somebody, who could tell her about the outside world'.[11] Both princesses were well informed politically, according to Charles-Roux:

They knew all sorts of things, such as where people were, what had happened and who one could trust, and so they were very much in the picture as sources of information. Socially the more brilliant was Princess Helen. The Revolution and so on had given her an experience of difficulties. So Princess Alice was a little second in line to her. Princess Helen saw the upper crust of the political world, the Ambassadors and so on. The Embassies were a little hesitant to ask Princess Alice.* But Princess Alice saw all sorts of people, and she certainly had a very sound and sharp political judgement on people. She had a rather objective view on the tricks of Greek politics.[12]

Alice was occasionally able to communicate with her mother through letters sent to the Greek Legation in London. In one such letter Alice declared that she had every intention of remaining in Athens, and could make no other plans until the end of the war. On 14 November Alice wrote to thank Dickie for inspiring the visit of Macmillan and in consequence the arrival of provisions. 'The last week before the liberation I had only eaten bread & butter & the servants were half starved. Also they shed tears of thankfulness when some army rations, including corned beef arrived promptly & they could have their first meal with meat for many, many months.'[13]

Alice was pleased when General Scobie invited her on board *Orion* in November to see the Noël Coward film *In Which We Serve*, based on Dickie's exploits in *Kelly*.

In the aftermath of the liberation, the political situation in Athens fluctuated dramatically. The Greek Communists were gathering strength and the threat of civil war loomed.

The British were in Athens to impose order and to arrange for

* Princess Nicholas also told newcomers that Alice was deaf and would prefer not to be invited. This was not true.

the return of George II. They aimed to demobilize the Greek National Army. But on the evening of 2 December, ELAS* overwhelmed the new National Guard at Megara. The next day a general strike was declared. A long column marched towards the main square of Athens in defiance of government orders. Firing broke out, and presently a scene of 'utmost confusion'[14] reigned. Twenty men were killed and frenzied crowds ran about. A bomb was lobbed into the Prime Minister's house. Martial law was then imposed with a nightly curfew at 7.00 p.m. The British spent the next thirty-three days fighting the 1st ELAS Army Corps (essentially urban guerrillas) in the centre of Athens.

Alice was confined to her house as the chaos got worse. In the midst of this strife came sad news. On the morning of 5 December, the Foreign Minister arrived at Alice's house bearing two telegrams, one from George II and one from the Greek Minister in Paris. They informed her that Andrea had died on 3 December, but gave no details.

'I was very lonely the first days as there was fighting all around the quarter & I could not communicate with Ellen,' Alice wrote to her mother.[15] Nor could she send any comforting words to her daughters, but, via Dickie, she was able to get a message to Philip, on board HMS *Whelp*, then in the Mediterranean, on his way to the Far East. It fell to Dickie to send him a naval message, deciphered on board: 'So shocked and grieved to hear of the death of your (?) father† and send you all my heartfelt sympathy. Following has been received from your mother: "Embrace you tenderly in our joint sorrow. Your loving mama."'[16]

There can have been no communication between Alice and Andrea since she last saw him in 1939. During these years Andrea had been stuck in the south of France, drifting between Cannes and Monte Carlo. Gilbert Beale had given his yacht to the British Royal Navy in 1940, after which Andrea had spent some of his

* ELAS, the military organization of EAM.

† The deciphering left the word 'father' with a (?) next to it, which would have been unnecessarily upsetting.

time aboard *Davida*, belonging to the Townsends. In 1940 he bought it from the Townsends for a nominal sum and then transferred ownership in 1942 to the Société Maritime Suisse. Meanwhile the yacht remained in the south of France.

In June 1943 Andrea had made a request to leave Monte Carlo for Portugal, but had been unable to obtain the necessary visa. Instead his Danish cousin, Erik, Count of Rosenborg,* came to the south of France and spent three months with him in *Davida*.

As early as the 1930s Andrea had formed a friendship with Comtesse Andrée de La Bigne, who had been brought up on the fringes of the intellectual world of Max Jacob and André Germain and was said to have enjoyed an undistinguished career on the stage. She was the granddaughter of Valtesse de La Bigne, a Second Empire courtesan and mistress of Napoleon III, who had also flirted lesbianically with the courtesan Liane de Pougy. The latter described Andrée de La Bigne in the 1920s as 'all golden in a dress of blue Japanese silk – really stunning, that girl'.[17]

When Alice's mother became aware of the liaison in the 1930s, she had consulted Andrea's former ADC, Menelaos Metaxas, who told her that Andrée de La Bigne was an 'adventuress, feathering her own nest'.[18] Alice thought better of her, describing her to Philip as 'the friend who looked after Papa so touchingly to the end'.[19] As much as anything, the friendship was based on Andrea's need for companionship.

Later, when the dismal state of Andrea's finances was revealed, Victoria concluded that he had become 'weak & apathetic', while 'his lady friend, who I had been told was unselfish, proved to have sucked him dry etc. as such women generally do'.[20]

Until 1931 Andrea had lived off £3,500 a year, the income from some shares in a Greek gold loan at the Westminster Bank, but this had collapsed. So he was then forced to depend on the annuity from the sale of Mon Repos to George II, as well as an extra £50

* Erik, Count of Rosenborg (1890–1950), son of Prince Valdemar, thus Andrea's first cousin. Married morganatically, 1924, Lois, daughter of John Booth, a Canadian lumber king. Divorced 1937.

a month that the King sent him to live on. His situation was worsened by premature arterial sclerosis and a more than social reliance on alcohol. For some time he had also been suffering from irregular pulsation of the heart.

By November 1944 the Hotel Metropole in Monte Carlo had become his more or less permanent home. He minded not being able to get news of his daughters or Philip, though contact was finally established with Louise and Victoria.

On 1 December Andrea went to Nice to attend a party given by the American General, based in Marseilles. He appeared animated and happier than he had been for a long time. Being tired, he stayed that night in Nice. On 2 December he returned to Monte Carlo to his room at the Metropole. Still feeling tired, he put on a dressing gown and went to bed early, something he never normally did.

In the early morning of 3 December he woke at 4.00 a.m. in a deep sweat. An hour later, he said: 'I have a pain there,' pointing to his heart. A minute later his heart just stopped.[21] These details Alice was told some months later by Andrée de La Bigne, presumably a witness to them.

Andrea's coffin was taken from Monte Carlo to the memorial chapel to the Tsarevich behind the gloriously onion-domed Russian cathedral in Nice. There it lay under the Greek flag.

Queen Mary summed up the sad end to the marriage of Alice and Andrea a little later, the details of which are more or less accurate. As this was presumably the accepted view, her letter is worth quoting:

> The trouble between Andrea & Alice started when she became Orthodox & religion went to her head (like poor Alix of Russia). She insisted on sleeping on the floor, & was too whacked for words. You will remember she lived in a Dr's house for some years, quite away from husband & children. By degrees she recovered more or less completely, but by that time the couple had no wish to rejoin each other, so she remained in their old house in Athens, & he lived on bd a yacht, near Cannes with a lady friend . . .[22]

Although separated from Andrea for many years, Alice assumed the status of his widow, mourning him as if he had still been with her. She was able to reclaim him in death, and as ever she behaved with stalwart dignity, subjugating her private feelings.

Meanwhile the fighting in Athens continued. Three days after hearing of Andrea's death, Alice had Ellen billeted on her 'without warning'.[23] Contrary to Alice's version of events, Major Green recalled that he had warned her of the need for Ellen to move in, her house being within the area protected by British troops. With customary generosity, Alice agreed readily. It then fell to Green to persuade Ellen that she was in danger at Psychico. Autocratic as ever, Ellen paced the floor, reminding Green that she had lived in the Royal Palace in Athens throughout the German occupation, but Green had some persuasive arguments with which to help her change her mind. On the way to the house, he had been slightly wounded in the head by a hand grenade and his driver had been shot dead at his side. Ellen relented.

On 21 December, writing in pencil in the absence of ink, Alice was able to give her mother an account of herself:

I am afraid you will be worrying about us but really we are all right & strongly guarded in our small free area of the town. We get British soldier's rations which are excellent & Ellen & I especially enjoy the meat rations as we have not had any for many months. I really think we are much better off than we have been for a long time in the way of food.

Although there is no electricity, we have a petroleum lamp to ourselves on the first floor, Ellen's rooms being next to mine is a great convenience. The servants have the ground floor petroleum lamp. Friends come daily to see us & in the evening we play card games & make jokes & try to forget our tragic circumstances.

Tell the girls we are both well & quite our usual calm selves. As it was impossible to go to church, we had a priest to say the funeral mass & panichida for Andrea in the big drawing room here (the girls will know it) & a few of Andrea's friends managed to come to it.[24]

Gerald Green was one of the regular visitors and he it was who brought the stable lamp. Having united the two princesses, he visited them daily. Popoulo confided to him that with the curfew which kept them all in for twenty-three hours a day, the ladies had little food but were too proud to say so. Green therefore arranged for provisions to arrive.

On these visits Green invariably found the princesses sitting politely together, but was not sure how much time they spent together at other times. A fire was often burning, and he discovered they were burning wood from packing cases. One evening, Ellen was sitting alone. It transpired that Alice had gone out, in contravention of the strict curfew. Presently she returned safely. Green recalled:

Princess Alice came in and instead of rising to my feet and bowing, I shot out of my chair and said: 'Where have you been?' I think Princess Helen was quite shocked and appalled by this. However, Princess Alice sat on a chair and said: 'You know, it's years since a man spoke to me like that.'

Princess Alice smoked like a chimney. She had saved all the chocolates that came with the cigarettes in the rations and had decided to go round the police who were being harassed by the Communists and cheer them up a bit. She had got some sort of perambulator and went alone to give the policemen a few cigarettes and sweets for their children.

I told Princess Alice that it was very dangerous and that she might well be shot, at which she replied: 'Well, they tell me that you don't hear the shot that kills you and in any case I am deaf, so why worry about that? I wouldn't know, would I?' She added: 'It's my duty. What else was I born to do?'

From that time started the great closeness that we had.[25]

Athens remained in a state of civil war into the new year of 1945. Churchill and Eden made their famous and unexpected visit on Christmas Day, living on board *Ajax*. There were many meetings. The leader of the Communist party went to see General Scobie and presented his terms. Scobie's reply was 'Good Morning'.[26] Archbishop Damaskinos, an imposing figure in his robes, arrived on board to see Churchill. In the midst of a seasonal fancy-dress party, some of the crew mistook him for a participant.

Churchill presided over a conference of Greek factions on Boxing Day, despite the failure of most of the ELAS representatives to arrive. The aim of the conference was to make terms for peace, prevent a massacre and seek to restore George II to the throne. Discussions were held by the light of eerie paraffin lamps, with sounds of fighting in the distance.

By the end of 1944 Damaskinos was installed as Minister for Foreign Affairs. By 3 January 1945 a new Cabinet was sworn in, with General Plastiras as Prime Minister. Two days later ELAS troops pulled out of the built-up area of Athens and the Piraeus. The British had re-established order, and peace reigned in Athens.

During this time, Alice and Ellen continued their curious phase of cohabitation under curfew. It was not until 21 January 1945 that Ellen returned to Psychico. Alice wrote several times of Ellen's comforting presence, while Ellen herself remained largely preoccupied with her own affairs. 'This last month has been a nightmare,' she wrote, 'but thank God since yesterday Athens has been freed thanks to General Scobie & his brave & splendid men.'[27]

Alice continued her work with her district nurses and charity institutions. Some thirty refugees came to the house daily, including eleven orphan boys from Alice's orphanage, which had been bombed. 'I am very grateful,' wrote Alice, 'as it takes my mind off so much misery, including my own loss, which I feel very deeply as I loved Andrea so very much.'[28] Philip wrote to her and she replied:

Your letter was such a comfort to me, to let me feel how wonderfully you took this great loss, for naturally I was sad for you being so far away & separated from all of us at such a moment. You know the deep love & understanding that united dear Papa & me & that I, like you, can feel him closer to me now. A great comfort also is to see with what veneration & love, all classes speak to me of Papa & how they rejoice that he has left a son to follow in his footsteps.[29]

Alice realized that Philip's duty now lay outside Greece, whereas she 'with more than 40 years experience here & a woman outside politics, could do more here than you could'.[30]

On 1 February 1945 Alice arrived in England, staying first with the Duchess of Kent at Coppins and then at Broadlands with her mother. She spent her sixtieth birthday with her mother, only returning to Athens on 25 March.

Alice had not seen Victoria since 1939. In the meantime Victoria had endured the deaths of the aunts she kept an eye on and of several friends, though the Pye-Crust was still with her, deaf in one ear and suffering from giddiness. Victoria had been bombed out of Kensington Palace, and in late June 1944 had been taken in by George VI and Queen Elizabeth at Windsor Castle.

It was impossible for a member of the Hesse family not to dwell on mixed loyalties. At the end of the war, Victoria wrote: 'When I think of my father, that just & kind-hearted man, I can only be glad he lived before the degradation with which Nazidom has poisoned the character of a whole people.'[31]

Reunited with her mother in 1945, Alice confirmed that she would stay on in Greece, which Victoria agreed would provide a suitable outlet for her energy and powers of organization. She was pleased when her daughter gradually looked less strained.

On the other hand, Alice was distressed to find conversation with her octogenarian mother rather confined. Victoria still possessed a clear mental outlook, though had lost a certain elasticity in her thoughts. Alice found it easier to listen than to attempt a rational argument, since Victoria was now unable to grasp a contrary point of view. Alice explained to Dickie:

> I am ashamed to say that at the beginning I was sometimes abrupt & sharp in my answers & I am now trying my best to remember her great age & that I must sadly renounce so much of the old Mama & let her talk on as she likes. It gives her so much pleasure to be allowed to say what she thinks without contradiction or interruption, so why should she not have that pleasure for the rest of her life.[32]

Queen Mary went to Coppins to see Alice on 23 February. Alice was able to give her news of various Brunswick, Baden, Hesse and Hohenzollern relations. 'Alice looked very old, I thought,' wrote the Queen, 'but was most talkative & nice.'[33]

As the war drew to its close, Alice came to terms with the plight of her daughters. In April 1945, Sophie was stranded in a wing of Schloss Friedrichshof at Kronberg, with nine children (her five children and Philipp's four) to feed. She told a reporter: 'We have reason to believe that at one time during the Allied invasion of Sicily my brother and my uncle [Philip and Dickie] were fighting on the same sector of the island where my husband was serving.'[34]

Darmstadt was extensively bombed and many of the Hesse family homes laid flat. In 1945 Queen Mary wrote to her brother in Canada: 'Poor Darmstadt has ceased to exist, everything gone. This was done by Americans, rather sad as Ernie had arranged everything so well in the old Schloss.'[35] By then Lu and Peg of Hesse had returned to Wolfsgarten from Switzerland. They took in numerous refugees from amongst their family, friends, retainers and others.

By May 1945, Sophie had moved there from Kronberg, the children conveyed under straw in the back of carts. Soon after her arrival, she learned that her sister-in-law, Mafalda, had died at Buchenwald.* 'Since 2 years my eyes have been open,' she wrote in a letter to Victoria, '& you can imagine what feelings one has now about those criminals.'[36]

Living in the country, Alice's other daughters, Margarita and Theodora, were better off. They were away from the fighting in the last months of the war, and had fresh vegetables to eat. Nevertheless Theodora was 'sad & depressed'.[37] Alice's Aunt Irène spent the later months of the war in western Silesia, sending news that she was being 'treated considerately'.[38]

After the war, Alice felt great distaste for the Germans and, for some time, she refused to go to Germany. Gradually she overcame this and applauded the steps taken in both her German and English

* Mafalda was killed accidentally by collateral damage when the Americans bombed an industrial site near the concentration camp.

families to rekindle friendly relations, to forgive and to work towards a lasting peace.

Alice was in England in 1945 to resolve Andrea's estate. The executor was a Monsieur Zagoréos, a temporary officer in the Greek navy, then stationed in Alexandria. He told Alice that the Comtesse de La Bigne was not mentioned in the will, which, meanwhile, could not be opened. Alice at once decided to give the Comtesse Andrea's car (largely so as not to have to pay the garage expenses), and any personal items that she wanted.

In London Alice spent a night at Claridge's where George II was based in exile.* They agreed that Andrea's will should be brought to London and opened before the Greek Consul. But it transpired that the will was lodged in a bank vault in Athens.

Alice finally saw the will on her return to Athens. It left Andrea's estate in divisions of roughly seven tenths to Philip and one tenth to each of the daughters. There was no remaining money in Greece since Andrea had spent it on uniforms at the time of the 1935 restoration. In Germany there were 60,000 Deutschmarks, which Andrea and Alice had inherited following the death of their granddaughter, Johanna, in 1939.† This, Alice decided, should go to her three daughters. In France there was a small sum left after debts had been paid and funeral expenses covered. This was deposited for Philip at the Greek Legation in Paris, but Alice warned him that he would get 'very little indeed & it will make a mere pocket-money to add to your pay'.[39]

Alice soon discovered that there were debts which were 'very large indeed'.[40] To pay off the first instalment of a large overdraft at the Westminster Bank, Alice sold the silver from Mon Repos, lately stored by Louise in Sweden, retaining only a monogrammed service for Philip. 'I calculated the things as being just what would

* Alice also saw 'Big George' and Marie. Her brother-in-law had now lost his voice completely because of cancer of the vocal chords.

† This was one of those situations worthy of a Wilkie Collins novel. After the 1937 air crash, Johanna had inherited money from her parents. At her death, this reverted to her maternal grandparents as her next of kin.

be needed in a modest household if you did not marry a rich wife, or for a captain's mess,'[41] she told him.

Andrea's debts were not resolved until 1947. Ernest Rehder, the family lawyer, advised that £12,500 should be paid in respect of a claim by a Mr Khalifa Boubli for payments to Andrea in French francs against Westminster Bank cheques. A further £4,000 was owed to the widow of Alexandre Ponisowsky for the same reason. But Rehder disputed claims from Mrs Townsend in respect of *Davida* and its silver.*

The various creditors were told to bring their claims to court in October 1947, but that summer the claims were settled out of court. In this Alice was assisted by Dickie, who held a meeting with Rehder to establish the order of priority in settling the debts. Nada Milford Haven's brother-in-law, Sir Harold Wernher, whose business acumen the family respected, also advised – to the extent of paying many of the debts himself.[42]

In March 1945 Alice made a private pilgrimage to the south of France. She flew to Nice and spent Holy Week there. She went to see Andrea's coffin in the chapel behind the Russian cathedral and took comfort from this. 'The site is too lovely for words,' she wrote to Philip. 'You can imagine the comfort of attending church services so near him.'[43] Alice returned to Greece with some of Andrea's papers.

In 1946 Andrea's coffin was transferred back to Greece and buried at Tatoï with none of the attendant pageantry that had so exercised Lincoln MacVeagh six years before.

War ended in Europe on 8 May 1945, and in August Alice enjoyed her first summer holiday for many years with Louise, Gustaf and her mother at Sofiero. 'One can hardly believe this nightmare is over,'[44] she wrote.

* Mrs Ida S. Townsend, living at the Villa Meunière, Prophète, near Marseilles, later claimed that Andrea's estate owed her £17,500. She claimed a further £25,000 for the silver on board, which had been consigned to Andrea's care. Ernest Rehder believed these claims to be exaggerated. The matter was settled out of court in the summer of 1947. By 1949, *Davida* was again registered in her name.

30. Philip's Engagement

As early as 1941, even as casual a visitor to Athens as 'Chips' Channon was happily speculating that Philip would one day marry Princess Elizabeth, a girl he had seen twice in his life, once at Princess Marina's wedding in 1934, and then more memorably at Dartmouth in 1939. Channon observed Philip at a cocktail party in Athens, and noted:

> He is extraordinarily handsome, and I recalled my afternoon's conversation with Princess Nicholas. He is to be our Prince Consort, and that is why he is serving in our Navy. He is charming, but I deplore such a marriage; he and Princess Elizabeth are too inter-related.*[1]

There is no contemporary evidence to support the conclusions Channon drew from his conversation with Princess Nicholas. Alice was inclined to dwell on potential dynastic alliances. She had spent most of the 1920s lining up potential husbands for her daughters, an endeavour crowned with no success. But as far as Philip was concerned, she played a passive role, observing the endeavours of others quietly and largely without comment.

At the outbreak of war, Philip had been training with the British Royal Navy. Alice had failed in her quest to turn him into a Prince of Greece. After George II sent him back to England in 1939, there was never any question of his doing other than becoming a British naval officer. Philip served with the Mediterranean Fleet, in Home Waters, and with the British Pacific Fleet in South East Asia and the Pacific. He was mentioned in dispatches at the Battle of Matapan, in the south of Greece, in February 1942.

* They were third cousins by descent from Queen Victoria and second cousins once removed by descent from Christian IX of Denmark.

From time to time during the war he materialized in London. In October 1941, George VI wrote to Victoria: 'Philip came here for the week end the other day. What a charming boy he is, & I am glad he is remaining on in my Navy.'[2]

At the beginning of 1944 Philip was in Britain, much in his grandmother's company, awaiting appointment to *Whelp*. While the destroyer was building, he undertook a tactical training course. He was then twenty-two and Victoria liked to compare him to his cousin David Milford Haven, who, in her view, lacked Philip's 'charm and easy manner'. She enjoyed observing 'the mixed character traits of their parents appearing in the cousins'.[3]

By 1944 Dickie was determined to get him naturalized as a British subject in order that he could continue to serve in the British Royal Navy. Furthermore, he would not be hindering the possibility that he might marry Princess Elizabeth. On the first plan, the entire family were happy to conspire; on the marriage question, wisely, they were more circumspect. They realized that nothing would happen unless the young couple wished it to happen, and so they waited. They loaded the gun for Philip, but left him to pull the trigger.

At first their messages to one another were rather coy. Following a meeting with Philip in February 1944, Victoria wrote to Dickie, then in India as Supreme Allied Commander of South East Asia: 'As he has not touched on the subject you spoke about to me with reference to his future, I also refrain from doing so.'[4] At the end of March, she was braver:

> I touched on the subject on which you gave him advice, but he was not inclined to confide in me, so I did not press him. There are no developments at present in the situation. He is, however, fully aware that he must give it careful consideration. His cousin [David], who is in England now, did not talk freely to him, when he broached the subject, but thought it a good idea. I gather his cousin is not inclined to mix himself in the matter.[5]

In June Alice mentioned this in a letter to Philip, sent as usual via Louise in Sweden: 'Through Ellen I heard you stayed with

23. Peace after the fray. Andrea and Alice sailing to New York, 1923.

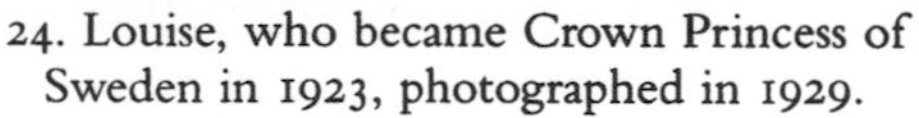

24. Louise, who became Crown Princess of Sweden in 1923, photographed in 1929.

25. Alice with Philip at Hemmelmark in 1929. The family would soon disperse.

26. Holiday at Arcachon 1923. Alice's family meet Louise's fiancé, Crown Prince Gustaf Adolf of Sweden: (*back row, left to right*) Theodora, Cécile, Ingrid of Sweden, Alice, Margarita, Louise; (*front row*) Victoria Milford Haven, Sophie, Andrea, Bertil of Sweden, Crown Prince Gustaf Adolf.

27. Victoria Milford Haven with her brother, Ernst Ludwig, Grand Duke of Hesse, facing a decision at Darmstadt, 1930.

28. Alice. A portrait.

29. Two betrothed couples: Christoph of Hesse with Sophie, and Cécile with Don of Hesse, Darmstadt, 1930.

30. (*top*) Dr Ernst Simmel's clinic at Tegel. Alice stayed there for some weeks in 1930.

31. (*left*) Dr Ludwig Binswanger, Alice's doctor from 1930 to 1932.

32. (*above*) Haus Maria, at the Bellevue Clinic, Kreuzlingen, Alice's home for two and a half years.

33. Breibach, near Cologne, home of the Markwitz family, where Alice was restored to health, 1937.

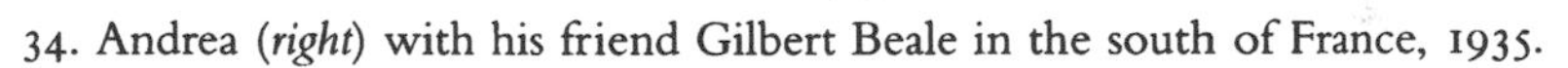

34. Andrea (*right*) with his friend Gilbert Beale in the south of France, 1935.

35. Greek children having their one meal of the day in Princess Alice's soup kitchen.

36. The Cohen family, members of which Alice hid in Athens in 1943, with George I (*foreground, in white*) and Andrea (*wearing a hat*). Beside Andrea is Mrs Haimaki Cohen, and behind him is Mr Haimaki Cohen. George I stayed with the Cohens in Tricala in 1912, when the city was flooded.

37. Alice about to board the royal yacht with her grandchildren, Charles and Anne.

38. Alice in full-length nun's robe, leading her family out of Westminster Abbey after the Queen's coronation, 1953. Following her are Theodora and Berthold of Baden and their son Max; Margarita and Friedel Hohenlohe and their daughter Beatrix; Sophie and George William of Hanover, and her daughter Christa of Hesse; and Prince and Princess George of Greece (Prince George in the robes of the Order of the Bath).

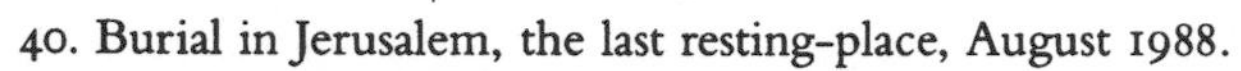

39. Alice in her dressing-gown, a last photograph by Godfrey Argent in King Edward VII Hospital, London, 1967.

40. Burial in Jerusalem, the last resting-place, August 1988.

Marina about Easter and paid an interesting visit, as well as lunching with a certain young lady & her parents before you left.'[6] Then Philip's grandmother began to report on the satisfactory departure from the stage of various potential rivals: the engagement of Harold Wernher's daughter, Gina, to Edwina's former lover, 'Bunnie' Phillips,* and that of a girl nicknamed 'Oslo' to Guy Millard.†[7]

Later in the year, Dickie had the chance to talk to Philip about the naturalization plan. Victoria was pleased:

It is a great relief to me to know that he wants it himself & that the others wish it & you have done good work by clearing up the situation. I think it is the best thing for him & it will give a firm basis for his life, which without a fixed career or home country it was wanting in, poor boy.[8]

The end of the war in Europe gave the family more chance to develop their plans. A letter survives from the Duchess of Kent to Dickie, indicating her complicity:

I did know from Georgie about Philip being given British nationality. I think it a very good idea & apart from it being a help in his naval career it might also be an asset for other 'matters'.

Of course the less said about the question we have sometimes discussed the better – & as you say it must take its course.[9]

In February 1945, while Alice was in England resolving matters concerning Andrea's will, Victoria spoke to her. The fruits of this conversation Victoria relayed to Dickie, still monitoring matters from afar:

Alice had had long talks with me & she is most sensible about everything regarding Philip. She knew about the future plans etc. for him. She is

* Georgina Wernher (b. 1919), married first, 1944, Lt.-Col. Harold Phillips (1909–80). Now Lady Kennard.

† Osla Benning (d. 1974), a Canadian. She was engaged to Guy Millard (later Ambassador to Sweden), but did not marry him. In 1946 she married John Henniker-Major (now Lord Henniker), later Ambassador to Denmark.

quite in agreement with us about the nationality question & has discussed it all now with G. of Greece. The only question is as to the time for taking this step. G. of Greece now seems to want it put off for a while, for what (possibly selfish) reason we can't fathom & we feel that the only unselfish judge in the matter is you & trust you will advise Philip what to do.

As to any future plans, Alice has a feeling that they lie in the hands of Providence & that she will not try to interfere in any way, which feeling I encourage.[10]

In late 1944 and early 1945 Dickie had obtained information about Alice's welfare by making high-level enquiries. In February 1945 he wrote to Anthony Eden to thank him and took the opportunity to remind him about Philip:

I . . . am more certain than ever that I was right to try and arrange for my sister's son, Philip of Greece, to be allowed to become a British subject and continue in our Navy, as I cannot believe there is any future in the Greek Navy. I suppose we shall have to wait a little bit for the excitement to die down before the naturalization comes through, but I do hope we can continue to count on the personal support you so kindly promised.[11]

Then both Dickie and George II suggested that Alice write to George VI to thank him for allowing Philip to become a British citizen. This she did, and when she later went to tea with the King on 13 March, he told her 'that the matter had been taken in hand now'.[12] The King had delayed because George II had asked him to wait. Alice reassured George VI that she had seen George II and he was now fully in favour.

In July Alice stayed with Dickie at Broadlands for a few quiet days. By this time, he was so confident of a happy conclusion to his plans that he was busily enquiring into the title of Prince Consort. Alice dutifully researched how the matter had been handled in respect of Prince Albert. On 6 July Victoria wrote to Dickie to say that George VI was keen for him 'to come over here for your consultations'.[13] On 24 July Victoria, Alice and Louise took tea with the King and Queen at Buckingham Palace.

There were long periods of inactivity. By the end of the Second World War, Philip was still in the Far East and did not return home from Tokyo until January 1946. Alice came over to London to see him, ending the second five-year phase in his life during which they had not seen each other.

In 1946 both Alice and Philip (then at the Naval Staff College, Greenwich) were much in England, Philip often spending his leave at Coppins, the Iver home of the Duchess of Kent. Her sister, Elisabeth, nicknamed 'Woolly' in the family, was sometimes there from Germany and furnished him with news of his sisters.

Sophie became engaged to Prince George Wilhelm of Hanover in January 1946. He was headmaster of Salem School and held in high esteem by Kurt Hahn. The union was much encouraged by Princess Peg of Hesse. Queen Mary was pleased that the 'pretty little widow Tiny' had found a new husband, and reckoned that with five children, they would need a large house.[14] Philip attended the wedding in Salem in April, bearing many gifts and provisions sent by Alice and Louise.

Then, accompanied by his naval friend Michael Parker, he went to Monte Carlo, where they met the Comtesse de La Bigne at the Café de Paris. She handed over Andrea's remaining books and other personal effects. Philip's affection for his father remained strong. He had any of his suits and jackets that were wearable adapted; he used his ivory shaving brush and, from that day on, wore his signet ring.

George II was restored to the throne of Greece in September 1946, following a plebiscite, and returned to Athens. Alice and Ellen, the two princesses who had spent the war there, greeted him in public. A Te Deum was sung in the cathedral.

There were times during his exile when George II had appeared to lack the will to return to face what *The Times* once called 'the hydra-headed monster of Greek politics'.[15] He was still in London in August 1946, at which time the Foreign Office reported that George VI believed George II 'was in a very bad way. He clearly dreaded going back to Greece and was talking of putting off doing so until the end of the year! . . . The Crown Prince and Princess on the other hand are . . . panting to go to Greece as soon as possible.'[16] The Foreign Office view was that if the King was looking forward to going back, he was 'quite mad'.[17] But in September 1946, back he went.

Alice was in Athens from the early spring of 1946 until she left for London at the end of April 1947. In that year she cemented her friendship with Major Green, seeing him often. She enjoyed the company of Sir Steven Runciman, then representing the British Council in Greece. They lunched together and he relished someone 'who combined wild dottiness with a sharp intellect and shrewd judgement'.[18] She would expound interesting theories about education in Denmark, then surprise him by explaining that the reason the Atlantic was so rough was that the sea hit high rocks and bounced back.

Alice's new son-in-law, Prince George of Hanover, confirmed Alice's habit of having a ready answer for everything. 'She would say: "That is because . . ." and then she would pause until she came up with an answer!'[19] Jean Charles-Roux never failed to pay her a visit before writing his dispatch to Paris, since she was well informed politically and he always learned something new. This phase in Greece was easier for Alice than hitherto and filled with stimulating company.

On 1 April 1947 Alice was shocked to hear that George II had died suddenly at the palace in Athens. On the day he died, he worked normally in the morning. His sister Katherine* was with him at the palace when he suffered a sudden stroke and by 2.00 p.m. he was dead. Alice wrote to Dickie:

It was indeed a great shock to us for Georgie was so nice & affectionate & the small remnants of the family in Athens met constantly in great

*Princess Katherine was about to marry an English officer, Major Richard Brandram. The wedding took place quietly in Athens a few days after the funeral on 21 April.

harmony & understanding. All news & events were openly & freely discussed & there was also much gaiety & good humour & so this sudden breaking-up of an intimate & happy circle was a great blow to all of us.

You know how shy & reserved Georgie was in society & public formerly, well he was quite changed when he arrived in September, so much softer & easier of manner, that he completely won all hearts both with the public in the streets as with the people he received in audience & he was liked & adored. Even the republican socialists were completely conquered by his manner & convinced that the monarchy must continue for some time still & they were terribly upset by his death.[20]

The King was succeeded by his brother Paul, who now accepted the throne with none of the reluctance that he expressed when it was first offered to him in 1920, on the death of his other brother, Alexander. Alice was optimistic that he would make a good King, while even the Communists admired the new Queen, Frederika, for visiting their wounded in Salonika and Thrace in 1946 and 1947, following the occupation and the civil war.

Alice was still in a state of shock when she arrived in London at the end of April. Spending the summer with her mother helped her regain her energy and kept loneliness at bay. 'She has heaps to do & worry over still,' wrote Victoria, 'but she is full of energy & good sense & she & Philip get on well together.'[21]

In the meantime, Philip finally renounced his rights to the Greek throne on 28 February 1947 and became a British subject. At his own request he ceased to be HRH Prince Philip of Greece and became Lieutenant Philip Mountbatten, RN.

Once his naturalization had been resolved, Philip's family waited patiently for the resolution of their further hopes. A lull occurred when George VI took Queen Elizabeth and Princesses Elizabeth and Margaret to South Africa between February and May 1947.

After his return from the Far East Philip became a frequent visitor to the palace and there were meetings at Coppins. The romance followed its private course, and in the summer of 1947 Philip proposed and was accepted. Alice, until then a passive onlooker, went to tea with the King and Queen and the bride-to-be.

Victoria's apartment at Kensington Palace became the focal point for her family. In preparation for the forthcoming nuptials, it was generally spruced up. And Victoria herself presided happily over the various comings and goings. Alice was permanently there, Philip appeared from time to time and David Milford Haven stayed there when on leave.

An entire upstairs room was suddenly filled with packing cases containing Andrea's books, clothes and papers which arrived from the Riviera that summer. Philip spent two spells of twenty-four hours with Alice, helping her sort them. He was often at Royal Lodge, Windsor Great Park, with his future in-laws, but Alice needed him for fittings as she had brought some silks and other fabrics from Athens as a present to him from various firms and individuals, 'so now he will look quite respectable'.[22]

George VI discussed with Alice the announcement of the engagement and it was settled for Wednesday 9 July, the day before a garden party so that the young couple could make a joint public appearance there. The day before, Philip arrived at Kensington Palace to collect his new clothes. Alice and her maid Augusta helped him to pack his trunk 'for he was so excited he hardly knew what he was doing'.[23]

Alice described the engagement to Dickie, away in India:

After all the congratulations in the morning, the family had a quiet lunch & then the young couple went to see Cousin May & returned for the garden party at 4 p.m. Mama did not go as it is too tiring for her, though she still could go last year.

It amused me very much to be waiting with the rest of the family, for Philip to come down grandly with Bertie, Elizabeth & Lilibet. The young couple made their rounds of the garden alone, accompanied by the court people & received ovations from the guests.

This morning the two came alone to visit Mama, who was delighted as she is very fond of Lilibet & likes her character very much.[24]

Queen Mary sent a message of congratulation to Alice, and she replied: 'The young couple seem very devoted to each other. They have had time to think such a serious decision over, & I pray they will find happiness & a great *friendship* in their future married life. Lilibet has a wonderful character & I think Philip is very lucky to have won her love.'[25]

31. Philip's Wedding

Alice adapted to the role as the bridegroom's mother with the same insouciance with which she faced the other dramas of her life. For a brief spell she was occupied with worldly affairs.

In June she was involved in the matter of an engagement ring. Her jewels had been deposited in the Paris branch of the Westminster Bank in Andrea's name since 1930 when she went to Kreuzlingen and the house at St Cloud was closed down. Signatures were needed from Philip and the three daughters, after which she could take possession of them. Theodora and Sophie signed promptly, while Margarita demurred, even making a claim on the estate. Eventually she too signed.

Alice took some of her diamonds to the jeweller Philip Antrobus at 6 Old Bond Street and had these designed as an engagement ring, a large diamond in the middle, surrounded by a cluster of five smaller stones, 'as Philip dare not show his face at jewellers, for fear of being recognized. I think the ring is a great success.'[1] The jeweller was later quoted in the press saying that he had no idea for whom the ring was intended.

In the late summer Alice left her base in London for Paris to have two grey velvet trains from Russia converted into her wedding outfit, acquiring a nasty glandular infection during the visit. She visited Louise in Sweden and in October she went to Paris once more to collect her dress and finally her jewels.

When the jewels were valued, there were some nasty surprises: Andrea's star of the Elephant of Denmark was missing and another star proved to have paste diamonds (Andrea having sold the originals and replaced them). At least Alice's Imperial Russian Order was in good condition. 'My St Katherine's star had exceptionally fine, white diamonds, much finer than Auntie Ellen's even,'[2] she wrote to Philip.

The Duke of Gloucester wrote round to the royal family, taking a collection for a joint wedding present, to which most members subscribed, though Dickie and Edwina did not. Dickie's excuse confirmed the quasi-paternal role he had played in Philip's life. Instead he and Edwina gave them a cinema for their weekend home, Windlesham Moor, in Berkshire: 'As Philip is really more of a son than a nephew to us (not having a son of our own!) we felt we ought to do them proud and said we would take this on.'[3]

Wedding fever increased. David Milford Haven, whom Philip had chosen as his best man, moved into Kensington Palace, as the family home, Lynden Manor, had been recently sold. Isa Buxhoeveden helped Victoria with her correspondence and the additional work that the wedding created. Alice and her niece, Lady Katherine Brandram, attended a Te Deum at the Greek cathedral in Moscow Road on the anniversary of Greece's entry into the war, 29 October.

Not everything went well. A controversial decision was made that none of Philip's sisters would be invited to the wedding. The war so recently ended was far from forgotten and it was deemed politically insensitive that they should come.

Philip's sisters longed to be there and failed to realize the depth of feeling in Britain against Germany, not to mention towards those who had been more directly linked to the Nazi regime. Sophie's three Hesse-Kassel brothers-in-law were awaiting denazification. One of them, Philipp, was still interned and would not be released until 1948. Palace advisers did not want Princess Elizabeth's groom tarnished by innuendo in the press. Philip's sisters considered it a necessary sacrifice that they would make for him. But they felt doubly hurt when invitations were sent to Queen Helen of Romania and her sister, the Duchess of Aosta, since Romania and Italy had been Hitler's chief allies in the war.*

* The Duchess of Aosta had been forbidden to come to Britain by Ernest Bevin in June 1946, though, following an intervention from George VI's private secretary, Sir Alan Lascelles, permission was eventually granted. But she was not allowed access to funds at the National Provincial Foreign Bank in London, as she was an enemy national.

Instead, Margarita, Theodora and Sophie joined the Duchess of Kent's sister, Elisabeth (Woolly), and Lu and Peg of Hesse at Marienburg, the home of Sophie's parents-in-law, the Duke and Duchess of Brunswick. They celebrated the wedding together, though Sophie wrote to Dickie: 'It is not very easy, I assure you, to make the press (who interview us continually) understand & they keep insisting that we must be estranged, which only makes a difficult & humiliating position even more unpleasant.'[4]

The wedding took place at Westminster Abbey on 20 November, Alice seated on the north side of the abbey opposite George VI, Queen Elizabeth, Queen Mary and the British royal family. Victoria was beside her, and Louise and Gustaf came from Sweden, and Dickie and Edwina came back from India. Queen Frederika came from Greece, though King Paul was ill and could not. Nor was Ellen on the invitation list. Philip's uncle, Big George, Aunt Marie and their daughter Eugénie, came from Paris. Queen Ena, Alice's Battenberg cousin, came from Switzerland. With Queen Helen of Romania came her son, King Michael, who would lose his throne at the end of that year. Even Philip's cousin Alexandra was there, now the wife of King Peter of Yugoslavia.

It was a glorious occasion, symbolic of a new age, looking to the future. For Alice in particular the marriage heralded the dawn of an exciting new phase of life and pointed towards some kind of security, a firm link reforged with the world of her childhood. The ceremony and the processions through the streets of London lightened the gloom of post-war Britain, still weighed down by rationing and other deprivations.

'How wonderfully everything went off,' wrote Alice to Philip, '& I was so comforted to see the truly happy expression on your face & to feel your decision was right from every point of view.'[5] She was happy to see photographs of Philip and Princess Elizabeth in the papers before she returned to Athens, her lady-in-waiting, Popoulo, prostrated with air-sickness.

The hurt feelings of her daughters remained a preoccupation. From Athens Alice wrote them a twenty-two page description of the wedding, which Queen Frederika took with her when she flew to stay with her parents* in Germany. The Duchess of Kent also went out there to see her sister 'Woolly' or Elisabeth, and so the Brunswicks kept their house party going an extra week so that all could meet. Alice felt that the sisters were by now 'really happy & consoled for their absence'.[6]

Back in Athens, Alice made a point of inviting her daughters to stay with her in turn. As she had to move out of Big George's house, she took rooms at 4 Heraklion Street, a side street off the Patissia Road, with windows overlooking the National Museum. The house belonged to a widowed friend of hers called Mrs Nasos.† This house was too small for guests so King Paul offered to house her daughters at the palace.

Margarita was the first to come with her three eldest children, Kraft, Beatrix and Andreas, arriving in Athens on 27 February 1948. Ostensibly Alice was paying for the trip, though in fact the money came from Edwina. It was Margarita's first return to Greece since King Paul's wedding ten years before and she was 'radiantly happy'[7] to be home. But, noted Alice: 'She has expanded very much, her legs and arms very fat, but her face quite unchanged & very fresh.'[8] They went on walks in the morning and in the afternoon the children cycled or played football. Margarita stayed until 3 April. She returned to Friedel, 'delighted with her stay'.[9]

Sophie came next, but Theodora's visit was postponed because of political unrest in Greece. Sophie's husband, Prince George, had been appointed headmaster at Salem, and in advance of this Kurt Hahn summoned him to Gordonstoun to show him how the school was run there. While Alice funded their trip to England, she prevailed on Philip to put them up in an hotel for five or six days

* Queen Frederika and Sophie's husband, Prince George of Hanover, were brother and sister.

† Edla Nasos, youngest daughter of Lord Abercromby. Her mother was Swedish, a cousin of the author Carl Heidenstam. Her husband, George, was a gifted Greek musician, and director of the Conservatory of Music in Athens for nearly half a century. He died in 1934.

and pay for their trip to Scotland and the return flight to Germany. This was an opportunity for Philip and Princess Elizabeth to break the ice by inviting them to stay with them at Birkhall, near Balmoral, establishing a practice of entertaining them privately, which has continued to this day.

On 10 June 1948 Alice attended the secret wedding of Queen Helen's son, the recently exiled King Michael of Romania to Princess Anne of Bourbon-Parma, the daughter of Andrea's cousins, Meg and René.* The wedding took place in Athens and had to be kept secret as Princess Anne's family were staunch Catholics, and the Pope had refused to sanction the marriage. The bride's parents had to take the position that they knew nothing of it, or they would risk excommunication.

Alice was one of those people who saw her needs as primarily spiritual. This meant that she avoided involvement with the more tedious aspects of her personal finances, while clear in her mind that she lived modestly and well within her means.

During these years, she received £30 a month from Edwina and £10 a month from Louise. During the war, the extra £10 had been sent to Popoulo, because of financial restrictions. She now began to receive a pension in Greece as a general's widow. This was enough to live on, but somehow Alice made frequent requests for extra funds, though never directly for herself. She thus enjoyed that rare position of being an occasional benefactress to one member of the family, while another was then prevailed upon to pay the tiresome bill.

In 1949 Alice was living on the Aegean island of Tinos, involved with the sisterhood she was founding.† But she decided that she needed a bachelor flat in Athens, with two rooms and a bathroom. Philip offered to help her, and she soon found an ideal one being built at 61 Patriarch Joachim Street, costing £6,000. She asked Philip if he could let her have the deposit of £2,000:

* They had been neighbours for some years at St Cloud in the 1920s.

† *See* Chapter 32, concerning her sisterhood.

I know it is a large sum I am asking you, & aunt Louise is also going to help but if you could possibly manage £2,000 now, immediately as it is urgent, I should be more than grateful. Besides, the flat is going to be inherited by your sisters, for it will let at a high rent & will enable the sisters to pay for their journey to Athens & buy clothing there for themselves & their children when I am gone. It is capital well invested & such a great help to the sisters once upon a time, for my English money which they will inherit cannot go to Germany for a good many years.[10]

Philip duly put up the deposit and Alice proceeded with the purchase.

In January 1950, Alice announced that she was going to sell the flat and move into a convent. Neither Dickie nor Louise approved of her selling the flat. On investigation they discovered that Alice's finances were in a muddle. Dickie learned that Alice had borrowed money from a Greek friend, Admiral Liambey,* to complete the purchase of the flat. The Admiral was now more than a little concerned as to whether he would be repaid. Philip had been kept in the dark about this, since Alice did not want to burden him with her problems at a time when he was still settling some of his father's outstanding debts.

Both Dickie and Louise thought the cost of Alice's flat to be exorbitant, but realized that this was inevitable in Athens. 'That does not excuse Alice's extravagance,'[11] commented her sister. Louise believed that Alice should have the flat as then 'Philip & we all can have a sort of assurance that Alice has got at least somewhere to live when she gets older.'[12] She did not want Alice to go into a convent, partly on grounds of health and partly because she did not think it would suit Alice from the religious point of view.

Louise did not think Alice would live long because for five successive winters Alice had suffered either from bronchitis or slight bronchial pneumonia. She had trouble with her liver which caused a brown patch on her face. Her gall bladder was poor and she had

* Admiral Liambey had generously given Philip silk for his shirts as a wedding present. He owned an artificial silk spinning factory in Greece.

digestive problems, especially when she suffered from bad chills. Alice was inclined to be greedy, and on occasions when she overate, she suffered and had to resort to tea and toast and medicine. All in all, there was cause for concern.

As ever, Philip stepped in. He paid the first instalment to the Admiral and by October 1950 the flat was in Philip's name, and Alice had a home for as long as she needed it.

Alice was delighted to receive a letter from her daughter-in-law in June 1948, confirming that she was pregnant, and later to receive a telegram from Philip on 14 November, announcing that her grandson Charles had been born.* It reached her in Tinos just before she set off to Athens to the dentist.

'I think of you so much with a sweet baby of your own,' Alice replied, 'of your joy & the interest you will take in all his little doings. How fascinating nature is, but how one has to pay for it in the anxious trying hours of the confinement.'[13]

Alice had known for a while that she would not see the baby until at least the summer of 1949, due to her various commitments. So she was glad to hear Louise's report, which she passed on to Dickie:

> She says that Lilibet was looking so well & fresh, a good recovery after a hard time she had, 30 hours in all. The baby is sweet with a well-shaped head, an oval face & a little bit of fair fluff of hair. She says he is like Philip, but Marina says he is like Lilibet, so you can choose. I am so happy for Philip for he adores children & also small babies. He carries it about himself quite professionally to the nurse's amusement.[14]

Alice finally saw Charles in July 1949, pronouncing him 'too sweet for words'.[15]

* Victoria wrote to Dickie of the birth of her 'latest & important great-grandson & let us hope he may live in a more peaceable & prosperous time than we & live to be some sort of reigning king'. [VMH to MtB, KP, 22 November 1948 – BA.]

32. The Sisterhood

The summer of 1948 marked Alice's final appearance in civilian clothes. In January 1949 a flurry of headlines in the world's press announced: 'Philip's Mother – Living as a Nun'.[1] Alice was traced to the Greek island of Tinos, and found to be living in four rooms of an old two-storeyed house, accompanied by a 45-year-old Greek Orthodox sister in black robes, Sophia Dimitriou Alberti. Alice undertook her own housekeeping and washing, and wore the austere grey habit of a nun. There was no telephone, and limited electricity in the night. She rose daily at six, attended services in the church, and over Christmas began her religious devotions at 4.30 a.m.

A reporter was sent by the *Daily Mail* to secure an interview with her. 'I don't like talking about my work,' she said. 'Duty is its own reward. I am not a politician or a film star. Taking pictures of me at work would be posing.'[2]

Alice's decision to go to Tinos was no sudden whim. She had declared her wish to found a sisterhood as long ago as 1930 during her sojourn at Kreuzlingen. But the idea had begun to form earlier still, when she was a witness to the founding of her Aunt Ella's convent in Moscow in 1908. Nor was 1949 the first time she wore the habit. She had worn it for practicality at times in the soup kitchens during the war.

In March 1948 she decided to eschew the expensive life of Athens in favour of Tinos, where 'life is cheap & food abundant'.[3] She had been given a piece of ground by the Church of the Virgin, a celebrated shrine for pilgrims who paid biannual visits there to see its miracle-working icon. There she intended to build a home and school for religious district nurses. Alice gave the Church of the Virgin her Russian Order of St Katherine to raise funds, to the irritation of some of her family. 'I am truly thankful to have an occupation,' she wrote to Dickie, 'as I love work & feel myself too young & active still to sit & do nothing.'[4]

On 17 July 1948 she 'withdrew from the world',[5] as she put it, and made what she hoped would be a permanent move to Tinos. She explained her reasons to Philip:

> I think I told you about the religious sisterhood of Martha & Mary I want to start along the lines of Aunt Ella's foundation in Moscow. Now that the last of my children is married & has a home, I feel the need of a whole time job to keep me occupied.[6]

Alice settled happily on Tinos, enchanted with the island and comparing it to Corfu and Mon Repos. Work began on the new building. In December Alice met the Bishop of Gibraltar, Rt. Revd Douglas Horsley, to ask him about the training of deaconesses in his church, and the administration of other Anglican religious orders. The Bishop observed that her sisterhood was to be 'something of a cross between the two'.[7]

Whereas it is usually possible to know exactly when Alice made a particular journey, one very important one remains elusive. It was probably in 1949 that Alice made the pilgrimage to Jerusalem to see where Ella's coffin lay. There, training to be Abbess of the Russian Orthodox Convent, was Princess Tatiana Bagration, who had taken the name of Abbess Tamara. She was devout and served full apprenticeship as a nun, in a way that even Ella had not. Abbess Tamara was the daughter of Grand Duke Constantine of Russia and the sister of the three Russian princes who died with Ella at Alapaievsk – John, Constantine and Igor. As a young girl, she had two suitors, Alexander I of Serbia and the Georgian Prince Constantine Bagration Moukhransky. Her father advised against the first – he did not trust '*ces trônes balkaniques chancelants*'[8] – and she married the other, whom in any case she loved, later giving birth to a son and daughter.*

* Prince Theimouraz (1912–92) and Princess Natasha (1914–84), who married Sir Charles Johnston.

Though she survived the Russian Revolution, Abbess Tamara's early life was as tragic as that of many members of the Russian Imperial family. She faced bereavements in close succession, including widowhood when her husband was killed in action. She raised her children, remarried, lived in exile and finally trained as a nun at the Russian Orthodox Convent of the Mount of Olives in Jerusalem.

Alice's mission was to create a sisterhood that would go out into the world to nurse. It was not a closed order, but one that sent its sisters out to work in a practical sense. Ella's order had been successful, but Ella had been rich, whereas Alice had little or no money of her own. The possession of money is not the first requisite for the founding of a religious order, though it brings certain practical advantages. Other princesses have founded religious orders: for example Princess Ileana of Romania, who founded a convent in Pennsylvania on no money. This survives today, though Mother Alexandra, as she was known, died in 1991.

Alice wore the grey habit because in Greece it was a help. It made it possible to raise funds for charity in a more direct manner than she could have done as a princess. It is therefore true that Alice was not a real nun, but disguised herself as one. The arrangement was practical too, as Prince Philip recalled: 'Her religion had no outward manifestation. It was something very private to her. But wearing the habit meant that she did not have to worry about clothes or getting her hair done.'[9]

The rules of Alice's sisterhood permitted only four weeks holiday each year. This rule she found she was unable to apply to herself. She came frequently to Athens when Dickie paid a visit or for some other social purpose. On these visits she combined committee meetings with other engagements. Later she made frequent trips from Greece, sometimes for months at a time, to see her family in England and Europe. In her absence, her sisterhood invariably began to flounder.

Ultimately, a lack of religious commitment and devotion undermined Alice's aspirations. Whereas Abbess Tamara was a real nun, Alice was not. As always she was well intentioned, but this was not enough. Her mother thought that by dressing as a nun, she was making a mockery of the achievements of Ella; she felt it was denigrating to her memory. Victoria expressed her opinion somewhat wryly: 'What can you say of a nun who smokes and plays Canasta?'[10]

These were not the only problems. There was the Greek attitude to young girls in training. Alice's experiments in training girls had served but to turn them into potentially excellent wives and mothers. By putting them into grey habits, Alice identified them more as nurses, but this raised a further problem. The Greek male had no great respect for nurses, equating them and sometimes treating them as prostitutes. Clearly, the families from which Alice sought girls to train had no desire for their daughters to be treated in this way. This may account for a setback in September 1949 when, following a prolonged absence by Alice in London and Switzerland, all her sisters asked to go on leave for various reasons.

In the late summer of 1949 Alice found a property on the outside of Athens to the north. Presently she decided to move her operation there and to relinquish the idea of building on Tinos as it was too expensive to transport materials there from the Piraeus. Alice paid a final visit to the island to collect her winter clothes and settled in Athens. It was at that point that she decided to buy a flat in Athens, one room of which would be used as the Athens office of her sisterhood.

The future of her enterprise still hung in the balance because of lack of funds. A bequest from a rich friend in Athens in gold pounds brought a temporary reprieve. But some of Alice's good intentions were undermined by Ellen, who discouraged her friends from giving their support. Alice grasped with glee the invitation of the new Patriarch of Constantinople (formerly Archbishop of America) to go to the United States in the new year to advise the new Archbishop there (a man previously in London) on the establishment of an American-Greek sisterhood similar to hers in the countryside outside New York.

This plan Alice relayed to her mother with some anxiety, 'for alas! she has the firm conviction that I am walking on the moon &

do not know what I am doing.'[11] Her mother commented: 'Alice . . . with her usual unrest is now planning a visit to America in the coming year. Well it is her affair & as my father used to quote when he used to stop us from criticizing other people's actions: "*Jedes Tierchen hat sein Pläsirchen.*" '*[12]

Before setting off for America, Alice went to Salem to be present at the birth of Sophie's seventh child, a boy† born safely and easily on 9 December. She felt 'quite an ancestor being there'.[13] She found Theodora unwell, suffering from a bad heart, which was to be a lasting problem.

After Salem Alice went to Margarita at Langenburg for Christmas and the new year, and then to Sweden to stay with Louise, who was pleased that Alice had gone to Germany as it proved that she had overcome her post-war 'repugnance about going there & seeing Germans'.[14]

Alice's proposed visit to the United States in January 1950 was problematic. Having no fixed plans until the autumn, Alice clung to the idea of going to help the Archbishop in New York, but his plans remained unsettled and eventually he wrote to say that he could not ask her to come. There then arose the diplomatic issue of Alice visiting the United States as a Greek princess in advance of the official visit of King Paul and Queen Frederika in the autumn. Both these issues were resolved by a widowed friend of Alice's in Boston inviting her to come over privately and Alice set off happily on 5 March, sailing back to Europe on 28 April.

Having missed the birth of Charles, Alice was determined to come to England for that of Philip's second child. She arrived in July to stay with her mother at Kensington Palace, coinciding her visit with Philip's naval leave in London. 'Poor Alice,' wrote Louise. 'She often is a problem. I do so hope Lilibet won't be too shy of

* 'Every man to his taste.'

† Prince George of Hanover, born 9 December 1949. Alice thought he had the same nose as his Aunt Frederika.

Alice. It is a pity that they can't make contact because I feel they could get on together.'[15]

Alice lunched with Princess Elizabeth, who told her that the birth was expected on about 6 August, so she was able to go to Cologne to visit her old friends, the Markwitzes at Breibach, before rather than after the birth. She went to Germany on 21 July and returned on 4 August, refreshed as ever by the company of her old friends.

Clarence House, where Princess Elizabeth and Philip were living, was surrounded by journalists and loyal well-wishers when the news broke that a much hoped-for daughter had been safely born to Princess Elizabeth on 15 August. The crowds were intrigued by the figure of a nun who made several calls, and the popular press were happy to identify Alice as 'one of the few remaining religious mystics in the Greek church'.[16] Alice was appointed one of Anne's godparents, along with Queen Elizabeth, Margarita, Dickie and the Hon. Andrew Elphinstone (a nephew of Queen Elizabeth).*

The summer of 1950 was the last in the long life of Alice's mother. As she grew older, her mind dwelt on the fate of Nicky, Alix and Ella. She could not blame the Russian people but she would always dislike the Bolsheviks. At certain times she felt she led 'a monotonous old woman's life';[17] at others, her apartment was overrun with great-grandchildren. If she became fractious with Dickie and lost her temper, she always apologized in shame. Almost impossibly thin, she smoked unceasingly, with a bronchial cough to match.

Victoria went to Broadlands in August, where Louise heard that she was 'well & content'.[18] Late that month she suffered a sudden heart attack. From this she made a reasonable recovery, but she knew the end was near. She returned to Kensington Palace, where Alice stayed with her. Gradually she weakened and Alice telegraphed Louise to come.

The doctors diagnosed deep-seated bronchitis. She was weakened by long-contained inflammation and phlegm retention, which

* Alice did not attend the christening in October.

was slowly poisoning her. But Victoria enjoyed a strong constitution and Alice awaited either recovery or decline.

The Pye-Crust helped nurse Victoria until she strained a muscle in her leg. Alice did her best, but sometimes felt inadequate because her deafness prevented her from understanding what was needed. Victoria asked to be nursed by Catholic nuns, but at first none seemed able to come. Finally the Mother Superior of the convent at Holland Park sent two Spanish nuns, because Victoria was the aunt of the Catholic Queen Ena of Spain.

The nuns were caring and Victoria was comfortable. She remained clear in her mind until a few hours before she died. On the night of Saturday 23 September, Victoria began to decline, so Alice and Louise summoned Dickie, who arrived with Edwina. Then she rallied a little, so they sent Edwina home, while Dickie slept on the sofa, and Alice and Louise in armchairs.

In the small hours of the night, Victoria became restless in her semi-conscious state. The doctors were summoned and she was given an injection, after which she relapsed into unconsciousness. One of the nuns called the family in at 7.40 a.m. and with the Pye-Crust, they all knelt by her bed. Writing later to Philip, Alice described those minutes:

> She was practically sitting up to ease the breathing & so we had a good view of her with such a calm & peaceful expression, as one who is having a good sleep & the breast rising & falling so evenly & gently, until it quietly stopped at 8 a.m., a beautiful end.[19]

Victoria's coffin was taken to the Chapel Royal, where a private funeral was held. Then the coffin was taken to Portsmouth and piped aboard HMS *Redpoll* on the orders of George VI. It sailed across the Solent to the Isle of Wight to lie beside her husband Louis in Whippingham churchyard.

Victoria left behind her a farewell letter, thanking her family for their love and devotion and urging the survivors to stick together and support each other. 'The bitterest grief in my life has been the loss of Georgie,' she wrote. 'You will miss me I know, but let it be a comfort to you to realize that the best part of my life & on the whole it has been a happy one, was ended when your dear father died & that I am ready & willing to enter into my rest at any time now.'[20]

Back in Greece, soon after this, Alice found it hard not to be writing to her mother to say she was safely home. 'Poor Alice, she is to be specially pitied so alone as she is,'[21] commented Louise.

There came the inevitable business of settling the estate. Alice gave her quarter share, amounting to about £2,000, to Philip in trust for Sophie, as she was the one sister who had received nothing from Victoria in earlier days, mindful that her husband was a schoolmaster, rather than a landowner like those of Margarita and Theodora. Victoria's papers were sorted by Isa Buxhoeveden, who drew Dickie's attention to some papers that Victoria had kept relating to Alice's illness, which she had 'intended to destroy but left'.[22] Her other possessions were distributed.

The family were pleased to hear that the Pye-Crust was allowed to stay on in Alice's old rooms at Kensington Palace. They were less pleased to hear that, a few weeks later, the Pye-Crust had received a visit from a Royal Household foreman, instructing her to hand back the keys to her late mistress's private garden.

33. The Coronation of Elizabeth II

Victoria had asked that her family should remain united and support each other. She would not have been disappointed. Dickie and Louise were in constant touch by letter despite busy lives and between them they kept a wary eye on Alice. Whenever possible Dickie, Louise and Alice met, in England, Sweden or Greece. They were sustained by sibling affection.

Alice was a less regular correspondent. In 1951 she sent Dickie a *Reader's Digest* article on flying saucers, and he responded with the first version of the Mountbatten genealogies that he had edited. By this time Alice never kept possessions for long. She immediately gave the handsome volume to Field Marshal Papagos, who needed a friendly sign, being on the point of resigning as Commander-in-Chief of the Greek armed forces due to hostility in King Paul's household.

In their letters, Alice, Louise and Dickie invariably invoked the memory of their mother, and a substantial bond between them was their mutual concern for the surviving band of their mother's friends, Nona and Dick Crichton, Baroness Buxhoeveden, the Pye-Crust and their penurious Aunt Anna, who would only accept money from Battenbergs. Dickie also monitored the progress and promotions of Christopher Jenkins, a boy taken in by the Milford Havens after losing his leg in the Dardanelles. Dickie reduced his mortgage at every opportunity and kept in touch with him until he died in 1974. The support they gave went beyond attention to financial welfare. They sought to stimulate the lives of these loyal friends, arranging treats and holidays to enliven existences less active than in previous days.

During the 1950s, Dickie served as Fourth Sea Lord until 1952, was Commander-in-Chief of the Mediterranean Fleet from 1952 to

1954, and concurrently Commander-in-Chief, Allied Forces, Mediterranean from 1953 to 1954. He then achieved his lifelong ambition to be First Sea Lord, serving from April 1955 until 1959. His last job was as Chief of The Defence Staff from 1959 until his retirement in 1965.

Exactly five weeks after Victoria's death, on 29 October 1950, Gustaf succeeded his father as King of Sweden and Louise became his queen consort. Louise accepted her change of status with shy modesty. 'It is quite frightful. I just can't get over people calling me your majesty,'[1] she wrote to Dickie. This reticence produced some stories cherished in Louise's family. At the funeral of George VI in 1952, the Queen of Sweden's car was announced and Louise did not recognize it was for her. Later, when she visited London, she was inclined to go shopping on her own. Lest she got run over and nobody knew who she was, she placed a card in her handbag, announcing: 'I am the Queen of Sweden.'[2]

Louise was sustained in her new role by her husband. She and Gustaf had enjoyed a happy marriage, boosted by his enthusiasm for everything he undertook, his scholarship and his benign nature. Their relationship had its funny side too. The Queen (of England) was in a car with both of them during the state visit to Sweden in June 1956, when Gustaf asked Louise to wind down the window. 'I will if you say please,'[3] was her unexpected reply.

In April 1951 Alice found herself working almost single-handed for her sisterhood, as some of her sisters succumbed to accidents, operations and illnesses. Her assistant spent a month in hospital and Alice ended up so tired that if she tried to write a letter in the evening, she promptly dropped off to sleep.

In the summer Alice began a long trail around her family. She went to Salem and Langenburg and on to Sofiero for most of August, where she found Louise rather frail, having got so overtired that she had had to spend five weeks in bed. But Alice was an easy guest. 'We are such good friends,' wrote Louise, '& we neither of us feel we must sit together all day.'[4]

At the end of August Alice arrived at Clarence House. When

Alice travelled, she invariably carried but one small suitcase, which she insisted on unpacking herself. She joined Philip and Princess Elizabeth at Birkhall, near Balmoral, for a week, where Sophie, George and her son, Karl, were staying, integrated at last into the British royal circle, without a whisper in the newspapers.

'It was hard leaving you,' wrote Alice to Philip when she got back to Greece, 'but my work occupies my mind & that is a help. I console myself with visions of next summer, when I hope to come again.'[5] In Greece Alice was preoccupied with Queen Frederika's open opposition to Field Marshal Papagos, who had unexpectedly stood in the elections and won a resounding majority. Politically sensitive, Alice was upset by this antagonism.

In England there was concern for the health of George VI. The family feared cancer and were relieved to hear that this was not the case. The proposed visit to Canada by Princess Elizabeth and Philip in October 1951 was able to proceed.

Early in 1952, Alice had planned another visit to America once more to raise money for her sisterhood. She cleared the visit with King Paul, informing him that she could not keep it a secret. She asked Philip if she could stay with him in London on the way and as a result, Queen Elizabeth asked Alice to stay at Sandringham. The two contrasting mothers never knew each other well, and years later Queen Elizabeth recalled that they had rather teased Alice about her nun's robes on account of their sartorial elegance: 'Very fetching, we said to her.'[6]

Alice flew to the United States, arriving at New York International Airport, Idlewild, on 18 January, attired in her grey habit. She was interviewed by the press, telling them that she had come to raise funds to enlarge the headquarters of her order to the north of Athens. Her sisters needed three years of training and at present there was only room for ten students. Her trip was sponsored by Spyros P. Skouras, the chairman of Twentieth Century Fox.

In New York Alice had success raising money. She then moved on to Boston for a few days and went from there to Chicago. She was staying at the Hotel Drake, when, on 6 February, she heard news of the sudden death of George VI, whose guest she had so lately been. Philip was with Princess Elizabeth in Kenya, but Alice wrote to him at once:

All my thoughts are with you in this sad loss. I know how fond you were of your father-in-law & how you will miss him. I think much of the change in your life this means. It means much personal self-sacrifice for you, as I am fully aware, but every sacrifice brings its reward in a manner we cannot foresee. Such has been my experience in my own life with its many ups & downs. Remember that Papa with his brilliant brains & sportsman like outlook (such as you were alas! too young to know) will be with you in spirit.

Commune with him & you will feel help & comfort in the responsible years to come as friend & adviser to your dear wife in her new position, whom I also love as a daughter.[7]

Alice then went to Washington where she saw Baron 'Steno' Stackleberg, a cousin through the von Hauke family, who invited her to a small dinner. He almost secured the Vice-President, Alben Barkley, but he was rushed to hospital for an eye operation. Mrs Robert W. Bliss, who had helped finance Louise's hospital at Nevers, gave two teas for her at Dumbarton Oaks, and both the Greek and British Ambassadors gave lunches for her.

On 15 February Alice attended a memorial service for George VI in Washington and then flew to New York. She went on briefly to Canada and flew to London on 26 February to be with Philip and the new Queen at Clarence House. She visited Dickie and Edwina at Broadlands for two days before returning to Athens. There she put the funds she had raised to good effect: she completed her building operations, creating a chapel and a second floor, and a rest home for elderly ladies.

From Athens Alice observed those changes that always attend the beginning of a new reign. The Queen and Philip moved into Buckingham Palace, sharing it for over a year with Queen Elizabeth The Queen Mother until her move to Clarence House in May 1953. Alice's main concern was for Philip, previously the master in his own house, who was now consort to the Queen. Inevitably, the courtiers served the Queen first, while he was relegated to an undefined role outside the constitution. Their attitude is demonstrated by the story of a patronizing courtier who said to him: 'You will like Windsor Castle when you get to know it.' To this he replied: 'Yes, my mother was born there.'[8] There was a more serious consequence. As Prince Philip observed some years later: 'The late King died in February 1952 and that effectively brought my naval career to an end.'[9]

In May Dickie was delighted to hear that old King Haakon of Norway intended to treat Philip as though he were a crowned head. 'I'm glad,' observed Dickie, 'as Philip has not been given adequate status in England yet in my opinion.'[10] Dickie was soon to be thwarted in the matter of the family name. Within days of the King's death, he boasted to Prince Ernst August of Hanover that the House of Mountbatten now reigned in England. The Prince took this thesis to Queen Mary, who placed the matter before Winston Churchill. The Prime Minister prevailed upon the Queen to declare that the reigning family should continue to be styled the House of Windsor, which declaration was made on 9 April 1952. This decision was disappointing, if not rather more than that, to Dickie.

At the end of the year Dickie asked the Duchess of Kent how she thought Philip was coping in his new role as consort. She replied:

> I think he is coping with it in the right way. He has a charming 'approach' with people & an easy manner & speaks (it seems) very well in public. Never too much in the background & yet not too much in front. Has his own opinions & plays an intelligent part in things. I think & pray 'They' are very happy.[11]

The summer of 1952 started badly for Alice, but improved. A bout of influenza was followed by a car accident. Alice was being driven by one of her sisters in her small Ford. Seeing a turning ahead, she issued the peremptory order: 'Turn left!' The astonished nun did so immediately, landing them both in a ditch.[12] Alice suffered a slight cut under her eye, which left no scar, as well as various bruises. Aware that Philip's finances were now on a more even keel, she did not hesitate to ask him to contribute £200 to a new £300 car, specifying that his private secretary, Lt.-Commander Michael Parker, should order it for her. This request was made in direct fashion: 'I want a new one to be sent out at once from the Regent Str. Shop where I got the last one.'[13] Once again, Philip obliged, though he was prodded by a rebuke from his mother: 'Mike is better at writing than you are & more prompt.'[14] Dickie, Louise and Gustaf stepped in to take care of the annual insurance of £50.

In July Alice went to Tatoï for a family lunch for Dickie and Edwina, and their daughters Patricia and Pamela. She then took them to see the house she was rebuilding and they met six of the sisters. Alice lunched aboard HMS *Surprise* (the Commander-in-Chief's dispatch vessel) and showed the Mountbatten family her flat.

In the autumn Dickie, then Commander-in-Chief of the Mediterranean Fleet, arranged a family reunion with Alice, Louise and Gustaf in Malta at the house next to 52 Strada Mezzodi, where the Battenbergs had lived forty-five years before. Lengthy discussions ensued about what police protection would be needed and whether Gustaf could be persuaded to invest in the tropical uniform of a British admiral (he could not). Alice's travel expenses were taken care of, and on 10 October Alice, Louise and Gustaf duly sailed from Italy to Malta in *Surprise*.

Dr Borg-Olivier, Malta's Prime Minister, insisted on greeting the royal party with the Governor, Sir Gerald Creasy, on the grounds that he was a genuine Maltese. The visit was a resounding success, as Alice wrote to Philip from Admiralty House in Valletta:

It is such fun being here after nearly 45 years, seeing all the old & new places, such as Gozo, which I had never visited. I have only 5 days here as I must get back to work, but the breathing space has done me a lot of good, as I was rather tired. Now I hear you are coming here next month & I so much regret that your visit does not coincide with mine. It would have been delightful to see you here in my second home.[15]

Alice went to Tatoï for Christmas Day lunch with King Paul, Queen Frederika, their young family and others. At the end of the year Alice wrote to Dickie: 'I still think constantly of Malta & that those days with you & Louise there were some of the happiest days of my life.'[16]

In June 1952 the Queen's coronation was proclaimed for 2 June 1953. The forthcoming ceremony dominated Alice's life as it did that of so many of her relations and friends. Margarita and Sophie were determined to be there. At least a year before they had 'fixed that in Philip's mind!!',[17] as Margarita put it. Louise was furious that being the wife of a king, she was not allowed to be there. King Paul and Queen Frederika also challenged that custom without success.

Dickie, lately appointed personal ADC to the new Queen, made his way back from Malta, and Queen Mary left instructions that if she died, court mourning was not to affect the plans.* Nona, who had attended the three previous coronations in attendance on Victoria, proved a problem. She much wanted to be invited but both Dickie and Louise felt that neither she nor Dick were up to the attendant problems of getting there. This was accepted until Nona heard that Philip had invited Isa Buxhoeveden as one of his guests.† Eventually she was invited to Alice's rooms at the palace to watch from there. 'Poor Nona,' commented Louise, who offered to pay for a hired car, 'she has always been like that, afraid to be forgotten when she considered she had a right to anything.'[18]

Alice arrived at Buckingham Palace on 28 May, Isa Buxhoeveden staying with her for ten days, and the Pye-Crust coming out of retirement from Kensington Palace to be her maid. Inevitably she

* Queen Mary died at Marlborough House on 24 March 1953. Court mourning lasted until 28 April.

† Baroness Buxhoeveden was an interesting presence in the abbey, having survived the vicissitudes of the Russian Revolution, when she served the Tsarina. Lately she had been gathering facts about Victoria's life for Dickie, and helping Philip's nieces on school visits to England, once moving into Clarence House to look after them.

became a focus of press attention in advance of her visit. She even granted an interview to a journalist from *The American Weekly*,[19] which was more about her work than the coronation. The media were fascinated by the idea of Mother Superior Alice Elizabeth emerging from her nunnery in Greece. Much was made of the austere conditions in which she now resided, much also of the special new nun's habit that she had ordered for the ceremony.

Here was the dichotomy of Alice's life: simplicity on the one hand, sudden extravagance on the other; and there is no doubt that she made more of an impression in her grey, contrasted to all the finery of the peers' robes and uniforms, than had she been more traditionally dressed. If Queen Salote of Tonga won all hearts in the rain in procession from Westminster Abbey, Alice's slow progress up the aisle did not pass unnoticed within. Even Cecil Beaton singled her out as 'a contrast to the grandeur, in the ash-grey draperies of a nun'.[20]

Alice sat in the royal box behind the Queen Mother and the royal princesses. With her were her three daughters and their husbands. Alice watched her daughter-in-law anointed and crowned, now occupying the position of her great-grandmother, Queen Victoria, and living in many of the homes that Alice had visited in the first fifteen years of life. She saw her son kneel before his wife and sovereign to become her 'liege man of life and limb'.

After further coronation festivities, always in the nun's robe, Alice returned to her life in Athens.

The Pye-Crust was thrilled to have served Alice during the festivities: 'I had a lovely time,'[21] she wrote to Edwina's secretary. She also wrote to Louise: 'Prince Dickie was simply magnificent! Absolutely a Coronation in himself!!' Louise passed this on to Dickie with the comment: 'Good, isn't it?'[22]

34. The Reign of King Paul

Since the death of George II in 1947, King Paul had reigned in Greece with the energetic, not to say manic, support of his wife, Queen Frederika. Alice and she were not able to appreciate the more admirable sides of their respective characters, Alice judging the German-born Queen insecure and capricious.

The 1950s was a difficult phase for a Greek king, but at few times in the troubled history of the Glückburgs in Greece were times ever other than difficult. The issue of Cyprus haunted relations between Britain and Greece during the decade,* preventing King Paul from paying the first state visit of a foreign king to Britain in 1954, and delaying his appointment to the Order of the Garter until 1963.

King Paul's character was delightfully informal, as evidenced by the British Ambassador's account of an incident early in his reign. Driving himself about Athens in an open car, the King had encountered a problem passing a taxi. Squeezing past with difficulty, he made 'what is considered a very rude gesture with his hand', and then noticed to his horror that the taxi was full of priests. 'What did you do then, Sir?' asked the Ambassador. The King replied: 'I turned down the nearest side street and crossed myself three times.'[1]

Queen Frederika, on the other hand, was more controversial. Her radiant smile was disarming. She could be all things to all people and in the early days her sense of fun and informality had 'an excellent softening effect'[2] on the various discords in Greek public life. Her charitable work was well received by the Greek

* Cyprus was a British crown colony from 1925 to 1960. A state of emergency existed between 1955 and 1959, when the United Kingdom, Greece and Turkey finally agreed that Cyprus should become a republic.

people and her fund for the welfare of the northern districts raised £300,000 in 1947. However, while King Paul invariably spoke with 'moderation', Queen Frederika was inclined to work herself 'into a highly emotional state'.[3] She never failed to express her views, which involved strong likes and dislikes. At the height of the Cyprus affair, Queen Frederika told a British MP that 'the British had received from Greece her most beautiful Princess (the Duchess of Kent) and her most popular Prince (the Duke of Edinburgh). Was it too much to ask that in return we should hand over Cyprus?'[4]

By March 1957 Alice was reporting 'the serious worries I have about their position here'.[5] And in May that year, another British Ambassador, Sir Roger Allen, described a meeting with Queen Frederika soon after the presentation of credentials:

> Most of the conversation was non-political but towards the end she said quite suddenly that she hoped that we should be able to 'look beyond' the present troubles and be happy here. She said that she and her husband indeed regarded these troubles as 'a thing of the past'. Whatever one may think about her being a bit over-optimistic, I am sure that it was meant kindly and that she intended to convey that the attitude of the King and herself towards the British was friendly. Since I gather that this has not always been 100% of the case in the past, I thought it just worth recording.[6]

To this memorandum was added a Foreign Office minute: 'Queen Frederika's charm is notorious, and deceptive.'[7]

Alice's visit to England for the coronation was the last major occasion on which she came to the attention of the British public. Those that were aware of her existence thought of her simply as Prince Philip's mother, who became a nun. Alice took some part in family events in Greece, but she made no public appearances in Britain, other than to attend family funerals or memorial services.

But she was often in the country, her arrivals and departures discreetly noted in the Court Circular. She could be at the palace during a busy court season, when the Queen and Philip were out doing royal duties. She did not even accompany them to the theatre, preferring to stay at home quietly, see her relations privately and play with her grandchildren.

She liked to shop at Selfridge's or Whiteley's, or pop into a chemist. Once she took tea at the Ritz, sent her car home and walked back to Buckingham Palace. Alice imagined herself more well known than she was. She told her niece Pamela that she was the perpetual prey for press photographers on her walks, but Lady Pamela recalled: 'I went out with her in London with Alice Egerton and nobody looked at her at all.'[8]

When she was sighted by an observant journalist and her excursion reported in the press, it was with the same delight that a mountaineer with raised binoculars might note the flight of a *rara avis*.

Occasionally there were photographs of her arriving in Britain, or escorting her grandchildren, Charles and Anne, on or off *Britannia*. Alice loved the Western Isles cruise to Scotland and went on several. Embarking at Southampton with Charles and Anne in August 1956, she was piped aboard by the bosun. She surprised Commander John Adams, Second in Command of the royal yacht, by seizing the pipe and playing it herself. 'My father taught me how to do this!'[9] she said.

The 1956 cruise was an official one, with the Queen and Philip being entertained by the great chieftains such as Dame Flora Macleod of Macleod at Dunvegan, but Alice never attended such occasions. Instead she accompanied the children and sometimes Princess Margaret to a beach. At times she just stood on deck gazing happily at the view.

Her departures also received press attention, especially on the occasion when Philip took the controls of his plane, flew her to Prestwick, kissed her on the cheek and then waved at her departing plane before flying back to Balmoral.

Members of the Queen's household remember her well from this period. At Christmas at Sandringham in 1957, Edward Ford, the Queen's assistant private secretary, sat next to her at dinner. He asked if she had seen the circus. His words did not penetrate her deafness and, to his increasing discomfort, he was forced to repeat the question several times. When the message finally reached Alice, she said: 'Oh, I thought you were saying something interesting.'[10]

Young guards officers, asked to dine at Windsor, might find themselves playing charades with the royal family after dinner. On these occasions, Alice would sit next to the Queen, helping to hand out the clues. James Fisher, one of the canons of Windsor, sat next to her at such a dinner and she outlined some sound views on 'the spreading of religion',[11] and on prayer:

> The first essential, she said, was the pause. Before speaking or acting, or praying, it was vital to make a momentary pause in one's flow of thought or purpose, just enough to stop the flow. When the pause had become customary, then an act of prayer or thanks might also become usual. But the pause was the first requisite . . . I was left with a very clear impression that she regarded this moment of pausing as vital to her own spiritual life.[12]

Alice was particularly close to Lady Alice Egerton, one of the Queen's long-serving ladies-in-waiting. Alice used to invite her to stay with her in Athens. A particular rapport was established between them when Lady Alice developed manic depression, as a result of which she relinquished her position in 1961. Alice was the only member of the family with first-hand knowledge of such things, her problems of the 1930s having given her insight into this much misunderstood condition.

The courtier to whom she was closest was Lt. Commander Michael Parker, Philip's private secretary from 1947 to 1957. With him she established a slightly conspiratorial friendship, often putting forward ideas but always exhorting him that these had not emanated from her. 'She was very sensitive about meddling,' Parker recalled. 'She was also a serious smoker!' When he took her out to dinner in Athens after leaving his job at the palace, he would bring her large packs of cigarettes and she would say: 'You're the only one to help me.'[13] Parker served as a good conduit between the increasingly busy Philip and the ever more isolated Alice. Part of his job was to keep Philip's mother happy and that he succeeded is evidenced by her fondness for him.

In August 1955, while in *Britannia*, Alice discussed with Parker some thoughts about Australia and its constitution. She thought there was too much centralization in Britain '& too few powers of local government in Scotland & Wales'; she learned that in Australia 'it seems there is too much decentralization of governing powers & the federal government has too few'.[14]

Later Alice suggested secretly to Dickie that Philip should be authorized to chair a commission to look into this when he went to Australia to open the Olympic Games in November 1956. She urged Dickie to push the idea independently: 'I cannot talk either to Philip or Lilibet as I do not live in England & my visits are purely family ones & I do not care to appear meddling with their affairs.'[15] Unfortunately Alice's ideas, however sound, were frequently deemed merely eccentric. Dickie was not prepared to foster this plan, which decision Alice accepted.

Alice was upset when, following his divorce, Mike Parker left Philip in 1957. 'What a tragedy for him,'[16] she wrote.

James Orr, the next private secretary from 1957 to 1970, used to meet Alice at the airport. He was impressed by her unfailing courtesy to the footmen and pages, shaking each by hand when she arrived at the palace. This is not to say that she could not express acerbic comments about other members of the household, her opinions invariably sound.

In Athens, Alice continued to work with her sisterhood. Her fundraising expedition to the United States and certain bequests had helped her expand her endeavours. In October 1953 new pupils arrived for training. The next summer she spent from June until autumn travelling incessantly between Athens and the island of Kalimnos in the Dodekanese, where she had placed some of her sisters in the island's small hospital. But by July 1954, she only had convalescents in her two rooms at Neon Heraklion – the little infirmary and the dormitory near by. There were six beds for patients, and the sisters lived on the top floor and in the room near the kitchen. To keep this stocked with provisions, Alice shopped energetically every day. She still had her car and a station wagon, but eventually sold this to pay for her daughters' visits to her.

By June 1959 the sisterhood had failed because of lack of impetus. Alice was then seventy-four and in indifferent health. The nuns dispersed, as did the cats that were a feature of the nunnery. The nurses' training school was closed and converted into a convalescent home with no religious connections. 'My mother clearly had organizational skills,' said Prince Philip. 'She was efficient, but needed a more professional organizer.'[17] Even then Alice did not renounce the grey habit, though she let it be known that she intended to live a life of semi-retirement.

While Alice's work continued during the 1950s, there were occasional diversions. Dickie brought his daughter Patricia and her husband, Lord Brabourne, to Athens in July 1953. In the evening Alice gave them the first ever dinner in her new flat, 7 Patriarch Joachim Street. Alice sent the Mountbatten family out for a walk, while she laid the table, and Popoulo was dispatched to shop at the back doors of various establishments, every shop being closed. The aptly named restaurant, Délicieux, sent in 'a really wonderful dinner', recalled Dickie, '& Alice was in wonderful form & regaled us with a lot of stories none of us had heard before'.[18] After dinner they went to look at the Acropolis in what appeared to be a full moon. It transpired that the Mayor of Athens had floodlit the monument in Dickie's honour. 'I did so enjoy our small dinner-party,' Alice wrote to Dickie, 'as it is an event for me in my quiet life here.'[19]

That day Dickie tried to persuade Alice to come to Petali Island, the summer residence of King Paul. He suspected that her growing antipathy to Queen Frederika was behind her insistent refusal. Though an exceptionally busy man, Dickie put his family before everything. Alice was 'overcome with surprise & emotion',[20] when, in October 1953, he sent her a generous gift for the fiftieth anniversary of her wedding day.

Alice was not known for keeping presents. When sent something she either gave it to somebody else or to charity. In May 1954 the Queen and Philip arrived in Malta at the conclusion of their coronation world tour. Dickie was there to greet them as Commander-in-Chief of the Mediterranean Fleet. He arranged a splendid welcome, the Fleet escorting the royal yacht, *Britannia*, to harbour. Dickie himself arrived on board by jackstay, which involved being whisked from his flagship to the royal yacht, the ships running parallel with each other.

In Malta there was a well-known shopkeeper called Mary Bugeja, who sold beautiful lace. She had got to know many members of the royal family, including the Queen, from their various visits there. The Queen had hoped to call on her, but was eventually too busy, so Dickie and Edwina went instead. They found the entire Bugeja family waiting 'in their best bib & tucker with bunches of flowers & boxes of chocolates', as they had done for five long days.

Mrs Bugeja showed the Mountbattens a special room where she was hoping to entertain the Queen, and Dickie looked in horror at the centrepiece, a special coronation photograph of the Queen and Philip, inscribed 'To Darling Mama with our love'. It did not take Dickie long to work out that it was Alice who had sent it. He urged Mrs Bugeja to remove it at once, or the Queen would be very unlikely to give her a signed photo. He told the story of 'our Beloved Alice' to Louise, adding, 'Don't scold her please.'[21] Louise worked out exactly what Alice had done:

> The story of Mary Bugeja & the photo is just unbelievable, it quite knocked me over . . . Till Alice dies she will do hurried impulsive jests, kind actions without proper thought behind it. I know why it was done. Mary B. sent her, like me, an Xmas present & Alice had nothing to give in return & this could give pleasure, but why not cut off *all* the writing.[22]

In September 1954 Alice watched in amusement as Queen Frederika entertained numerous young princes and princesses on a cruise, an ambitious and not unsuccessful attempt at matchmaking.*

* Queen Frederika used to exhort her family to marry well. 'Never marry a *Schnibbelfipps*,' she would say.

Alice lunched at Tatoï with them, and found it 'bewildering',[23] despite knowing five of Ellen's grandchildren and ten of her own.

In November she held a lunch party for Ellen, her daughter Marina and her sister 'Woolly'. It was therefore a shock when Woolly died suddenly in Munich in January 1955. Further tragedy was to follow. Alice attended a memorial service for Woolly at the church at Tatoï, taking Popoulo with her. Popoulo was suffering from high blood pressure and the emotion of the occasion proved too much for her. She suffered a stroke and died a few days later.

Alice lost a lady-in-waiting who had served her loyally for most of forty-three years. As Prince Philip put it: 'She was a tiny little woman, very tough and saw my mother through many crises.'[24] Alice paid for the funeral with money given her by Louise.

After Popoulo's death, Kitty Valaoritis, a widow and neighbour, came to help Alice with her business affairs. She was the granddaughter of an Irishman, and had many friends in England and Scotland. Alice assured Philip: 'She is a very capable business woman so that I am well looked after, but naturally there is not the same friendship.'[25]

In February Alice celebrated her seventieth birthday at Salem, to which Philip flew himself from London with Louise and Theodora's daughter, Margarita.

Relations between Alice and Queen Frederika descended to their lowest ebb at the time of the death of Princess Nicholas. In her declining years, Ellen had enjoyed relatively good health, although her house at Psychico was 'swarming with cats',[26] as King Constantine recalled. But on 15 March 1957, she died at home at the age of seventy-five.

Her surviving daughters, Olga and Marina, arrived at her bedside the night before she died. Crown Prince Constantine was likewise summoned to see his favourite great-aunt. 'Hello darling,' said Aunt Ellen, opening her eyes to see him. But Alice was not at the death bed. For some reason, not a kind one, Queen Frederika gave specific instructions that news of Ellen's illness was to be withheld from her. She was not even told that she had died. Alice had to make do with attending the funeral, after which Ellen was buried next to Prince Nicholas at Tatoï.

By June, when she attended the wedding of Alice's granddaughter, Margarita of Baden, to Prince Tomislav of Yugoslavia at Salem, the *froideur* between them had developed into open hostility. As Dickie wrote to Louise: 'Now she [Alice] has explained to me how Freddy deliberately withheld news of Ellen's illness and even death from Alice, I am on her side in her treatment of F. . .d at Salem.'[27] Louise replied: 'I am glad Alice was not in the wrong this time. I fear Freddy will end by getting her husband turned out.'[28] Even at Christmas 1958, Alice declined to join King Paul and Queen Frederika for the festivities. Eventually Queen Frederika was forced to apologize.

Alice felt increasingly lonely in Athens. In the autumn of 1956, after returning from her holiday in Britain, she suddenly departed for Salem. Louise was worried by the reasons for this, which Alice explained:

> Everything went wrong in my inside, not only my liver & finally the heart became a bit weak, so I was not fit for work any more. There is nowhere I could go in Greece. In winter hotels shut, & too long & tiring journeys to get away anywhere else. So the least tiring & shortest journey was to come here for a complete rest. I am already better.[29]

Louise wondered how ill Alice really was, thinking her 'just run down & lonely for her children. She is often very lonely in Athens as practically all her real old friends have died, & relations.'[30]

In November 1953, Alice's last Hesse aunt, Irène, had died at Hemmelmark aged eighty-seven, and there was criticism in the German press that there was no representation of the Queen or Philip, he being a great-nephew, who had stayed with her as a youngster.

The death of Ellen in March 1957 was followed at the end of the year by that of 88-year-old Big George. He and Marie were about to celebrate their Golden Wedding on 12 December and Alice was set to be there. But on 25 November Big George died at St Cloud. At the end of one of the more extraordinary marriages of the twentieth century, his widow Marie recorded: 'I bent over his cold forehead and kissed it. Not his lips, which he had always refused me.'[31]

Alice stayed in Athens to greet the arrival of the coffin by destroyer from Marseilles and attended the funeral. Marie lived on until 21 September 1962. She is well remembered today in Freudian circles as a much respected psychoanalyst.* After her death Alice was the last survivor of her generation in the Greek royal family.

And in February 1960, Alice's cousin, Drino Carisbrooke, died.† He was the last surviving grandson of Queen Victoria. 'Poor lonely old man,' wrote Louise. 'It was for the best.'[32] On the other hand, the new generation multiplied and on 18 July 1957 Alice became a great-grandmother when Sophie's daughter Christina‡ gave birth to her daughter Tatiana, known as Tania.

★

* A favourite story in the Greek royal family concerned her encounter with a 'flasher' in the Bois de Boulogne. Unfazed, she presented the hapless figure with her card and offered him a free session of analysis. He bounded off.

† Drino's last years were spent ensuring himself a suitable memorial. To this end he designed niches for the ashes of his wife Irene and himself in the Battenberg chapel in St Mildred's Church, Whippingham. In his negotiations, he was mindful that 'the chapel was given to my mother as our burial place' [Marquess of Carisbrooke to MtB, 1958 – BA]. A year before his death, Drino tried to have Louis's flag as Vice-Admiral, aboard HMS *Drake*, removed from the Battenberg chapel. Letters winged their way between the local vicar and Broadlands, and Dickie became increasingly irritated with his pompous cousin, the more so when he remembered that Drino had served in *Drake*. Drino tried to assure Dickie that his admiration for Uncle Louis remained undimmed, but he needed the space for his Order of the Bath banner.

As usual Dickie won. Drino died, Louis's flag remained in the chapel and Dickie more or less took the whole chapel over, placing in it memorial tablets to his branch of the family. This would have horrified Drino, a cousin with an excess of self-importance and time on his hands.

In a final irony, in the summer of 1997, vandals stole Drino's ashes, which were eventually retrieved in a nearby field.

‡ Princess Christina of Hesse, Sophie's daughter, had married Prince Andrej of Yugoslavia in 1956. They were divorced in 1962.

Because Alice had so little money, she could be of little practical assistance to the old friends of the family in their decline. But she helped when she could. Dickie and Louise offered more assistance, Dickie ever ready to employ Edwina's fortune to alleviate hardship, while Louise was quick to pay a bill here or supplement a pension there.

The Pye-Crust had stayed on at Kensington Palace after Victoria's death, but the family wondered how long she could remain there. In June 1957, Alice motored her to the country to see a 'Friends of the Poor' home, but that did not appeal to her. In 1960 the family thought she should go to the Distressed Gentlefolks Aid Association home in Vicarage Gate. Because the home only took gentlefolk, Dickie wrote to them, mentioning that she had handed him to Queen Victoria for his christening, worked as secretary and companion to Alice on her visits to London, was 'a lady of the finest feelings' and would regale the other residents with stories of 'travelling in Russia with my mother before the Revolution'.[33] But Matron rejected the Pye-Crust. She explained that Miss Pye was 'too well & active for our Nursing Home', and would find 'such surroundings rather depressing'.[34]

So the Pye-Crust continued to live at Kensington Palace, supported by Dickie and Louise, until the day in May 1962 when she suddenly collapsed with heart failure in the courtyard and died on her way to St Mary Abbot's Hospital in Marloes Road. Louise arranged a wreath from herself and Alice.

Isa Buxhoeveden died aged seventy-two in November 1956. For Louise and Alice her death severed a link that took them back to childhood and memories of their tragic Russian cousins.

The decline of Nona and Dick Crichton weighed heavily on Alice, Louise and Dickie. They owed so much to Nona, that faithful confidante of their mother and of themselves, and they did not desert her in her last years, which were dogged by ill-health. In December 1955 Dickie invited them to Broadlands when the Queen and Philip were staying and Nona was thrilled to sit next to Philip, who had so often been her guest in his youth.

Year after year the Crichtons staggered to Sofiero for a holiday with Louise, until 1959 when the visit had to be cancelled. Nona died on 28 December 1960. Louise was as sanguine as ever: 'For beloved Nona we must not grieve. She was so old & mercifully was spared a long illness. How my heart aches for poor lonely Dick! For you & me darling Nona was our last link with our childhood. How we will miss her.'[35]

Dick survived two more years, refusing offers of a television set, adamant that he would not have 'the "beastly thing" near him'.[36] After the Pye-Crust's death in 1962, Dickie and Louise increased his annual allowance from £800 to £1,000. Dickie called on him that November to hear Dick describe himself as 'nothing but "a blithering idiot"'.[37] He died a few days later. Alice described this death as 'a last break with our past family life'.[38]

Alice had numerous surviving grandchildren. In Germany there were five Hohenlohes, three Badens, five Hesses and three Hanovers (Sophie producing her eighth and last child at the age of forty). Eventually there would be four more in England. The eldest grandchild was Margarita, born in 1932, and the youngest Edward, born in 1964. To them all she was 'Yaya', the Greek for grandmother.

Many of the grandchildren found Alice a distant, forbidding figure, isolated as she was by her deafness, and wearing her nun's habit. But she took an interest in their fortunes and found plenty to preoccupy her as they grew up and pursued their conventional or unconventional lives.

When at Buckingham Palace, Alice doted on Philip's children, Charles and Anne. They both profess considerable affection for her. To Charles Alice used to say: 'Punctuality is the prerogative of Princes.' The Prince of Wales recalled: 'She used to come and lunch with us in the nursery, I remember. We were terrified if we were late. She was very strict.'[39] She did not discuss religion with either of them, nor ever mention her favourite Schuré book, *Les Grands Initiés*. 'I remember her lecturing me about the power of the brain,'[40] recalled the Prince of Wales. Here Alice returned to a theory she had discussed with Dr Binswanger about the division between the conscious and subconscious part of the brain. She believed the brain should be 'compartmentalized' and urged this concept on to the heir to the throne.

The Princess Royal did not regret the fact that Alice was not 'a cuddly granny'. She was a little alarmed by her in early years, because no one, not least Alice herself, had explained the deafness. Therefore she would come and see her grandmother in her rooms on the second floor of the palace (rooms which she later occupied), finding her in a cloud of smoke – 'I've known a few worse, I suppose, but not many' – and have to gain her attention. Later, when she learned how to talk to her, they established a good rapport. To both grandchildren Alice told fascinating stories about Queen Victoria and the past, but she remained 'something of a mystery figure',[41] with areas of her life unexplained.

In those nursery days there would be occasional phases when Alice was with them, but even longer times when she was quietly in Athens and quite out of touch. She did not, for example, write to them at school.

Most summers Alice stayed a few weeks with Louise and Gustaf. She much admired the modest way that Louise conducted herself as Sweden's queen. Alice invariably arrived exhausted, but soon regained her energy. They went on expeditions and in the evenings they played cards. Lord Brabourne, staying there on one occasion, was amused when Alice accused the King of cheating.[42]

Alice was just as concerned about Louise's health as vice versa. Each was solicitous to the other and this could lead to misunderstandings.

In the early summer of 1958 Louise fell ill with flu and eye trouble and made the mistake of writing to tell her sister. Alice, 'bored with nothing to do', announced that she would come and keep Louise company. Louise did not want company, but Alice was soon flying in. But the would-be nurse was soon the patient, as Louise explained:

What happened was Alice went to the 'ladies loo' after Copenhagen, just crossing the Sound, & an air pocket gave such a bump Alice hung on to some thing & wrenched muscles in her back & the pain from it goes all down her right leg. She really was in agony yesterday & the night we arrived, a wee bit better today.[43]

Alice developed sciatica and her plan to read to Louise was dropped. During her four-week visit to Ulriksdal, Alice saw only her room, the dining room and the big living room, but at least the sisters were able to talk.

Alice established a good rapport with Dickie's daughter, Pamela. In October 1958 Pamela went to stay with Alice in Athens. She asked if she could bring her cousin, Mary Anna Marten, with her, to which Alice gave reluctant permission: 'I suppose you think you'll be bored.'[44] Lady Pamela remembered the eccentric arrangement by which Alice's driver was given only just enough money for his petrol for each journey, leading to endless problems.

Alice surprised Pamela by taking her aside and suggesting that it was possible she was in love with her brother-in-law, Lord Brabourne. The idea had never occurred to Pamela but it worried her sufficiently to put the thesis to her father. Dickie reassured her: 'Don't worry. Alice has always had a thing about brothers-in-law.'[45]

The visit was a success, Alice praising Pamela to Dickie: 'She is so sweet & gentle & good company. Also she is a fine character with high principles & I am glad to have known her properly at last.'[46] Alice made friends with Mary Anna Marten too, and visited her more than once at Crichel, happy to find a new friend from a younger generation.

Alice liked to stay with Dickie and Edwina at Broadlands. In 1957 she went there after spending Christmas with the Queen and Philip at Sandringham. Dickie commented that she seldom gave him much notice of her plans, but nor did she mind in the least if the visit therefore did not happen.

At that time Alice had conceived a new plan, which she outlined to Dickie. She wanted to found a Women's University College in

Greece, and to this end she visited Oxford, and then spent a day in Paris hoping to raise funds. Nothing came of this scheme, but Dickie told Louise: 'I do admire her.'[47]

35. India and Bahrain

In September 1959 Alice had met Rajkumari Amrit Kaur,* the former Indian Minister of Health, in Athens at a Red Cross conference. Amrit Kaur invited Alice to come to India, with all expenses paid, to see the women's work there. The Rajkumari wrote to Dickie:

> It was a great pleasure and privilege to meet your sister, HRH Princess Alice, in Athens. She was kind enough to invite me to her flat and I was singularly impressed with the beauty of her character which is written so clearly on her lovely face. I had no idea that she had so dedicated her life.
>
> I invited her to India because she seemed to be so intensely interested in Indian philosophical thought, and in the theory of achieving spiritual uplift through contemplation and meditation, that I thought she would enjoy coming out and meeting persons like Vice-President Radhakrishnan and others. Since she would prefer possibly not to stay at Government House I offered her hospitality in my own home and I do hope she will come. Her life's example would greatly appeal to Indians.[1]

Alice took up Amrit Kaur's invitation in January 1960. She asked Philip to tell the High Commissions of Pakistan and India that her visit was strictly private and that there should be no official receptions. Alice stayed in Amrit Kaur's compound at Willingdon Crescent in the shadow of the President's house.

Amrit Kaur was a legendary figure in India, and a close personal friend of both Dickie and Edwina. The daughter of Sir Harnam Singh, of the princely house of Kapurthala, she worked tirelessly to promote the full enfranchisement of women and the ending of the caste and purdah systems. She became a follower of Gandhi and

* Rajkumari Amrit Kaur (1889–1964), Minister of Health in India 1947–57.

served as his secretary at his ashram near Wardha in the central provinces. She was the first woman member of the Central Advisory Committee on Education. Like so many others, she was arrested in 1942 and imprisoned until 1945.

Amrit Kaur became the only woman in the central government of 1947 and the first woman Minister of Health, serving until 1957. She was a passionate supporter of the work of the Red Cross in India. She and Alice were natural soulmates.

Edwina happened to be in Delhi during Alice's stay. After the wedding of her daughter Pamela to David Hicks in January (which Alice had missed), she had left London for a tour of India. She had many engagements, but took the trouble to call on her sister-in-law:

I saw Alice this morning after I arrived – very well and happy and I think enjoying herself *hugely*. She is talking to a variety of groups – students included and is thrilled by India and Indians and all the varied religions and cultures and languages. She says people have been *wonderful* to her and Amrit of course an angel. I lunched with them both today and showed her all wedding cuttings and photos and gave her a graphic description of the 'Day'. I said how much we had missed her which is so true especially as she has always been so wonderful to Pammy. She goes next week to Calcutta for a week to stay with the Governor Padmaja Naidu, then to Bombay for another week and will stay with the Governor Sri Prakassa but we are arranging for her to be looked after by my great friend Jena Duggan (a Parsee) and widow of the world famous surgeon. Jena is very prominent in all fields of nursing medicine, social works and philosophy so I am sure they will get along very well. Then I think Alice returns to Athens.[2]

But soon after this, everything went wrong. Edwina was about to set off on the next lap of her trip, leaving at 5.30 a.m., but she filled Dickie in, urging him only to quote her to those who '*really understand*' Alice:

You remember I wrote to you how happy she was at Amrit's and in what grand form and that I had seen her twice and lunched with her there. She suddenly developed a bad *chill* and bronchitis & liver trouble and was *most* difficult looking after herself in her room and refusing to let the Dr. come or Amrit to help her. She then got better and I went round to see her & we all persuaded her *not* to continue her visits to Calcutta & Bombay as she really wasn't well enough & we all felt the changes of climate would upset her again. She quite agreed and really said she felt too weak and I did persuade her to see the Dr. He said there was nothing serious but she should take care & recommended her giving up her 'Talks' & returning to Athens the end of this week. She *agreed.*

Imagine my amazement on going to Amrit's house the next morning to see if all was fixed up satisfactory for her journey to find that she had walked out of Amrit's house – sent for the Greek Ambassador and gone to the Ashoka *Hotel* for the last *3* days this without any warning to poor old Amrit who had taken infinite trouble to make her as comfortable as possible for the last 3 weeks! I think they had something of a row as Alice was adamant (as she can be!) that she wanted to leave and Amrit was obviously hurt beyond words.

I have seen Alice twice at the Ashoka & I think calmed Amrit. Alice's story is that she was too cold and ill and alone and wanted a woman to talk to and look after her. You know what Indian households are – all bearers – but wonderful and Amrit is of course desperately busy but spent hours with Alice all the same & really devoted all the time she had to her.

Don't say too much or indeed anything about all this except vy. discreetly but Alice's story may be somewhat distorted.

It was useless my arguing with her as she was already at the hotel!!

I do love her so much but she can do strange things!!! She was never *seriously* ill altho' she says she was. But she was very unwell and that may account for it. Oh dear, oh dear![3]

Alice returned safely to Athens. Later she told her granddaughter Anne that while in India she had had 'an out of body experience', that she had sensed herself floating away to the next world and then come back again.[4]

After Alice left India, Edwina continued on the 'pretty stiff tour ahead of me'.[5] After a dinner in Jesselton, North Borneo, on 19 February, she lost her balance and caught the railing up to the Acting

Governor's house. The next day, despite a chronic headache, she attended two parties and an evening reception for 120 people. Edwina sat on the sofa and received batches of guests, four at a time. That night she returned to her room, went to bed and never woke up. She was fifty-eight.

Alice travelled to England. Edwina had left the wish that she should be buried at sea. Alice and Philip joined Dickie and the coffin at Portsmouth Dockyard on 25 February, Alice's seventy-fifth birthday. They boarded the frigate, *Wakeful*, sailed out to sea and the coffin was launched into the water. Dickie was left a widower, with his two daughters and his two older sisters to keep an affectionate eye on him. He received thousands of letters of sympathy, one of which came from Amrit Kaur:

I am sure that Princess Alice must have been very upset also by Edwina's passing because she told me more than once how much she cared for her and how very understanding Edwina had always been as far as her having become a Sister was concerned. I do hope she is now completely recovered from the illness which she unfortunately had here. If you write to Princess Alice do tell her that I have nothing in my heart except respect and affection for her and I am only sorry that I could not prevent her falling ill and that her stay in India had to be kept short.[6]

With Edwina's death, the various allowances paid to members of her extended family ceased. Alice was one affected. Under a deed dated 15 April 1954, she received £46 a month, which supplemented her annual widow's pension of £430. She needed Philip to take on a monthly payment of at least £16, apologizing for being a financial burden, but pointing out: 'I have left my share of the flat to you in my Greek will, so whenever you decide to sell it one day, you will receive the whole sum back. That is all I can do for you.'[7] Philip obliged.

Neither Alice nor Philip were particularly concerned with questions of his status in Britain. But the matter was taken seriously by Dickie, passively supported by Louise in Stockholm. Dickie was not satisfied that Philip was properly recognized in Britain. Together, they had discussed the delays in his appointment as Admiral of the Fleet, Field Marshal and Marshal of the RAF. Certain courtiers had been less than friendly.

There was also the question of his style and surname. By a curious constitutional oversight, when George VI had created his son-in-law a Royal Highness and Duke of Edinburgh (with subsidiary titles), he had failed to create him a Prince of the United Kingdom. Louise hoped that this situation would be rectified on Philip's thirty-fourth birthday in 1955, but when this did not happen, she concluded, correctly, that Philip 'must have disapproved of the suggestion'.[8] Nearly two years went by before Dickie was able to report: 'Lilibet has got the new Prime Minister [Harold Macmillan] – in consultation with Commonwealth colleagues – to ask for Philip to be made "The Prince" on return from this tour* & we all hope he'll agree this time!'[9]

Louise was still concerned in March 1957: 'When is Philip to be called Prince Philip?'[10] she demanded. In fact, the grant had been gazetted on 22 February. Alice read of the announcement in the Greek papers with no great interest. Her comment to Dickie was succinct: 'Anyway your wish has been fulfilled.'[11]

But Dickie was not satisfied. He felt that Philip had been denied his right to found a new dynasty.† He continued to agitate. He sought the introduction of a new family called Mountbatten-Windsor. Neither name was of ancient origin, and Philip only became a Mountbatten in 1946. Alice herself had never borne that name.

Finally, in February 1960, Dickie reported that the Queen had dined with him. 'She is very well‡ and told me that the idea of the hyphenated name had been agreed by the Cabinet & would be

* Philip had been absent for four months, touring Australia, New Zealand and elsewhere.

† If anything, Philip would have liked to found the House of Edinburgh, after his dukedom.

‡ The Queen was pregnant and about to give birth to her third child, Andrew, now Duke of York.

announced when the Baby is born about the 18th. I think I told you about this but it must be kept a complete secret until announced.'[12]

The announcement was made on 8 February. Even then, it was not clear under which circumstances members of the royal family would bear the name Mountbatten-Windsor. This did not prevent Dickie from seeking every possible opportunity to cement the matter in a number of different and devious ways.*

After Edwina's funeral, Alice met her new grandson and was thrilled that he was to be called Andrew, a name that Louise thought doubly appropriate since his other grandmother was Scottish. Back in Greece, Alice wrote to Philip: 'I am so happy about

* Twelve years later Dickie was invited by Hugh Montgomery-Massingberd to write a foreword to *Burke's Guide to the Royal Family* (1973). He agreed to do so only if an introductory article by Dermot Morrah was altered to strengthen the name issue. The Queen and the Prince of Wales discussed the matter, and her private secretary, Sir Martin Charteris, wrote that an appropriate paragraph should read: 'It has been ascertained that the Queen's pleasure is that her children shall use the compound name on documents on which a surname is required by law.' [Sir Martin Charteris to MtB, October 1972 – MB/K194 – HL.] Princess Anne's marriage certificate in 1973 bore the hyphenated name. In 1981, the Prince of Wales's did not.

Also in 1972 Dickie obliged Clare Forbes Turner, the daughter of his archivist, to type out an article which was in fact written by him, and submit this to the Society of Genealogists, of which he happened to be President. Correspondence in the Mountbatten archives contains a letter from the archivist, saying: 'He has written the article and would like you to type it out on your machine . . . There is little chance that you will be traced as being my daughter.' Dickie sent copies of the article to various royal households. To Sir Martin Charteris he wrote: 'I gather the article was vetted by various constitutional experts, and was amended by them to what they presume to be absolutely legally correct.' [MtB to Charteris, 2 November 1972 – MB/K194 – HL.] Charteris may not have been deceived. 'I have read it with profit,' he wrote. [Charteris to MtB, 7 November 1972 – MB/K194 – HL.]

The 1999 decision that Prince Edward's children would not be Royal Highnesses means that any such children will be born Mountbatten-Windsors. Prince Edward's surname was thus given on his marriage certificate.

Papa's name being given to the baby. The people's delight here about this is really touching. Unknown people waved to me in the streets, calling out Andreas. He is not forgotten here & still much loved.'[13]

The summer of 1960 brought further bereavement with the death of Margarita's husband, Friedel Hohenlohe, after some months of poor health. When he deteriorated, Alice flew to Frankfurt to comfort Margarita, arriving just too late. Friedel had died that day, 11 May. Later Alice encouraged Margarita to take a more active part in life and in 1961 she attended the wedding of the Duke of Kent to Katharine Worsley, and a dinner at Buckingham Palace for the President of the United States and Mrs Kennedy.

After Friedel's funeral in Langenburg, Alice went to see her old friends the Markwitzes at Breibach for a week in June. There was a visit to London in July. During the state visit of the King and Queen of Siam, she moved from Buckingham Palace to the Hyde Park Hotel, where Louise and Gustaf were staying. One afternoon Alice was spotted walking in the grounds of Hampton Court. There was speculation that she might take on Wilderness House, the grace-and-favour Wren house recently made vacant following the death of her friend Grand Duchess Xenia of Russia in April.

Alice had remained in touch with her friend, Major Gerald Green, who had exchanged life in Greece for a job in Bahrain. He was now commanding the military wing of public security in Bahrain.

In January 1961 Alice flew alone to Bahrain, sure in the knowledge that Major Green would look after her. He had employed a personal maid, but Alice promptly dismissed her. He had also cleared it with the Emir that he had a royal guest. The Emir duly received Alice, who spoke to him in her most formal royal manner, and then asked Green later: 'Did I behave nicely?'[14]

Mindful of what had occurred in India the year before, Dickie instructed Rear-Admiral Fitzroy Talbot, Flag Officer in the Arabian Seas, to be solicitous. Alice was not pleased to hear this. Major Green asked whether the Admiral and Mrs Fitzroy Talbot should be invited to lunch or dinner, but Alice replied that a glass of sherry would suffice. Worse, she extended but two fingers to the Admiral when he shook hands, and he was presently dispatched with peremptory haste.

Green worked in the mornings, leaving Alice almost alone in his house, reading happily. 'I am very busy & have no time to make a long description of things which could take volumes to fill,'[15] Alice wrote to Louise. Her account to Dickie was clearly written to please him:

> My stay in Bahrain was most enjoyable. Not only did I visit the Ruler and his family more than once & admired them for their unselfish work in the island, but I found the English colony charming, including Admiral F. Talbot & his wife, who gave me a charming dinner, as did the other officials. I was there during their very short winter, which was as cold as Athens some days.
>
> While my host, Major Green, was at his office, I did some work too; some lectures I wrote down to be translated into Arabic.[16]

Alice left Bahrain for Athens on 12 February, which Dickie judged 'a relief'.[17] She did not stray as far afield again.

Dickie was still leading an active working life, but Alice and Louise were conscious of his loneliness following Edwina's death. Their visit to Classiebawn Castle, his Irish holiday retreat, in August 1961, was undertaken to cheer him up. Every detail of their journey was planned by Dickie with military exactitude.

Alice thought Classiebawn like the Queen Mother's Castle of Mey. There were expeditions in fishing boats, lobster pots were inspected, crabs collected, and mackerel fished as bait for pollock. They even caught five small sharks, and watched delighted as sharks leapt out of the water to snatch the pollocks. These were expeditions like that more fateful one, eighteen years later, when Dickie sailed out at Mullaghmore and was blown up by the IRA.

Alice and Louise saw Yeats's grave and crossed to Enniskillen. In the streets people occasionally stopped Alice to tell her how much they admired Philip. With Dickie's elderly sisters on this holiday was the incongruously glamorous Paula Long,* Edwina's great friend, for whose presence Dickie had asked their permission.

Much as they loved their visit, neither Alice nor Louise emerged well from it. Louise broke her finger, slipping down some stone stairs, and developed lumbago. When Alice arrived at Sofiero with her, she suffered from liver and bilious trouble, the result, wrote Louise, 'of me not behaving like a queen & telling her what not to eat'.[18] The sisters stayed together for a further month, Alice looking disapproving when Louise sent Gustaf on errands or when she grumbled that his old beret was too shabby.

Alice was next in Sweden for Gustaf's eightieth birthday celebrations in November 1962:

> The birthday festivities were splendid, especially the lunch in the magnificent gold hall of the town hall, over 700 people sitting down. Most touching was the devotion of the people to their King. Louise was so happy all the time. It was a real pleasure to see. She was well, luckily, for all these fatigues, & only developed a violent cold & sore throat & went to bed when all was over.[19]

Both sisters reported to Dickie how compatible they had been. Alice found Louise and Gustaf 'so well & so happy . . . we had wonderful talks',[20] while Louise wrote: 'Alice & I got on so well this time, & I really felt how fond she is of me. She told me just a little about her work, religious philosophy! I don't ask her, not to seem just inquisitive.'[21]

Alice's life in Athens was less eventful. She often sat alone in Kolonaki Square in her habit, reading a newspaper. Yet from time to time her routine was alleviated by a family visit, a state occasion, a crisis or some political development.

Alice relished any connection with Philip and his family. He paid a rare visit to Athens in December 1961. Alice was pleased

*Paula Long (1898–1986) was a foundling, who became a Modigliani-esque beauty. She married the Marquis de Casa Maury, and then a lawyer called Bill Allen. She had an affair with the Duke of Kent. Later she married 'Boy' Long, and lived in Kenya at the time of the Erroll murder.

that there was a dance at the Yacht Club, which he enjoyed. He stayed in Andrea's old rooms at the palace, which again pleased her.

The following February Alice was in London, staying with the Queen, while Philip was away on a two-month tour of South America. Charles welcomed a visit from his Greek grandmother, especially as she often brought stamps from Greece. He once wrote to her with a request for a postcard. He asked that she 'pretty well fill up the card with stamps and not worry so much about the writing part'.[22] These were good for swapping at his prep school, Cheam.

Charles was recovering from an operation to remove his appendix, so Alice paid him frequent visits in hospital, sometimes taking Anne and Andrew with her. On 19 February she attended a tea party for Andrew's second birthday to which her two Yugoslav great-grandchildren were invited, four-year-old Tania giving her a spontaneous hug and saying: 'It is nice to see you again.'[23]

In May 1962, Alice found herself at the heart of her family in Athens, when there was a large gathering of royalty for the glamorous wedding of King Paul's daughter, Sophie.* Margarita stayed with Alice for a busy fortnight, during which Alice held open house at noon every day for drinks and lunch.

Dickie was at this wedding, but Alice, who had originally invited him to stay, thought it better that he stay at the Embassy, because she was tired as a result of flu and thought that 'for all the changings of clothes for an official occasion'[24] he would be more comfortable there. Dickie brought a cine-camera with him and filmed the guests, none more so than Princess Marie Gabriella of Savoy, with whom he was somewhat infatuated, to the disapproval of his daughter, Patricia, and of Louise.

Alice followed the repercussions of this wedding later that year. A notable absentee had been Queen Frederika's mother, the Duchess of Brunswick. In Germany the old Duchess was interviewed by a journalist working for *Athenaiki*, and gave the reason: 'No one

* Sophie married Prince Juan Carlos, Prince of the Asturias, who General Franco had tentatively decided should become King of Spain on his death. Juan Carlos had been trained for this since 1947. He was officially appointed heir in 1969, and became king on Franco's death in 1975.

invited me.'[25] It was further suggested that the Duchess had been 'ruthlessly abandoned by her children'.*[26] The publisher and editor were arrested, and following a three-day trial were sent to prison for fifteen months for 'offending the Queen'.[27]

The Duchess telegraphed King Paul: 'The knowledge that I, though quite innocent, appear to be the cause for this punishment is causing me deep concern, particularly now in the Christmas season.'[28] No fan of the Queen of Greece, Alice concluded: 'Sissy's reckless interview with a Greek journalist has done Freddy a lot of harm, unfortunately.'[29]

Alice had reason to worry about her two elder daughters. Margarita suffered a profound shock in January 1963, when she lost every personal possession, either valuable or of sentimental attachment, in an extensive fire at Langenburg. One side of the castle was totally gutted and Margarita's private rooms were destroyed. The only good luck was that she was not in them at the time and was wearing the pearls inherited from Victoria Milford Haven.

Theodora was a greater worry. After the wedding in Athens the previous year, Alice had commented upon how 'old & haggard'[30] her daughter looked, and now she was shocked as the extent of her ill health became fully apparent, as she reported to Philip:

There are days, she speaks with great difficulty & can't manage her legs & then after some hours that passes & she talks & walks normally. For that reason, she walked about with a stick here as she never knows when these periods come on. It is the arteries narrowing so much more & preventing blood going to her head. Also her heart is much worse. I thought I would warn you, as no one warned me.[31]

In July 1963 Alice saw Theodora at Schloss Ebers.ein, a Baden home near Oberstrot. Her daughter had had her teeth extracted,

* The Foreign Office took the view that the fault was on the side of the Duchess: 'Basically the trouble is that the Duchess of Brunswick has never reconciled herself to her impoverished post-war state and blames her children for not supporting her in the style to which she is accustomed.' [FO minute, 1 July 1963 – Political Central Greece FO 371 169102.]

now sporting what Alice called 'a dazzling smile to which one has to get accustomed'.[32] At the end of September Theodora toured Italy. Thus she had not seen her husband Berthold for a month, when, on 27 October, he slumped dead in the car on the way to Baden-Baden with his son Ludwig.

Alice's own health was less than stable. In the summer of 1963 she became unwell at Broadlands. Louise attributed this to her bad liver and was glad that she had gone to Buckingham Palace, 'as Lilibet is the only person who can do anything & Alice likes Lord Evans'.*[33] The family relished a story in which pressure was put on Alice to see the doctor. 'I am much too ill to see the doctor,' said Alice. Then a few days passed and she said: 'Now I am feeling better. Now I will see the doctor!'[34]

It transpired that Alice had a germ in the blood, causing undue tiredness. At Sofiero that August, she succumbed to a serious bilious attack and high fever, which lasted thirty hours. She was taken to hospital by ambulance, highly doped and very muzzy. After a day on a drip she perked up. Tests revealed that while her liver was in poor condition, her heart and blood pressure were fine.

In the summer of 1963, nobody realized that King Paul's reign was approaching its end. Alice was pleased that after interminable problems over Cyprus, relations between Britain and Greece now permitted him to make a state visit to London. But the visit was undermined by demonstrations over political prisoners in Greece.† At last King Paul received the Order of the Garter, and as usual, the politicians and diplomats declared that the visit had strengthened Anglo-Greek relations, dismissing the incidents as 'a mere drop in the ocean'.[35]

A few months later, in January 1964, King Paul was diagnosed

* Horace Evans (1903–63), created a baron 1957. The Queen's physician. Formerly physician to George VI and to Queen Mary. He died on 26 October. His grand piano, never played, was the repository for a considerable number of signed photographs from grateful patients of varied celebrity.

† The scenes were worse than the behaviour of media and veterans during the 1998 visit of Emperor Akihito of Japan.

as having cancer of the stomach. His health deteriorated nor could he be saved by the Holy Icon of Tinos, brought to his bedside when medical treatment failed. On 6 March, at the age of sixty-two, he died.

Alice was at the palace in Athens on the evening that Mrs Lyndon B. Johnson, wife of the President of the United States, called to pay her respects to Queen Frederika. Mrs Johnson described being received by the Queen in black velvet, after which she walked out into the hall. 'There I encountered one of the most remarkable members of the whole entourage,' she wrote, 'a very elderly lady, who floated along in a gray habit of some religious order.'[36]

Alice was joined at the funeral on 11 March by Philip, who came to represent the Queen, safely delivered of her fourth child, Edward, the day before. After the service in the cathedral, Philip walked in the mile and a half procession to the Hilton Hotel, from which they then drove to Tatoï. Next to him in the procession were Prince Rainier of Monaco and Mrs Johnson. He told the latter: 'We measure our pace to the oldest priest, and he is ninety-two.'[37]

There were numerous wreaths. The Queen sent one, as did Dickie and Ellen's daughters, Olga and Marina. But when the bills came, there was a row. The Queen's cost over £65 and the others over £53 each. Princess Marina commented that there must be some mistake and Dickie's office queried it, as did Philip's. Princess Olga wrote: 'I am *aghast* at such a blatant act of thievery . . . Neither of these wreaths was ever seen, so far as I know, and *never* has anyone paid such a sum for a wreath before.'[38] The British Ambassador explained that not for the first time had the Greek court florists multiplied their prices, but, he added: 'It appears also that some alert Greek had made a quick corner in laurel which raised the prices even higher than otherwise might have been the case and that it was a bad moment for flowers when to a large extent they had to be flown in from Italy.'[39] Dugald Malcolm, Vice-Marshal of the Diplomatic Corps, pacified the royal households by reminding them of what happened to George III, when his carriage broke down and he wanted to buy some eggs: 'Being charged an exorbitant price, he asked if eggs were so scarce in that part of the world. The farmer replied: "No Sir, but Kings are!"'[40]

Gustaf was also at King Paul's funeral. Mrs Johnson thought Gustaf 'spry and elderly'.[41] Louise, whose frail health kept her in Sweden, reported:

I am proud of my old husband's physical strength. He stood for practically 5½ hours, only time he sat during the funeral was in the cathedral before the service began & then the drive up to Tatoï. Some minor official got fussed & soon after they got to the burial place he made all the royal relations line up & there they stood for one hour. Mercifully a chair was got for Alice.[42]

A chair was also obtained for President Harry Truman.*

Eventually King Paul was buried at the spot where he had placed a stone to mark each passing year.

* This led to a curious exchange between the former president and the young official. When offered the chair, Truman said: 'You are going to make an old man out of me yet,' to which the young man, thinking he referred to the delay, replied: 'I'm afraid it's going to be quite a long while.' Truman said: 'I hope so.' [Lady Bird Johnson, *A White House Diary* (Weidenfeld & Nicolson), p.93.]

36. The Reign of King Constantine

Crown Prince Constantine succeeded his father as King of Greece, and there were auguries for a glittering future. The 23-year-old King, known in the family as 'Tino', was handsome and popular. He had won a gold medal as a yachtsman in the 1960 Olympic Games at Naples. Furthermore he was in love with his seventeen-year-old third cousin, Princess Anne-Marie of Denmark, Gustaf's granddaughter.

Yet worries were expressed in diplomatic circles. Sir Ralph Murray, the British Ambassador, pointed out that the position of a Greek king was always 'extremely exacting', and that the Greeks liked to think of themselves as of a 'democratic temperament', and were inclined to regard their King as 'being permanently on probation'. Along with his natural abilities and advantages, the new King had 'a headstrong side to his temperament'. He was ill-trained, had not 'seemed hitherto to bear boredom gladly', while 'his easy manner sometimes slips into off-handness which has given offence'.[1] There were pitfalls awaiting him 'and the most obvious of these is the suspicion that it will be his mother, Queen Frederika, who will call the tune'.[2]

King Constantine had always been fonder of Princess Nicholas than of Alice. Thus the new reign isolated Alice yet more in Athens. Dickie found her 'slightly thin & frail',[3] when she attended his sixty-fourth birthday lunch in London in June.

Presently Alice was at Sofiero, relaying to Philip the news that Gustaf was investing in a special white Admiral's uniform for his granddaughter's wedding in Athens. Louise found her 'older but otherwise she was better in health by being more careful about her food'.[4] Alice walked badly, but only because she had not bothered to walk much earlier in the year.

Just before the wedding, one of Louise's projects came to fruition.

Some years before, she had commissioned Miss E. M. Almedingen, a doughty author who adorned herself in magnificent tweed from head to foot, to write a biography of her Aunt Ella, which was published in time for her centenary. In choosing Miss Almedingen, Louise had found an excellent writer and a scholar. 'One is proud to have been so nearly related to that saintly woman, whom I remember so well,'[5] wrote Queen Ena to Louise. There have been many books on Ella since 1964, but hers ranks amongst the finest. Louise was delighted, though slightly irritated with Dickie for giving the Queen a copy of this biography. 'It is *my* book,'[6] she pointed out.

The Greek royal wedding was due to take place on 18 September, but it preoccupied the royal family and the diplomats all that summer. As early as April, the young King had invited the Queen, Philip, Charles and Anne to attend. Philip was able to accept at once, but the Queen had to be more cautious. Philip wrote to the King: 'I am afraid that it is still impossible to decide whether Lilibet can come while the Cyprus situation remains critical,' but added that Charles and Anne were delighted to serve as crown holder and bridesmaid 'and unless something dreadful happens in the meantime they will report for duty on the appointed day'.[7]

By September there had been 'two acute war scares'.[8] Louise hoped to accompany Gustaf but her failing health prevented this. Thus she missed a last joint meeting with Alice and Dickie.

The wedding was the most splendid in Greece's history, with the men in white uniforms and the royal ladies at their most beautiful. Seven reigning monarchs attended with their consorts, two reigning princes, two ex-Kings, two Queen Mothers, and a profusion of princes and princesses, but in the end Britain's Queen did not come.*

Alice lunched with King Constantine and Queen Anne-Marie at the palace at Christmas, but otherwise she kept away. In the new year she had accepted an invitation from the Emir of Bahrain, via

* Philip, Charles, Anne, Prince Richard of Gloucester, Princess Marina, Prince Michael and Princess Alexandra and Hon. Angus Ogilvy were there, however.

Major Green, to visit that country again as his guest with her fare paid by the Emir. There she would pass her eightieth birthday, but she urged Philip not to tell Dickie, 'for he behaved idiotically about my last visit there'[9] – a reference to the ministrations of Admiral Talbot.

In December 1964 Louise suffered a heart attack and remained in hospital until 6 February 1965. In Greece Alice sensed that Louise's health was worse than she was intimating. As usual, Louise did all she could not to alarm Alice. 'How lucky I am,' she wrote to Dickie on 27 January, 'a wonderful dear brother and a touching sister. I had to write so carefully otherwise I feared Alice would come here.'[10] A few weeks later, Louise wrote again to Dickie:

> Alice arrived alright on the 23rd [February], had a good flight & surprisingly little tired after such a long day. She is about the same as when she was at Sofiero, perhaps her knees a bit stiffer & uncertain as she never walks all winter. Well she gets a bit of exercise as her room is quite a bit away from our dining room & big living room. It is so very nice having her. We sit & talk in the morning for an hour or so before lunch. Then I go to bed after lunch for a rest & a little massage. We sit together after tea quite a while. So you see we do not tire each other. We produced a sponge cake with light icing & one candle & put her few presents on a table. Alice says she is very pleased over our bag.* Gustaf gave her a shawl for the evening & some money for the additional old ladies' & mens' home [another scheme, supported by Alice] . . . I think Alice had quite a nice day, letters & telegrams.[11]

On 3 March Louise experienced great pain. She was taken by ambulance to St Goran's Hospital, and operated on for the removal of a blood clot in the main artery of her heart. She survived the operation but lost consciousness on 6 March and died the next day, so peacefully that only the monitoring instruments registered the moment of death.

* Dickie and Louise had bought Alice a grey leather bag for her birthday.

Alice accompanied Gustaf to the funeral on 13 March, in her nun's habit and heavy grey coat. Back in Athens she wrote to Dickie:

I don't feel recovered enough to tell you now about the operation & after. But this I will tell you now. That the sudden decision to spend my birthday with Louise was the result of a strong feeling that if I delayed till later, I would not see her once more. As it was, I only had one week with her before she went to hospital. Both she & I knew it was our last meeting, but we were determined to ignore that. So, we had such a peaceful & truly *happy* week together, for which I thank God with all my heart.[12]

Queen Anne-Marie invited Gustaf to come to Athens in April. Alice was happy that Dickie could also be there. 'I do need to see you so badly,' she wrote, '& I am calmer now. To have written to you all the details would have made my letter unreadable with tears.'[13] On St George's Day, brother, sister and bereaved husband met at Alice's flat in Patriarch Joachim Street. 'It was most harrowing to see the state the two men were in, talking over A. Louise's operation,' Alice wrote to Philip, 'but it did them both good to get it over.'[14]

For many years Alice had longed for better amity between Germany and Britain. She welcomed the first state visit to Germany (including Berlin) by the Queen and Philip, in May 1965, an important step towards reconciliation. Alice asked Philip to arrange that her old cousin and wartime ally in Greece, Victor Erbach, be presented to the Queen.

The ten-day visit was Philip's opportunity to take the Queen to Wolfsgarten, for him as for so many others in the family a true home from home. They dined there on 20 May, spent the weekend at Salem with Theodora and were entertained by Margarita at Langenburg.

Alice's next months were divided between Greece and England. In June 1965 she came to London. 'As the Filibets will be away,' she wrote to Dickie, 'I can come to you for lunch or supper any day you like.'[15] Alice loved her summer in London, staying longer than usual, now that Sweden was no longer a summer refuge. She joined the Queen, Philip, Charles, Anne, Andrew and Dickie in *Britannia* for a review of the Home Fleet in the Clyde in August and spent most of the summer at Balmoral. 'Dear Bubby-kins,' she wrote to Philip, 'you do not know how happy you have made me this summer & I am so sad it was over so quickly.'[16]

In September Alice attended the christening of King Constantine's first-born, Alexia, born at Mon Repos on 10 July. To the annoyance of the retrograde Prince Peter, a scourge of the Greek royal family at this time, Alexia became Crown Princess of Greece.

In the early months of 1966 the Queen and Philip went on an official visit to the Caribbean. Hardly had they left England than Alice suddenly arrived in London, ostensibly to be with the children in their parents' absence but also to avoid a political demonstration planned in Athens for 16 February. Alice was keen to justify this to Philip on his travels, but it is hard not to detect her loneliness – the more acute since the death of Louise – and a wish, then half-formed, to take sanctuary with her English family.

Charles was then at school in Australia, which Alice thought 'quite an experiment, but a good way to get to know Australia before official visits begin'.[17] In London Andrew and Edward played in Alice's room after breakfast and lunched with her every day. 'So nice for me, who am so lonely in Athens,'[18] she wrote. Young Edward used to run in and jump on his grandmother's bed. Halma was a favourite game.

On 19 February Alice helped Andrew celebrate his sixth birthday. There was a film and twelve other children came. But, she noted archly: 'An odd thing, their granny never sent a present or even a phone message on Andrew's birthday, which she has done other times, when you were away. He never noticed that luckily, as he never sees her.'[19]

At first Alice was going to remain in London until the Queen and Philip returned, but when the demonstration in Athens passed by without alarm and she received a letter from Eugénie's daughter,

Tatiana, inviting her 'urgently'[20] to attend her wedding there, she went home.

The political situation in Greece was deteriorating fast. Alice sought information and found her best source in Queen Helen of Romania, who was staying with King Constantine, and who took 'the keenest interest in Greek politics' and had not 'lost her nerve or morale',[21] as Alice put it. Queen Helen came round to Kitty Valaoritis's flat, where Alice was staying, and told her that she worried for the dynasty, while Alice told her she thought it was safe as long as the army was loyal. Queen Helen doubted this, saying that the Prime Minister Georges Papandreou's son had received large sums from Russia and that she feared the officers would accept substantial bribes to oust the King.

Alice assessed King Constantine's position, finding him well advised by his private secretary, a man called Bitsios, and thus aware of what was going on. But she thought he suffered from 'the optimism of the young that destiny will not let him leave the country'.[22] Alice, who had endured exile on more than one occasion, was all too aware of the historical precedents. Thus she alerted Philip privately of these dangers and asked him to be ready to rescue the King if necessary.

The Queen and Philip went to some trouble to get Alice to Windsor for Easter. Greeted by the Queen, Alice announced: 'I don't want to be here, but the King of Greece insisted that I came.'[23] This was probably inspired by nervousness, but sounded somewhat ungrateful.

Presently Alice went to the Hague for the wedding of her grandson Karl and thence to Sweden to stay with Gustaf at Ulriksdal. Dickie, Patricia, Pamela and her husband, David Hicks, were also there. The visit was notable for Alice's complaint that Patricia and Pamela were not properly seated at an official dinner. Bothered by this, she took the matter up with the King's chamberlain, Admiral H:son-Ericson, and almost with the King himself. The matter rumbled on for some time after the visit was over. The Admiral explained to Dickie that if British and Swedish precedence were mixed, then this would 'give the Master of the Ceremonies a strong headache'.[24] Dickie wound it up with a few diplomatic lines, which somewhat understate the importance in which he himself held such matters:

I am sorry my sister, Princess Alice, spoke to you about the placing of my daughters at the luncheons and dinners in Sweden. I hope I don't need to assure you that neither they nor I ever gave the matter any thought. My sister is much more '*placement* conscious' and told me she intended talking to you about it. I said I would only agree if she made it clear that we were not in any way upset ourselves. My sister belongs to a generation that set great store by such matters and of course the placing at the British Court is on the lines she explained rather than on the lines you use in Sweden.[25]

Alice decided not to go to Sweden again. At the end of May she went to Salem for Theodora's sixtieth birthday, celebrated with singing, speeches and a luncheon for 150. Alice met an old friend there, the Queen of Portugal, whom she used to see in London before the First World War, and she had a long talk to Kurt Hahn, now eighty, and to Jocelin Winthrop-Young, King Constantine's former tutor.

Alice suffered intermittent bouts of illness, from which she made good recoveries. These years provide a litany of complaints, involving the liver, her mobility and a series of coughs, colds and influenza, all of which gradually undermined her general well-being. This was punctuated with worries about politics in Greece, the deaths of numerous friends and relations and concerns about the frailty of Theodora and others.

The British public were occasionally made aware of Alice's ill-health, particularly on the occasions when Philip flew to her rescue. One such occasion was in June 1966, when Alice fell ill while staying with Sophie. She felt giddy and sick and was taken to the Rote Kreuz Krankenhaus in Munich by ambulance.

Alice diagnosed that the trouble stemmed from her heart, which had given her trouble as far back as the summer of 1904 when she had suffered from rheumatic fever. Now a sudden, sharp drop in the barometer caused the heart to be unable to send enough blood to certain veins near the centre of the brain. This caused the giddiness and sickness, she explained.

Philip paid her hospital bill and Alice hoped to go on to Margarita at Langenburg. But a month later she was still in the clinic. On 1 August Alice was sufficiently worried to write to Philip warning him that a combined infected liver and weak heart was the problem and that 'the end may come suddenly or slowly as a result of a general deterioration caused by this state of affairs'. She urged him: '*Be brave* & remember I will never leave you & you will always feel me when you need me most. All my devoted love, your old Mama.'[26]

Alice's daughters kept a watchful eye on her in turn, while she followed plans for the wedding at Persenberg of her grandson, Max of Baden, to which she could not go. Alice saw her old cousin, Victor Erbach, and his wife, and was pleased that her floor maid watched the final of the World Cup on television and spotted Philip, who happened to wave in the direction of the German cameras.

From her sickbed, with a drip infusion in her arm, Alice returned to the theme of Anglo-German relations and congratulated Philip on what he had achieved.

The doctor assures me that there is not a man in the whole of Germany who is not devoted to you, a fact much helped by your shooting & yachting visits here. Every visit of yours here strengthens the ties between two countries & he thinks that nothing will alter them now. But the pleasant atmosphere round the match is certainly [due] to yours & L's visit last year.[27]

Philip now invited his mother to come to live at Buckingham Palace, which Alice declined, pointing out that her lady-in-waiting, Kitty Valaoritis, was in Athens, and the hospital at Munich was nearer to Athens. 'Then I have a great longing to live in a place which has been my home for 63 years. I would be out of place at Buckingham Palace & I don't know any London hospitals & doctors. I do hope you will understand.'[28]

From the clinic Alice followed a reunion between Charles, coming from Australia, with his father and Anne in Jamaica for the Commonwealth Games. When Philip had deposited his children at Balmoral on 17 August, he enquired of his mother's health and on finding she was well enough to return to Athens, he flew from Scotland in an RAF aircraft, took her on board, flew her to Athens, stayed one night to see her safely re-established, and then flew back to Scotland, an expedition which involved sixteen and a half hours of flying. Margarita stayed with her and she soon moved back to her flat, where the doctor hoped she would eat better and regain her health.

October found Alice at home again, boosted by injections, able to walk around at home, but not well enough for drives yet. She felt 'sort of betwixt & between. I don't get better & I don't get worse.'[29]

37. Alice at the Palace

There were two overriding concerns for Alice in the new year of 1967: her failing health and Greek politics, which soon reached a critical point. Her state of health caused her to have a young nurse looking after her and she then lost the help of her lady-in-waiting, Kitty Valaoritis, because of a cancer operation. But she was cheered by two visits from Philip, on his way to and from Australia in February. On one of the visits he bought a new carpet for the flat.

Within three years of succeeding his father, King Constantine was being seen as the cipher of his overly political mother. In 1965 he had confronted the colonels and dismissed Georges Papandreou, the ardently socialist Prime Minister, from office. The issue then turned to whether the young King would reign or rule. Keen to rule, King Constantine seemed to have the support of the Greek people in this, and elections were scheduled for May.

The situation was highly unstable and Athens was hardly the appropriate place for an ailing princess of eighty-one to contemplate her last years, yet Alice was determined to remain.

On 21 April 1967 came the 'Colonels' Coup', in which the military seized power in the name of the King. Athens came under fire, but no blood was shed. Philip made immediate enquiries as to how his mother was. He found she had already moved into the Royal Palace for greater safety. She was able to send him a message via the British Embassy bag to tell him that she was well and to remind him that 'revolutions & wars have never disturbed me & this also did not'.[1] Nevertheless she told a harrowing version of events:

That day of the coup was like the occupation time, shops shut, no buses or taxis, no telephone or telegraph & curfew too. Luckily there was some food in the house, so I did not starve. Our news came from the concierge, who heard the military announce news from the army radio. Of course I can't get reliable news yet, as the Palace & Tatoï are circled by troops & no one is allowed into the Palace yet, although the shops are now opened, buses & taxis circulate & one can telephone, but not abroad yet. The only news is what the chauffeur told Kitty & that is that, at 2 a.m. Friday 21st tanks & troops were in all the main points of the city, that army officers went to wake Tino and told him that he was not allowed out of the house. They also told Freddy she could not leave her house, but she made such a clamour to join Tino that finally some officers drove her to Tatoï. But Tino, under military escort, was allowed to come to town at 7 p.m. that day for the new cabinet to be sworn in. He also came the day after (Saturday 22nd) to town, but escorted to have a talk with his political adviser at the latter's house. Beyond that I know nothing except that Papandreou intended to go to Salonica & form his own government there, Sat. 22nd, & this coup was to forestall this, as the army realized that a democratic government & a constitutional King could not take dramatic measures. All the leading Communist agitators were sent to the islands. The arrested politicians are housed in an unknown building. The son Papandreou, the Communist, was arrested with an American passport, intending to leave by the first plane there. No officers came here & I was left in peace.[2]

It was announced that the army had saved Greece, and this news was well received. The Communist headquarters were searched, guns and other ammunition found, hordes of money and the uniforms of policemen and gendarmes. The King was confined until the end of the month, when he was suddenly set free. Eight top generals were dismissed from their commands with no reason given. The people were afraid that these generals might have supporters in the army, and that a counter-movement might follow. Alice followed every detail and manoeuvre, assuring Philip: 'I am well & terribly interested of course.'[3]

Presently Alice returned to her flat, where she received a message from Philip with as much reliable information as he could send. Theodora arrived to see her, but with a streaming cold. Political uneasiness continued into May, the people wondering what was happening, as 'Tino was completely silent & they did not know if he were going to accept the "coup" or leave the country until normal elections.'[4]

By this time it was clear to the Queen and Philip, if not to Alice, that history was likely to repeat itself and the King would probably have to leave Athens in a precipitous hurry. He had his aeroplane, which could take him and Queen Anne-Marie, his baby daughter Alexia, Queen Frederika and his unmarried sister Irene. The only other princess still in Athens was Alice. But there would be no room in the aeroplane for her.

There was an additional problem. It was impossible to telephone Alice, since she could not hear what was said. She had the disconcerting habit of telephoning Kitty Valaoritis to give her instructions and then hanging up without waiting for a reply. This sometimes left the lady-in-waiting in a quandary.

Sophie arrived to visit Alice on her way to India. She came with an invitation, this time from the Queen, to come to live at Buckingham Palace. She warned her mother of the dangers of staying in Greece, as outlined to her by Philip in England, and by her husband, Prince George, who had been briefed by his sister Queen Frederika.

Alice had been fiercely independent for many years but lately her sense of isolation and loneliness had intensified. She listened with interest to Sophie's proposal and the problem of the King's plane. When she heard that it was the Queen herself who had issued the invitation her eyes brightened. 'Lilibet said that?' she asked. 'We go this afternoon.'[5]

In the event her departure took longer to organize. In preparation, Alice gave away her furniture and her worldly goods. Later that month, King Constantine's plane was going over to England to be re-fitted. Soon afterwards, Alice, who had first arrived in Greece in the royal yacht some sixty-three years before as a beautiful bride, greeted by enthusiastic crowds and the inevitable Te Deum, slipped quietly out of the country, never to return, to make her home in the land of her birth.

*

At Buckingham Palace, Alice moved into two rooms on the first floor overlooking the Mall*. At first she was restless, unhappy and full of complaints, but just as suddenly she relaxed and appreciated her good fortune.

For a time she travelled about much as before, spending weekends at Windsor Castle. It was the time when the royal family all got to know her best, including the Queen, who was particularly good to her. Charles and Anne were often at the palace or at Windsor and invariably looked in to see her. The small princes were taken to her rooms to play. When they were very small, she had alarmed the children with her deep voice. The Prince of Wales told his valet that as he grew older, he came to appreciate 'her sense of fun and lively mind'.[6] Alice was pleased that Charles played the cello, since Andrea had done so in his youth.

The servants at the palace had become used to Alice staying for increasingly long periods in the 1960s. She still wore her nun's habit and they remembered that she was

> eccentric and deaf, and smoked like a chimney. If we could tell when the Queen was coming by the pattering of the corgis' feet, we always knew when Princess Andrew was about from the clouds of smoke that followed her. And the coughing. The poor lady coughed incessantly as she lit another cigarette. Not surprisingly, she was often in the hospital with bronchitis.

The staff thought her 'strange but likeable'.[7] A bell was installed in Alice's rooms, so that she could summon help. There was some grumbling about the extra work this might entail in the pages' room, though Alice rarely used it. The pages liked to jest that the bell rang more often in the days after Alice's death than while she was alive.

By the end of May 1967, the British press had detected that Alice

* These rooms are to the right of the balcony room, as you face the palace, towards the Constitution Hill side. The Duchess of Windsor was to stay in them before the Duke's funeral in 1972 and a memorable photograph was taken of her watching the return of The Queen's Birthday Parade procession. Senior members of foreign suites use these rooms during state visits.

was installed at the palace, and this fact was noted in the English newspapers. A palace press officer said: 'Although she is based here, we never know her movements. She likes to see a lot of her grandchildren and she also goes to stay with various relatives – including her brother, Lord Mountbatten. She will be in England for several weeks.'[8]

Above all, Alice loved being near Philip. Occasionally, however, there were what the Princess Royal called

> not arguments, but let's say slight differences of agreement. My father would then go off down the corridor muttering and she would be in her room muttering too. I realized that she could not hear a word he was saying and yet the conversation followed completely coherently. Maybe he had already made his point, and she knew what he would be saying.[9]

The Princess Royal thought it strange that when the family left for Balmoral that summer, Alice stayed in London. The first year, no one seemed quite sure what to do with her, while she had clearly decided it was better for her health not to make the journey north. In August a few days after Philip left for Cowes, Alice moved into the Hyde Park Hotel, that favourite old haunt of Gustaf and Louise, while the palace closed down for the summer.

'I was so sad to see you all go off,' wrote Alice to Philip, '& I miss my talks with you. I am so grateful that my health permitted me to travel to England & have such a wonderful time with you in consequence.'[10] Margarita came to London to see her mother, and there was a dinner for Dickie in her sitting room. Young Edward, who had not gone with the rest of the family and was himself a bit lonely in the palace, came over to the hotel each morning with his nanny, Mabel Anderson.

Soon afterwards, on 29 August, Alice fell ill with bronchitis and was taken to the King Edward VII Hospital, Marylebone. Philip flew down to see her for the day on 1 September. The next day she was reported to be 'critically ill',[11] but she recovered.

On 22 September Alice was well enough to have her portrait photograph taken by Godfrey Argent in hospital. She sat in the chair in her dressing-gown, her face expressing many moods, her hands clasped in characteristic poses. The whole session was over within twenty minutes and there was no conversation between photographer and subject.

On 3 October Alice was discharged from hospital. A vigilant press photographer took a snap of her in her nun's habit, the last time the British public ever saw her. She was driven back to Buckingham Palace, never to leave it again.

In due course two full-time nurses arrived to care for her. As she became more infirm, and particularly in the last year of her life, she travelled about the palace in a wheelchair, pushed by the Queen's page, Bennett, or the Duke's page.

In December 1967, King Constantine instigated his counter coup, but the army failed to support him. He and his family were forced to flee to Rome. This made any return to Athens by Alice yet more unlikely, though in response to enquiries from the press the Greek Embassy stated: 'She would be most welcome at home. She is much loved by the people.'[12]

It has sometimes been suggested that Alice was some kind of strange recluse, locked up in Buckingham Palace. She was infirm, but she was totally *compos mentis*. She received many visitors, Gustaf, who came to see her at the palace on every London visit, noting: 'It always struck me that she was not only well looked after there but in fact was feeling both comfortable and even happy there.'[13]

Her daughters would take it in turn to come and stay, as Alice was not well enough to leave the palace. When Alice's eighty-third birthday in 1968 fell on a Sunday, the Queen and Philip stayed in London specially for the weekend.

Dickie came to see her on his weekly visits to London, armed with news from the outside world. One project on which they put their heads together was the biography of Louise, being written by Margit Fjellman.* Alice enjoyed her younger brother's visits but did not hesitate to berate him. She complained: 'He only comes to see me to write letters on Buckingham Palace writing paper!'[14]

* Margit Fjellman, *Louise Mountbatten, Queen of Sweden* (Allen & Unwin, 1968).

In October 1968 Alice appointed the palace solicitor as trustee of her will, and was still alert to the news: 'The papers are full of the Olympics Committee's fury at the political demonstrations & Jack. [Jacqueline] Kennedy's marriage.'[15]

In February 1969, Alice passed her eighty-fourth birthday. In April her Battenberg cousin Ena died in Lausanne, and then on 16 October Theodora died suddenly in the Sanatorium Buedingen in Constance. Philip was away on a tour of Canada and the United States, so Charles flew to the funeral at Salem. A few days later Alice sent her last letter to Philip. Most of it she dictated to her nurse:

> The funeral guests from here went by helicopter, leaving in the morning and returning same evening, otherwise the funeral was exactly the same as for her husband.
>
> I got such nice letters from Margarita and Tiny.
>
> Margarita is the most upset because there was only one year between them and also she has become closer to her during this past year.
>
> Edward was not told anything. Charles and Anne paid me the most touching visits.
>
> The doctor does not find me any worse.
>
> My thoughts are always with you.[16]

Alice lived for less than two months. She did not want to live longer. She was annoyed when an injection from the doctor set her right again when she was sure she was slipping away. Princess Margaret recalled that 'she made a pact with God and decided she was going to die that Thursday. She summoned Dickie and he changed all his plans to come and see her on the Wednesday. Then she didn't die and he was furious!'[17]

By the end of her life the general public scarcely remembered that she was alive, and were largely unaware that she was at Buckingham Palace. But there were a handful of Alice followers. Harold Albert, who wrote books under the name of Helen Cathcart, had recently written a chapter on her life for a forthcoming book,* and one

* Helen Cathcart, *The Royal Bedside Book* (W. H. Allen, 1969).

evening he walked in the Mall and observed the lights in the rooms which he assumed, correctly, were lived in by Alice.

In November Alice saw her priest, Father Gregory,* and she told him that she was going to die soon. 'She was a very brave woman,'[18] he said. Later he gave her the last rites.

Dickie happened to call on her on the last evening of her life: 'I saw her at 6.15 on the night that she died and she was very peaceful and seemed happy and talked of recollections of the past.'[19]

Alice died peacefully in her sleep on 5 December. Both the Queen and Philip were at the palace at the time. All she left in the world were three dressing-gowns, which Sophie gave to the nurses who had cared for her, and there was a letter from her old friend, Gerald Green, on which she had begun to write a reply. This Sophie returned to him.

It happened that Anne had not paid her usual visit to Alice on the day she died. She therefore asked the undertakers if she could go into her grandmother's room and see her. 'I am glad I did that. She looked very peaceful. All the lines in her face had gone and for the first time I could see the resemblance to the de László portrait.'[20]

The coffin was taken from her bedroom along the corridors of the palace to the small part of the private chapel that had survived wartime bombing. From there it was conveyed to Windsor for the funeral in St George's Chapel, arriving at the Albert Memorial Chapel on Tuesday 9 December. Family mourning was ordered for a week.

Alice's death was briefly noted in British newspapers and there were obituaries in some of them. The Court Circular, which had recorded her birth at Windsor eighty-four years earlier, announced that the Queen had 'heard' of Alice's death 'with great regret'.†[21]

Tributes came in from various quarters. Gustaf wrote to Dickie:

* Archimandrite Gregory Theocarous, Chancellor of the Greek Orthodox Archdiocese of Thyateira and Great Britain.

† Normally such news is 'received', but this subtle wording indicated that the Queen was under the same roof at the time.

I am glad to be able to say that Alice and I always remained friends and also that we understood each other. I shall never forget her whole attitude of kindness and of understanding when darling Louise was taken from me . . . I am also glad to be able to say that in my opinion the two sisters seemed to draw closer together and to understand one another.[22]

Dickie's daughter Patricia recalled her devotion to her grandmother and continued: 'Aunt Alice too was so much of a character one will never forget her – & indeed all those *bons mots* she never failed to produce!'[23]

Alice was eighty-four when she died. Nevertheless, one of the messages came from her old Aunt Anna in her room in Territet. Aunt Anna was then ninety-five.* An unlikely sympathizer, but a sound one, was the former Gaiety Girl Ruby Miller, who wrote: 'When a young girl, I always admired her tremendously. I thought she would make a most beautiful queen. She certainly produced a wonderful son in Prince Philip.'[24]

Alice's funeral took place at St George's Chapel, Windsor, on 10 December. She had been born in the castle in the days of Queen Victoria and now she returned to the castle after what Philip described as 'a life of wars, revolutions, separations and tragedies'.[25]

Margarita and Philip walked behind the coffin, followed by Sophie and Dickie. Gustaf could not come because of the Nobel Prize ceremony. The Queen brought Charles, Anne and nine-year-old Andrew with her. The British royal family turned out in force, and some twenty-two royal visitors from overseas arrived at Windsor despite a thick veil of fog which caused the cancellation of numerous flights. King Constantine, who was staying with King Baudouin of the Belgians, asked for a car and outriders and came by ferry to Dover. Princess Olga and Princess Eugénie would have come but were grounded in Paris by the fog.

Amongst the mourners was that 'other little Alice', as Queen Victoria called her – Princess Alice, Countess of Athlone, who had

* Princess Anna died at Montreux on 22 April 1971, aged ninety-six. For a long time she was the oldest European princess.

been born on the same day as Alice but two years earlier. The other surviving granddaughter of Queen Victoria, Lady Patricia Ramsay, was also there, accompanied by her peppery old husband, Admiral Sir Alexander Ramsay, whose loud voice, made less inhibited by his own deafness, could be heard asking numerous questions before the service: 'Do we have to go to Frogmore? Beastly cold at Frogmore.'[26]

In the quire were the royal nannies and Alice's nurses, overseen as ever by Miss Alice Saxby, Matron of King Edward VII Hospital. Father Gregory, the Archimandrite, was there in his dark robes and tall hat. The service was partly in English and partly in Greek. The lesson came from St Luke and dealt appropriately with Martha and Mary. Robin Woods, the Dean of Windsor, ended the service by commending Alice for 'the memory of her long life, for her service to those in need, for her courage in the face of adversity and for her devotion to her Lord and to his Church'.[27] Then, for the third time in over a decade, a royal coffin descended into the royal vault, the old lift working silently, yet dramatically, and the coffin disappearing from view.

After the funeral the fog descended yet more heavily. The Queen stayed an extra night at Windsor Castle, where she was joined by various fog-bound mourners.

Not long before she died, Alice had given verbal instructions that she wished to be buried near her Aunt Ella in Jerusalem. When the family protested that this was a long way away and that it would be hard to visit her there, she retorted: 'Nonsense! There is a perfectly good bus service.'[28]

Nothing happened for some years, Alice's coffin resting on one of two catafalques in the royal vault. After Michael Mann was installed as sixty-second Dean of Windsor in 1976, he opened negotiations to fulfil Alice's wishes. Little did he know the long journey that lay ahead.

Religious, political and diplomatic problems all stood in the way. Alice was Greek Orthodox, but the convent belonged to the White Russians. Furthermore, since the Middle East war of 1967, Britain had refused to recognize East Jerusalem, the location of the convent, as Jordanian rather than as part of Israel. It was not until 3 August 1988 that it was possible to lay Alice to rest in a vault under the convent in which Aunt Ella's coffin was buried.*

Today the coffin rests on its small marble bier, still covered with the Greek royal standard. On the far wall is a simple inscription:

ALICE
PRINCESS ANDREW
OF GREECE
PRINCESS OF BATTENBERG
25 – FEBRUARY 1885
5 – DECEMBER 1969

Underneath, in Greek, are the words 'Thy will be done'.

On 11 April 1993, a posthumous award to Alice as 'Righteous among the Nations' was approved by the Holocaust Memorial, Yad Vashem, in Jerusalem, recognizing that 'during the Holocaust period in Europe' she had 'risked her life to save persecuted Jews'.[29] The lengthy process of obtaining the medal had been initiated by Freddy Cohen, one of the family Alice had hidden in the Second World War, after he learned in 1988 that Alice was buried on the Mount of Olives. Freddy died in 1989 and it fell to his widow, Stella, and to his brother, Jacques, to follow the matter through. The award,† the highest award for a non-Jewish foreigner, 'was not so easy to obtain,'[30] recalled Jacques Cohen.

On 31 October 1994, her two surviving children, Prince Philip and Princess George of Hanover, went together to Jerusalem to receive the award on behalf of Alice. In a ceremony they jointly laid a wreath in the Holocaust Museum and planted a tree at Yad Vashem. They then listened to the description of what Alice had

* For full details of this dramatic saga, see the Appendix.

† Alice's number is Greece (5643). Other famous recipients include Oskar Schindler, of *Schindler's List* fame, Archbishop Damaskinos, the Regent of Greece, and Queen Helen of Romania.

done. In his acceptance speech, Prince Philip said: 'As far as we know she had never mentioned to anyone that she had given refuge to the Cohen family at a time when Jews throughout Greece were in danger of being arrested and transported to the death camps. I suspect that she never thought of it as something special. She was a person with deep religious faith and she would have considered it to be a totally natural human action to fellow human beings in distress.'[31]

Afterwards they went together to the beautiful spot where Alice lies, near to the aunt she loved and whose life had been her inspiration.

In a life often touched by tragedy, Alice never allowed adversity, penury, near starvation, wars or revolutions to bring her down. She was isolated by her deafness, brought low by ill health. But, like Ella, she wanted to serve humanity in a practical way, and when a challenge presented itself, she rose to the call.

Her work in the Balkan Wars, her care of the afflicted in the Second World War, and her attempts to emulate Ella's example in Greece by creating a nursing sisterhood were tackled with determination, and if failure sometimes resulted, it was not for want of effort.

Shy, sometimes austere, remote, self-sufficient beyond the point of coping, she put much into life. Had she lived in different times, it might have been possible for her to achieve more. Had she been less determined, less obstinate, her life might have been gentler. But in spite of all the disappointments and sorrows, she never flinched. Above all, she saw hers as a life of service, in which she did her best to help those less fortunate than herself.

Appendix: The Burial of Alice

Alice's coffin was still in the royal vault, still covered in the Greek royal standard, when, in 1976, the new Dean of Windsor, Rt. Revd Michael Mann, undertook a tour of inspection of St George's Chapel. He was told by the Lord Chamberlain that one of his jobs was to bury Princess Alice in Jerusalem. Prince Philip gave him permission to proceed.

The Dean began by writing to the Patriarch in Jerusalem, Diodoros I, to ask if he had any objections:

> The answer I got back was: Yes, he'd have every objection. A: She was Greek Orthodox and should be buried in a Greek Orthodox Church. B: The Church was White Russian Orthodox, and the man in charge of it was a person he found difficult. No way were they prepared to have any dealings with this. So at that point I wrote to the Russian Patriarch in Moscow, and said 'This is the position all right, it is a White Russian Church, but this is a dying woman's wishes. Does it really matter?' And he wrote back a most charming letter saying 'Of course not, they would have no objection at all.' Then, having got this, I went back to Diodoros and said: 'The Russians have no objection at all, do you still maintain yours?' And he said: 'In principle, no, but we don't like the set-up in the White Russian Church.' So then I got in touch with the man in charge, Archimandrite Anthony Grabbe,* and he welcomed the idea.[1]

All this took some time. Negotiations were further delayed by the Queen and Prince Philip undertaking a five-day state visit to Jordan at the end of March 1984. It was deemed imprudent to advance the plans until after this visit had taken place.

* Archimandrite Anthony Grabbe, Chief of the Russian Ecclesiastical Mission in Jerusalem until 1986.

Completely without warning, Archimandrite Grabbe decided to pay a call on Prince Philip to discuss what he called the matter 'of your pious concern'.[2] He made the journey to Amman, and found that the royal party had moved to Aqaba. He followed them there, made his presence known to the Court Chamberlain to King Hussein and asked to meet Prince Philip. Grabbe failed to get the point across that he had come in connection with the burial. As no one knew anything about him, and time was short, he was not received. Grave offence was taken and Grabbe wrote to Prince Philip in London, telling him that he had concluded that he must have changed his mind about burying his mother in his church, expressing surprise that neither the Dean nor the local Anglican Bishop had taken the time to inform him, and ending that Prince Philip must feel free of any further obligation to him.[3]

The subtle negotiations of the Dean appeared to come to nought at a stroke, and after seven years they were back where they started. Prince Philip wrote personally to Grabbe, apologizing for the unintentional slight and assuring him that he wished to proceed as before. He explained that he had thought the border between Jordan and Israel was closed and said he had been told that 'there was a Russian priest who claimed to know my father. As I was in Aqaba at the time, and due to leave the following morning, I did not see what I could do about it.'[4]

The Dean also wrote, but Grabbe remained in high dudgeon, reiterating, amongst other grievances, his annoyance at not having been received by Prince Philip and telling the Dean that he had therefore informed his superiors, the Synod of Bishops, that the matter was closed.[5] For good measure, he added that he would now be away until December.

The Dean wrote a further conciliatory letter, saying that he was most distressed and adding: 'I have spoken to His Royal Highness The Duke of Edinburgh, who is equally upset.'[6] He attempted to reassure the tricky Archimandrite on every point raised.

A further problem then arose when the Dean was telephoned by Sir Antony Acland, the Permanent Under-Secretary at the Foreign Office, telling him to drop the negotiations at once, since the burial of a royal body on the West Bank would give the Israelis the chance to exploit the issue to get the British government to recognize their occupation of the West Bank. The Dean recalled:

So I had a chat with Prince Philip about this, which he thought was nonsense, and so I wrote to King Hussein, with whom I had some connections and explained the situation and asked him if he would have any objection or be embarrassed politically by this. And then I got on to Evelyn de Rothschild* and asked him to speak to the Israeli authorities so that they didn't make a fuss. King Hussein was charming and said they had no objection. But at that point it became very clear that if the thing succeeded, there was no way that the Duke of Edinburgh could come out to the funeral.† It would have to be done very privately.[7]

Meanwhile Grabbe fell silent until November 1985. At that point he wrote to the Dean proposing that a special vault be built to house the coffin and he asked the Dean to submit plans for this and to declare how much Prince Philip might like to contribute towards its construction.[8] In December the Dean wrote back with a strategic withdrawal, pointing out that with all the changes and new conditions, it was clear to him and to Prince Philip that no further purpose was likely to be achieved.

In the interim period the Dean had written a letter appealing for help to Metropolitan Filaret of the Russian Church, in New York. The letter went unanswered because the Metropolitan had died. Only some time later was the letter found amongst his papers. Meanwhile there was a local dispute in Jerusalem concerning some funds raised for the regilding of the golden domes of the convent. This had been done cheaply and, all too soon, the domes had lost their lustre. Grabbe was dismissed in January 1986 for 'moral

* (Sir) Evelyn de Rothschild (b. 1931), chairman of N. M. Rothschild & Sons Ltd.

† The Foreign Office made it clear that such a visit was too dangerous. They could not guarantee Prince Philip's safety. For the same reason, the Prince of Wales was unable to visit the coffin when he attended the funeral of Yitzak Rabin in 1995.

turpitude, gross misappropriation of church funds and unauthorized sale of church property and relics',[9] dividing the congregation at the White Russian Church, some of whom supported him, while others did not. He then formed a splinter group, which represented a latent threat to these burial plans.

The Dean pressed on undeterred and his persistence steered him into calmer waters. He contacted a friend at the Cathedral of St John the Divine in New York, Canon Edward West.* He led him to Prince Theimouraz Bagration Moukhransky, President of the Orthodox Palestine Society/USA, a courteous and helpful aristocrat of the old school, and coincidentally, related to Grand Duchess Elisabeth and indeed to Alice.†

Prince Bagration was the perfect man to deal with all the disparate factions. Calmly and quietly, he addressed the issues and resolved them one by one. In April 1986 he was able to reassure the Dean: 'I hope that we are finally on the good track. We have good will and discretion and with this the rest will be easier.'[10]

By June the Dean was providing the Prince with the measurements of the coffin and discussing means of reducing the size if necessary. By July the Prince was negotiating with the Greeks in Jerusalem, noting that they were 'very touchy and our people have to be careful in dealing with them, observing strictly all rules of protocol'.[11] By September 1987 the proposed burial of Alice had been approved by the Greek Patriarch in Jerusalem, the Bishops of

* Canon Edward West (1909–90), Sacrist at the Cathedral of St John the Divine 1941–81. Theologian, author, expert in the design of altar cloths and episcopal rings, and leading authority on liturgical celebrations. An exuberant figure, invariably clad in black cassock, cape and skull cap, he organized the funerals of Duke Ellington and George Balanchine and was much in evidence during the Queen Mother's visit to the cathedral in 1954.

† Prince Theimouraz Bagration (1912–92), descended from the royal dynasty of Georgia and son of Princess Tatiana of Russia (1890–1979), later Abbess Tamara of the Russian Orthodox Convent on the Mount of Olives, Jerusalem. She was a daughter of Grand Duke Constantine ('K.R.'), and it was his Uncle John whose arm was bandaged by Grand Duchess Ella when they were both thrown down the mine shaft at Alapaievsk in July 1918.

the Russian Church in Exile and the Supreme Council of the Orthodox Palestine Society.

A new problem arose as to who owned the Church of St Mary Magdalen and this had to be resolved between the Russian Orthodox Church in Exile and one of its dismissed clerics. The matter went to arbitration in February 1988. Prince Bagration turned to two lawyers, Mrs Lena S. Zezulin in Washington and Mr David Martin in Jerusalem, and with exemplary skill, they helped a satisfactory agreement to be reached in July 1988.

Then there was fear that the floor in the church was not strong enough to bear the weight of the coffin. The Dean wrote to Prince Bagration: 'I must say that this particular exercise has been fraught with delays and unforeseen difficulties and I only hope that this is the final one.'[12]

The Dean himself went out to Jerusalem, at a time when he had dislocated his back and had to be fork-lifted on to the aeroplane. He met the new Russian Orthodox Archimandrite, an Australian called Alexis. The Greek Patriarch told him that all would be well, provided that the coffin came to the Greek Orthodox Church first for the full burial mass and then went to the Russian Church to be interred.* The Dean went to the church and saw the coffins of Grand Duchess Elisabeth and Sister Barbara lying in the main body of the church, because of their recent canonization. The Archimandrite told him that Princess Alice's coffin could not go there as she was not canonized, but that there were open vaults, then piled high with builder's rubble, either side of the steps up to the church. One of these could be cleared and could serve as a place of interment. The Dean related:

* During his visit the Dean was invested as Knight Grand Cross of the Order of the Holy Sepulchre. The Foreign Office did not mind, but he was told that he was not allowed to wear it. But he did wear it at Princess Alice's interment. He was also taken on a trip to Masada by one of the nuns from the convent. 'I don't think I've ever been so frightened. She drove me in a Peugeot at about 150 miles an hour on a narrow road with buses coming the other way.' [Bishop Mann to author, 11 February 1997.]

And I thought 'Oh Heavens'. Knowing what time scales are like, they probably wouldn't start doing it until the coffin had actually arrived. However that was fine,* and after all that, I went back and explained it to Prince Philip and said: 'I think what I have to say is that my reconnaissance tells me that it may happen, it may not. The risk we have to take is that I may go out with the coffin and come back with it, but that is the worst that could happen. It's worth a try.' So he said to go ahead.[13]

The journey was as memorable as the negotiations. On the evening of 2 August, Alice's coffin was taken privately from the royal vault of St George's Chapel, where it had now lain for nearly nineteen years. Father Gregory came to say some prayers, and then the small group set off. They were the Dean, Alice's daughter Princess George of Hanover, the Dean's wife, Jill, acting as lady-in-waiting, and Christopher Kenyon, the undertaker. They took a scheduled flight from Heathrow to Jerusalem, arriving at about 4.30 a.m. They were escorted to a VIP room, where to his surprise, the Dean was asked for £100 in cash. They were met there by an Israeli undertaker and driven up the winding roads to the Mount of Olives, arriving at 6.00 a.m.

The coffin was taken straight into the church and the Greek Orthodox service began immediately, a requiem, all participants standing, as is usual in an Orthodox church. The Dean managed to get a chair for Princess George. The Patriarch then invited the party to an enormous breakfast, which seemed unending, during which the Dean presented the Patriarch with a signed photograph of Prince Philip. At about 10.30 a.m., they set off again to the Garden of Gethsemane. The final stage of Alice's journey was as dramatic as so many other parts of her long life. The Dean recalled:

We found television and crowds of people there. Christopher Kenyon, on the advice of the Israeli undertaker, had in fact employed a lot of strong-arm men. Luckily the Garden is surrounded by a considerable wall

*The Archimandrite personally cleared the rubble, redecorated the crypt and painted beautiful modern icons on the walls.

and iron gates, and once we had got inside, the security men fought the press and pushed them out, and up we went. The nuns of the White Russian Orthodox Church then began the Russian Orthodox liturgy for the dead, and as they started, the Greeks rushed in and started singing. The Russians behaved immaculately. They just stopped and waited and let the Greeks sing themselves out.

Then they started the liturgy which was beautifully and movingly sung and the coffin was taken and put on the bier, and Princess George was obviously very moved and really felt that they had fulfilled her mother's dying wishes.[14]

The burial safely realized after hazards innumerable, the small party attended a very long lunch. Then they checked in at their hotel. It was 3.30 p.m. and they had been on their feet for almost twenty-four hours.

Shortly after Alice's burial in Jerusalem in August 1988 the Dean of Windsor wrote to Prince Theimouraz to thank him for his help, and the Prince replied: 'The last will of Princess Alice has been executed and her children can have peace of mind.'[15]

WHOEVER SAVES ONE LIFE IS AS THOUGH HE HAD SAVED THE ENTIRE WORLD

כל המקיים נפש אחת ... כאילו קיים עולם מלא

תעודת כבוד

Certificate of Honour

THIS IS TO CERTIFY THAT IN ITS SESSION
OF MARCH 11, 1994 [illegible]
THE COMMISSION [illegible]
OF THE RIGHT[illegible]
YAD VASHEM [illegible]
& MARTYRS [illegible]
ON THE BA[illegible]
BEFORE [illegible]

Princess A[illegible] of Greece

WHO, DU[illegible]
IN EUROP[illegible]
SAVE PERS[illegible]
THE COMM[illegible]
ACCORDED [illegible]
RIGHTEOUS AMO[illegible]
HER NAME SHALL [illegible]
ENGRAVED ON THE HONOUR WALL IN
THE GARDEN OF THE RIGHTEOUS, AT
YAD VASHEM, JERUSALEM.

וזאת לתעודה שבישיבתה
מיום יח אדר תשנ"ד
החליטה הוועד[illegible]
חסידי אומות [illegible]
שליד רשות [illegible]
על יסוד [illegible]
שהובאו [illegible]
ויקר ל[illegible]
הנסי[illegible]
מיוון
על אש[illegible]
באירופה [illegible]
להצלת [illegible]
מידי רודפיה [illegible]
את המדליה [illegible]
העולם.
שמה יונצח לעד על
כבוד בחורשת חסידי אומות
העולם ביד ושם.

Jerusalem, Israel
OCTOBER 31. 1994

ניתן היום בירושלים
כו חשון תשנ"ה

Avner Shalev
בשם רשות הזכרון יד ושם
ON BEHALF OF THE YAD VASHEM DIRECTORATE

בשם הועדה לציון חסידי אומות העולם
ON BEHALF OF THE COMMISSION FOR THE DESIGNATION OF THE RIGHTEOUS

Notes

Abbreviations

People

Alice – Princess Andrew of Greece
Andrea – Prince Andrew of Greece
B – Dr Ludwig Binswanger
Cécile – Princess Cécile of Hesse
Edwina – Countess Mountbatten of Burma
GMH – George, Marquess of Milford Haven
KGV – George V
KGVI – George VI
Louise – Queen Louise of Sweden
Margarita – Princess Margarita of Hohenlohe-Langenburg.
MtB – Earl Mountbatten of Burma
NK – Nona Kerr
PL – Prince Louis of Battenberg
QM – Queen Mary
QV – Queen Victoria
Theodora – Margravine of Baden
VMH – Victoria, Marchioness of Milford Haven

Places

BP – Buckingham Palace
KP – Kensington Palace

Sources

BA – Broadlands Archive
BP – Buckingham Palace
FO – Foreign Office
HL – Mountbatten papers, Hartley Library, University of Southampton
PRO – Public Records Office
RA – Royal Archives
TB – Bagration papers
UT – Binswanger papers, University of Tübingen

Introduction

1. Viscount Lambton to author, Italy, 7 September 1998.

1. The Infant Princess

1. Empress Frederick [of Germany] to QV, Berlin, 27 February 1885 [RA VIC/Z 37/61]; and QV to Duke of Connaught, 24 April 1885 [RA VIC/Add. 15/4462].
2. VMH memoirs [HL].
3. VMH memoirs, p. 1 [HL].
4. QV Journal, 25 February 1885 [RA VIC/QVJ].

2. *The Battenbergs*

1. VMH memoirs, p. 49 [HL].
2. VMH memoirs, p. 26 [HL].
3. VMH memoirs, p. 69 [HL].
4. VMH memoirs, p. 72 [HL].
5. Queen Elizabeth The Queen Mother to author, Castle of Mey, 22 August 1998.
6. *The Times*, 12 September 1921.
7. Antony Lambton, *The Mountbattens* (Constable, 1989), p. 42 and *passim*.
8. VMH memoirs, p. 58 [HL].
9. Prince von Bülow, *Memoirs 1849–1897*, (Putnam, 1931), pp. 603–4.
10. *Dictionary of National Biography 1912–1921*, entry by T. M., p. 394.
11. PL memoirs, p. 59 [HL] (copy specially bound for Queen Louise of Sweden by Lord Mountbatten).
12. PL memoirs, p. 74 [HL].
13. PL memoirs, p. 149.
14. MtB office file note on Lillie Langtry affair [MB, T116 – HL].
15. PL memoirs, p. 235 [HL].
16. Copy of baptismal record, no. 266, church Marboeuf, Paris, dated 20 June 1881. Parents' names listed as not known [MB, K166a – HL].
17. PL memoirs, p. 308 [HL].
18. VMH memoirs, p. 73 [HL].
19. Ibid.
20. Michaela Reid, *Ask Sir James* (Hodder & Stoughton, 1987), p. 64.

3. *Early Days*

1. *The Times*, 20 March 1885.
2. Empress Frederick to QV, 27 February 1885 [RA VIC/Z 37/61].
3. QV journal, 21 March 1885 [RA VIC/QVJ].
4. QV to VMH, in the train between Dijon and Chalon, 1 April 1885 [RA VIC/Add U 173/110].
5. Sir George Buchanan, *My Mission to Russia and Other Diplomatic Memories* (Cassell, 1923), p. 26.
6. David Duff, *Hessian Tapestry* (Frederick Muller, 1967), p. 197.
7. Norman Rich and M. H. Fisher (eds), *The Holstein Papers, Volume II – Diaries* (Cambridge University Press, 1957), p. 131.
8. Meriel Buchanan, *Diplomacy and Foreign Courts* (Hutchinson, 1923), p. 18.
9. VMH to GMH, 24 April 1921 [MB Y27 – HL].
10. Grand Duchess Serge of Russia to QV, 3 March 1885 [RA Z 88/73].

11. Baroness Sophie Buxhoeveden, *The Life & Tragedy of Alexandra Feodorovna* (Longman, 1930), p. 19.
12. Meriel Buchanan, *op.cit.*, p. 20.
13. QV journal, 25 April 1885 [RA/VIC/QVJ].
14. PL to Hon. Francis Spring-Rice, Sennicotts, 23 June 1885, quoted in Mark Kerr, *Prince Louis of Battenberg* (Longman, 1934), pp. 108–9.
15. QV to VMH, Osborne, 21 August 1885 [RA VIC/Add U 173/117].
16. VMH to QV, Osborne, 22 August 1885 [RA VIC/Add U 166/13].
17. VMH memoirs, p. 84 [HL].
18. VMH memoirs, Chapter 9 [HL].
19. The Princess Royal to author, BP, 24 March 1999.
20. G. K. A. Bell, *Randall Davidson* (Oxford University Press, 1938), pp. 77–8.
21. VMH memoirs, Chapter 9 [HL].
22. See Michaela Reid, *Ask Sir James* (Hodder & Stoughton, 1987), pp. 83–4.
23. VMH to QV, [Sennicotts, Chichester], 9 June 1885 [RA VIC/U 166/10].
24. QV journal, 11 July 1885 [RA VIC/QVJ].
25. VMH to QV, Darmstadt, 17 November 1885 [RA VIC/Add U 166/18].
26. VMH to QV, [Darmstadt], 25 February 1886 [RA VIC/Add U 166/21].
27. VMH to QV, Darmstadt, 20 February 1886 [RA VIC/Add U 166/20].
28. VMH to QV, [Darmstadt], 25 February 1886 [RA VIC/Add U 166/21].
29. VMH memoirs, p. 88 [HL].
30. VMH memoirs, p. 107 [HL].
31. VMH memoirs, Chapter 9 [HL].
32. VMH to QV, [Darmstadt], 7 January 1887 [RA VIC/Add U 166/29].
33. VMH to QV, Darmstadt, 9 March 1889 [RA VIC/Add U 166–58].
34. VMH to QV, Heiligenberg, 21 May 1889 [RA VIC/Add U 166–59].
35. VMH memoirs, p. 149 [HL].
36. Prince Tomislav of Yugoslavia to author, London, 16 March 1998.
37. Princess Eugénie of Greece to author, St Cloud, 18 February 1980.
38. VMH to Grand Duke of Hesse, 29 March 1893 [MB/T107 – HL].
39. *Hansard's Parliamentary Debates*, Vol. CCCXVIII (Cornelius

Buck, 1887), 1 and 2 August 1887, pp. 720 and 924.

40. VMH to QV, San Antonio Palace, 2 November 1887 [RA Add U 166–41].

4. *Growing Up*

1. VMH to QV, Darmstadt, 22 December 1888 [RA VIC/Add U 166–55].
2. QV to VMH, Osborne, 29 December 1888 [RA VIC/Add U173/146].
3. QV to VMH, Windsor Castle, 21 February 1888 [RA VIC/Add U173/139].
4. VMH to QV, Heiligenberg, 3 August 1889 [RA VIC/Add U 166/60].
5. VMH memoirs, p. 154 [HL].
6. VMH to QV, Heiligenberg, 11 August 1889 [RA VIC/Add U 166/61].
7. VMH to QV, Darmstadt, 14 October 1889 [RA VIC/Add U 166/62].
8. VMH memoirs, p. 123 [HL].
9. QV Journal, 31 March 1895 [RA VIC/QVJ].
10. Princess Marie zu Erbach-Schönberg, *Reminiscences* (George Allen & Unwin, 1925), p. 270.
11. VMH to QV, Darmstadt, 9 April 1890 [RA VIC/Add U 166/67].
12. Empress Frederick of Germany to QV, 19 August 1891 [RA VIC/Z51/letter 13].
13. Arthur S. Gould Lee, *The Empress Frederick Writes to Sophie* (Faber & Faber, 1955), p. 92.
14. Queen Alexandra of Yugoslavia, *Prince Philip: A Family Memoir* (Hodder & Stoughton, 1959), p. 27.
15. VMH to QV, Darmstadt, 21 February 1892 [RA VIC/Add U 166/82].
16. *The Times*, 14 March 1892.
17. Princess Marie zu Erbach-Schönberg, *op.cit.*, pp. 170–71.
18. Arthur S. Gould Lee, *op.cit.*, p. 110.
19. PL to MtB [MB/I 170–HL].
20. Queen Marie of Roumania, *My Life*, Vol. 1 (Cassell, 1934), p. 6.
21. VMH memoirs, p. 107 [HL].
22. Hector Bolitho, *A Biographer's Notebook* (Longman, 1950), p. 44.
23. Sophie Hahn diary, 21 June 1892 [Hesse State Archives, Darmstadt/copy at BP].
24. VMH to QV, Jugenheim, 26 July 1892 [RA VIC/Add U 166/86].
25. Sophie Hahn diary, 30 July 1892 [BP].
26. VMH memoirs, pp. 143–6 [HL].

27. Sophie Hahn diary, 30 July 1892 [BP].
28. VMH memoirs, pp. 143–6 [HL].
29. Meriel Buchanan, *Queen Victoria's Relations* (Cassell, 1954), p. 172.
30. Meriel Buchanan, *op.cit.*, p. 173.
31. QV to Duke of York, Balmoral, 26 May 1893 [RA GV AA 10 – letter J3].
32. James Pope-Hennessy, *Queen Mary* (George Allen & Unwin, 1959), p. 260 [Hessische Hausstiftung Archives].
33. QV Journal, 8 July 1893 [RA VIC/QVJ].
34. VMH to QV, London, 14 October 1893 [RA VIC/Add U 166/95].
35. VMH memoirs, p. 149 [HL].
36. QV Journal, 10 February 1894 [RA VIC/QVJ].
37. VMH memoirs, p. 151 [HL].
38. Andrei Maylunas and Sergei Mironenko, *A Lifelong Passion* (Weidenfeld & Nicolson, 1996), pp. 73–4.
39. VMH memoirs, p. 160 [HL].
40. QV to VMH, Balmoral, 18 October 1895 [RA VIC/Add U 173/198].
41. Empress Frederick to Crown Princess Sophie of Greece [undated, but September 1896], quoted in Arthur S. Gould Lee, *op.cit.*, p. 233.

5. *Alice with Queen Victoria*

1. QV Journal, 11 March 1896 [RA VIC/QVJ].
2. QV Journal, 12 March 1897 [RA VIC/QVJ].
3. VMH memoirs, p. 180 [HL].
4. PL to NK, Halifax, Nova Scotia, 23 September 1905 [MB1/T72 – HL].
5. PL to NK, KP, 25 January 1915 [MB1/T72 – HL].
6. Meriel Buchanan, *Queen Victoria's Relations* (Cassell, 1954), p. 174.
7. VMH to QV, [London], 15 October 1899 [RA VIC/Add U 166/144].
8. Louise to MtB, Sofiero, 16 June 1952 [BA].
9. QV Journal, 25 June 1900 [RA VIC/QVJ].
10. Margit Fjellman, *Louise Mountbatten, Queen of Sweden* (Allen & Unwin, 1968), p. 73.
11. QV Journal, 26 June 1900 [RA VIC/QVJ].
12. QV Journal, 17 July 1900 [RA VIC/QVJ].
13. J. G. Lockhart, *Cosmo Gordon Lang* (Hodder & Stoughton, 1949), pp. 139–140.
14. Ibid.

6. Falling in Love

1. Alice to Fräulein C. von Riedesel zu Eisenach, London, 3 February 1901 [Princess George of Hanover].
2. VMH memoirs, p. 208 [HL].
3. Lord Carisbrooke, 27 July 1949 [private source].
4. VMH memoirs, p. 212 [HL].
5. The Prince of Wales to author, Sandringham, 24 March 1999.
6. VMH memoirs, p. 216 [HL].
7. Meriel Buchanan, *Queen Victoria's Relations* (Cassell, 1954), p. 175.
8. VMH to NK, 23 July 1902 [BA].
9. Tsarina of Russia to VMH, 16 August 1902, quoted in Sophie Buxhoeveden, *The Life & Tragedy of Alexandra Feodorovna* (Longman, 1930), p. 99.
10. J. E. C. Bodley, *The Coronation of Edward the Seventh* (Methuen, 1903), pp. 248–9.
11. Meriel Buchanan, *op. cit.*
12. HRH Prince Andrew of Greece, *Towards Disaster* (John Murray, 1930), Preface by Alice, Princess Andrew of Greece, p. v.
13. Alice to Fräulein C. von Riedesel zu Eisenach, Konigliches Schloss, Kiel, 1 January 1903 [Princess George of Hanover].
14. Alice to Fraulein C. von Riedesel zu Eisenach, 70 Cadogan Square, London, 4 February 1903 [Princess George of Hanover].
15. Edward VII to Grand Duke of Hesse, BP, 11 March 1903 [BA].
16. Alice to Fräulein C. von Riedesel zu Eisenach, 70 Cadogan Square, London, 11 April 1903 [Princess George of Hanover].
17. VMH to NK, 70 Cadogan Square, London, 6 April 1903 [BA].
18. *The Times*, 16 May 1903.
19. Grand Duchess of Mecklenburg-Strelitz to QM (Princess of Wales), Strelitz, 14 May 1903 [RA GV/CC/30/35].
20. Grand Duchess of Mecklenburg-Strelitz to QM (Princess of Wales), Strelitz, 20 May 1903 [RA GV/CC/30/36].
21. VMH to NK, Sopwell, 16 July 1903 [BA].
22. Alice to Fräulein C. von Riedesel zu Eisenach, Jugenheim, 7 August 1903 [Princess George of Hanover].
23. Ibid.

7. The Wedding

1. Grand Duchess of Mecklenburg-Strelitz to QM (Princess of Wales), Strelitz, 8 October 1903 [RA GV/CC/30/58].

2. Mark Kerr, *Land, Sea and Air* (Longman, 1927), pp. 129–30.
3. Princess Marie zu Erbach-Schönberg, *Reminiscences* (George Allen & Unwin, 1925), p. 293.
4. Duke of Teck to Duchess of Teck, Palais Darmstadt, 5 October 1903 [RA GV/CC/50/691].
5. Princess Marie zu Erbach-Schönberg, *op. cit.*, p. 294.
6. Mark Kerr, *op.cit.*, pp. 131–2.
7. VMH memoirs, p. 233 [HL].
8. QM to Grand Duchess of Mecklenburg-Strelitz, Frogmore, 23 June 1907 [RA GV/CC/24/84].

8. The Greek Royal Family

1. Charles des Graz to Marquess of Lansdowne, Athens, 7 January 1904 [FO 32 751 1904, Consular – PRO].
2. Lincoln MacVeagh note re death of Prince Christopher, to Secretary of State, Washington, 25 January 1940 [Political Southern Greece FO 371/1946 – 58845 – PRO].
3. Prince von Bülow, *Memoirs 1849–1897* (Putnam, 1931), p. 423.
4. Captain Walter Christmas, *King George of Greece* (Eveleigh Nash, 1914), p. 66.
5. Princess Eugénie of Greece to author, St Cloud, 18 February 1980.
6. Prince von Bülow, *op. cit.*, pp. 423–4.
7. QV to Empress Frederick of Germany, 9 April 1888, quoted in Hannah Pakula, *An Uncommon Woman* (Weidenfeld & Nicolson, 1996), p. 519.
8. Prince Michael of Greece, *The Royal House of Greece* (Weidenfeld & Nicolson, 1990), p. 9.
9. Princess George of Hanover to author, BP, 20 May 1997.
10. HRH Prince Nicholas of Greece, *My Fifty Years* (Hutchinson, 1926), p. 33.
11. Lady Pamela Hicks to author, London, 27 July 1999.
12. Alastair Forbes to author, 5 April 1996.
13. Prince Francis of Teck to Prince of Wales, Athens, 15 May 1904 [RA GV/CC 52/379].
14. George Criticos, *George of the Ritz* (Heinemann, 1959), pp. 8 and 9.
15. VMH Memoirs, p. 235 [HL].
16. VMH to NK, Moscow, 2 March 1905 [BA].

17. VMH Memoirs, p. 241 [HL].
18. PL to Louise, HMS *Drake*, 9 June 1905 [MB/T90 – HL].
19. VMH Memoirs, pp. 243–4 [HL].
20. Louise to PL, Heiligenberg, 29 August 1905 [BA].
21. HRH Prince Andrew of Greece, *Towards Disaster* (John Murray, 1930), Preface by Alice, Princess Andrew of Greece, p. v.
22. Alice to Fräulein C. von Riedesel zu Eisenach, Tatoï, 20 September 1906 [Princess George of Hanover].
23. Referred to in letter of VMH to NK, Wolfsgarten, 28 August 1907 [BA].
24. Ibid. (*Acropolis*, 14 February 1907).
25. Ibid. (*Chronos*, 15 February 1907).
26. Sir Francis Elliot to Sir Edward Grey, Athens, 4 March 1907 [Greece FO 286/507 1907 – PRO].
27. Ibid.

9. Political Intrigue

1. QM to Grand Duchess of Mecklenburg-Strelitz, Frogmore, 23 June 1907 [RA GV/CC/24/84].
2. Prince Philip to author, December 1999.
3. VMH to GMH, Heiligenberg, 9 July 1907 [MB/Y27 – HL].
4. *Dictionary of National Biography, 1931–1940*, entry by Herbert B. Grimsditch, p. 526.
5. Major Gerald Green to author, London, 21 August 1996.
6. Celia Bertin, *Marie Bonaparte* (Harcourt Brace Jovanovich, New York, 1982), p. 92.
7. Celia Bertin, *op.cit.*, p. 90.
8. Sir Francis Elliot to Sir Edward Grey, Athens, 13 December 1907, supplemented by Elliot to Sir Charles Hardinge, Athens, 13 December 1907 [Greece FO 286/507 1907 – PRO].
9. Elliot to Hardinge, Athens, 13 December 1907 [Greece FO 286/507 1907 – PRO].
10. Hardinge to Elliot, [London], 25 December 1907 [Greece FO 286/507 1907 – PRO].
11. NK diary, 2 June 1908 [BA].
12. NK diary, 4 June 1908 [BA].
13. Hugo Mager, *Elizabeth, Grand Duchess of Russia* (Carroll & Graf, New York, 1998), pp. 243–4.
14. NK diary, 12 June 1908 [BA].
15. Mr Young to Grey, Athens, 31 August 1908 [Greece FO 286/514 1908 – PRO].

16. Elliot to Grey, Athens (very confidential), 31 August 1909 [Greece FO 286/521 1909 – PRO].
17. Alice to Philip, Royal Palace, Athens, 24 April 1967 [Prince Philip papers, BP].
18. Quoted in VMH to NK, Heiligenberg, 10 September 1909 [BA].
19. HRH Prince Andrew of Greece, *Towards Disaster* (John Murray, 1930), Preface by Alice, Princess Andrew of Greece, pp. vi–vii.
20. Elliot to Grey, Athens, 1 September 1909 [Greece FO 286/521 – PRO].
21. Elliot to Grey, Athens, 3 June 1909 [Greece FO 286/521 1909 – PRO].
22. Elliot to Grey, Athens, 27 October 1909 [Greece FO 286/ 521 1909 – PRO].
23. Ibid.
24. Louise to NK, Heiligenberg, 17 September 1909 [BA].
25. Elliot to Grey, 27 October 1909 [Greece FO 286/521 1909 – PRO].
26. HRH Prince Andrew of Greece, *op.cit.*, p. vii.
27. Elliot to Grey, Athens, 7 January 1910 [Greece FO 286/531 – PRO].
28. Ibid.
29. Louise to NK, Dover, 31 March 1910 [BA].
30. VMH memoirs, p. 281 [HL].
31. Ibid.
32. Louise to NK, Heiligenberg, 4 August 1910 [BA].
33. Louise to NK, Heiligenberg, 30 August 1910 [BA].
34. Elliot to Grey, Athens, 13 April 1911 [Greece FO 286/542 1911 – PRO].
35. VMH to NK, Wolfsgarten, 31 August 1911 [BA].
36. Louise to MtB, Athens, 25 February 1912 [BA].
37. Tsarina of Russia to the Tsar of Russia, 3 April 1916, quoted in *Letters of the Tsaritsa to the Tsar 1914–1916* (Duckworth, 1923), p. 315.
38. Compton Mackenzie, *First Athenian Memories* (Cassell, 1931), p. 160.

10. The First Balkan War

1. Alice to VMH, Servia, Macedonia, 26 October 1912 [RA VIC/Add A 17/1129].
2. Ibid.
3. Ibid.
4. Ibid.
5. Ibid.
6. Alice to VMH, Verria, 2

November 1912 [RA VIC/Add A/17/1130].
7. Ibid.
8. Ibid.
9. GMH to VMH, Berehaven, 11 November 1912 [MB/Y8 – HL].
10. Letter from Schwester Anna, of the Alice Hospital, Darmstadt, from Elassona, 18 November 1912 [Hesse State Archives, Darmstadt].
11. NK diary, 24 October 1912 [BA].
12. NK to VMH, *Amphitrite*, Katerina, 13 November 1912 [BP].
13. NK to VMH, Hadji Lazaro, Salonika, 15 November 1912 [BP].
14. Ibid.
15. NK to VMH, Royal Palace, Athens, 1 December 1912 [BP].
16. NK to VMH, Royal Palace, Athens, 3 January 1913 [BP].
17. NK to VMH, Royal Palace, Athens, 31 December 1912 [BP].
18. NK to VMH, Philippiada, 25 January 1913 [BP].
19. NK to VMH, Jannina, 9 March 1913 [BP].
20. Alice to Grand Duchess Eleonore of Hesse, Corfu, 5 October 1914 [Hesse State Archives, Darmstadt].
21. *The Times*, 8 November 1913.

11. The Murder of King George

1. Sir Francis Elliot to Sir Edward Grey (copied to Queen Alexandra), Athens, 1 April 1913 [Greece FO 285/558 1913 – PRO].
2. Elliot to Grey (copied to Queen Alexandra), Athens, 1 April 1913 [Greece FO 286/558 1913 – PRO].
3. *The Times*, 14 April 1913.
4. NK to VMH, Salonika, 18 December 1912 [Prince Philip Papers, BP].
5. NK to VMH, Salonika, 10 January 1913 [Prince Philip Papers, BP].
6. VMH to NK, Mall House, London, 2 February 1913 [BA].
7. NK to VMH, Philippiada, 26 February 1913 [BP].
8. Elliot to Grey (copied to Queen Alexandra), Athens, 1 April 1913 [Greece FO 286/558 1913 – PRO].
9. NK to VMH, Salonika, 22 December 1912 [BP].
10. VMH to NK, Mall House, London, 27 December 1912 [BA].
11. VMH Memoirs, p. 292 [HL].
12. HRH Prince Andrew of Greece, *Towards Disaster* (John Murray,

1930), Preface by Alice, Princess Andrew of Greece, p.vii.
13. VMH to NK, Mon Repos, Corfu, 21 June 1914 [BA].
14. VMH to NK, Mon Repos, Corfu, 26 June 1914 [BA].
15. Ibid.

12. *The First World War*

1. Alice to Grand Duchess Eleonore of Hesse, Corfu, 5 October 1914 [Hesse State Archives, Darmstadt].
2. Louise to Alice, Mall House, London, 22 September 1914, quoted by Alice, 5 October 1914 [Hesse State Archives, Darmstadt].
3. Tsarina of Russia to Alice, Tsarskoe Selo, 14 August 1914, quoted by Alice, 5 October 1914 [Hesse State Archives, Darmstadt].
4. Alice to Grand Duchess Eleonore of Hesse, 5 October 1914 [Hesse State Archives, Darmstadt].
5. PL to NK, Kent House, Isle of Wight, 20 November 1914 [MB1/T72 – HL].
6. Oliver, Viscount Esher (ed.), *Journals and Letters of Viscount Esher, Vol. 3 (1910–1915)* (Ivor Nicholson & Watson, 1938), p. 61.
7. VMH to NK, Mall House, London, 30 October 1914 [BA].
8. VMH to NK, Kent House, Isle of Wight, 22 August 1916 [BA].
9. VMH to NK, Hotel Rubens, London, 12 May 1915 [BA].
10. Grand Duke of Hesse to Tsarina of Russia, quoted in VMH to NK, 12 May 1915 [BA].
11. VMH to NK, Kent House, Isle of Wight, 9 April 1916 [BA].
12. PL to Louise, [undated, but July 1916], [MB/T90 – HL].
13. Alice to Grand Duchess Eleonore of Hesse, Athens, 2 May 1915 [Hesse State Archives, Darmstadt].
14. VMH to NK, 17 January 1915 [BA].
15. VMH to NK, Grand Hotel, Nevers, 25 September 1915 [BA].
16. Ibid.
17. Obituary of Alexander Stuart-Hill, *The Times*, 24 February 1948.
18. Alice to Grand Duchess Eleonore of Hesse, Athens, 18 September 1915 [Hesse State Archives, Darmstadt].
19. Lord Granard to KGV, Salonika, 29 October 1915 [RA PS/GV/Q 832/86].
20. Ibid.
21. Alice to MtB, Salonika, 5 January 1916 [BA].
22. Quoted in VMH to NK, Kent House, Isle of Wight, 3 May 1916 [BA].

23. *The Times*, 7 July 1916.
24. Meriel Buchanan, *Queen Victoria's Relations* (Cassell, 1954), p. 183.
25. PL to Louise, Kent House, Isle of Wight, 29 August 1916 [MB/T90 – HL].
26. Louise to NK, Nevers, 23 October 1916 [BA].
27. Sir Francis Elliot to Sir Edward Grey, Athens, 16 September 1916 [Greece – FO 286/586 1916 – PRO].
28. Elliot to Grey, Athens (urgent), 1 December 1916 [Greece – FO 286/586 1916 – PRO].
29. Meriel Buchanan, *op.cit.*, p. 183.
30. Elliot to A. J. Balfour, Athens (private and secret), 29 April 1917 [Greece – FO 286/602 – PRO].
31. Compton Mackenzie, *First Athenian Memories* (Cassell, 1931), p. 161.
32. Elliot to Balfour, Athens, 16 June 1917 [Greece – FO 286/632 – PRO].

13. The First Exile

1. Dayrell Crackanthorpe to FO, [Athens], 20 June 1917 [Greece – FO 286/633 – PRO].
2. PL to Louise, Cambridge, 23 June 1917 [MB/T90 – HL].
3. Earl Granville to A. J. Balfour, Athens, 30 October 1917 [Greece – FO 286/633 – PRO].
4. Alice to Grand Duchess Eleonore of Hesse, Zurich, 14 December 1917 [Hesse State Archives, Darmstadt].
5. VMH to NK, Kent House, Isle of Wight, 8 September 1917 [BA].
6. VMH to NK, Kent House, Isle of Wight, 20 September 1917 [BA].
7. VMH to NK, Kent House, Isle of Wight, 7 June 1917 [BA].
8. PL to Louise, Kent House, Isle of Wight, 6 June 1917 [MB/T90 – HL].
9. Ibid.
10. Alice to Grand Duchess Eleonore of Hesse, Zurich, 14 December 1917 [Hesse State Archives, Darmstadt].
11. VMH to NK, Kent House, Isle of Wight, 8 September 1917 [BA].
12. Louise to NK, Kent House, Isle of Wight, 14 July 1917 [BA].
13. Ibid.
14. Alice to Grand Duchess Eleonore of Hesse, Lucerne, 8 December 1918 [Hesse State Archives, Darmstadt].
15. Alice to Grand Duchess Eleonore of Hesse, Lucerne, 21 May 1919 [Hesse State Archives, Darmstadt].

16. Will of Alexander Stuart-Hill, proven 1948 [Somerset House].
17. Alice to Grand Duchess Eleonore of Hesse, Zurich, 14 December 1917 [Hesse State Archives, Darmstadt].
18. VMH to NK, Kent House, Isle of Wight, 16 April 1916 [BA].
19. Alice to Grand Duchess Eleonore of Hesse, Grand Hotel, Zurich, 14 December 1917 [Hesse State Archives, Darmstadt].
20. Ibid.
21. FO note [RA – GeoV/M1226].
22. Lord Hardinge to Lord Stamfordham, FO, London, 3 December 1917 [RA PS/GV/M 1226/1].
23. Granville to BP, Athens, 17 December 1917 [RA PS/GV/P 1204/5].
24. VMH to NK, Kent House, Isle of Wight, 3 January 1917 [BA].
25. VMH to NK, Kent House, Isle of Wight, 18 March 1917 [BA].
26. Alice to Grand Duke of Hesse, Lucerne, 31 July 1918 [Hesse State Archives, Darmstadt].
27. *The Times*, 5 December 1918.
28. VMH to NK, Kent House, Isle of Wight, 10 November 1918 [BA].
29. General I. S. Smolin, *Alapalevsk Tragedy* [Hoover Institute on War, Revolution and Peace, Stanford University, California, stored in Russian Revolution Institute, eighteenth floor/copy in BA].
30. Alice to Grand Duchess Eleonore of Hesse, Lucerne, 6 November 1918 [Hesse State Archives, Darmstadt].
31. Obituary of Grand Duke Ernst Ludwig of Hesse, *The Times*, 22 October 1937.
32. *The Times*, 11 February 1919.
33. *The Times*, 10 July 1919.
34. *The Times*, 4 August 1919.
35. *The Times*, 6 August 1919.

14. Veering towards Religion

1. Édouard Schuré, *The Great Initiates* (William Rider, 1922), p. x.
2. Édouard Schuré, *op.cit.*, pp. x–xi.
3. Lincoln MacVeagh to Secretary of State, Washington, 25 January 1940 [Political Southern Greece – FO 371/1946 – 58845 – PRO].
4. Louise to NK, Sofiero, 25 August 1929 [BA].
5. VMH statement, Kreuzlingen, 8 May 1930 [case history UT].
6. Margarita to MtB, Lucerne, 7 June 1919 [BA].
7. British Consul, Geneva to FO, 23 May 1920 [Greece – FO 286/723 1920 – PRO].

8. Louise to NK, Thun, 5 July 1919 [BA].
9. Alice to Grand Duchess Eleonore of Hesse, Lucerne, 1 July 1919 [Hesse State Archives, Darmstadt].
10. Louise to NK, Vulpera, 8 August 1919 [BA].
11. Ibid.
12. VMH to NK, Pension Villa Maria, Vulpera, 15 August 1919 [BA].
13. Earl Granville to A. J. Balfour, [Athens], 7 November 1917 [Greece – FO 286/658 – PRO].
14. Balfour to Granville, London, 28 April 1918 [Greece – FO 286/633 – PRO].
15. Granville to Balfour, Athens, 8 May 1918 [Greece – FO 286/633 – PRO].
16. Ibid.
17. *The Times*, 29 May 1920.
18. Memorandum from the Greek Minister, London, 7 September 1920 [Political Central Balkans FO 371/1920 4681 – PRO].
19. Howard Kennard, Rome, telegram to FO, 26 September 1920 [Political Central Balkans FO 371/1920 4681 – PRO].
20. Kennard to Lord Curzon, Rome, 29 September 1920 [Political Central Balkans FO 371/1920 4681 – PRO].
21. Commander N. W. Diggle, naval attaché, to HBM Chargé d'Affaires, British Embassy, Rome, 28 September 1920 [Political Central Balkans FO 371/1920 4681 – PRO].
22. *The Times*, 18 October 1920.
23. *The Times*, 1 November 1920.
24. *The Times*, 19 November 1920.
25. George Raymond to Granville, Corfu, 22 November 1920 [Greece FO 286/732 – 1920 – PRO].
26. HRH Prince Andrew of Greece, *Towards Disaster* (John Murray, 1930), Preface by Alice, Princess Andrew of Greece, p.ix.
27. Granville to Curzon, Athens, 23 November 1920 [Greece – FO 286/732 1920 – PRO].
28. Curzon to Granville, 2 December 1920 [Greece – FO 286/732 1920 – PRO].
29. *The Times*, 20 December 1920.

15. *The Birth of Prince Philip*

1. VMH to NK, Rome, 28 February 1921 [BA].
2. HRH Prince Andrew of Greece, *Towards Disaster* (John Murray, 1930), p. 21.
3. Ibid.
4. Queen Alexandra of Yugoslavia, *Prince Philip: A Family Portrait* (Hodder & Stoughton, 1959), p. 29.

5. VMH to GMH, Fishponds, Netley, 24 April 1921 [MB/Y27 – HL].
6. Alice to Grand Duchess Eleonore of Hesse, Corfu, 3 July 1921 [Hesse State Archives, Darmstadt].
7. VMH to NK, Fishponds, Netley, 14 June 1921 [BA].
8. Alice to Grand Duchess Eleonore of Hesse, [Corfu], 3 July 1921 [Hesse State Archives, Darmstadt].
9. Alice to Grand Duchess Eleonore of Hesse, Fishponds, Netley, 28 September 1921 [Hesse State Archives, Darmstadt].
10. Alan Clark, *A Good Innings* (John Murray, 1974), p. 212.
11. *The Times*, 12 September 1921.
12. KGV to VMH, Balmoral, 13 September 1921 [BA].
13. VMH to Father Seraphim, [undated, but December 1922], [BA].
14. HRH Prince Andrew of Greece, *op.cit.*, p. x.
15. Winston S. Churchill, *The World Crisis, Vol. 5, The Aftermath* (Thornton Butterworth, 1929), p. 379.
16. Andrea to Ionnis Metaxas, 1 January 1922, quoted in Michael Llewellyn Smith, *Ionian Vision* (Allen Lane, 1973), p. 245.
17. Andrea to Metaxas, 1 January 1922, quoted in Michael Llewellyn Smith, *op.cit.*, p. 246.
18. HRH Prince Andrew of Greece, *op.cit.*, p.1.
19. HRH Prince Andrew of Greece, *op.cit.*, p.4.
20. MtB to NK, New Delhi, 21 February 1922 [MB1/A2-HL].
21. VMH to NK, KP, 20 February 1922 [BA].
22. VMH to NK, Rome, 28 February 1922 [BA].
23. Margarita to MtB, Mon Repos, Corfu, 5 April 1922 [BA].
24. Quoted in Louise to NK, Mon Repos, Corfu, 6 April 1922 [BA].
25. VMH to NK, Mon Repos, Corfu, 20 March 1922 [BA].
26. Ibid.
27. VMH to GMH, Mon Repos, Corfu, 7 May 1922 [MB/Y27 – HL].
28. Louise to NK, Mon Repos, Corfu, 21 March 1922 [BA].
29. Louise to NK, Mon Repos, Corfu, 6 April 1922 [BA].
30. MtB to NK, 22 March 1922 [MB1/A2 – HL].
31. Louise to NK, 8 September 1922 [BA].
32. Ibid.

16. The Greeks in Defeat

1. Harold Nicolson, *Peacemaking 1919* (Constable, 1933), p. 173.
2. Francis Lindley to Lord Balfour, 27 June 1922 [Greece FO 371/7585 – PRO].
3. C. H. Bentinck, Athens, to Lord Curzon, 6 September 1922 [Greece FO 371/7585 – PRO].
4. Francis Lindley, telegram 489 to FO, 26 September 1922 [Greece FO 371/7585 – PRO].
5. Harold Nicolson, file note on the new Greek King, no. 209, 2 October 1922 [Greece FO 371/7585 – PRO].
6. Lindley, telegram 517 to FO, 4.00 p.m., 29 September 1922 [Greece FO 371/7585 – PRO].
7. VMH to MtB, KP, 25 October 1922 [BA].
8. VMH to NK, KP, 28 October 1922 [BA].
9. Alice to VMH, Corfu, [*c.* 9 November 1922], passed on to KGV [RA PS/GV/M 1823/2].
10. *The Times*, 28 October 1922.
11. George Raymond to Private Secretary of State for Foreign Affairs, from Corfu, 27 October 1922 [Greece FO 371/5786 – PRO].
12. Lindley, telegram 623 to FO, 2.00 p.m., Athens, 27 October 1922 [Greece FO 371/5786 – PRO].
13. Lindley, report 635, 3 November 1922 [Greece FO 371/5786 – File 71 – PRO].
14. Ibid.
15. *Memoirs of HRH Prince Christopher of Greece* (Hurst & Blackett, 1938), p. 174.
16. Ibid.
17. Sir Eyre Crowe to Lindley, telegram, 7.00 p.m., FO, London, 22 November 1922, (private) [RA PS/GV/M 1823/8].
18. Lindley to Crowe, (private), 10.00 p.m., 23 November 1922, [RA PS/GV/M 1823/10].
19. H. G. Mayes to R. P. M. Gower, Junior Naval and Military Club, London 20 November 1922 [Greece FO 371/5787/2 – File 23 – PRO].
20. Lindley to London, telegram, 9.00 p.m., 26 November 1922 [Greece FO 371/5787/2 – File 23 – PRO].
21. Michael Llewellyn Smith, *Ionian Vision* (Allen Lane, 1973), p. 328.
22. Hardinge to Curzon, no. 631, France, 29 November 1922 [Greece FO 371/5787/2 – File 23 – PRO].
23. Lindley, telegram, 8.30 p.m., 28 November 1922 [RA PS/GV/M 1823/15].

24. Harold Nicolson, Report in FO, 13 September 1922 [Greece FO 371/7585–109].
25. Compton Mackenzie, *First Athenian Memories* (Cassell, 1931), pp. 301–2.
26. Curzon to Crowe, 1.30 a.m., 29 November 1922 [RA Geo V M 1823/17].
27. Ibid.
28. *Daily Express*, 29 December 1922.
29. Bentinck to Crowe (most urgent, private and most secret), Athens, 29 November 1922 [RA PS/GV/M 1823/23].
30. Princess Helen of Romania to Prince Carol of Romania, quoted in Prince Paul of Hohenzollern-Romania, *King Carol II* (Methuen, 1988), pp. 80–81.
31. Queen Olga of Greece to KGV, Paris, 1 December 1922 [RA PS/GV/M 1823/37].
32. Bentinck to Curzon, Athens, telegram, 11.45 a.m., 3 December 1922 [RA PS/GV/M 1823/41].
33. Bentinck to Curzon, 4 December 1922 [RA PS/GV/M 1823/44].
34. Ibid.
35. Margarita to MtB, Schloss Langenburg, 13 October 1977 [BA].

17. *'Alice's Royalist Plots'*

1. *New York Times*, 21 March 1923.
2. Colonel Waterhouse to Lord Stamfordham, record of telephone message from Downing Street, 4 December 1922 [RA PS/GV/M 1823/45].
3. Miles Lampson file note, FO, London, 7 December 1922 [Political Greece – File 13 1922].
4. Stamfordham to KGV, BP, 7.30 p.m., 7 December 1922 [RA PS/GV/M 1823/53].
5. VMH to Alice, telegram, quoted in VMH to Stamfordham, KP, 4 December 1922 [RA PS/GV/M 1823/48].
6. VMH to Stamfordham, KP, 7 December 1922 [RA PS/GV/M 1823/54].
7. Ibid.
8. Sir Eyre Crowe to Lord Hardinge, telegram, 10.45 a.m., 8 December 1922 FO [RA PS/GV/M 1823/57].
9. Stamfordham to VMH, BP, 8 December 1922 [RA PS/GV/M 1823/56].
10. Hardinge to Crowe, British Embassy, Paris, 8 December 1922 [RA PS/GV/M 1823/62].
11. Ibid.
12. Louise to NK, 15 December 1922 [BA].

13. KGV diary, 19 December 1922 [RA].
14. Louise to NK, KP, 20 January 1923 [BA].
15. *New York Times*, 12 January 1923.
16. Andrea to VMH, St Cloud, 29 May 1923 [BA].
17. *New York Times*, [undated but January 1923].
18. Prince Peter of Greece to *Life International* [undated, but January 1952] (in reply to an article by Jack Winocour, *Life International* 8 October 1951).
19. Princess George of Hanover to author, Wolfsgarten, 16 January 1996.
20. *Life International* [undated, but January 1952].
21. MtB to VMH, Casa Medina, Malta, 1 November 1927 [MB/M65 – HL].
22. *New York Times*, 12 January 1923.
23. *The Times*, 19 December 1923.
24. *The Times*, 20 February 1924.
25. *The Times*, 26 March 1924.
26. VMH to NK, St Cloud, 7 April 1926 [BA].
27. R. G. Leigh to Stamfordham, 2 September 1926 [RA PS/GV/M 2062/28].
28. Sir Eric Drummond, record of interview [with Princess Alice of Greece], 1 July 1927 [RA PS/GV/M 2537/2].
29. Ibid.
30. Lord Crewe to Stamfordham, British Embassy, Paris, 9 July 1927 [RA PS/GV/M 1273/62].
31. Ibid.
32. John O. Iatrides, *Ambassador MacVeagh Reports* (Princeton University Press, 1980), p. 121.
33. Alice to Drummond, Toscana Park, Gmunden, 16 September 1927 [RA PS/GV/M 2537/3].
34. Ibid.
35. Drummond to Alice, Geneva, 21 September 1927 [RA PS/GV/M 2537/4].
36. Sir Austen Chamberlain to KGV, 17 October 1927 [RA PS/GV/M 2537/1].
37. KGV to Stamfordham, BP, 19 October 1927 [RA PS/GV/M 2537/5]. (Relayed to Sir Austen Chamberlain by Stamfordham, 20 October 1927.)

18. Family Life

1. Princess George of Hanover to author, Wolfsgarten, 16 January 1996.
2. VMH to NK, KP, 26 May 1942 [BA].
3. VMH to NK, KP, 16 April 1925 [BA].
4. VMH to Princess Nicholas of Greece, [undated] 1927 [MB/N4A – HL].

5. Princess George of Hanover to author, BP, 23 November 1997.
6. Louise to NK, 5 March 1924 [BA].
7. *The Times*, 7 July 1924.
8. *The Lady*, 2 July 1925.
9. Louise to NK, [Sweden], 28 February 1927 [BA].
10. Ibid.
11. Ibid.
12. Princess George of Hanover to author, 11 December 1998.
13. Alice to MtB, 5 rue du Mont-Valérien, St Cloud, 27 June 1923 [BA].
14. Louise to NK, KP, 15 June 1923 [BA].
15. Ibid.
16. Nicky Mariano, *Forty Years With Berenson* (Hamish Hamilton, 1966), p. 87.
17. Princess George of Hanover to author, BP, 23 November 1997.
18. VMH to NK, KP, 13 June 1923 [BA].
19. Louise to NK, KP, 15 June 1923 [BA].
20. Louise to MtB, Southsea, 25 June 1923 [BA].
21. Louise to NK, St Cloud, 28 July 1923 [BA].
22. Louise to NK, KP, 22 July 1923 [BA].
23. Sir Colville Barclay to Lord Curzon, 14 December 1923 [Political Northern Sweden FO 371/9379 – 1923 – PRO].
24. Louise to NK, Ulriksdal, 10 June 1925 [BA].
25. Alice to MtB, St Cloud, 24 November 1924 [BA].
26. Alice to MtB, London, [19] November 1925 [BA].
27. Major Gerald Green to author, London, 21 August 1996.
28. Alice to MtB, St Cloud, 28 August 1924 [BA].
29. VMH to NK, KP, 20 June 1926 [BA].
30. VMH to NK, Blakeney Hotel, Norfolk, 21 August 1926 [BA].

19. Descent into Crisis

1. Record of lady-in-waiting, Kreuzlingen, 27 June 1930 [case history UT].
2. Hermann von Keyserling, *The World in the Making* (Jonathan Cape, 1927), p. 69.
3. Hermann von Keyserling, *The Travel Diary of a Philosopher, Volume 1* (Harcourt, Brace, New York, 1925), biographical note, p. 7.
4. Hermann von Keyserling, *The World in the Making, op.cit.*, p. 71.
5. Hermann von Keyserling, *The World in the Making, op.cit.*, p. 78.
6. Alice to Georgina von

Rotsmann, St Cloud, 9 October 1928 [Hesse State Archives, Darmstadt].

7. Louise to MtB, Ulriksdal, 22 September 1928 [BA].
8. Alice to Miss M. Edwards, St Cloud, 8 September 1928 [RA – Geo V AA68 – 211].
9. Alice to MtB, St Cloud, 9 October 1928 [BA].
10. VMH to GMH, 23 October 1928 [MB/Y27 – HL].
11. MtB to VMH, Casa Medina, Malta, 4 November 1928 [MB/M65 – HL].
12. B note, 27 June 1930 [case history UT].
13. Louise to NK, Sofiero, 25 August 1929 [BA].
14. Alice to Louise, November 1929, quoted in Louise to NK, Ulriksdal, 6 January 1930 [BA].
15. VMH to B, 8 May 1930 [UT].
16. Virginie Simopoulos to B, 27 June 1930 [case history UT].
17. Princess Eugénie of Greece to author, St Cloud, 18 February 1980.
18. VMH to NK, St Cloud, 2 January 1930 [misdated as 1929] [BA].
19. Louise to NK, Ulriksdal, 6 January 1930 [BA].
20. Ibid.
21. VMH to NK, St Cloud, 11 January 1930 [BA].
22. Princess Eugénie of Greece to author, St Cloud, 18 February 1980.

20. Tegel and Kreuzlingen, 1930

1. Sigmund Freud to Ernest Jones, 11 October 1928 [*Complete Correspondence of Sigmund Freud & Ernest Jones 1908–1939*, Belknap Press, 1993, p. 649].
2. Dr Ernst Simmel to B, 15 May 1930 [UT].
3. Ibid.
4. Alice to Cécile, Tegel, 17 February 1930 [Hesse State Archives, Darmstadt].
5. Alice to Cécile, St Cloud, 8 April 1930 [Hesse State Archives, Darmstadt].
6. VMH to NK, KP, 11 April 1930 [BA].
7. VMH to NK, Neue Palais, Darmstadt, 21 April 1930 [BA].
8. VMH to NK, Darmstadt, 4 May 1930 [BA].
9. Professor Wilmanns to B, Heidelberg, 5 May 1930 [case history UT].
10. VMH to NK, Darmstadt, 4 May 1930 [BA].
11. Wilmanns to Binswanger, Heidelberg, 3 May 1930 [UT].
12. Prince Philip to author, December 1999.

13. Alice to Philip, Broadlands, 29 September 1950 [BP].
14. Manfred Bosch, *Bohème am Bodensee – Literarisches Leben am See von 1900 bis 1950 (Ludwig Binswanger und das 'Belle-Vue'),* (Libelle, Switzerland, 1997), p. 402.
15. Norbert Jacques, *Skizzen und Erlebnisse*, pp. 35ff (quoted in Manfred Bosch, *op.cit.*, p. 403).
16. Alfred Döblin, *Destiny's Journey* (Paragan House, New York, 1992), p. 332.
17. Robert Faesi, *Erlebnisse, Ergebnisse* (Zurich, 1963), p. 209.
18. Joseph Roth, *The Radetsky March* (Penguin, 1995), p. 186.
19. Anton Dolin, *Ballet Go Round* (Michael Joseph, 1938), pp. 243–5.
20. Dr E. Wenger note, Kreuzlingen, May 1930 [case history UT].
21. Ibid.
22. Wilmanns to B, 5 May 1930 [case history UT].
23. B note, 8 May 1930 [case history UT].
24. B note, 15 May 1930 [case history UT].
25. Alice to Cécile, Kreuzlingen, 17 May 1930 [Hesse State Archives, Darmstadt].
26. Cécile to Alice, St Cloud, 22 May 1930 [Hesse State Archives, Darmstadt].
27. B note, 9 June 1930 [case history UT].
28. Cécile to Alice, 15 June 1930 [Hesse State Archives, Darmstadt].
29. Alice to Cécile, Kreuzlingen, 21 June 1930 [Hesse State Archives, Darmstadt].
30. B note, 25 June 1930.
31. VMH to B, Hemmelmark, 22 July 1930 [case history UT].
32. Alice, 'Recommendations for the Constitution' [case history UT].
33. B note, 26 July 1930 [case history UT].
34. Ibid.
35. Alice to Cécile, Braunwald, 20 August 1930 [Hesse State Archives, Darmstadt].
36. Schwester Lina to B, Braunwald, 23 August 1930 [case history UT].
37. Ibid.
38. B note re letter from Nurse Lina, 1 September 1930 [case history UT].
39. Ibid.
40. Ibid.
41. Alice to MtB, Grand Hotel, Lucerne, August 1930 [BA].
42. B note, 20 September 1930 [case history UT].
43. Alice to B, 18 September 1930 [case history UT].
44. Cécile to Alice, Paris, 25 November 1930 [Hesse State Archives, Darmstadt].

45. VMH to NK, Darmstadt, 18 December 1930 [BA].
46. Louise to NK, Drottingholm, 26 December 1930 [BA].
47. Ibid.

21. *Kreuzlingen, 1931*

1. B note, 21 January 1931 [case history UT].
2. VMH to GMH, Neue Palais, Darmstadt, 8 February 1931 [MB/Y27 – HL].
3. B note, 22 February 1931 [case history UT].
4. Alice to B, 23 February 1931 [case history UT].
5. B note, 4 March 1931 [case history UT].
6. Alice to B, 24 March 1931 [case history UT].
7. VMH to B, KP, 29 March 1931 [case history UT].
8. Alice to B, 30 March 1931 [case history UT].
9. Louise to NK [Sweden], 28 April 1931 [BA].
10. Alice to B, 23 May 1931 [case history UT].
11. B note, 26 May 1931 [case history UT].
12. B note, 27 May 1931 [case history UT].
13. VMH to B, KP, 29 May 1931 [case history UT].
14. B to VMH, 25 July 1931 [case history UT].
15. Louise to NK, Sofiero, 15 July 1931 [BA].
16. Louise to NK, Wolfsgarten, 19 August 1931 [BA].
17. VMH to B, KP, 5 October 1931 [case history UT].
18. Alice to VMH, 6 October 1931, quoted in VMH to B, KP, 12 October 1931 [case history UT].
19. VMH to B, KP, 12 October 1931 [case history UT].
20. Hermann von Keyserling, *The World in the Making* (Jonathan Cape, 1927), p. 69.
21. Alice to the Grand Duke of Hesse [undated] [case history UT].
22. Quoted in B to Louise, 23 November 1931 [case history UT].
23. B to Andrea, 26 November 1931 [case history UT].
24. Andrea to B, Paris, 27 November 1931 [case history UT].
25. Theodora to B, Salem, 16 December 1931 [case history UT].
26. Dr Wenger to Theodora, 18 December 1931 [case history UT].
27. Ibid.
28. B note, 19 December 1931 [case history UT].

29. B note, 20 December 1931 [case history UT].
30. Ibid.

22. *Escape*

1. B note, 9 January 1932 [case history UT].
2. B note, 31 January 1932 [case history UT].
3. B note, nurse report, 12 February 1931 [case history UT].
4. VMH to NK, Salem, 5 March 1932 [BA].
5. VMH to MtB, Darmstadt, 16 March 1932 [BA].
6. VMH to B, Darmstadt, 20 March 1932 [case history UT].
7. B note, 30 April 1932 [case history UT].
8. Dr Kr. report, 7 July 1932 [case history UT].
9. Dr Kr. report, 9 July 1932 [case history UT].
10. Ibid.
11. Dr Kr. report, 18 July 1932 [case history UT].
12. VMH to MtB, Salem, 29 July 1932 [BA].
13. B note, 3 August 1932 [case history UT].
14. Wilmanns to B, Heidelberg, 8 September 1932.
15. VMH to B, Wolfsgarten, 2 September 1932 [case history UT].
16. VMH to MtB, KP, 27 October 1932 [BA].
17. B note, 23 September 1932 [case history UT].

23. *Alice Itinerant*

1. VMH to B, KP, 19 October 1932 [case history UT].
2. VMH to NK, Rome, 5 December 1932 [BA].
3. Louise to NK, Stockholm, 8 December 1932 [BA].
4. Dr von Kaan to B, Merano, 23 December 1932 [case history UT].
5. VMH to NK, Darmstadt, 28 February 1933 [BA].
6. VMH to MtB, Darmstadt, 20 March 1933 [BA].
7. VMH to MtB, Stockholm, 11 April 1933 [BA].
8. B to VMH, Kreuzlingen, 1 May 1933 [case history UT].
9. Ibid.
10. Louise to NK, Sofiero, 19 September 1933 [BA].
11. Almuth Schmidt-Reuter to Rainer von Hessen, Cologne, 13 July 1997.
12. VMH to MtB, Fishponds, Netley, 20 September 1933 [BA].

13. Ibid.
14. VMH to MtB, KP, 21 June 1934 [BA].
15. B note, 9 July 1934 [case history UT].
16. VMH to NK, Wolfsgarten, 14 July 1934 [BA].
17. VMH to NK, Wolfsgarten, 1 June 1935 [BA].
18. VMH to MtB, KP, 5 November 1935 [BA].
19. VMH to MtB, KP, 31 December 1935 [BA].
20. VMH to NK, Hemmelmark, 5 August 1936 [BA].
21. Princess Louise, Duchess of Argyll, to VMH, KP, 28 August 1936 [BA].
22. Louise to NK, Hotel St Gellért, Gellért Sza, Budapest, 2 September 1936 [BA].
23. Ibid.
24. Official request for passport from Mayor of Breibach to Markwitz, 27 November 1936.
25. *Rheinisch-Bergischer Kalender*, 1992, p. 227.
26. *Rheinisch-Bergischer Kalender*, 1992, p. 130.
27. Quotation from Markwitz book, cited in *Rheinisch Bergischer Kalender*, 1992, pp. 230–31.
28. Alice to Cécile, Breibach, Kürten, 28 December 1936 [Hesse State Archives, Darmstadt].

24. *Philip and Andrea*

1. VMH to MtB, Neue Palais, Darmstadt, 7 April 1937 [BA].
2. VMH to NK, Darmstadt, 13 April 1937 [BA].
3. VMH to Nada Milford Haven, 18 December 1931 [MB/Y27 – HL].
4. VMH to NK, Stockholm, 6 April 1933 [BA].
5. VMH to GMH, Wolfsgarten, 18 July 1934 [MB/Y27 – HL].
6. VMH to MtB, KP, 5 November 1935 [BA].
7. VMH to MtB, KP, 12 January 1936 [BA].
8. Prince Philip to author, BP, 20 May 1997.
9. VMH to GMH, [undated, but April/May 1937] [MB/Y27 – HL].
10. Hon. Sir Patrick Ramsay to Lord Wigram, 23 May 1931 [Political Central Greece FO 371 15240 – 1931 – 87 – PRO].
11. Andrea to MtB, 1 rue Basse, Monte Carlo, 3 October 1932 [BA].
12. MtB to VMH, HMS *Daring*, Corfu, 9 July 1934 [MB/M66 – HL].
13. Hon. Sir Patrick Ramsay to Sir John Simon, 4 June 1932 [Political Central Greece FO 371 15966 – 1932 – 166 – PRO].

14. Andrea to MtB, Monaco, 3 October 1932 [BA].
15. Mrs Maurice Hare to author, Suffolk, 20 November 1999.
16. Quoted in Sydney Waterlow to Sir John Simon, from Athens to FO, 2 January 1935 [Political Southern Greece FO 371 1935 – 19504/124 – PRO].
17. Information derived from John Van der Kiste, *Kings of the Hellenes, The Greek Kings 1863–1974* (Alan Sutton, 1994), pp. 145–53.
18. David Horbury, *The Red Aunts* (*Royalty Digest*, April 1999), p. 290.
19. *The Times*, 8 July 1935.
20. Robert Bruce Lockhart, *Diaries, Volume One* (Macmillan, 1973), p. 382.
21. VMH to MtB, KP, 5 November 1935 [BA].
22. Henry Colyton, *Occasion, Chance and Change* (Michael Russell, 1993), p. 138.
23. Waterlow to Sir Robert Vansittart, from Athens to FO, 30 May 1935 [PSG FO 371 1935 19507/179 – Athens PRO].
24. Waterlow, telegram, Athens, 18 November 1935 [PSG FO 371 1935 19509/324 – PRO].
25. John O. Iatrides, *Ambassador MacVeagh Reports* (Princeton University Press, 1980), p. 62.
26. Mrs Maurice Hare to author, Suffolk, 20 November 1999.
27. Quoted in Waterlow to Anthony Eden, Athens, 27 May 1936 [PSG FO 371 1936 28389/113 – PRO].
28. Ibid.
29. Ibid.
30. R. C. S. Stanley to Major Wright, Larnaca, 26 April 1937 [PSG FO 371 1937 21142/154 – PRO].
31. Ibid.
32. Police report, Limassol, 25 April 1937 [PSG FO 371 1937 21142/161 – PRO].
33. H. R. Palmer, Government House, Cyprus, to A. J. Dawe, Colonial Office [April 1937] [PSG FO 371 1937 21142/151 – PRO].
34. Ibid.

25. *Recovery and Tragedy*

1. VMH to NK, Darmstadt, 13 April 1937 [BA].
2. Alice to Philip, [undated, but June 1937] [BP].
3. Alice to Cécile, Kirchberg [undated, but June 1937] [Hesse State Archives, Darmstadt].
4. Alice to Cécile, Kirchberg

[second letter – undated, but June 1937] [Hesse State Archives, Darmstadt].

5. Cécile to VMH, Wolfsgarten, 16 July 1937 [BA].
6. B note, 29 July 1937 [case history UT].
7. VMH to NK, Langenburg, 5 August 1937 [BA].
8. VMH to Philip, KP, 29 October 1937 [BP].
9. Cécile to MtB, Wolfsgarten, 12 November 1937 [BA].
10. *The Times*, 17 November 1937.
11. Herausgegeben von Eckhart G. Franz und Karl-Eugen Schlapp. *Margaret, Prinzessin von Hessen und bei Rhein* (Verlag H. L. Schlapp, Darmstadt, 1997), p. 9.
12. Louise to NK, Ulriksdal, 18 November 1937 [BA].
13. Rainer von Hessen to author, 30 December 1998.
14. Louise to NK, 22 November 1937 [BA].
15. Andrea to VMH, The Travellers Club, Paris, 11 December 1937 [BA].
16. QM to VMH, Marlborough House, 21 November 1937 [BA].
17. VMH to B, KP, 7 December 1937 [case history UT].
18. B note, 10 March 1947 [case history UT].

26. Separate Ways

1. Andrea to VMH, The Travellers Club, Paris, 11 December 1937 [BA].
2. Louise to NK, 1 December 1937 [BA].
3. Alice to MtB, Sweden, 13 December 1937 [BA].
4. E. E. P. Tisdall, *Royal Destiny* (Stanley Paul, 1955), p. 210.
5. MtB to VMH, Brook House, London, 5 April 1938 [MB/ M66-HL]
6. VMH to NK, KP, 21 April 1938 [BA].
7. Ibid.
8. Prince Alexander Romanoff to author, 15 May 1997.
9. Alice to Frau Hedwig Markwitz, Plaxtol, 3 August 1938 [Stockmann papers, Cologne].

27. Return to Greece

1. VMH to NK, Sofiero, 28 August 1938 [BA].
2. Alice to Philip, KP, 5 December 1938 [BP].
3. Sir Sydney Waterlow to Viscount Halifax, Athens, 19 December 1938 [PSG FO 371 1938 22371 – PRO].
4. Ibid.

5. Louise to NK, 22 January 1939 [BA].
6. VMH to MtB, Le Cannet, 1 March 1939 [BA].
7. Alice to Frau Hedwig Markwitz, 8 rue Coumbari, Athens, 1 March 1939 [Stockmann papers, Cologne].
8. Alice to Markwitz, 8 rue Coumbari, Athens [undated, but *c.* April 1939] [Stockmann papers, Cologne].
9. Alice to MtB, 8 rue Coumbari, Athens, 12 March 1939 [BA].
10. Mr Mountain, Admiralty, to P. B. B. Nichols, Foreign Office, 18 April 1939 [PSG FO 371 1939 23773/185 – PRO].
11. Ibid.
12. Alice to Philip, Wolfsgarten, 15 June 1939 [BP].
13. VMH to NK, Adsdean, Chichester, 19 June 1939 [BA].
14. Alice to Philip, Breibach, 24 June 1939 [BP].
15. VMH to NK, KP, 6 August 1939 [BA].
16. Alice to MtB, Athens, 14 September 1939 [BA].
17. VMH to MtB, Lynden Manor, 26 September 1939 [BA].
18. Alice to Philip, Athens, 1 December 1939 [BP].
19. Lincoln MacVeagh to the Secretary of State, Washington, 25 January 1940 [PSG FO 371 58845/99 – PRO].
20. Ibid.
21. Ibid.
22. Ernest A. Rehder, Rehder & Higgs, London, to Edwina, 21 May 1940 [MB/A84 – HL].
23. Quoted in Louise to NK, [Sweden], 20 November 1940 [BA].
24. VMH to NK, KP, 14 August 1940 [BA].
25. Quoted in Louise to NK, [Sweden], 20 November 1940 [BA].
26. Henry Colyton, *Occasion, Chance and Change* (Michael Russell, 1993), p. 143.
27. Sir Henry Channon diary, 9 January 1941 [Robert Rhodes James (ed.), *The Diaries of Sir Henry Channon* (Weidenfeld & Nicolson, 1967), p. 283].
28. George II of Greece to VMH, Royal Palace, Athens, 20 January 1941 [BA].
29. Queen Frederica of the Hellenes, *A Measure of Understanding* (Macmillan, 1971) p. 42.
30. VMH to QM, Broadlands, 23 May 1941 [RA GV/CC 45/1285].

28. Greece under Occupation

1. Foreign Office note, 30 April 1941 [PSG FO 371 1941 29884 R 4677 – PRO].
2. VMH to MtB, Broadlands, 17 May 1941 [BA].
3. Lincoln MacVeagh to Secretary of State, Athens, 15 May 1941, no. 4915 [*Foreign Relations of the United States 1941*, Vol. 2, (US Department of State), p.740].
4. Secretary of State to Ambassador Winant, Washington, 3 December 1941, no. 5630 [*Foreign Relations, op.cit.*, p. 724].
5. Tsouderos to Roosevelt, 22 December 1941, no. 3683 [*Foreign Relations, op.cit.*, p. 726].
6. Mary Henderson, *Xenia – A Memoir* (Weidenfeld & Nicolson, 1988), pp. 47–8.
7. Major Gerald Green to author, London, 8 December 1999.
8. Private information, 1 August 1997.
9. Alice to Philip, Athens, 11 December 1941 [BP].
10. Alice to Philip, Ulriksdal, 25 May 1942 [BP].
11. Louise to VMH, quoted in VMH to NK, KP, 5 June 1942 [BA].
12. Alice to MtB, Ulriksdal, 25 May 1942 [BA].
13. Alice to Philip, Ulriksdal, 31 May 1942 [BP].
14. Alice to Philip, [Greece], 21 September 1942 [BP].
15. Ibid.
16. Alice to Philip, [Greece], 14 November 1942 [BP].
17. Alice to Philip, [Greece], 5 October 1943 [BP].
18. VMH to MtB, KP, 16 November 1943 [BA].
19. Alice to Philip, [Greece], 5 October 1943 [BA].
20. All the above information comes from documents written by Jacques Cohen, Paris, and made available by him, and a conversation with Jacques Cohen and his brother, Michel, in Paris, 23 May 1997. This is further supported by a memorandum from Jacques Cohen, 13 March 2000.

29. Alice in Germany

1. Landgravine Margaret of Hesse-Kassel, June 1942 [Archives of Hessische Hausstiftung, Schloss Fasanerie, Eichenzell].
2. VMH to NK, KP, 16 October 1943 [BA].
3. VMH to MtB, KP, 4 February 1944 [BA].

4. Alice to Philip, [Athens], 23 April 1944 [BP].
5. Alastair Forbes to author, 5 April 1996.
6. Harold Macmillan, *War Diaries* (Macmillan, 1984), p. 558.
7. Harold Macmillan, *op. cit.*, pp. 558–9.
8. Major Gerald Green to author, London, 21 August 1996.
9. Major Gerald Green to author, London, 17 March 1998.
10. Father Jean Charles-Roux to author, February 1997.
11. Father Jean Charles-Roux to author, London, 5 March 1997.
12. Ibid.
13. Alice to MtB, [Athens], 14 November 1944 [BA].
14. General Scobie diary, 3 December 1944 [Imperial War Museum].
15. Ref. Alice to VMH, Athens, *c.* December 1944 [BA].
16. MtB to Philip, immediate naval message [December 1944] [BP].
17. Liane de Pougy, *My Blue Notebooks* (André Deutsch, 1979), p. 104.
18. VMH to MtB, KP, 19 February 1946 [BA].
19. Alice to Philip, [Athens], 20 January 1945 [BP].
20. VMH to MtB, KP, 19 February 1946 [BA].
21. Details drawn from a letter, Alice to Philip, Athens, 10 May 1945 [BP].
22. QM to Earl of Athlone, Badminton, 12 March 1945 [RA GV/CC 53/1369].
23. Alice to VMH, 10 December 1944 [copied in VMH to MtB, undated, but late December 1944] [BA].
24. Alice to VMH, 21 December 1944 [copied in VMH to MtB, undated, but late December 1944] [BA].
25. Major Gerald Green to author, London, 21 August 1996.
26. General Scobie diary, 12 December 1944 [Imperial War Museum].
27. Princess Nicholas of Greece to Natasha Johnston, Athens, 6 January 1945 [author's papers].
28. Alice to MtB, [Athens], 2 January 1945 [BA].
29. Alice to Philip, [Athens], 2 January 1945 [BP].
30. Ibid.
31. VMH to MtB, Broadlands, 29 April 1945 [BA].
32. Alice to MtB, KP, 19 March 1945 [BA].
33. QM to Earl of Athlone, Badminton, 26 February 1945 [RA – Geo V CC 53 – 1364].
34. *News Chronicle* [undated, but April 1945].

35. QM to Earl of Athlone, Badminton, 26 February 1945 [RA GV/CC 53/1564].
36. Princess Sophie of Hesse to VMH, Wolfsgarten, 14 May 1945 [BA].
37. VMH to MtB, KP, 10 June 1945 [BA].
38. Quoted in VMH to MtB, KP, 6 October 1945 [BA].
39. Alice to Philip, rue Demokritou 2, Athens, 8 April 1945.
40. Alice to Philip, KP, 26 July 1945 [BP].
41. Alice to Philip, Claridge's, London, 9 September 1945 [BA].
42. Private information, 25 July 1999.
43. Alice to Philip, Athens, 10 May 1945 [BP].
44. Alice to Philip, Claridge's, London, 9 September 1945 [BP].

30. Philip's Engagement

1 Sir Henry Channon diary, 21 January 1941 [Robert Rhodes-James (ed.), *The Diaries of Sir Henry Channon* (Weidenfeld & Nicolson, 1967), pp. 286–7].
2. KGVI to VMH, BP, 31 October 1941 [BA].
3. VMH to MtB, Broadlands, 9 January 1944 [BA].
4. VMH to MtB, KP, 4 February 1944 [BA].
5. VMH to MtB, KP, 2 April 1944 [BA].
6. Alice to Philip, [Athens], 10 June 1944 [BP].
7. VMH to MtB, 4 June 1944 [BA].
8. VMH to MtB, Broadlands, 20 September 1944 [BA].
9. Duchess of Kent to MtB, 28 January 1945 [BA].
10. VMH to MtB, Broadlands, 8 February 1945 [BA].
11. MtB to Anthony Eden, South East Asia Command, 19 February 1945 [Avon papers, University of Birmingham].
12. Alice to MtB, KP, 19 March 1945 [BA].
13. VMH to MtB, KP, 6 July 1945 [BA].
14. QM to Princess Alice, Countess of Athlone, Sandringham, 26 January 1946 [RA GV/CC 53/1452].
15. *The Times*, 2 December 1935.
16. Sir Orme Sargent, FO minute, 7 August 1946 [PSG FO 371 1946 58854/135 – PRO].
17. Ralph Selby, FO minute, 12 August 1946 [PSG FO 371 1946 58854/134 – PRO].
18. Hon. Sir Steven Runciman to author, London, 5 February 1996.

19. Prince George of Hanover to author, Hampshire, 15 May 1998.
20. Alice to MtB, KP, 8 May 1947 [BA].
21. VMH to MtB, KP, 12 May 1947 [BA].
22. Alice to MtB, [KP], 20 June 1947 [BA].
23. Alice to MtB [KP], 11 July 1947 [BA].
24. Ibid.
25. Alice to QM, [KP], 10 July 1947 [RA GV/CC 45/1519].

31. Philip's Wedding

1. Alice to MtB [KP], 20 June 1947 [BA].
2. Alice to Philip, KP, 25 November 1947 [BP].
3. MtB to Duke of Gloucester, 21 August 1947 [BA].
4. Princess George of Hanover to MtB, Wolfsgarten, 10 November 1947 [BA].
5. Alice to Philip, Athens, 2 December 1947 [BP].
6. Ibid.
7. Alice to Philip, Athens, 4 March 1948 [BP].
8. Ibid.
9. Prince Gottfried of Hohenlohe to MtB, 16 May 1948 [BA].
10. Alice to Philip, Tinos, 7 March 1949 [BP].
11. Louise to MtB, Stockholm, 22 January 1950 [BA].
12. Ibid.
13. Alice to Philip, Athens, 24 November 1948 [BP].
14. Alice to MtB, Tinos, 14 December 1948 [BA].
15. Alice to Philip, KP, 6 September 1949 [BP].

32. The Sisterhood

1. *Daily Mail*, 11 January 1949.
2. *Daily Mail*, 14 January 1949.
3. Alice to Philip, Athens, 23 March 1948 [BP].
4. Alice to MtB, Athens, 23 March 1948 [BA].
5. Associated Press report by L. S. Chakales, *Philadelphia Evening Bulletin*, 7 February 1949.
6. Alice to Philip, Athens, 25 June 1948 [BP].
7. Bishop of Gibraltar to Prince Philip, Rome, 16 December 1948 [BP].
8. Sir Charles Johnston diary, 2 February 1979 [author's papers].
9. Prince Philip to author, BP, 20 May 1997.
10. Countess Mountbatten of Burma to author, London, 16 June 1998.
11. Alice to MtB, Salem, 9 December 1949 [BA].

12. VMH to MtB, 28 December 1949 [BA].
13. Alice to MtB, Stockholm, 14 January 1950 [BA].
14. Louise to MtB, Stockholm, 10 January 1950 [BA].
15. Louise to MtB, Sofiero, 14 July 1950 [BA].
16. *Daily Mail*, [undated, but August 1950].
17. VMH to MtB, KP, 9 September 1949 [BA].
18. Louise to MtB, [Sofiero], 19 August 1950 [BA].
19. Alice to Philip, Broadlands, 29 September 1950 [BP].
20. VMH letter, Broadlands, dated 22 April 1945, copied by Alice for Philip, 29 September 1950 [BP].
21. Louise to MtB, Stockholm, 31 October 1950 [BA].
22. Baroness Buxhoeveden to MtB, KP, 10 November 1950 [MB1/G49 – HL].

33. The Coronation of Elizabeth II

1. Louise to MtB, Ulriksdal, 29 October 1950 [BA].
2. Margit Fjellman, *Louise Mountbatten, Queen of Sweden* (Allen & Unwin, 1968), p. 208.
3. Private information, 9 April 1999.
4. Louise to MtB, Ulriksdal, 27 June 1951 [BA].
5. Alice to Philip, [Athens], 14 September 1951 [BP].
6. Queen Elizabeth The Queen Mother to author, Castle of Mey, 22 August 1998.
7. Alice to Philip, Chicago, 6 February 1952 [BP].
8. Private information, 22 August 1998.
9. Obituary of Lord Lewin, *The Weekly Telegraph*, 3–9 February 1999.
10. MtB to Louise, Wilton Crescent, London, 9 May 1952 [BA].
11. Duchess of Kent to MtB, Coppins, Bucks, 2 December 1952 [BA].
12. Countess Mountbatten of Burma to author, 12 June 2000.
13. Alice to Philip, Athens, 14 May 1952 [BP].
14. Alice to Philip, Athens, 7 June 1952 [BP].
15. Alice to Philip, Valletta, Malta, 15 October 1952 [BP].
16. Alice to MtB, Athens, 31 December 1952 [BA].
17. Margarita to MtB, 5 March 1952 [BA].
18. Louise to MtB, Ulriksdal, 12 May 1953 [BA].
19. *The American Weekly*, 24 May 1953.

20. Cecil Beaton, *The Strenuous Years* (Weidenfeld & Nicolson, 1973), p. 143.
21. Edith Pye to Miss Ward, KP, 27 October 1953 [MB/R175 – HL]
22. Louise to MtB, [Sweden], 19 July 1953 [BA].

34. *The Reign of King Paul*

1. Sir Clifford Norton to Ernest Bevin, Athens, 16 October 1947 [Political Southern Greece FO 371 1947 67124 – PRO].
2. Norton to Bevin, Athens, 26 May 1947 [Political Southern Greece FO 371 1947 67124 – PRO].
3. Charles Mott-Radclyffe to Sir Charles Peake, 19 April 1954 [Political Southern Greece FO 371 1954 112845 – PRO].
4. Ibid.
5. Alice to Philip, Athens, 1 March 1957 [BP].
6. Sir Roger Allen to W.H. Young, Athens, 9 May 1957 [Political Southern Greece FO 371 1957 130066].
7. Ibid.
8. Lady Pamela Hicks to author, London, 27 July 1999.
9. Rear-Admiral John Adams to Anne Griffiths, relayed to author, 29 April 1999.
10. Sir Edward Ford to author, London, 1996.
11. Canon J.A. Fisher to author, St George's Chapel, Windsor, 21 January 1968.
12. Canon J.A. Fisher to author, 11 December 1999.
13. Lt.-Commander Michael Parker to author, July 1998.
14. Alice to MtB, HM yacht *Britannia*, 11 August 1955 [BA].
15. Ibid.
16. Alice to Philip, Athens, 1 March 1957 [BP].
17. Prince Philip to author, BP, 20 May 1997.
18. MtB to Louise, HMS *Glasgow*, Dardanelles, 26 July 1953 [BA].
19. Alice to MtB, Athens, 16 August 1953 [BA].
20. Alice to MtB, Athens, 9 October 1953 [BA].
21. MtB to Louise, Malta, 24 May 1954 [BA].
22. Louise to MtB, Sofiero, 14 June 1954 [BA].
23. Alice to MtB, Athens, 4 September 1954 [BA].
24. Prince Philip to author, BP, 20 May 1997.
25. Alice to Philip, Athens, 5 February 1955 [BP].
26. King Constantine of Greece to author, London, 20 March 1996.
27. MtB to Louise, Admiralty, London, 26 June 1957 [BA].

28. Louise to MtB, Sofiero, 28 June 1957 [BA].
29. Alice to Louise, quoted in Louise to MtB, Stockholm, 3 December 1956 [BA].
30. Louise to MtB, Stockholm, 3 December 1956 [BA].
31. Celia Bertin, *Marie Bonaparte* (Harcourt Brace Jovanovich, New York, 1982), p. 254.
32. Louise to MtB, Stockholm, 25 February 1960 [BA].
33. MtB to E.C. Godfrey, 22 January 1960 [MB/R175 – BA].
34. E.C. Godfrey to MtB, London 29 January 1960 [MB/R175 – BA].
35. Louise to MtB, [Sweden], 5 January 1961 [BA].
36. Helen Fanshawe to MtB, London, 27 May 1961 [MB/028 – HL].
37. MtB to Helen Fanshawe, 12 November 1962 [MB/028 – HL].
38. Alice to MtB, Athens, 29 November 1962 [BA].
39. The Prince of Wales to author, Sandringham, 24 March 1999.
40. Ibid.
41. The Princess Royal to author, BP, 24 March 1999.
42. Lord Brabourne to author, London, 16 June 1998.
43. Louise to MtB, Ulriksdal, 13 May 1958 [BA].
44. Lady Pamela Hicks to author, London, 27 July 1999.
45. Ibid.
46. Alice to MtB, Athens, 18 October 1958 [BA].
47. MtB to Louise, Broadlands, 9 February 1958 [BA].

35. India and Bahrain

1. Rajkumari Amrit Kaur to MtB, New Delhi, 9 October 1959 [MB1/J255 – HL].
2. Edwina to MtB, Prime Minister's House, New Delhi, 25 January 1960 [BA].
3. Edwina to MtB, Prime Minister's House, New Delhi, 4/5 February 1960 [BA].
4. The Princess Royal to author, BP, 24 March 1999.
5. Edwina to Rajkumari Amrit Kaur, 11 December 1959 [MB/R127 – HL].
6. Rajkumari Amrit Kaur to MtB, New Delhi, 11 March 1960 [MB1/J255 – HL].
7. Alice to Philip, Athens, 22 March 1960 [BP].
8. Louise to MtB, 19 June 1955 [BA].
9. MtB to Louise, Ashford, 17 February 1957 [BA].
10. Louise to MtB, [Sweden], 21 March 1957 [BA].

11. Alice to MtB, Athens, 1 March 1957 [BA].
12. MtB to Louise, Ministry of Defence, 8 February 1960 [BA].
13. Alice to Philip, Athens, 6 April 1960 [BP].
14. Major Gerald Green to author, London, 21 August 1996.
15. Alice to Louise, 16 February 1961 – quoted in Louise to MtB, [Sweden], 23 February 1961 [BA].
16. Alice to MtB, Athens, 28 February 1961 [BA].
17. MtB to Louise, Singapore, 15 February 1961 [BA].
18. Louise to MtB, Sofiero, 20 August 1961 [BA].
19. Alice to MtB, Athens, 29 November 1962 [BA].
20. Alice to MtB, Athens, 20 December 1962 [BA].
21. Louise to MtB, [Sweden], 19 December 1962 [BA].
22. *Daily Express*, [after 18] February 1960.
23. Alice to Philip, BP, 21 February 1962 [BP].
24. Alice to MtB, Athens, 22 March 1962 [BA].
25. *The Times*, 4 December 1962.
26. *The Times*, 7 December 1962.
27. Ibid.
28. *The Times*, 14 December 1962.
29. Alice to Philip, Athens, 14 December 1962 [BP].
30. Alice to Philip, Salem, 7 June 1962 [BP].
31. Alice to Philip, Athens, 10 April 1963 [BP].
32. Alice to Philip, Schloss Eberstein, 30 July 1963 [BP].
33. Louise to MtB, [Sweden], 10 July 1963 [BA].
34. Princess George of Hanover to author, Wolfsgarten, 16 January 1996.
35. Dick Barnes to FO, Athens, 13 July 1963 [Political Southern Greece FO 371 1963 169104].
36. Lady Bird Johnson, *A White House Diary* (Weidenfeld & Nicolson, 1970), p. 87.
37. Lady Bird Johnson, *op. cit.*, p. 92.
38. Princess Olga to Sir Philip Hay, quoted in Hay to Dugald Malcolm, KP, 3 September 1964 [FO 372/7923 – PRO].
39. Sir Ralph Murray to FO, Athens, 14 August 1964 [FO 372/7923 – PRO].
40. Dugald Malcolm to Rear-Admiral Christopher Bonham Carter, FO, London, 17 August 1964 [FO 372/7923 – PRO].
41. Lady Bird Johnson, *op.cit.*, p. 87.
42. Louise to MtB, [Sweden], 14 March 1964 [BA].

36. The Reign of King Constantine

1. Sir Ralph Murray to R. A. Butler, Athens, 21 March 1964 [Political Southern Greece FO 371 1964 174837].
2. Ibid.
3. MtB to Louise, London, 25 June 1964 [BA].
4. Louise to MtB, Sofiero, 2 September 1964 [BA].
5. Queen Ena of Spain to Louise, Lausanne, 9 September 1964 [BA].
6. Louise to MtB, [Sweden], 9 September 1964 [BA].
7. Philip to King Constantine, quoted in Sir Michael Adeane to Sir Harold Caccia, 10 July 1964 [FO 372 1964/7925 – PRO].
8. Sir Ralph Murray to Sir Harold Caccia, Athens, 2 September 1964 [FO 372 1964/7920 – PRO].
9. Alice to Philip, Athens, 21 December 1964 [BP].
10. Louise to MtB, Sophiaheim, 27 January 1965 [BA].
11. Louise to MtB, Drottingholm, 26 February 1965 [BA].
12. Alice to MtB, Athens, 16 March 1965 [BA].
13. Alice to MtB, Athens, 3 April 1965 [BA].
14. Alice to Philip, Athens, 24 April 1965 [BP].
15. Alice to MtB, Langenburg, 24 June 1965 [BA].
16. Alice to Philip, Ritz Hotel, London, 27 August 1965 [BP].
17. Alice to Philip, Athens, 16 December 1965 [BP].
18. Alice to Philip, BP, 24 February 1966 [BP].
19. Ibid.
20. Ibid.
21. Alice to Philip, Royal Palace, Athens, 23 March 1966 [BP].
22. Ibid.
23. Private information, 9 April 1999.
24. Admiral S. H:son-Ericson, Stockholm, to MtB, 24 May 1966 [BA].
25. MtB to Admiral S. H:son-Ericson, Broadlands, 4 June 1966 [BA].
26. Alice to Philip, Munich, 1 August 1966 [BP].
27. Ibid.
28. Alice to Philip, Munich, 15 August 1966 [BP].
29. Alice to Philip, Athens, 18 October 1966 [BP].

37. Alice at the Palace

1. Alice to Philip, Royal Palace, Athens, 24 April 1967 [BP].
2. Ibid.

3. Alice to Philip, Royal Palace, Athens, 28 April 1967 [BP].
4. Alice to Philip, 7 Patriarch Joachim St, Athens, 12 May 1967 [BP].
5. Princess George of Hanover to author, Wolfsgarten, 16 January 1996.
6. Stephen P. Barry, *Royal Secrets* (Villard Books, New York, 1985), p. 77.
7. Stephen P. Barry, *op. cit.*, p. 76.
8. *Sunday Express*, 3 June 1967.
9. The Princess Royal to author, BP, 24 March 1999.
10. Alice to Philip, Hyde Park Hotel, London, 12 August 1967 [BP].
11. Message from Kyleski Post Office, Scotland, Esther Clark, to Philip, 2 September 1967 [BP].
12. *Sunday Express*, [undated but March 1968].
13. King Gustaf VI Adolf to MtB, Stockholm, 13 December 1969 [BA].
14. Princess George of Hanover to author, Wolfsgarten, 16 January 1996.
15. Alice to Philip, BP, 19 October 1968 [BP].
16. Alice to Philip, BP, 25 October 1969 [BP].
17. Princess Margaret to author, Hampshire, 1 January 1996.
18. *Daily Express*, 6 December 1969.
19. MtB reply to sympathy letter, 12 December 1969 [BA].
20. The Princess Royal to author, BP, 24 March 1999.
21. *The Times*, 6 December 1969.
22. King Gustaf VI Adolf to MtB, Stockholm, 13 December 1969 [BA].
23. Lady Brabourne to MtB, Luton Hoo, 5 December 1969 [BA].
24. Ruby Miller to MtB, Ardwick Bay, 6 December 1969 [BA].
25. Prince Philip to Cecil Beaton, Balmoral, 19 December 1969 [papers, St John's College, Cambridge].
26. Unpublished memoirs of Captain A. V. Yates, RN, p. 342 [author's copy].
27. Funeral service sheet, St George's Chapel, Windsor, 10 December 1969 [author's copy].
28. Princess George of Hanover to author, Wolfsgarten, 16 January 1996.
29. Certificate of Honour, Yad Vashem, Jerusalem, 31 October 1994 [BP].
30. Jacques Cohen to author, Paris, 23 May 1997.
31. Speech by Prince Philip, Jerusalem, 31 October 1994 [quoted in the *Jerusalem Post*, 1 November 1994].

Appendix: The Burial of Alice

1. Rt. Revd Michael Mann to author, London, 11 February 1997.
2. Archimandrite Anthony Grabbe to Prince Philip, 4 April 1984 [TB].
3. Ibid.
4. Prince Philip to Grabbe, BP, 30 April 1984 [TB].
5. Grabbe to Mann, Jerusalem, 5 June 1984 [TB].
6. Mann to Grabbe, Windsor, 12 July 1984 [TB].
7. Mann to author, London, 11 February 1997.
8. Grabbe to Mann, Jerusalem, 9 November 1985 [TB].
9. Press release, Orthodox Palestine Society, 23 August 1987.
10. Prince Theimouraz Bagration to Mann, New York, 22 April 1986 [TB].
11. Bagration to Mann, New York, 16 July 1986 [TB].
12. Mann to Bagration, Windsor, 25 March 1988 [TB].
13. Mann to author, London, 11 February 1997.
14. Ibid.
15. Bagration to Mann, New York, 21 August 1988 [TB].

Bibliography

This bibliography is intended to recommend the published sources which were particularly useful in the research for this biography. I cannot mention every book from which I drew a fact or a line. However, all books from which direct sources were taken are listed in the source notes.

This is the first full biography of Princess Andrew of Greece. There are summaries of her life in Meriel Buchanan, *Queen Victoria's Relations* (Cassell, 1954), and Helen Cathcart, *The Royal Bedside Book* (W. H. Allen, 1969), and in other books listed below.

The history of the Mountbatten family is best covered in David Duff, *Hessian Tapestry* (Frederick Muller, 1967). There are also Alden Hatch, *The Mountbattens* (W. H. Allen, 1966), E. H. Cookridge, *From Battenberg to Mountbatten* (Arthur Barker, 1966), Brian Connell, *Manifest Destiny* (Cassell, 1953) and Antony Lambton, *The Mountbattens* (Constable, 1989). The two volumes by Richard Hough, *Louis and Victoria* (Hutchinson, 1974) and *Advice to a Grand-Daughter* (Heinemann, 1975), were especially helpful with the life of Princess Alice's parents. I relied heavily on the unpublished memoirs of Prince Louis of Battenberg, and his wife, Victoria, Marchioness of Milford Haven, of which there are copies in the Mountbatten papers at the Hartley Library, University of Southampton, supplemented by Mark Kerr, *Prince Louis of Battenberg* (Longman, Green & Co, 1934).

There are a great number of biographies of individual members of Princess Alice's immediate family, and volumes of memoirs, in particular, Margit Fjellman, *Louise Mountbatten, Queen of Sweden* (Allen & Unwin, 1968), Philip Ziegler, *Mountbatten* (Collins, 1985), Richard Hough, *Mountbatten – Hero of Our Time* (Weidenfeld & Nicolson, 1980), Janet Morgan's *Edwina Mountbatten* (Harper Collins, 1991), Basil Boothroyd, *Philip: An Informal Biography* (Longman, 1971), Denis Judd, *Prince Philip* (Michael Joseph, 1980) and Tim Heald, *The Duke* (Hodder & Stoughton, 1991). The biography, *Prince Philip – A Family Portrait* (Hodder & Stoughton, 1959), by Queen Alexandra of Yugoslavia (ghosted by Harold Albert, *alias* Helen Cathcart) is generally mistrusted, but contains some useful family material.

Other members of the family are to be found in Princess Marie zu Erbach-Schönberg, *Reminiscences* (Allen & Unwin, 1925), Gerard Noel, *Princess Alice* (Constable, 1974), Princess Christian, *Alice, Grand Duchess of Hesse* (John Murray, 1884), David Duff, *The Shy Princess* (Evans Brothers, 1958), Peter Ednay, *H.R.H. Princess Beatrice, Island Governor* (Vectis Research, Isle of Wight, 1994), Rowland E. Prothero, *H.R.H. Prince Henry of Battenberg, K.G.* (John Murray, for private circulation, 1897), Gerard Noel, *Ena, Spain's English Queen* (Constable, 1984), Raleigh Trevelyan, *Grand Dukes and Diamonds* (Secker & Warburg, 1991) and Grand Duchess Marie of Russia, *Things I Remember* (Cassell, 1931).

The life and times of Queen Victoria have been extensively written about. For this book, I consulted many of them, including Elizabeth Longford, *Victoria R.I.* (Weidenfeld & Nicolson, 1964), Sir Frederick Ponsonby, *Recollections of Three Reigns* (Eyre & Spottiswoode, 1951), Michaela Reid, *Ask Sir James* (Hodder & Stoughton, 1987) and Gabriel Tschumi, *Royal Chef* (William Kimber, 1954).

The Greek royal family have inspired many books: Arthur S. Gould Lee, *The Royal House of Greece* (Ward, Lock & Co., 1948), E. E. P. Tisdall, *Royal Destiny* (Stanley Paul, 1955), John Van der Kiste, *Kings of the Hellenes, The Greek Kings 1863–1974* (Alan Sutton, 1994), Captain Walter Christmas, *The Life of King George of Greece* (Royalty Digest Reprint, 1998), H.R.H. Prince Nicholas of Greece, *My Fifty Years* (Hutchinson, 1927), H.R.H. Prince Andrew of Greece, *Towards Disaster* (John Murray, 1930), H.R.H. Prince Christopher of Greece, *Memoirs of H.R.H. Prince Christopher of Greece* (Hurst & Blackett, 1939), Stelio Hourmouzios, *No Ordinary Crown* (Weidenfeld & Nicolson, 1972), Queen Frederica of the Hellenes, *A Measure of Understanding* (Macmillan, 1971), Arthur S. Gould Lee, *The Empress Frederick Writes to Sophie* (Faber & Faber, 1955) and Celia Bertin, *Marie Bonaparte* (Harcourt Brace Jovanovich, New York, 1982).

Books on the Hesse-Darmstadt family include Manfred Knodt, *Ernst Ludwig, Grossherzog von Hessen und bei Rhein* (Verlag H. L. Schlapp, Darmstadt, 1978), Ernst Ludwig, Grossherzog von Hessen und bei Rhein,

Erinnertes (Eduard Roether Verlag, Darmstadt, 1983), Herausgegeben von Eckhart G. Franz und Karl-Eugen Schlapp, *Margaret, Prinzessin von Hessen und bei Rhein* (Verlag H. L. Schlapp, Darmstadt, 1997), John Van der Kiste, *Princess Victoria Melita* (Alan Sutton, 1991) and Michael John Sullivan, *A Fatal Passion* (Random House, New York, 1997).

There are too many books about the Russian royal family to list each individually, but I relied on Robert K. Massie, *Nicholas and Alexandra* (Victor Gollancz, 1968), Sir Bernard Pares, *Letters of the Tsaritsa to the Tsar 1914–1916* (Duckworth & Co, 1923) and Andrei Maylunas & Sergei Mironenko, *A Fatal Passion* (Weidenfeld & Nicolson, 1996).

There are several biographies of Grand Duchess Elisabeth of Russia, most notably the one commissioned by Queen Louise of Sweden, E. M. Almedingen, *An Unbroken Unity* (The Bodley Head, 1964). The others are: Ludmila Koehler, *Saint Elisabeth, The New Martyr* (The Orthodox Palestine Society, New York, 1988), Lubov Millar, *Grand Duchess Elizabeth of Russia* (Nikodemus Orthodox Palestine Publication Society, Redding, California, 1991) and Hugo Mager, *Elizabeth, Grand Duchess of Russia* (Carroll & Graf, New York, 1998).

For Greek politics, I relied on Michael Llewellyn Smith, *Ionian Vision* (Allen Lane, 1973), Compton Mackenzie, *First Athenian Memories* (Cassell, 1931), G. F. Abbott, *Greece and the Allies 1914–1922* (Methuen, 1922), John O. Iatrides (ed.), *Ambassador MacVeagh Reports: Greece, 1933–1947* (Princeton University Press, New Jersey, 1980), Mary Henderson, *Xenia – A Memoir* (Weidenfeld & Nicolson, 1988) and P. Constantopoulou and T. Veremis (eds.), *Documents on the History of the Greek Jews* (Kastaniotis Editions, Athens, 1999).

There are several books containing material on Dr Ludwig Binswanger: Jacob Needleman (ed.), *Being-in-the-World (Selected Papers of Ludwig Binswanger* (Basic Books, New York, 1963), Ludwig Binswanger, MD, *Sigmund Freud: Reminiscences of a Friendship* (Grune & Stratton, New York, 1957), Herausgegeben von Max Herzog, *Ludwig Binswanger und die Chronik der Klinik 'Bellevue' in Kreuzlingen* (Quintessenz, Berlin, 1995) and Manfred Bosch, *Bohème am Bodensee – Literarisches Leben am See von 1900 bis 1950* (Libelle, Switzerland, 1997).

Also useful were Hermann von Keyserling, *The World in the Making* (Jonathan Cape, 1927), and Princess Alice's favourite book, Édouard

Schuré, *The Great Initiates* (William Rider, 1922), though she read it in the French edition.

Finally, there are the well-thumbed reference books, never far from my side during the research and writing: Hugh Montgomery-Massingberd (ed.), *Burke's Royal Families of the World, Volume 1, Europe & Latin America* (Burke's Peerage, 1977) and Marlene A. Eilers, *Queen Victoria's Descendants* (Rosvall Royal Books, Sweden, 1997).

Family Trees

The British Royal Family: A Select Family Tree

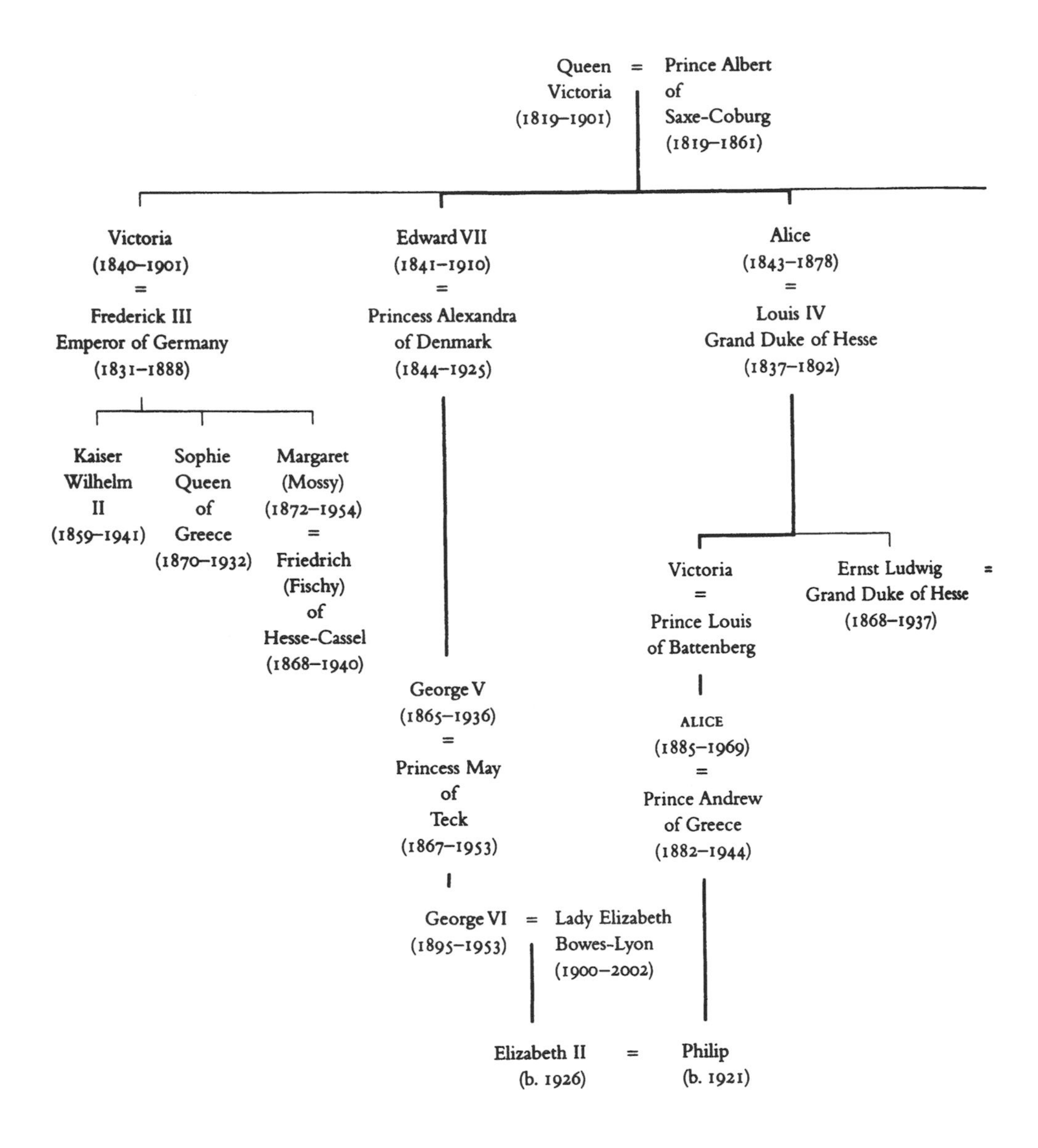

- Alfred Duke of Edinburgh (Duke of Saxe-Coburg) (1844–1900) = Grand Duchess Maria of Russia (1853–1920)
  - Victoria Melita (1876–1936)
  - Beatrice (Baby Bee) (1884–1966)
- Helena (1846–1923) = Prince Christian of Schleswig-Holstein (1831–1917) ↓
- Louise (1848–1939) = Duke of Argyll (1845–1914)
- Arthur Duke of Connaught (1850–1942) = Princess Louise Margaret of Prussia (1860–1917) ↓
- Leopold Duke of Albany (1853–1884) = Princess Helena of Waldeck (1861–1922)
  - Alice (1883–1981) = Earl of Athlone (1874–1953) ↓
- Beatrice (1857–1944) = Prince Henry of Battenberg (1858–1896) ↓

The Greek Royal Family: A Select Family Tree

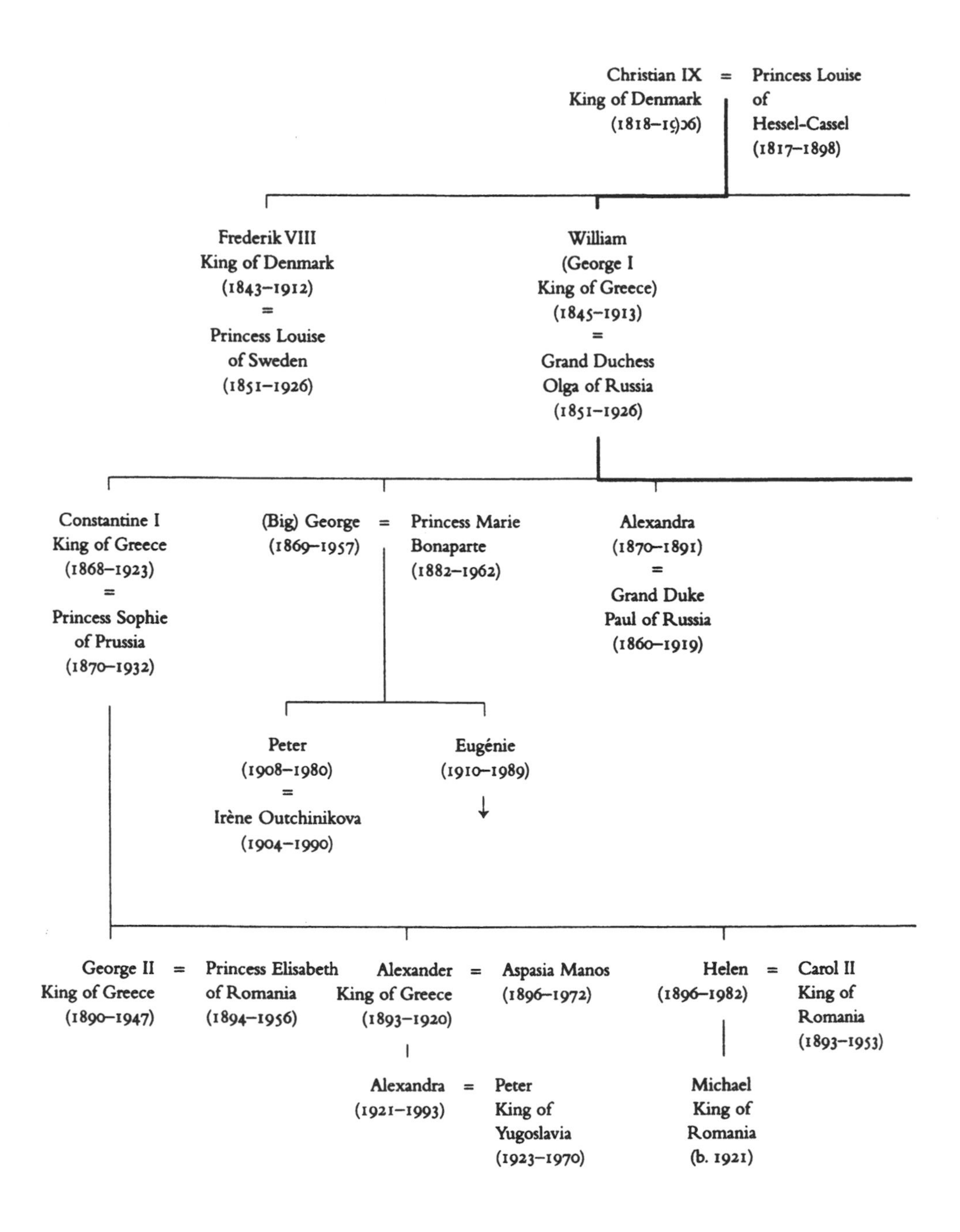

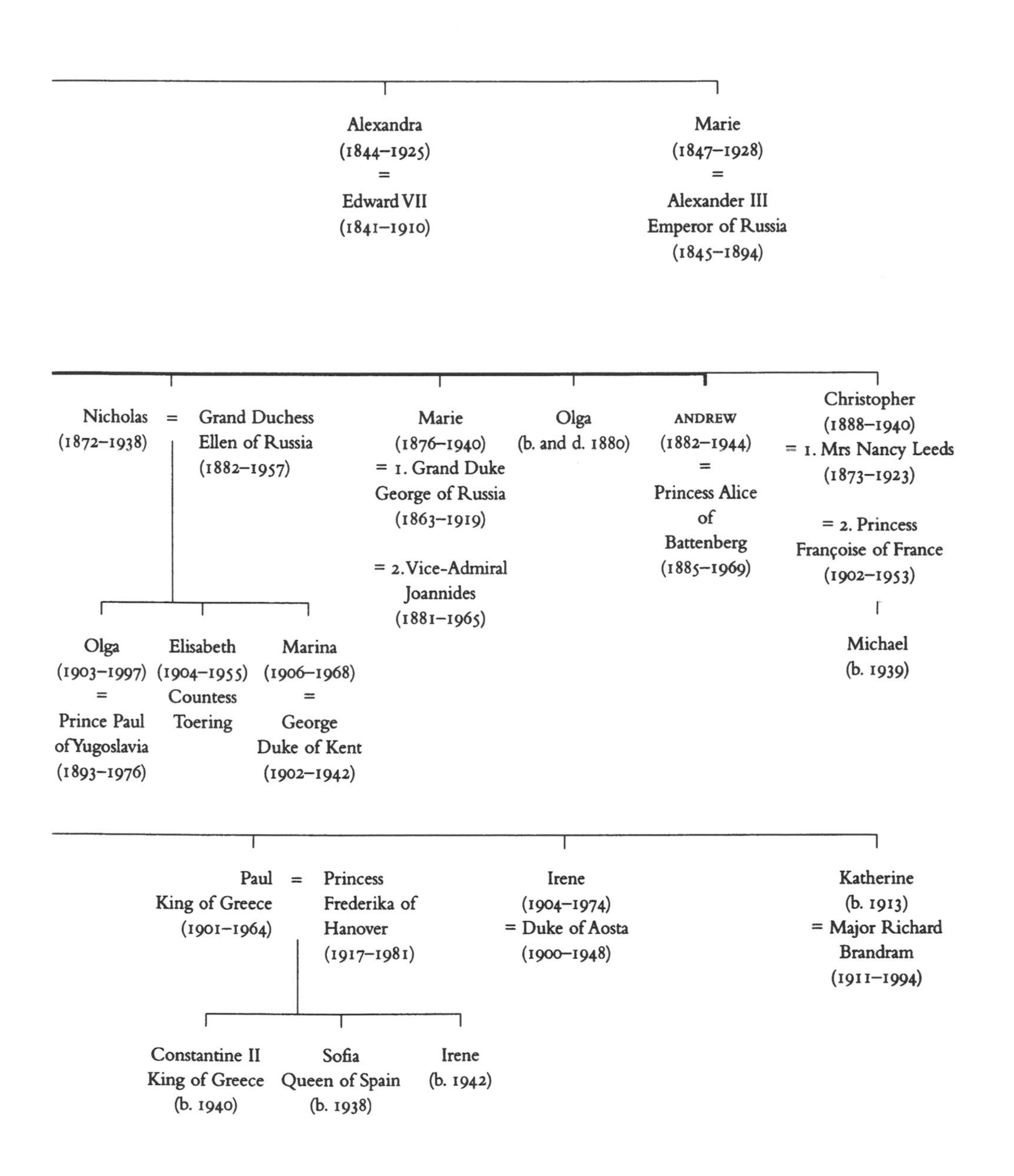

Alexandra
(1844–1925)
=
Edward VII
(1841–1910)
Marie
(1847–1928)
=
Alexander III
Emperor of Russia
(1845–1894)
Nicholas
(1872–1938)
=
Grand Duchess
Ellen of Russia
(1882–1957)
Marie
(1876–1940)
= 1. Grand Duke
George of Russia
(1863–1919)
= 2. Vice-Admiral
Joannides
(1881–1965)
Olga
(b. and d. 1880)
ANDREW
(1882–1944)
=
Princess Alice
of
Battenberg
(1885–1969)
Christopher
(1888–1940)
= 1. Mrs Nancy Leeds
(1873–1923)
= 2. Princess
Françoise of France
(1902–1953)
Michael
(b. 1939)
Olga
(1903–1997)
=
Prince Paul
of Yugoslavia
(1893–1976)
Elisabeth
(1904–1955)
Countess
Toering
Marina
(1906–1968)
=
George
Duke of Kent
(1902–1942)
Paul
King of Greece
(1901–1964)
=
Princess
Frederika of
Hanover
(1917–1981)
Irene
(1904–1974)
= Duke of Aosta
(1900–1948)
Katherine
(b. 1913)
= Major Richard
Brandram
(1911–1994)
Constantine II
King of Greece
(b. 1940)
Sofia
Queen of Spain
(b. 1938)
Irene
(b. 1942)

Hesse-Darmstadt : A Select Family Tree

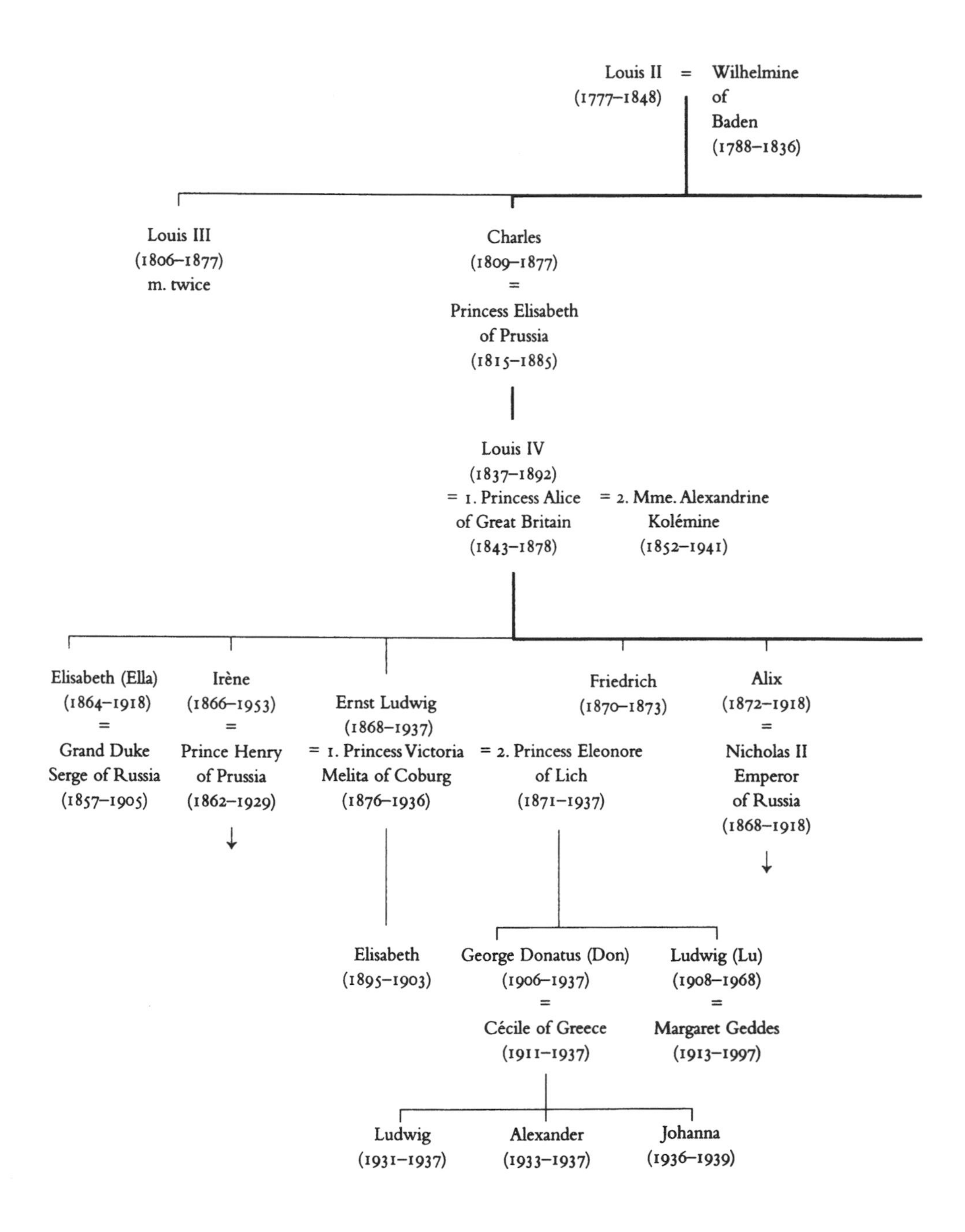

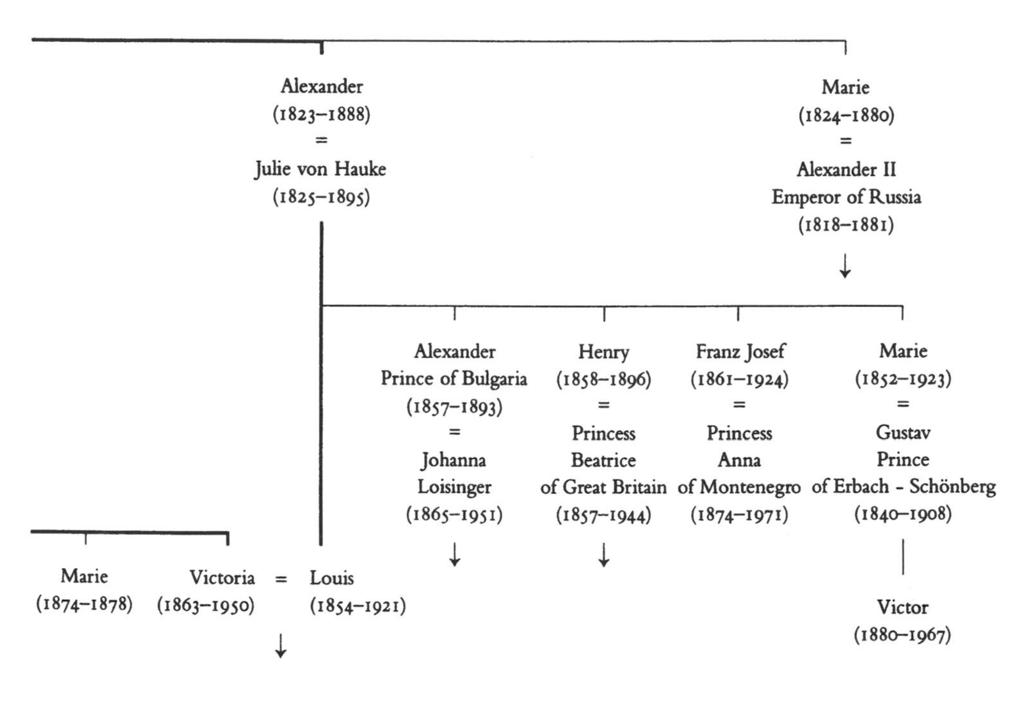
Alexander
(1823–1888)
=
Julie von Hauke
(1825–1895)
Marie
(1824–1880)
=
Alexander II
Emperor of Russia
(1818–1881)
Alexander
Prince of Bulgaria
(1857–1893)
=
Johanna
Loisinger
(1865–1951)
Henry
(1858–1896)
=
Princess
Beatrice
of Great Britain
(1857–1944)
Franz Josef
(1861–1924)
=
Princess
Anna
of Montenegro
(1874–1971)
Marie
(1852–1923)
=
Gustav
Prince
of Erbach - Schönberg
(1840–1908)
Victor
(1880–1967)
Marie
(1874–1878)
Victoria
(1863–1950)
=
Louis
(1854–1921)
ALICE

The Battenbergs : A Select Family Tree

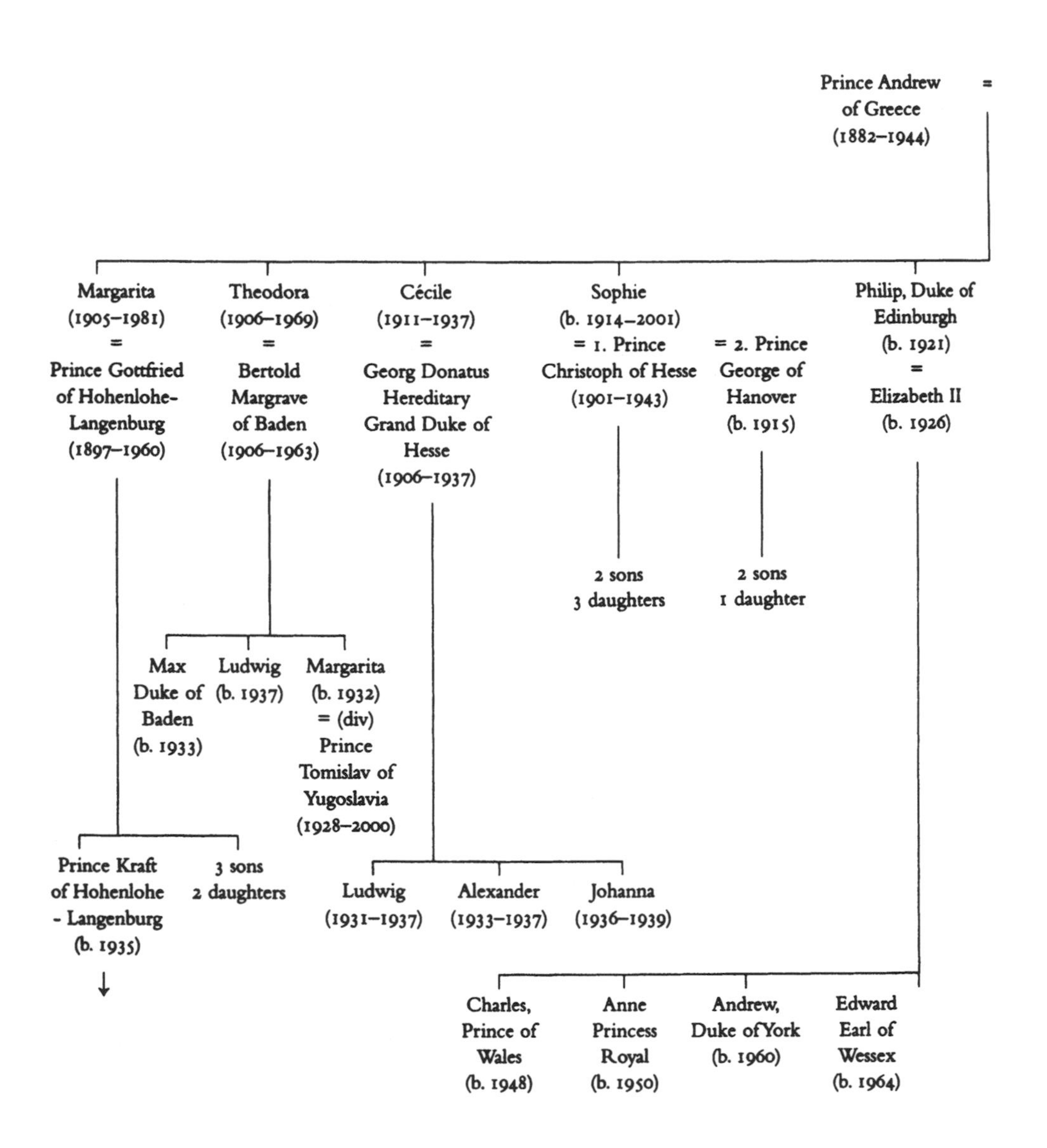

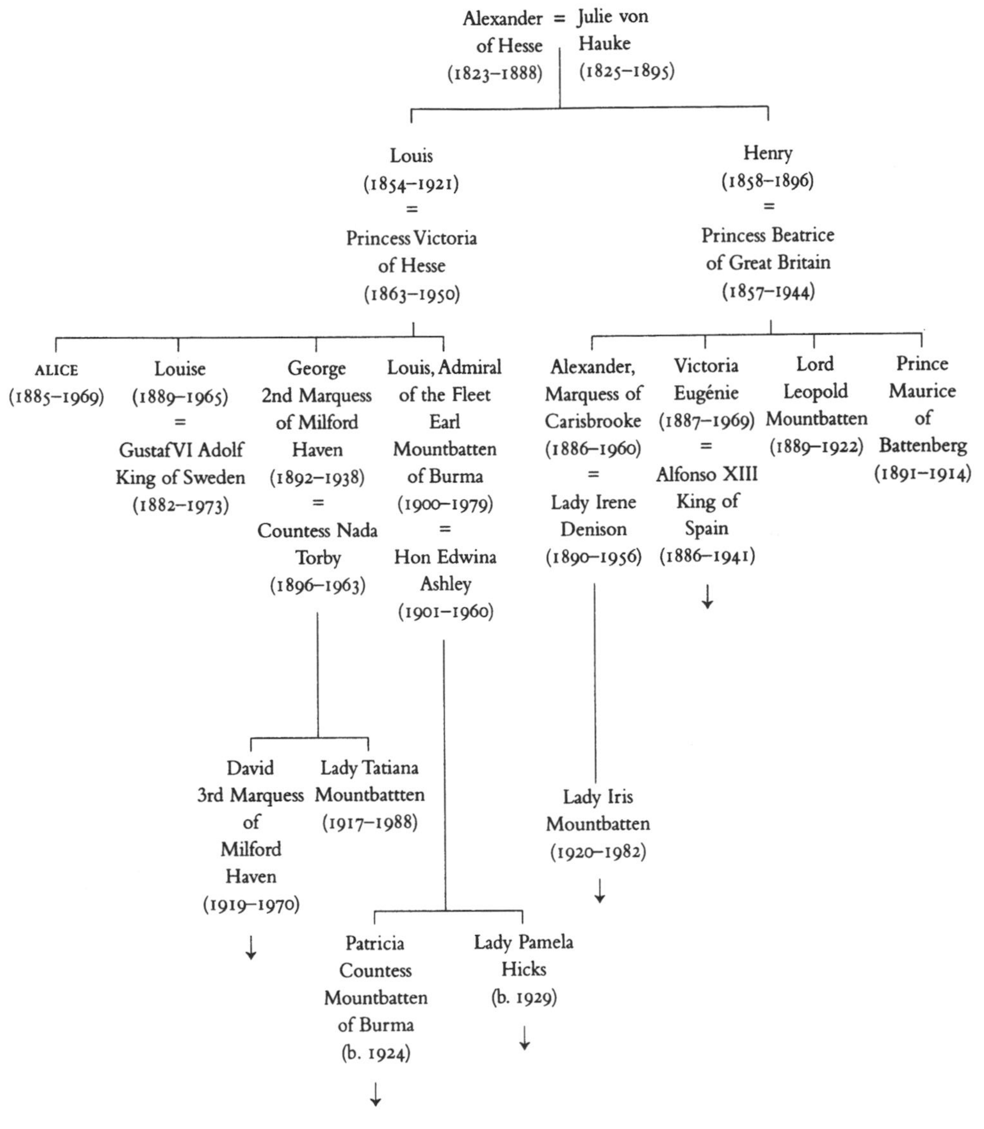
Alexander of Hesse (1823–1888) = Julie von Hauke (1825–1895)
Louis (1854–1921) = Princess Victoria of Hesse (1863–1950)
Henry (1858–1896) = Princess Beatrice of Great Britain (1857–1944)
ALICE (1885–1969)
Louise (1889–1965) = Gustaf VI Adolf King of Sweden (1882–1973)
George 2nd Marquess of Milford Haven (1892–1938) = Countess Nada Torby (1896–1963)
Louis, Admiral of the Fleet Earl Mountbatten of Burma (1900–1979) = Hon Edwina Ashley (1901–1960)
Alexander, Marquess of Carisbrooke (1886–1960) = Lady Irene Denison (1890–1956)
Victoria Eugénie (1887–1969) = Alfonso XIII King of Spain (1886–1941)
Lord Leopold Mountbatten (1889–1922)
Prince Maurice of Battenberg (1891–1914)
David 3rd Marquess of Milford Haven (1919–1970)
Lady Tatiana Mountbattten (1917–1988)
Lady Iris Mountbatten (1920–1982)
Patricia Countess Mountbatten of Burma (b. 1924)
Lady Pamela Hicks (b. 1929)

Index

'There are too many Georges in your book', said my editor. In order to help discriminate between the characters, I have added dates of birth and death where possible. Most royal names are given under Christian names.

Made in the USA
Las Vegas, NV
05 January 2023